CHALLENGING THE LEGAL BOUNDARIES OF WORK REGULATION

Focusing on paid work that blurs traditional legal boundaries and the challenge this poses to traditional forms of labour regulation, this collection of original case studies illustrates the wide range of different forms of regulation designed to provide decent work. The case studies cover a diversity of workers from across developed and developing countries, the formal and informal economies and public and private work spaces. Each deals with the failings of traditional labour law, and several explore the capacity of different forms of regulatory techniques, such as commercial law, corporate codes of conduct, or supply chain regulation, to protect workers.

Oñati International Series in Law and Society

A SERIES PUBLISHED FOR THE OÑATI INSTITUTE
FOR THE SOCIOLOGY OF LAW

General Editors
Rosemary Hunter   David Nelken

Founding Editors
William L F Felstiner   Eve Darian-Smith

Board of General Editors
Carlos Lugo, Hostos Law School, Puerto Rico
Jacek Kurczewski, Warsaw University, Poland
Marie-Claire Foblets, Leuven University, Belgium
Roderick Macdonald, McGill University, Canada

Recent titles in this series

**For the complete list of titles in this series, see
'Oñati International Series in Law and Society' link at
www.hartpub.co.uk/books/series.asp**

Challenging the Legal Boundaries of Work Regulation

Edited by

Judy Fudge
Shae McCrystal
and
Kamala Sankaran

Oñati International Series in Law and Society

A SERIES PUBLISHED FOR THE OÑATI INSTITUTE
FOR THE SOCIOLOGY OF LAW

·HART·
PUBLISHING

OXFORD AND PORTLAND, OREGON
2012

Published in the United Kingdom by Hart Publishing Ltd
16C Worcester Place, Oxford, OX1 2JW
Telephone: +44 (0)1865 517530
Fax: +44 (0)1865 510710
E-mail: mail@hartpub.co.uk
Website: http://www.hartpub.co.uk

Published in North America (US and Canada) by
Hart Publishing
c/o International Specialized Book Services
920 NE 58th Avenue, Suite 300
Portland, OR 97213-3786
USA
Tel: +1 503 287 3093 or toll-free: (1) 800 944 6190
Fax: +1 503 280 8832
E-mail: orders@isbs.com
Website: http://www.isbs.com

© Oñati IISL 2012

British Library Cataloguing in Publication Data
Data Available

ISBN: 978-1-84946-279-2

Typeset by Compuscript Ltd, Shannon
Printed and bound in Great Britain by
CPI Group (UK) Ltd, Croydon, CR0 4YY

Preface

The chapters in this collection were first presented at a workshop with a group of researchers from across the developed and the developing world held at the International Institute for the Sociology of Law (IISL) in Oñati, Spain on 1–2 July 2010. The collection benefited from the lively and collegial discussion in the quiet and lovely surroundings of the Institute. Adelle Blackett, Beata Nasca, Ashwini Sukthankar and Anne Trebilcock contributed to the book through their participation in the workshop; we hope we have reflected some of their insight and knowledge. We would also like to thank IISL for hosting the workshop and providing financial assistance to enable some of our participants to attend the workshop. At the Institute, Malen Gordoa Mendizabal provided seamless and attentive logistics, Cristina Ruiz graciously guided us through the publication process, and Sol Picciotto offered us intellectual support and hospitality. In addition, we are indebted to Gregor Murray and the Inter-University Research Centre on Globalisation and Work (Centre de recherche interuniversitaire sur la mondialisation et le travail—CRIMT) for providing additional financial support to enable developing world scholars to attend the workshop.

We were delighted when Hart Publishing agreed to publish the collection as an edited book in the Oñati International Series in Law and Society. We would like to thank the Series Editors and the external anonymous reviewers for their helpful and perceptive feedback. For her careful work in preparing the manuscript for publication, we would like to thank Tashina Orchiston. Our thanks also go to Richard Hart and Rachel Turner for making publishing a pleasure and an honour, and to the copy editor.

Contents

Contributors

Einat Albin is a Lecturer in the Faculty of Law, Hebrew University of Jerusalem.

Lizzie Barmes is Professor of Labour Law, Queen Mary University of London.

Stéphanie Bernstein is Professor, Département des sciences juridiques, Faculté de science politique et de droit, Université du Québec à Montréal, Montreal, Canada.

Poornima Chikarmane is Reader and Assistant Director, Department of Continuing and Adult Education and Extension Work, SNDT Women's University.

Guy Davidov is Professor and Elias Lieberman Chair in Labour Law, Hebrew University of Jerusalem.

Judy Fudge is Professor and Lansdowne Chair in Law, University of Victoria and a member of the Inter-University Research Centre on Globalisation and Work (Centre de recherche interuniversitaire sur la mondialisation et le travail—CRIMT).

Alan Hyde is Distinguished Professor and Sidney Reitman Scholar, Rutgers University School of Law, Newark NJ, USA.

Brendan Johnson is a Solicitor for Maurice Blackburn Lawyers, Melbourne.

Richard Johnstone is Professor, Griffith Law School, Griffith University; Adjunct Professor, National Research Centre for Occupational Health and Safety Regulation, Australian National University; Honorary Professor, Department of Ageing, Work and Health, University of Sydney.

Juan-Pablo Landa Zapirain is Professor of Labor and Social Security Law, Law Faculty, University of the Basque Country, Spain.

Roopa Madhav is an Independent Law Researcher based in Bangalore.

Shae McCrystal is a Senior Lecturer in the Faculty of Law, University of Sydney.

Guy Mundlak is Professor, Faculty of Law and Department of Labour Studies, Tel Aviv University.

Lakshmi Narayanan is General Secretary of the Kagad Kach Patra Kashtakari Panchayat (KKPPKP), Pune, India.

Anna Pollert is Emerita Professor of the Sociology of Work, Centre for Employment Studies Research, Faculty of Business and Law, University of the West of England.

Joellen Riley is Professor, Faculty of Law, University of Sydney.

Kamala Sankaran is Professor, Campus Law Centre, Faculty of Law, University of Delhi.

Dzodzi Tsikata is Associate Professor, Institute of Statistical, Social and Economic Research, University of Ghana.

1

Blurring Legal Boundaries: Regulating for Decent Work

INTRODUCTION

DECENTRALISED PROCESSES OF production and service provision, which are facilitated by digital technologies and an international trading and financial regime that promotes the free movement of capital, goods and services across national borders, are transforming labour markets and paid work in both developing and developed countries.[1] Policies that emphasise labour market flexibility and deregulation have resulted in deteriorating working conditions and labour standards for a large proportion of the working population.[2] These changes have led to the informalisation and commercialisation of employment processes by which work arrangements are constructed outside the scope of employment and labour protection. At the same time, a large proportion of the population in developing countries engage in subsistence activities, some of which, such as street vending, are not connected with the formal economy, and others, such as waste picking, are linked to the formal economy through complex networks of intermediaries and firms. Moreover,

* I would like to thank the Social Sciences Research Council of Canada for support for my research. I would like to thank Anne Trebilcock, Shae McCrystal and Kamala Sankaran for very helpful comments on an earlier draft. All errors are my own.

[1] Benería, L and Floro, M, 'Distribution, Gender, and Labor Market Informalization: A Conceptual Framework with a Focus on Homeworkers' in N Kudva and L Benería (eds), *Rethinking Informalization: Poverty, Precarious Jobs and Social Protection* (New York, Cornell University Open Access Repository, 2005) 6, available at: www.wiego.org/publications/Rethinking_Informalization.pdf and Teklè, T (ed), *Labour Law and Worker Protection in Developing Countries* (Oxford, Hart Publishing, 2010). The nomenclature for describing groups of countries in terms of their type and level of economic development is controversial and ideological. In this Chapter, the terms 'developed' and 'developing' countries are used.

[2] International Labour Organization, *Declaration on Social Justice for a Fair Globalization* (Declaration presented to the International Labour Conference, 97th Session, Geneva, 2008), available at: www.ilocarib.org.tt/projects/cariblex/conventions_24.shtml.

many women in both developed and developing countries continue to be paid to perform domestic work in households that are not their own. Some of this work is performed on an informal basis outside the scope of regulation, while in other cases it is officially recognised and regulated.

Globalisation and neo-liberalism are the economic and political forces fuelling the transformation of labour markets.[3] However, in order to understand the 'enormous increase in precarious employment and informalised production that has resulted from the implementation of neo-liberal policies', Lourdes Benería has advised that it is necessary to examine the 'changes taking place at the level of the firm'.[4] Firms have segmented production through outsourcing and subcontracting in order to meet the pressures of global markets. Tzehainesh Teklè links the process of informalisation, which places workers beyond the scope of labour protection, to the 'externalization of either production or labour'.[5] Common to the wide range of different forms of externalisation, from off-shoring production through labour-only contracting to the use of migrant workers to perform dangerous and dirty jobs in host countries, 'is the transfer of risks and responsibilities that are linked to an employment relationship from the enterprise receiving the product or service to third parties (either enterprises or workers)'.[6] Productive activities that used to be performed in core firms have been relocated to the periphery of smaller and often geographically distant firms and households. The outsourcing of intra-firm services has also expanded.[7] These processes are related; as Jane Kelsey has remarked, 'internationally integrated supply chains [have] made the traditional economic and legal distinction between trade in goods or agriculture commodities and services increasingly anachronistic'.[8]

These processes of decentralisation, externalisation, fragmentation, and reconfiguration of production and services have resulted in a great deal of heterogeneity in work arrangements. In highly developed countries, self-employment, for example, ranges from freelance professionals to women who provide childcare in their homes, and to men who drive trucks or operate franchises for a living. Informal work, which proliferates in developing countries, is even more varied, ranging from waste picking to employment

---

[3] Harvey, D, *A Brief History of Neoliberalism* (Oxford, Oxford University Press, 2005); Castells, M, *The Rise of the Network Society. The Information Age: Economy, Society, and Culture*, 2nd edn (Oxford, Blackwell, 2000).

[4] Benería, L, 'Shifting the Risk: New Employment Patterns, Informalization, and Women's Work' (2001) 15 *International Journal of Politics, Culture and Society* 272, 48.

[5] Teklè, T, 'Labour Law and Worker Protection in the South: An Evolving Tension Between Models and Reality' in T Teklè (ed), *Labour Law and Worker Protection in Developing Countries* (Oxford, Hart Publishing, 2010) 3, 20.

[6] *Ibid*.

[7] Kelsey, J, *Serving Whose Interests: The Political Economy of Trade in Services Agreements* (Abingdon, Routledge-Cavendish, 2008) 7.

[8] *Ibid* at 7.

in unregistered factories, street vending, and paid domestic work performed in households by migrants. Not only are these work arrangements diverse, they are also fluid, shifting across boundaries such as formal and informal employment and, especially for women, paid and unpaid work.[9] One common feature that unites these different types of paid work is that they trespass traditional economic and legal boundaries—such as the informal and formal economies, employment and commercial law, the productive and reproductive economy, trade and labour, public and private spaces—that are used to distinguish different economic activities for the purposes of regulation. These forms of work also tend to be associated with poor working conditions and low labour standards.[10]

In both the developed and developing world the forms of work and numbers of workers outside the scope of labour law has proliferated, and the resulting 'crisis' in labour law has led to calls for its reconsideration or rejuvenation by labour law scholars.[11] These proposals range from modernising existing concepts, such as the employment contract, to devising new bases of social entitlement, such as social drawing rights.[12] One important consequence of the crisis of labour law is that the search for normative resources and regulatory tools is no longer confined to the field of employment law. Heed has been taken of Mark Freedland's warning that the belief that the law regulating employment is 'an oasis of social justice regulation in a desert of neo-liberal laissez-faire for contracts in general ... overlooks the considerable and fast-developing body of regulation addressing issues of unfairness in the making and performance of contracts in general'.[13] Greater attention is now placed on exploring a wider range of tools and institutions for regulating work that falls outside the traditional regulatory repertoire of labour law.

The focus of this collection is on paid work that blurs traditional legal boundaries and the challenge this poses to traditional forms of labour regulation. Many of the Chapters concentrate on work arrangements that fall outside the employment relationship and several examine forms of

---

[9] Benería and Floro, above n 1, at 6; Carr, M and Chen, MA, *Globalization and the Informal Economy: How Global Trade and Investment Impact on the Working Poor* (Geneva, International Labour Organization, 2002); Carr, M and Chen, MA, 'Globalization, Social Exclusion and Gender' (2004) 143 *International Labour Review* 129.

[10] International Labour Organization, above n 2.

[11] Teklè, above n 5, at 3.

[12] See Davidov, G and Langille, B (eds), *Boundaries and Frontiers of Labour Law* (Oxford, Hart Publishing, 2006); Supiot, A, *Beyond Employment: Changes in Work and the Future of Labour Law in Europe* (Oxford, Oxford University Press, 2001); Vosko, L, *Managing the Margins: Gender, Citizenship, and the International Regulation of Precarious Employment* (Oxford, Oxford University Press, 2010); Davidov, G, and Langille, B (eds), *The Idea of Labour Law* (Oxford, Oxford University Press, 2011).

[13] Freedland, M, 'From the Contract of Employment to the Personal Work Nexus' (2006) 35 *Industrial Law Journal* 1, 24.

regulation that do not fit within the classification of labour law. Some of the Chapters look at the regulation of work arrangements in developing countries, and this focus provides a useful counterpoint to labour law's traditional preoccupation with models of employment that are embedded in the political economy of the developed world.[14] The collection has been designed to decentre traditional legal categories and norms of employment by examining forms of work that deviate from these categories and norms. Moreover, the emphasis on the heterogeneity of work arrangements is perfectly compatible with an attention to a hierarchy of work arrangements ranked in terms of the security of the work and the adequacy of the income generated.[15] In developing this hierarchy, it is important to be attentive to how the social location of the worker—gender, family status, migration status, race and ethnicity, and age, for example—is linked to different forms of work and the working conditions and employment security of the worker.[16] It is also important to recognise that neither the hierarchy of work arrangements or social locations are stable. The goal of the collection is to explore the capacity of different legal approaches and techniques to protect the dignity of these workers, promote their self-determination, and protect them against social risks.

Before looking at the specific examples of paid work and regulatory techniques that are presented in the following Chapters, it is necessary to provide the broader context and interlocking themes that connect the different case studies. The terminology used to describe the changes in the contemporary world of work differ from country to country. The goal in this introduction is not to stipulate nomenclature, but, rather, to identify broader processes that tend to shift work outside the scope of labour protection. The next section is devoted to explaining how the process of 'informalisation' helps to understand the changes that are occurring to work arrangements. It begins by discussing informal work in developing and developed countries, and traces the changes in the meaning of 'informal' as it pertains to economic activities since the early 1970s when the term 'informal sector' was coined. Adopting an approach that encompasses subsistence work in the developing world and the process of informalisation that is changing work around the globe, this section identifies a hierarchy of work arrangements and links this hierarchy with the social location of the workers who perform the work. Informalisation is linked with commercialisation, which is discussed

---

[14] Teklè, above n 1 and Blackett, A 'Labor Law and Development: Perspectives on Labor Regulation in Africa and the African Diaspora' (2011) 32 *Comparative Labor Law & Policy Journal* 303 are very important recent contributions that revise the dominant narrative of labour law by turning to the global south.

[15] Carr and Chen, *Globalization and the Informal Economy*, above n 9; Carr and Chen, 'Globalization, Social Exclusion and Gender', above n 9.

[16] Lamphere, L, Zavella, P and Gonzales, F, *Sunbelt Working Mothers: Reconciling Family and Factory* (Ithaca, Cornell University Press, 1993).

in the following section. Commercialisation is a multidimensional process that is transforming labour markets at the local, national, and global levels. It refers to the contraction of the standard employment relationship,[17] the disintegration of vertically integrated firms, and the shift in the legal framework for regulating international services. Commercialisation has also affected the provision of care, which increasingly involves paid work performed in the household or other institutional settings. The examination of paid care work in the fourth section is critical because it blurs boundaries between productive and reproductive activities, and the spheres of the market and the family. Moreover, paid care work demonstrates the significance of the institutions in which the work is embedded for the effectiveness of labour regulation. These themes are then drawn together in the fifth section of this Chapter, which considers how the blurring of the boundaries between employee and independent contractor, between formal and informal employment, between productive and reproductive work creates problems for defining and achieving the goals of labour law. If protection is the justification for employment law, there is a range of work relationships in which the individuals may be in as much need of protection as employees.[18] If the goal of labour law is to secure workers' rights and dignity, the traditional boundaries continue to create arbitrary distinctions. The section ends by touching upon the capacity of the International Labour Organization's (ILO) Decent Work Agenda to provide labour and social protection to all workers regardless of their employment status. The concluding section briefly describes the following Chapters in this collection, and links them to the key themes discussed in this introductory Chapter.

INFORMALISATION

Over the past 40 years, the prediction that the informal sector, which was characterised as a residual sector in developing countries, would be absorbed into the formal, or modern capitalist, economy as economies modernised, was proven to be incorrect. In fact, the informal sector has expanded in developing and developed countries, and with it low-skilled, poorly paid, intermittent and insecure employment.[19] Changes in the economy, the types

---

[17] I am using the term 'standard employment relationship' to refer to the regulatory norm. See Tham, J-C 'Towards an Understanding of Standard Employment Relationships under Australian Labour Law' (2007) 20 *Australian Journal of Labour Law* 123; Vosko, above n 12.

[18] Hyde, A, 'What is Labour Law?' in G Davidov and B Langille (eds), *Boundaries and Frontiers of Labour Law: Goals and Means in the Regulation of Work* (Oxford, Hart Publishing, 2006).

[19] Benería, above n 4; Sankaran, K 'The ILO, Women and Work: Evolving Labor Standards to Advance Women's Status in the Informal Economy' (2002) 3 *The Georgetown Journal of Gender and the Law* 851, 854.

of activities measured, the nature of statistics collected, and different foci of study have led to a proliferation of different conceptions of informality.[20]

During the 1950s and 1960s it was assumed that poor traditional economies could be transformed into dynamic modern economies and that, in the process, the traditional sector comprising petty traders, small producers, and a range of casual jobs would be absorbed into the formal, or modern capitalist, economy. However, by the mid-1960s, concerns about widespread unemployment led the ILO to send a series of large, multi-disciplinary missions to several developing countries.[21] Significantly, the mission to Kenya reported in 1972 that the traditional sector had expanded to include profitable and efficient enterprises as well as marginal activities. Relying on a study of economic activities in urban Ghana by the British economist Keith Hart, in 1972 the ILO used the term 'informal sector' to describe the activities of the working poor who were working very hard but who were not recognised, recorded, protected, or regulated by the public authorities.[22] Hart's emphasis 'on the productivity and growth potential of informal economic activities in developing economies' prompted a debate about economic development and the role of the informal sector, and led to a range of approaches to examining the informal sector.[23]

Instead of focusing on the dichotomy between the informal and formal sectors, in the 1980s Alejandro Portes and his colleagues conceptualised the relationship as a process of informalisation, which they understood as a specific feature of global capitalism.[24] Thus, they expanded research on informal economic activities to include changes that were occurring in advanced capitalist economies, where production was reorganised into small-scale, decentralised, and more flexible economic units. The significance of this approach, according to Elizabeth Hill, is that 'the social processes that underlie the development of the informal economy are highlighted and significant emphasis is put on the relationship between social processes and the wider context of economic change in the world economy'.[25]

[20] Trebilcock, A, 'Using Development Approaches to Address the Challenges of the Informal Economy for Labour Law,' in G Davidov and B Langille (eds), *Boundaries and Frontiers of Labour Law* (Oxford, Hart Publishing, 2006) 64, 64–6.

[21] International Labour Organization, *Women and Men in the Informal Economy: A Statistical Picture* (Geneva, International Labour Office, 2002).

[22] International Labour Organization, *Employment, Incomes and Equality: A Strategy for Increasing Productive Employment in Kenya* (Geneva, International Labour Office, 1972).

[23] For a succinct account of this debate see Hill, E, *Worker Identity, Agency and Economic Development: Women's Empowerment in the Indian Informal Economy* (London, Routledge, 2010) 12.

[24] *Ibid* at 20.

[25] Hill, above n 23, at 20 citing A Portes, M Castells and LA Benton (eds), *The Informal Economy: Studies in Advanced and Less Developed Countries* (Baltimore, John Hopkins University Press, 1989).

Castells and Portes described the informal economy not as 'an individual condition but a process of income-generation characterized by one central feature: *it is unregulated by the institutions of society, in a legal and social environment in which similar activities are regulated*'.[26] They emphasised the links between informal and formal economic activities, and their focus was on changes in production and the ways in which firms pursue flexible forms of labour, such as casual labour, contract labour, outsourcing, home working, and other forms of subcontracting that offer the prospect of minimising fixed non-wage costs. The link between informalisation and labour market flexibility was taken up by Guy Standing, who argued that there has been an 'informalisation' of employment in developed countries, such that 'a growing proportion of jobs possess what may be called informal characteristics, i.e. without regular wages, benefits, employment protection, and so on'.[27]

As the Chapter by Kamala Sankaran in this collection demonstrates, this process of informalisation is also occurring in developing countries such as India.[28] Alongside this shift from regulated to precarious employment, developing countries have continued to experience the growth of subsistent activities generated by the inability of their economies to absorb the unemployed and underemployed.[29] These activities constitute the more traditional urban informal activities in developing countries, as typified by the street vendors and waste pickers in many urban centres. Some of these informal workers, such as the waste pickers described by Poornima Chikarmane and Lakshmi Narayanan in their Chapter,[30] are connected to the formal economy; however, others are not.

Focusing on informalisation recognises the tremendous heterogeneity of informal activities and gets beyond the informal/formal divide. Far from being the low-productivity, 'backward' sector described in the early literature, the informal economy has proved to be dynamic and a source of growth in many areas and sectors, even if representing extreme forms of precariousness in others.[31] The blurred boundary between formal and

---

[26] Castells, M and Portes, A, 'The World Underneath: The Origins, Dynamics, and Effects of the Informal Economy' in A Portes, M Castells and LA Benton (eds), *The Informal Economy: Studies in Advanced and Less Developed Countries* (Baltimore, John Hopkins University Press, 1989) 12 (emphasis in original).

[27] Standing, G, 'Global Feminisation Through Flexible Labor: A Theme Revisited' (1999) 27 *World Development* 583, 585.

[28] Sankaran, K, 'Flexibility and Informalisation of Employment Relationships' in this collection.

[29] Benería and Floro, above n 1. See also Tsikata, D 'Toward a Decent Work Regime for Informal Employment in Ghana: Some Preliminary Considerations' (2011) 32 *Comparative Labor Law & Policy Journal* 311.

[30] Chikarmane, P and Narayanan, L, 'Transform or Perish: Changing Conceptions of Work in Recycling' in this collection.

[31] Guha-Khasnobis, B, Kanbur, R and Ostrom, E (eds), *Linking the Formal and Informal Economy Concepts and Policies* (New York, Oxford University Press, 2006).

informal economic activities has led to the recognition of a continuum of informal economic activities.

In June 2002, the International Labour Conference adopted a resolution containing Conclusions concerning Decent Work and the Informal Economy that focuses on activities that are 'appropriate for regulation or protection under labour or commercial law'.[32] This approach recognises a continuum of production and employment relations and stresses the linkages between formal and informal activities. However, it also excludes activities that are treated as criminal, as well as the reproductive or care economy that consists of unpaid domestic work and care activities.[33] Criminalised sex work would, for example, fall outside even the ILO's expanded definition of work. In its report, *Decent Work and the Informal Economy*, the ILO identified the following broad range of informal workers:

> [O]wn-account workers in survival-type activities, such as street vendors, shoeshiners, garbage collectors and scrap- and rag-pickers; paid domestic workers employed by households; homeworkers and workers in sweat-shops who are 'disguised wage workers' in production chains; and the self-employed in micro-enterprises operating on their own or with contributing family workers or sometimes apprentices/ employees.[34]

Despite their heterogeneity, these different groups of workers 'share one important characteristic: *they are not recognised or protected under the legal and regulatory frameworks. This is not, however, the only defining feature of informality. Informal workers and entrepreneurs are characterised by a high degree of vulnerability*'.[35] Not only are these workers outside the scope of labour law, and thus deprived of legal and social protection and legal enforcement regimes, 'they are rarely able to organise for effective representation and have little or no voice to make their work recognised and protected'.[36]

However, the informal nature of these activities does not mean that the workers lack agency. Chikarmane and Narayanan's discussion of waste pickers in Pune demonstrates that informal workers are able to establish a collective occupational identity as workers, and that if they do they will express demands for social protection and formal recognition of their work.[37] Their Chapter also demonstrates that simply because work is informal does not entail 'that there are no rules or norms regulating the activities

---

[32] International Labour Conference, 90th Session, *Decent Work and the Informal Economy: Report VI* (Geneva, International Labour Office, 2002) 4.

[33] *Ibid* at 31 for a copy of the Guidelines concerning a statistical definition of informal employment, endorsed by the Seventeenth International Conference of Labour Statisticians (November–December 2003).

[34] *Ibid* at 2.

[35] *Ibid* (emphasis in original).

[36] *Ibid* at 3.

[37] Chikarmane and Narayanan, above n 30.

of workers or enterprises'.[38] These workers have their own group rules, arrangements, institutions, and structures. The key question is what 'these informal rules or norms are based on and whether or how they observe the fundamental rights of workers'.[39]

Marilyn Carr and Martha Chen have developed a hierarchy of employment statuses in the informal economy.[40] At the top of the pyramid they locate employers in unregulated or unregistered business, followed by own-account self-employed, wage workers, casual day labourers who are placed above domestic workers, and contract workers (workers who are provided to producers through a third party) who are situated at the bottom of the hierarchy. While they acknowledge that the exact shape of the pyramid of employment statuses is temporally and geographically specific, this hierarchy also tends to map onto vulnerabilities to exploitation that results from a worker's social location. Social location refers to the way in which regional and local political economy interact with social relations of subordination that are linked to workers' attributes, such as sex, ethnicity, caste, race, immigration status, linguistic group, and skill and ability levels.[41] For example, rural workers who migrate to urban areas are overrepresented amongst own-account workers such as street vendors.[42] Women, who are often either intra- or inter-national migrants, predominate within domestic work, and they are often drawn from groups that are subordinated on the basis of race, ethnicity, caste, or language.[43] Social location combines with work arrangements to increase a worker's vulnerability to exploitation within informal employment.

It is important, however, not to reify the distinction between formal and informal employment. As employment relations are individualised with the contracting scope of unionisation and collective representation, employees who are entitled to legal protection may not, in fact, be able to access employment-related rights. Research by Anna Pollert and Andy Charlwood indicates that many employees who fit within the paradigmatic standard employment relationship are unable to avail themselves of

---

[38] International Labour Office, above n 22, at 3.

[39] *Ibid.*

[40] Carr and Chen, *Globalization and the Informal Economy*, above n 9; Carr and Chen, 'Globalization, Social Exclusion and Gender', above n 9.

[41] Lamphere, Zavella and Gonzales, above n 16.

[42] Sankaran, K, Sinha, S and Madhav, R, *WIEGO Law Pilot Project on the Informal Economy: Street Vendors in India* (undated), available at: http://previous.wiego.org/informal_economy_law/india/content/sv_background_note.pdf.

[43] Razavi, S, *The Political and Social Economy of Care in a Development Context: Conceptual Issues, Research Questions and Policy Options* (Gender and Development Programme Paper No 3, United Nations Research Institute for Social Development, Geneva, June 2007).

their employment rights.[44] Anna Pollert's contribution to this collection describes problems in the United Kingdom in ensuring compliance with, and enforcement of, employment and labour laws for workers who are not represented by trade unions, and it suggests that is not possible to regard even standard employees in developed countries as effectively protected by employment and labour laws.[45]

COMMERCIALISATION

The commercialisation of employment refers to the breakdown of the boundary between commercial activities and employment, on the one hand, and the erosion of the separation between work and care, on the other hand.[46] Like informalisation, it is part of the broader process of externalisation of risk through production and service changes and organisations. However, commercialisation is also involved in the shift of care work from unpaid care work by women in the home into paid care work, performed predominantly by women, either in the home or other institutions.

In developed countries, commercialisation takes many forms. Employment is increasingly project-, task-, or term-limited rather than ongoing, and pay has been individualised. Self-employment—often in the form of 'freelancers'—has increased, and the distinction between employment and self-employment is blurring as employment practices rapidly change.[47] Labour-only subcontracting, franchises, joint ventures, and project employment are examples of the commercialisation of employment.

The standard employment relationship, which is the target of labour regulation and the platform for many economic and social rights, is conceptualised as involving a bounded relationship: a contract between a single employer and an employee. However, changing organisational forms have weakened this platform. Vertical disintegration of firms and the breakdown of internal labour markets have resulted in the transformation of employees into independent contractors who are outside the scope of labour

[44] Pollert, A and Charlwood, A, 'The Vulnerable Worker in Britain and Problems at Work' (2009) 23 *Work, Employment & Society* 343.

[45] Davidov, G, 'The Enforcement Crisis in Labour Law and the Fallacy of Voluntarist Solutions' (2010) 26 *International Journal of Comparative Labour Law and Industrial Relations* 61; Weil, D and Pyles, A, 'Why Complain? Complaints, Compliance and the Problem of Enforcement in the U.S. Workplace' (2005) 27 *Comparative Labour Law and Policy Journal* 59; Pollert, A, 'How Britain's Low Paid Non-Unionised Employees Deal with Workplace Problems' in this collection.

[46] Marchington, M *et al* (eds), *Fragmenting Work: Blurring Organizational Boundaries and Disordering Hierarchies* (Oxford, Oxford University Press, 2006).

[47] Davidov, G, 'Freelancers: An Intermediate Group in Labour Law?' in this collection.

protection.[48] The boundaries of the firm have proved to be quite porous, 'making it difficult to know where the firm ends and where the market or another firm begins'.[49] Emerging organisational forms, such as networks, have combined with older, pre-Fordist organisational forms—especially subcontracting and employment agencies—to blur the traditional boundary of the firm. Prominent researchers have suggested 'it is more plausible to regard 'market', 'hierarchy', and 'network' as concepts that have proven valuable in differentiating elements or dimensions of organising practices within and between organisations, rather than as alternative designs of economic organisation'.[50] Decentralisation and fragmentation of production has contributed to the commercialisation of employment.

The structure of enterprises determines not only what form the work arrangements take, but also which entity in a common enterprise bears the responsibility for employing labour and the attendant work-related obligations. The blurring of organisational boundaries affects whether a worker falls within the scope of labour protection and which entity bears the responsibility for legal obligations owed to employees in different legal contexts. Moreover, the organisational form that an enterprise takes has a profound impact upon equity in employment conditions.[51]

The ease with which firms can adopt different organisational forms enables them to disaggregate different components of production and service provision around the globe. Global production and supply chains proliferate, and new technologies have resulted in the expansion of global services. Manuel Castells explains how

> the core activities of production, consumption, and circulation, as well as their components (capital, labour, raw materials, management, information, technology, markets) are organised on a global scale, either directly or indirectly though a network of linkages between economic agents.[52]

However, while capital, goods and services move easily across national borders, the mobility of people across borders is very restricted.[53]

---

[48] Collins, H, 'Independent Contractors and the Challenge of Vertical Disintegration to Employment Protection Laws' (1990) 10 *Oxford Journal of Legal Studies* 353.

[49] Powell, WW, 'The Capitalist Firm in the Twenty-First Century: Emerging Patterns in Western Enterprise' in P DiMaggio (ed), *The Twenty-First Century Firm: Changing Economic Organization in International Perspective* (Princeton, Princeton University Press, 2003) 58.

[50] Rubery, J 'Introduction: Fragmenting Work Across Organizational Boundaries' in Marchington *et al*, above n 46, at 10.

[51] Collins, H, 'Multi-segmented Workforces, Comparative Fairness, and the Capital Boundary Obstacle' in G Davidov and B Langille (eds), *Boundaries and Frontiers of Labour Law: Goals and Means in the Regulation of Work* (Oxford, Hart Publishing, 2006) 317; Earnshaw, J, Rubery, J and Cooke, FL, *Who is the Employer?* (London, Institute of Employment Rights, 2002) 2.

[52] Castells, above n 3, at 6.

[53] Trebilcock, M and Howse, R, *The Regulation of International Trade*, 3rd edn (London, Routledge, 2005) ch 19.

Organisational forms interact with the structure of markets to influence work arrangements. Some markets are structured in ways that increase the vulnerability of workers to poor outcomes and labour market risk. For example, David Weil has shown how the presence of large, concentrated business entities that have greater market power than the large set of small-scale organisations with which they interact has this effect.[54] He describes four types of monopsony markets with distinctive competitive dynamics that cause or exacerbate worker vulnerability; they are: strong buyers sourcing products in competitive supply chains; central production co-ordinators managing large contracting networks; small workplaces linked to large, branded national industries; and small workplaces and contractors linked together by common purchasers. Brendan Johnson's study of truck owner drivers in this collection is an example of workers providing services in the first type of monopsony market[55] and Shae McCrystal's study of postal delivery workers is an example of workers operating in the third type of market.[56]

The changes in how enterprises are organised combined with the structure of markets have resulted in a transformation in, and polarisation of, work arrangements.[57] At the high end of the spectrum are the knowledge workers, who are associated with the rise of the 'new economy' and networked organisations.[58] Although they fall outside the standard employment relationship, these workers are not typically considered to be in need of labour protection.[59] Moreover, such 'workers' tend to come from privileged social locations; they are highly educated or have access to social and economic capital, and typically are not obligated to engage in unpaid domestic and caring activities.

[54] Weil, D, 'Rethinking the Regulation of Vulnerable Work in the USA: A Sector-Based Approach' (2009) 51 *Journal of Industrial Relations* 411.

[55] Johnson, B, 'Developing Legislative Protection for Owner-Drivers in Australia: The Long Road to Regulatory Best Practice' in this collection.

[56] McCrystal, S, 'Organising Independent Contractors: The Impact of Competition Law' in this collection.

[57] In the context of South Africa, Jan Theron describes this process of the externalisation of work as leading to a hierarchy of work relations in the extended workplace; Theron, J, 'Re-inventing Inequality in the Post-apartheid Workplace' in O Dupper and C Garbers (eds), *Equality in the Workplace: Reflections from South Africa and Beyond* (Cape Town, Juta & Co, 2009) 133.

[58] Dickens, L, 'Problems of Fit: Changing Employment and Labour Regulation' (2004) 42 *British Journal of Industrial Relations* 595; Stone, KVW, *From Widgets to Digits: Employment Regulation for the Changing Workplace* (Cambridge, Cambridge University Press, 2004); Hyde, A, *Working in Silicon Valley: Economic and Legal Analysis of a High-Velocity Labor Market* (Armonk, NY, ME Sharpe, 2003).

[59] However, in a labour market in which knowledge workers are oversupplied, they too are easily transformed into contingent workers who may well be in need of labour protections. See Purcell, J, Purcell, K and Tailby, S, 'Temporary Work Agencies: Here Today, Gone Tomorrow?' (2004) 42 *British Journal of Industrial Relations* 705.

At the other end of the spectrum are 'precarious' or vulnerable workers who are associated with sub-contracted labour.[60] These workers are poorly paid and employed in atypical and unstable jobs, which more often than not fall outside the scope of collective representation or legal regulation. They tend to be drawn from vulnerable social locations. Women, people from ethnic minorities and racialised groups, and workers with precarious immigration statuses, whether temporary or undocumented, are overrepresented in precarious work arrangements that fall outside the norm of the standard employment relationship.

In the middle, are an increasing number of workers, such as independent contractors, freelancers, and franchisees, who enjoy some control over, and independence in, their work process as well as some capital (human or otherwise). Although they are not legally subordinated to a specific employer, these workers are also exposed to a number of risks—such as illness and lack of work—that individuals are not well placed to meet. Moreover, they often operate in markets in which individuals have little bargaining power. While some of these workers are drawn from social locations that make them vulnerable to exploitation, others, especially those who have access to capital or professional qualifications, are not.

Commercialisation also refers to how the flow of labour across national boundaries is being recharacterised as a matter of the free trade in services and not migrant, labour, or immigration law. As a matter of international law, migrant workers who are working temporarily within the national territory of a host state are entitled to the same laws and terms and conditions of employment as permanent residents or citizens of the host state.[61] The effect of this rule is to provide equality of treatment between temporary migrant workers and the residents of a host state by raising the conditions of the former to the latter. However, the logic of the General Agreement on Trade in Services (GATS), especially Mode 4, which deals with the provision of services by the presence of an individual in another territory, is to treat labour as just another commodity and, as such, subject to the principle that the sending country should be able to take advantage of the fact that its workers earn lower wages.[62] However, highly developed democracies have resisted Mode 4. While GATS Mode 4 has made it easier for managerial and professional workers to cross borders in order to engage in services, it has not made it easier for the vast majority of workers without formal credentials or recognised skills to migrate in order to find work.

---

[60] Fudge, J and Owens, R, 'Precarious Work, Women and the New Economy: The Challenge to Legal Norms' in J Fudge and R Owens, *Precarious Work, Women and the New Economy: The Challenge to Legal Norms* (Oxford, Hart Publishing, 2006) 7–9.

[61] Wickramasekara, P, 'Globalisation, International Labour Migration and the Rights of Migrant Workers' (2008) 29 *Third World Quarterly* 1247, 1256.

[62] Kelsey, above n 7, at 190–3.

These workers are still subject to temporary migration schemes under which receiving countries impose mobility restrictions on migrant workers (typically by tying them to the sponsoring employer) and the workers are vulnerable to exploitation.[63] Kelsey explains the sleights of hand that support these segmented streams of migration:

> First, to substitute 'trade' for a 'labour' paradigm, the 'market' that is being accessed must be reclassified as the *services* market of the purchaser, instead of the *employment* market of the host state (at least for those professionals, executives and skilled workers that inhabit the privileged tier in the international labour market). Second, the argument that mode 4 'conceptually does not fall under the administrative machinery applicable to permanent migration' rests on a sharp, objective and illusory distinction between foreign workers engaged in services and non-services activities, and between short-term and longer-term foreign services workers.[64]

The globalisation of services helps to create a new international division of immaterial labour. 'Immaterial labour' is a term coined by Michael Hardt and Antonio Negri to describe labour that 'produces an immaterial good, such as a service, a cultural product, a knowledge, or communication', and they identify three forms of immaterial labour: the first involves industrial production that has incorporated information technologies; the second is analytic and symbolic labour, which can either involve creative manipulation or be routine; and the third is affective labour that has traditionally been regarded as women's caring work.[65] Moreover, these 'categories are infused with class relations':

> At one level, transnational corporations require international mobility for their executives, managers, and specialists, and for associated professions. At the same time, they seek to minimise the cost of the mundane labour component of services, whatever the mode of delivery—remotely across the border (call centre operators); to visiting foreign consumers (hotel workers); by contractors for foreign-owned enterprises (cleaners); or through temporary migrants (construction labourers or domestic services).[66]

PAID DOMESTIC AND CARE WORK

Domestic work is an example of immaterial labour, and it includes the activities of caring for other, often dependent, people and household tasks

---

[63] Martin, JP, 'Temporary Labour Migration: An Illusory Promise?' (2008) *International Migration Outlook: SOPEMI 2008* 17, 20.

[64] Kelsey, above n 7, at 193 (emphasis in original), quoting Chanda, R, *Movement and Presence of Natural Persons: Issues and Proposals for the GATS Negotiations* (Geneva, South Centre, 2004) 1.

[65] Hardt, M and Negri, A, *Empire* (Cambridge, MA, Harvard University Press, 2000) 209 (footnote omitted).

[66] Kelsey, above n 7, at 189.

that have traditionally been performed by women, especially mothers, primarily for affective reasons and as part of deeply rooted social and cultural roles.[67] A defining characteristic is that this work takes place in the home, the private domain of the family. The boundaries between home/ market and private/public are deeply inscribed in contemporary legal doctrines, discourses and institutions. When performed for wages in the household, domestic work troubles boundaries that distinguish different spheres of social activity, which are associated with specific discourses and technologies of legal regulation.[68] Moreover, when they cross national boundaries, domestic workers also cross a number of different legal fields or jurisdictions.[69] Adelle Blackett explains how

> the law at once jealously guards the public borders of the state through immigration laws, while reifying the private borders of the home despite the public activity that proliferates behind its doors. Restrictive regulation of the immigration dimensions of the trans-national 'maid trade' stands in stark contrast to the abject neglect of the employment and labour law dimensions of domestics' workforce participation.[70]

Over the past 30 years, women's labour force participation has increased substantially and a growing proportion of care work has been commercialised, 'even though much is still performed within the household, either as unpaid work by family members or as paid activities performed by hired domestic help'.[71] Moreover, neoliberal policies have subjected women across the globe to similar pressures. Privatisation in developed countries has weakened the welfare state, and in developing countries, social protection has contracted. In the developed world, the emphasis is on increasing women's labour force participation, and policies designed to reconcile the competing pressures of paid work and care work emphasise paid maternity, parental, and (very occasionally) paternal leave, flexible hours of work, and childcare services.[72] In the developing world, the availability of inexpensive

---

[67] Following the lead of Adelle Blackett, I am deliberately using the terms 'care work' and 'domestic work' interchangeably. See Blackett, A, 'Introduction: Regulating Decent Work for Domestic Workers' (2011) 23 *Canadian Journal of Women and the Law* 1. See also the discussion in footnote 1.

[68] Albin, E, 'From "Domestic Servant" to "Domestic Worker"' in this collection.

[69] Fudge, J, 'Global Care Chains, Employment Agencies and the Conundrum of Jurisdiction: Decent Work for Domestic Workers in Canada' (2011) 23 *Canadian Journal of Women and the Law* 235.

[70] Blackett, A, 'Promoting Domestic Workers' Human Dignity through Regulation' in A Fauve-Chamoux (ed), *Domestic Service and the Formation of European Identity: Understanding the Globalization of Domestic Work, 16th–21st Centuries* (Bern, Peter Lang, 2005).

[71] Benería, L, 'The Crisis of Care, International Migration, and Public Policy' (2008) 14(3) *Feminist Economics* 1, 2. See also Razavi, S and Staab, S, 'Underpaid and Overworked: A Cross-National Perspective on Care Workers' (2010) 149 *International Labour Review* 407.

[72] Benería, above n 71, at 5.

domestic service, the large informal economy, and the feminisation of migration as a form of survival strategy suggest that the policies needed in developing countries for balancing different types of work may differ from those in developed ones.[73]

Rural to urban migration historically has provided a supply of domestic workers.[74] Moreover, historically and across a diverse range of countries, both developed and developing, women from disadvantaged racial and ethnic groups have tended to provide care services to meet the needs of more powerful social groups, while their own care needs have been downplayed and neglected.[75] Nowhere is this process of racialisation and subordination more evident than when it comes to the globalisation of care and social reproduction.

Arlie Hochschild coined the term the 'global care chain' to refer to 'a series of personal links between people across the globe based on the paid or unpaid work of caring'.[76] Global care chains are transnational networks that are 'formed for the purpose of maintaining daily life'; these networks comprise households that transfer their caregiving tasks across borders on the basis of power axes as well as employment agencies, governments and their departments, and other agents, institutions, and organisations.[77] Elaborating on the concept of global care chains, Nicola Yeates emphasises the great diversity of agents involved in the provision of care services, which 'include recruitment and placement agencies, overseas job promoters and job brokers provided by commercial and non-commercial, governmental and non-governmental bodies'.[78] These agents operate in different contexts and according to different logics; they are governed internally by '[r]elations of power and authority' that operate within the chain and externally by immigration and labour regulation.[79]

A defining characteristic of paid domestic work is that it is located in the employer's home. However, care work, as Guy Mundlak's Chapter so clearly shows, can take place in a number of different institutional settings. Paid child care, for example, can take place either in the child's or the carer's home, a for-profit enterprise, a not-for-profit agency, a worker-owned and operated

---

[73] *Ibid*, at 6.

[74] Tsikata, D, 'Employment Agencies and Domestic Work in Ghana' in this collection.

[75] Razavi, above n 43, at 2.

[76] Hochschild, AR, 'Global Care Chains and Emotional Surplus Value' in W Hutton and A Giddens (eds), *On the Edge: Living with Global Capitalism* (London, Jonathon Cape, 2000) 131.

[77] Pérez Orozco, A, *Global Care Chains* (Gender, Migration and Development Series, Working Paper 2, (United Nations International Research and Training Institute for the Advancement of Women, Santo Domingo, Dominican Republic, 2009).

[78] Yeates, N, *Global Care Chains: A Critical Introduction* (Global Migration Perspectives Paper No 44, Global Commission on International Migration, Geneva, September 2005) 9.

[79] *Ibid*. See also Yeates, N, *Globalizing Care Economies: Explorations in Global Care Chains* (Houndmills, Palgrave Macmillan, 2009). Yeates expands the conception of global care chains to examine highly skilled care workers such as nurses.

co-operative, or it can be delivered as a public service by government. The question of the institutional setting in which work is performed is critical to whether or not the work is precarious or well regulated. As Alice Sindzingre explains, 'all institutions are characterised by their forms—their definitions, names, and modes of organisation—and "contents"—their meanings, function, relevance, and elements'.[80] Institutional setting, rather than the dichotomy of formality versus informality might explain better the quality of certain kinds of paid work.[81]

REGULATING FOR DECENT WORK

In response to the broad changes in the standard employment relationship and to the recognition of the growth in informal employment, the ILO initiated a major organisational review, which led to its Decent Work Agenda. Launched in 1999, the Decent Work Agenda radically broadens the ILO's traditional constituencies to focus on people at the periphery of formal systems of labour and social protection. Its goal is to promote opportunities for women and men to obtain decent and productive work in conditions of freedom, equity, security, and human dignity. Decent work is captured in four strategic objectives or pillars: fundamental principles and rights at work and international labour standards; employment and income opportunities; social protection and social security; and social dialogue and tripartism. Significantly, these objectives hold for all workers, women and men, in both formal and informal economies; in wage employment or working on their own account; in the fields, factories, and offices; in their homes or in the community.[82]

The June 2002 International Labour Conference adopted a resolution concerning decent work and the informal economy that called for the needs of workers and economic units in the informal economy to be addressed, with emphasis on an integrated approach from a decent work perspective.[83] A crucial component of the decent work perspective is the emphasis on the ILO's 1998 *Declaration on Fundamental Principles and Rights at Work*, which articulates fundamental rights: freedom of association and the

[80] Sindzingre, A, 'The Relevance of the Concepts of Formality and Informality: A Theoretical Appraisal' in B Guha-Khasnobis, R Kanbur and E Ostrom (eds), *Linking the Formal and Informal Economy Concepts and Policies* (New York, Oxford University Press, 2006) 70.
[81] Mundlak, G, 'The Wages of Care-Workers: From Structure to Agency' in this collection; Bernstein, S, 'Sector-Based Collective Bargaining Regimes and Gender Segregation: A Case Study of Self-Employed Home Childcare Workers in Quebec' in this collection.
[82] International Labour Conference, 87th Session, *Decent Work: Report of the Director General of the International Labour Organization* (Geneva, International Labour Organization, 1999).
[83] International Labour Office, above n 22, at 2.

effective recognition of the right to collective bargaining; the elimination
of all forms of forced or compulsory labour; the effective abolition of child
labour; and the elimination of discrimination in respect of employment and
occupation.[84] The ILO is clear that the fundamental principles and rights
at work, and the conventions with which they are associated, apply to all
workers, and that 'there should not be a two-tiered system or separate regulatory framework for formal and informal workers—although there may be
a need for different modalities and mechanisms for guaranteeing them in
the less regulated, less formal parts of the economy'.[85]

According to the ILO, 'informal work can be treated as a legal
problem'.[86] This problem can arise in a number of ways. Workers could
be covered by legislation that is not enforced. Or it may be the case that
labour legislation has lagged behind changes in forms of work organisation
such that workers, such as temporary agency workers, are excluded from its
scope. Another possibility is that workers are excluded from labour legislation because such legislation only applies to formal and narrowly defined
employment relationships.

In 2008, the ILO adopted its third major statement of principles and
policies since the 1919 Constitution, the *Declaration on Social Justice
for a Fair Globalisation*.[87] The Social Justice Declaration enshrined the
four strategic objectives of the Decent Work Agenda in a major policy
document. However, at the same time, the ILO has largely moved to 'soft'
law techniques and away from its traditional Convention-based system.
The 1998 Declaration signalled the beginning of this shift in direction, as
it established follow-up procedures based on country and ILO reports. The
Decent Work Agenda, although it expanded the ILO's focus beyond the
four fundamental principles and rights at work, continued with the 'soft'
law approach, and is directed at reducing poverty and creating sustainable
development.[88]

At the same time, the ILO's Decent Work Agenda has begun to make
greater inroads in breaking down the conceptual and regulatory barriers
between the workplace and the household. The 2010 International Labour
Conference discussed the report *Decent Work for Domestic Workers*
and voted to bring an international convention for domestic workers

---

[84] International Labour Organization, *Declaration of Fundamental Principles and Rights at
Work* (Declaration presented to the International Labour Conference, 86th Session, Geneva,
1998).
[85] International Labour Office, above n 22, at 40.
[86] *Ibid* at 48.
[87] International Labour Organization, above n 2.
[88] International Labour Conference, 96th Session, *Strengthening the ILO's Capacity to
Assist Members' Efforts to Reach Its Objectives in the Context of Globalization: Report V*
(Geneva, International Labour Office, 2007) iv.

to the 2011 Conference, where it was adopted.[89] The Convention, and accompanying recommendation, goes a long distance towards providing a regulatory regime that recognises domestic work as valuable and productive work deserving of the same protections as any other forms of work. Specifically designed for care work that is performed in private households, the Convention formalises the employment relationship by requiring written contracts or collective agreements, setting maximum hours and hours of rest, and requiring the payment of wages.[90] Among other things, it also calls attention to the need to protect domestic workers, especially migrants, who are recruited or placed by private agencies.[91]

Migrant workers, especially workers who are working in the host country for a temporary period without rights to permanent settlement, also challenge legal boundaries, but in this case the boundaries between immigration and labour law, on the one hand, and trade and labour law, on the other. The Global Commission on International Migration, the International Organisation for Migration, the ILO and the World Bank have all called for the expansion of legal migration through temporary and circular migration programmes. With the exception of the OECD,[92] which has introduced a note of caution that temporary migration 'does not appear to be a foundation upon which one can construct a solid migration policy', there is an 'emerging global consensus on the need to expand legal opportunities for migration to potential migrants, especially the low-skilled workers, from developing countries'.[93]

The ILO is taking some steps towards recognising the increasing importance of international migration in challenging the boundaries of labour law. At the 92nd Session of the International Labour Conference in 2004, it adopted a resolution on a '*Fair Deal for Migrant Workers in the Global Economy*', which noted the need for 'a rights-based international regime for managing migration' that rests 'on a framework of principles of good governance developed and implemented by the international community'.[94] Instead of a convention, the Conference opted for a non-binding multilateral framework for a rights-based approach to labour migration that takes account of national labour market needs. In 2005, the ILO Tripartite Meeting of Experts adopted the *ILO Multilateral Framework on Labour*

---

[89] International Labour Conference, 99th Session, *Decent Work for Domestic Workers: Report IV(1)* (Geneva, International Labour Office, 2009), available at: www.ilo.org/wcmsp5/groups/public/---ed_norm/---relconf/documents/meetingdocument/wcms_104700.pdf. For discussion see Albin, above n 68.

[90] *Domestic Workers Convention* 2011 (ILO C189).

[91] *Ibid*, at Art 15(1).

[92] Martin, above n 63, at 20.

[93] Wickramasekara, above n 61, at 1256.

[94] International Labour Conference, 92nd Session, *Towards a Fair Deal for Migrant Workers in the Global Economy: Report VI* (Geneva, International Labour Office, 2004) 139.

Migration: Nonbinding principles and guidelines for a rights-based approach to migration, which was authorised by the ILO's Governing Body in 2006.[95] Its goal is to create a virtuous circle of migration for sending and receiving countries that also benefits migrant workers by fostering co-operation and consultation among and between the tripartite constituents of the ILO within the broader commitment of promoting decent work for all.

However, at the same time that the ILO and other United Nations institutions are attempting to secure human, including labour, rights for migrant workers, other transnational and international institutions are trying to subsume labour under the category of services. This is the logic of the GATS,[96] and it can also be discerned in the controversial negotiations that resulted in the services directive in the European Union and in a series of European Court of Justice decisions that limit the ability of host countries to regulate the employment conditions of workers who are posted temporarily in another member state in order to perform services.[97] The boundaries between trade, labour, and immigration laws are increasingly blurred, as 'multiple international legal regimes—in human rights law, refugee law, labor law, trade law and criminal law—address, to some degree, the rights and privileges that should be accorded to aliens working within the territories of states parties'.[98]

By contrast, the boundary between competition law, on the one hand, and labour law, on the other, creates real problems for devising mechanisms to promote collective organisation and action for individuals who are engaged in commercialised work arrangements.[99] Less controversial, although still the exception rather than the rule, are regulations that are designed to improve the terms and conditions of small contractors such as franchisors[100]

---

[95] International Labour Organization, *ILO Multilateral Framework on Labour Migration: Non-binding principles and guidelines for a rights-based approach to labour migration* (Geneva, International Labour Organization, 2006) 61.

[96] Kelsey, above n 7.

[97] Bercusson, B, 'The Trade Union Movement and the European Union: Judgment Day' (2007) 13 *European Law Journal* 279, 279–80; Syrpis, P and Novitz, T, 'Economic and Social Rights in Conflict: Political and Judicial Approaches to their Reconciliation' (2008) 33 *European Law Review* 411, 416–18; Ashiagbor, D, 'Collective Labour Rights and the European Social Model' (2009) 3 *Law and Ethics of Human Rights* 223.

[98] Thomas, C, 'Convergences and Divergences in International Legal Norms on Migrant Labor' (2011) 32 *Comparative Labor Law and Policy Journal* 405, 405.

[99] McCrystal, S, 'Regulating Collective Rights in Bargaining: Employees, Self-Employed Persons and Small Businesses' in C Arup *et al* (eds), *Labour Law and Labour Market Regulation* (Sydney, Federation Press, 2006); McCrystal, S, 'Collective Bargaining by Independent Contractors: Challenges from Labour Law' (2007) 20 *Australian Journal of Labour Law* 1; McCrystal, above n 56.

[100] Riley, J, 'Regulating Unequal Work Relationships for Fairness and Efficiency: A Study of Business Format Franchising' in C Arup *et al* (eds), *Labour Law and Labour Market Regulation* (Sydney, Federation Press, 2006); Riley, J, 'A Blurred Boundary between Entrepreneurship and Servitude: Regulating Business Format Franchising in Australia' in this collection.

or self-employed workers.[101] More promising are various forms of supply chain regulation that operate within and across jurisdictions.[102] But, while there are examples of innovative forms of regulation that target commercialised work arrangements at the national and subnational levels, the ILO has continued to take a conservative approach in developing instruments that address the problems of workers who fall outside a formal employment relationship.[103]

The major problem with relying on international labour standards as a way of improving the working conditions and living standards of workers who fall outside the traditional boundaries of labour law is the failure of nation states both to ratify and to enforce international standards. Since tying labour standards to trade regimes has proved to be politically infeasible because many developing countries consider it to be a form of trade protection, voluntary co-operative codes of conduct have been regarded as an important form of 'soft' regulation.[104] There is a great deal of debate about the effectiveness of these codes in guaranteeing labour standards, and whether they can be considered a form of responsive regulation or simply window-dressing.[105]

Historically, effective labour standards have depended on workers' collective self-organisation. Trade unions have been the most widespread and durable vehicle for workers' self-organisation, and one of their explicit goals has been to regulate the labour market. However, trade union strength is

[101] Fudge, J, 'A Canadian Perspective on the Scope of Employment Standards, Labour Rights, and Social Protection: The Good, the Bad, and the Ugly' (2010) 31 *Comparative Labor Law & Policy Journal* 101; Sanchez Torres, E, 'The Spanish Law on Dependent Self-Employed Workers: A New Evolution in Labor Law' (2010) 31 *Comparative Labor Law & Policy Journal* 231; Landa Zapirain, J-P, 'Regulation of Dependent Self-Employed Workers in Spain: A Regulatory Framework for Informal Work?' in this collection.

[102] Weil, above n 54; Johnstone, R, 'Regulating Occupational Health and Safety in a Changing Labour Market' in C Arup *et al* (eds), *Labour Law and Labour Market Regulation* (Sydney, Federation Press, 2006); Nossar, I, 'Cross-Jurisdictional Regulation of Commercial Contracts for Work Beyond the Traditional Relationship' in C Arup *et al* (eds), *Labour Law and Labour Market Regulation* (Sydney, Federation Press, 2006); Rawling, M, 'A Generic Model of Regulating Supply Chain Outsourcing' in C Arup *et al* (eds), *Labour Law and Labour Market Regulation* (Sydney, Federation Press, 2006); Johnson, above n 55.

[103] Fudge, J, 'Self-Employment, Women, and Precarious Work: The Scope of Labour Protection' in J Fudge and R Owens (eds), *Precarious Work, Women and the New Economy: The Challenge to Legal Norms* (Oxford, Hart Publishing, 2006); Fudge, J, 'The Legal Boundaries of the Employer, Precarious Workers, and Labour Protection' in G Davidov and B Langille (eds), *Boundaries and Frontiers of Labour Law: Goals and Means in the Regulation of Work* (Oxford, Hart Publishing, 2006); Hyde, A, 'Legal Responsibility for Labour Conditions Down the Production Chain' in this collection.

[104] Kolben, K, 'The New Politics of Linkage: India's Opposition to the Workers' Rights Clause' (2006) 13 *Indian Journal of Labor Studies* 225.

[105] Trebilcock and Howse, above n 53, at 563–6; Kolben, K, 'Integrative Linkage: Combining Public and Private Regulatory Approaches in the Design of Trade and Labor Regimes' (2007) 48 *Harvard International Law Journal* 203; Madhav, R, 'Corporate Codes of Conduct in the Garment Sector in Bangalore' in this collection.

dependent on specific forms of employment, workplaces, types of firms, and political support.[106] The increase in self-employed workers has resulted in the establishment of different types of organisation to represent them. These organisations exhibit a range of different logics of action and they mobilise different work-related identities.[107] Similarly, informal workers in developing economies have adopted a range of different organisational forms, from co-operatives to traditional trade unions, to represent their interests.[108] Whether, and the extent to which, these organisations can secure labour standards and protect workers is an open question.

THE STRUCTURE OF THE BOOK

The Chapters in this collection are organised thematically, and each of the four Parts that follow corresponds to one of the themes discussed earlier in this introductory Chapter. The three Chapters in Part I focus on informal work, beginning with Kamala Sankaran's discussion of how processes of informalisation in India have eroded workers' protections and led to a deterioration in their living standards. She examines the feasibility of treating workers employed in these flexible forms of production as employees of the main enterprise, and considers the ILO's recommendation on the employment relationship from this vantage.[109] Sankaran's discussion of processes of informalisation in India is followed by a case study of informal subsistence workers in one city in India. In 'Transform or Perish: Conceptions of Work in Recycling', Poornima Chikarmane and Lakshmi Narayanan explore attempts by subsistence waste pickers in Pune to organise in order to improve the terms and conditions of their work. They describe how these informal workers adopted two organisational forms, a traditional trade union structure and a co-operative, in order to assert their demands for decent work.[110] The final Chapter in this Part, by Richard Johnstone, examines occupational health and safety regulation in developing countries, where workers disproportionately suffer from work-related death, injury, and ill-health. His Chapter questions the utility of borrowing regulatory models for occupational health and safety from developed countries for labour markets in developing countries that have a significant amount of informal employment and that depend upon transnational supply and

---

[106] Silver, B, *Forces of Labor: Workers' Movements and Globalization since 1870* (New York, Cambridge University Press, 2003).

[107] D'Amours, M, 'The Logic of Collective Action of Self-Employed Workers' Associations' (2010) 65 *Relations Industrielles* 257.

[108] Selcuk, FU, 'Labour Organisations in the Informal Sector' (2004) 3 *South-East Europe Review* 93.

[109] Sankaran, above n 28.

[110] Chikarmane and Narayanan, above n 30.

commodity chains. Johnstone begins to map out some of the possible regulatory approaches that might be taken to effectively regulate occupational health and safety in developing countries.[111]

The six Chapters included in Part II probe the gap between employment law and commercial law, a regulatory space into which increasing numbers of workers fall. These Chapters begin with work arrangements that deviate the greatest from traditional norms of employment and traditional techniques of employment and labour regulation. Alan Hyde's Chapter examines the process of commercialisation from a broader, economic perspective, and considers how this process plays out in the United States as well as in global labour markets.[112] Based upon an economic perspective that treats different forms of contracts as interchangeable, Hyde attempts to synthesise a workable concept of responsibility for labour conditions, under which purchasers of those services could realise efficiency gains from freedom of contract, while remaining legally responsible for violations of labour standards or human rights.

Hyde's Chapter is followed by three Chapters from Australia that look at regulatory devices rooted in commercial law. Australia is distinctive amongst Anglo-common law countries in offering a variety of mechanisms that either promote collective representation or secure decent labour standards. All three Chapters are case studies of different groups of workers operating in distinct commercially based regulatory regimes. The Chapter by Joellen Riley examines the regulation of franchise operators.[113] This group of workers experience contractual arrangements more closely resembling dependent employment than 'entrepreneurial business ownership', a situation Riley coins 'entrepreneurial servitude'. She evaluates the capacity of codes to ensure decent work for this group of 'entrepreneurs'. Brendan Johnson examines a range of regulatory regimes affecting truck owner drivers in light of a 2008 report by the Australian National Transport Commission that suggested existing regulation in the transport industry has failed to correct market failures that lead to unsafe and dangerous driving practices.[114] He concludes that these different commercial regimes for regulating this practice of subcontracting fail to address the inequality in bargaining power. The third case study, by Shae McCrystal, examines the impact of competition laws on the ability of independent contractors to engage in collective bargaining through a case study of contractor workers in the Australian postal industry.[115] In particular, McCrystal examines the

---

[111] Johnstone, R, 'Informal Sectors and New Industries: the Complexities of Regulating Occupational Health and Safety in Developing Countries' in this collection.
[112] Hyde, above n 103.
[113] Riley, 'A Blurred Boundary between Entrepreneurship and Servitude', above n 100.
[114] Johnson, above n 55.
[115] McCrystal, above n 56.

response of competition regulators to arguments by contractor workers about the pro-competitive effects of collective bargaining. Together, these Chapters demonstrate the challenges of regulating labour from within commercial law as each Chapter highlights a key regulatory failing of the models under evaluation. These failures include the continued litigation over contractual disputes involving franchisees (Riley), the failure of the market in the transport sector to produce 'safe rates' of pay for owner drivers (Johnson) and competition based solutions producing outcomes which fail to correct workers' imbalance of bargaining power (McCrystal).

The last two Chapters in Part II explore the question of how to classify and treat for regulatory purposes workers who do not fit easily into the categories of employee or entrepreneur. Juan-Pablo Landa Zapirain examines the new regulatory regime applying to self-employed workers in Spain, drawing parallels with other European attempts to regulate such workers.[116] This Chapter effectively demonstrates the difficulties (both legal and practical) of implementing a regime designed to facilitate freedom of contract while also providing protection for the workers susceptible to exploitation. The Chapter by Guy Davidov proposes more widespread recognition of an intermediate category of workers, between employees and independent contractors, commonly called 'dependent contractors'.[117] Davidov argues that the identification of such a group would allow workers who are economically dependent, but not legally subordinate, to be protected by labour law regulation that is appropriate to their working arrangements and enacted for that purpose, while at the same time to be excluded from other legislation designed to protect legally subordinate workers.

Part III focuses on care and domestic work, and the Chapters in it examine the on-going significance of institutions for obtaining decent work for care workers and the historical legacy of legal categories for contemporary regulatory strategies for care work. It begins with two Chapters that emphasise the significance of the institutional setting in which the care work is performed in influencing collective strategies and occupational identities. Using Israel as his case study, in 'The Wages of Care Workers from Structure to Agency', Guy Mundlak examines four different arrangements for delivering care work, which provides an overview of different care arrangements and the collective strategies that were used in pursuit of change.[118] In the next Chapter, Stéphanie Bernstein's case study of the recently created sector-based collective bargaining regime for home childcare providers in Quebec demonstrates the utility of Mundlak's typology of care arrangements in welfare states.[119] Bernstein illustrates the contradictory goals embedded in the regulatory

---

[116] Landa, above n 101.
[117] Davidov, 'Freelancers: An Intermediate Group in Labour Law?', above n 47.
[118] Mundlak, above n 81.
[119] Bernstein, above n 81.

regime. On the one hand, the regime's goal is to contain the rising costs to the state of subsidised childcare, and on the other, the regime's goal is to appease unions' demands in the political and judicial arenas for the full recognition of home childcare providers' collective bargaining rights. She concludes with reflections on its potential pitfalls and on the regime's effectiveness in eliminating deeply-ingrained gender-based discrimination in relation to care work.

The second pair of Chapters in Part III concentrate on domestic work performed in private households. Albin's Chapter begins on an historical note, as she explores the legacy of the legal category of 'domestic servant' in British labour law on the current legal treatment of domestic workers.[120] She proceeds to assess whether, and to what extent, the ILO's *Domestic Workers Convention* 2011 (ILO C189) addresses the problems encountered by domestic workers in the British field of labour law. The final Chapter in the Part shifts attention to the developing world, and the relationship between formality and informality when it comes to domestic work. Dzodzi Tsikata describes how domestic work in Ghana has been largely informal and unregulated, and she explores the role of employment agencies in providing some predictability in the terms and conditions of domestic work.[121]

Part IV comprises three Chapters that look at the capacity of legal mechanisms to provide decent work. The Chapter by Roopa Madhav moves from the domestic realm of adjudicative tribunals and courts to the transnational space of voluntary codes of conduct.[122] She concludes that overall the move away from 'hard' law to the 'soft' law of codes of conduct as a means of protecting labour rights has created yet another forum to which workers can appeal, but provides little by way of substantial and sustainable benefits to the workers. She emphasises the continuing need for state inspection and enforcement mechanisms, as well as union organisation.

The recurring and increasing difficulty of enforcing employment and labour law suggests that any solution to the problem of the declining scope of employment protection must go beyond designing new forms of regulation to tackling the sticky and enduring problem of enforcement. Using data from the United Kingdom, Anna Pollert's Chapter demonstrates that many workers in standard employment relationships, in what is clearly a developed country, do not exercise their employment rights.[123] This Chapter reminds us that collective organisation and representation is essential to any form of effective regulation.

---

[120] Albin, above n 68.
[121] Tsikata, 'Employment Agencies and Domestic Work in Ghana', above n 74.
[122] Madhav, above n 105.
[123] Pollert, above n 45.

In 'Learning from Case Law Accounts of Marginalised Working', Lizzie Barmes questions how adjudicative tribunals and courts in the United Kingdom characterise the working arrangements, conditions, and choices of vulnerable and precarious workers.[124] Focusing on a recent case that went to the Court of Appeal and involved migrant workers she probes the significance of immigration status in creating a hierarchy in the labour market. She demonstrates how the abstract nature of the Court of Appeal's reasoning demonstrates little awareness of the situation of vulnerable migrant workers and little commitment to doing anything to improve it. Barmes provides a compelling account of the extent to which legal categories serve to distance adjudicators from the reality of vulnerable and precarious workers.

The goal of the collection is to provide a glimpse of the heterogeneity of contemporary work arrangements in order to challenge the traditional legal boundaries of work regulation. By broadening the field of vision, it has been necessary to shift focus away from traditional norms of employment and techniques of labour law that predominate in developed countries. This introduction has attempted to provide a framework for understanding how these different forms of work are related and a different conceptual lens for examining them. It has also sought to identify the key regulatory challenge, which is to identify and institutionalise 'innovative forms of participatory governance alive to workers' social locations', for achieving decent work.[125]

[124] Barmes, L, 'Learning from Case Law Accounts of Marginalised Working' in this collection.
[125] Blackett, above n 14, 309.

Part I

Informality at Work

2

Flexibility and Informalisation of Employment Relationships

KAMALA SANKARAN[*]

THIS CHAPTER EXAMINES the patterns of increased flexibility and informalisation of work that have taken place in India in the recent past in order to understand how production and employment processes have shifted and have resulted in greater levels of informal employment. The Chapter focuses on one aspect of the informalisation process, namely the movement from formal to informal employment relationships that have characterised a part of the growth of informal employment in the last couple of decades. Employers have rearranged the nature of work relations in order to reduce costs and to increase the degree of flexibility available to them to determine the number of employees within their enterprise/ establishment.[1] Some of these shifts have taken place in a manner '*external*' to the enterprises; that is, their effects are reflected outside the immediate enterprise when enterprises resort to product outsourcing decisions.[2] The effect of these decisions has often been to exclude several workers from the scope of labour protection and has contributed to the increase in the numbers in informal employment. The Chapter traces the manner in which labour law has contributed to and responded to the growth of informal employment.

[*] I am grateful for comments by anonymous reviewers, Judy Fudge, and participants at the workshop in Oñati where an earlier version of the Chapter was presented.
[1] Rajeev, M, *Contract Labour Act in India: A Pragmatic View* (IGIDR Proceedings/Project Reports Series, PP-062-33, 2009).
[2] I have borrowed this expression from the schema of numerical and functional flexibility developed by P Auer. See Auer, P, *Security in Labour Markets: Combining Flexibility with Security for Decent Work*, Economic and Labour Market Papers (Geneva, International Labour Organization, 2007), available at: www.ilo.org/wcmsp5/groups/public/---ed_emp/---emp_elm/---analysis/documents/publication/wcms_113923.pdf. See also Jha, P and Golder, S, *Labour Market Regulation and Economic Performance: A Critical Review of Arguments and Some Plausible Lessons for India*, Economic and Labour Market Papers (Geneva, International Labour Organization, 2008), available at: www.ilo.org/wcmsp5/groups/public/---ed_emp/---emp_elm/---analysis/documents/publication/wcms_113926.pdf.

FORMAL AND INFORMAL EMPLOYMENT RELATIONSHIPS

The past couple of decades have seen high rates of economic growth in India. Together with the rise in population, there has also been a rapid increase in the size of the labour force, from 345 million in 1993–94 to 429 million in 2004–05.[3] The labour force consists of all those who are either working or employed or 'seeking or available for work' (ie unemployed).[4] This increase in the rates of growth of the economy and the labour force has been accompanied by significant changes in the nature of employment and work relationships.

A recent government-appointed Commission has defined the terms 'informal sector' and 'informal employment', and by implication, 'formal sector' and 'formal employment', as follows:

> *Informal sector*: The unorganized sector consists of all unincorporated private enterprises owned by individuals or households engaged in the sale and production of goods and services operated on a proprietary or partnership basis and with less than ten total workers. *Informal worker/employment*: Unorganized workers consist of those working in the unorganized sector or households, excluding regular workers with social security benefits provided by the employers and the workers in the formal sector without any employment and social security benefits provided by the employers.[5]

Based on this definition, this Chapter uses the term 'formal employment relationships' to indicate those employees whose terms and conditions of employment are governed by labour laws and who obtain social security benefits.

Workers in formal employment relationships, that is, those covered by labour regulations and obtaining social security benefits, are a small proportion of workers in countries such as India. The formal sector employs a little over 10 per cent of workers in India (62.6 million out of a total of over 450 million in 2004–05). There are a miniscule number of formal workers (who get protected by labour law) in the informal sector. This section of

---

[3] National Commission for Enterprises in the Unorganised Sector (NCEUS), *The Challenge of Employment in India: An Informal Economy Perspective*, vol 1 (New Delhi, Government of India, 2009) 8. Detailed data from the 66th Round of the National Sample Survey conducted in 2010 is not yet available; however, preliminary data from this round indicates that the Labour Force Participation Rate has marginally declined to 400 persons per 1,000 in the last round. See National Sample Survey Office, *Key Indicators of Employment and Unemployment in India, 2009–10* (New Delhi, Government of India, 2011) available at: http://mospi.nic.in/Mospi_New/upload/Press_Note_KI_E&UE_66th_English.pdf.

[4] 'Labour force refers to that segment of population which supplies or offers to supply labour for production and therefore, includes both employed and unemployed persons.' See Labour Bureau, *Report on Employment & Unemployment Survey 2009–10* (Chandigarh, Government of India, 2010) 15, 29. The definition of the labour force in India includes all those who are 'employed' whether in employment relationships or as self-employed workers.

[5] NCEUS, *The Challenge of Employment in India*, above n 3, at 3.

workers comprises 0.5 per cent of total employment in India and has been ignored for the present Chapter.[6]

The early 1990s saw a major shift in economic and trade policies, including reforms in the process of industrial licensing and the removal of restrictions on import requirements in India, resulting in what has often been termed a period of liberalisation and a paradigm shift of the economy.[7] The net growth in employment since the onset of liberalisation and opening up of the economy during the past couple of decades in India has been largely of an informal kind. Formal employment relationships within large enterprises have not grown as significantly as have forms of informal employment with their attendant lack of job and social security.

Informal forms of employment in the labour market comprise those employed within *both* the formal and informal sectors. Informal employment relationships are not necessarily located only in enterprises in the informal sector, which covers those enterprises/establishments employing fewer than 10 workers. There is a sizeable, and growing, proportion of informal employment relationships within larger-sized enterprises in the formal sector. For instance, in 1999–2000, 23.1 million workers were employed as informal workers (ie those in informal employment relationships) in the formal/organised sector, and they comprised 42.1 per cent of those employed in that sector. The number of informal workers in the formal sector rose to 28.9 million in 2004–05, comprising 46.2 per cent of those employed within the formal sector.[8] The number of workers in formal employment relationships has remained more or less constant. Although employment in the formal sector grew from 54 million to 63 million between 1999–2000 and 2004–05, the number of people with social security benefits remained constant at 34 million.[9] One can conclude that most of the increase in formal sector employment took the form of *informal* employment in the formal sector.

The increase in formal sector employment has come either in the form of 'contract labour', ie workers engaged via intermediaries and contractors, who are often deprived of the benefits available to directly employed workers, or through an increase in the employment of casual workers. Casual

---

[6] NCEUS, *Conditions of Work and Promotion of Livelihoods in the Unorganised Sector* (New Delhi, Government of India, 2007) 4.

[7] The liberalisation following the economic crisis of 1991 'involved a sharp devaluation of the rupee; removal of quantitative restrictions on imports; reduction of import tariffs; and a unification of the exchange rate as the rupee was made convertible for current-account transactions. On the domestic front of the reform process the system of industrial licensing was removed and the list of items reserved for the small-scale producers was shortened considerably'. See Mazumdar, D and Sarkar, S, *Globalization, Labor Markets and Inequality in India* (Ottawa, International Development Research Centre, 2008) 2.

[8] NCEUS, *Conditions of Work*, above n 6, at 3.

[9] Dewan, R, 'Manufacturing Fragmentation and Flexibility: Book Review of Jeemol Unni and Uma Rani, Flexibility of Labour in Globalizing India: The Challenge of Skills and Technology (New Delhi: Tulika Books), 2008' (2009) 44(7) *Economic and Political Weekly* 31.

workers are engaged on a daily or intermittent basis, and because they are not employed for a minimum number of days per year (the number varies from 240 days per year for coverage under laws dealing with employment protection, to 80 days for social security benefits) they are classified as falling within informal employment relationships. Casual workers may be governed by minimum wage laws, yet the nature of their employment relationships are precarious and devoid of social security protection, and as a result they are treated as informal workers. Casual workers form a sizeable proportion of all those who work. Data indicates that for the country as a whole, the self-employed constituted the majority of workers (56.6 per cent) while casual workers were 28.1 per cent and only 15.3 per cent of workers were regular salaried/wage workers in 2004–05.[10] The proportion of casual workers for the country as a whole rose to 33.5 percent in 2009–10.[11] Casual workers fall outside the protection of many labour laws.

The development of labour law protection covering, mainly, the small section of the formal sector workforce can perhaps be explained by the nature of the social compact which underpinned the early industrialisation of newly independent India in the middle of the twentieth century.[12] Trade unions were made partners in the process of planned industrial development and workers were provided with employment security and social security in the key industries that were to be vehicles of India's industrial growth. The legal framework for this social compact was mainly contained in the Industrial Disputes Act 1947 (IDA),[13] the Industrial Employment (Standing Orders) Act 1946 (SOA) and several other laws providing for social security and regulating conditions of work. The IDA and SOA, inter alia, regulate terms of employment and impose several limitations upon employers against wrongful termination of employment. The IDA requires large-scale enterprises to obtain permission from the government prior to the retrenchment of any worker. This requirement has often been described as a rigidity, and seen as constituting a hurdle when reasons of efficiency require downsizing. Managerial prerogatives to determine work on the shop floor are also curtailed by provisions that require employers to get 'standing orders'[14] certified and to give prior notice of change before modifying any conditions of work or work arrangements, or while assigning alternative

---

[10] NCEUS, *Challenge of Employment in India*, above n 3, at 57.

[11] National Sample Survey Office, *Key Indicators of Employment and Unemployment in India 2009–10*, above n 3.

[12] For an overview of the development of the labour laws in the region see Sankaran, K, 'Labour Law in South Asia: Need for an Inclusive Approach' in T Tekle (ed), *Workers' Protection and Labour Law in Developing Countries* (Oxford, Hart Publishing, 2010) 225.

[13] The IDA applies to 1.4 per cent of the total work force, comprising 3 per cent of those who are in employment relationships.

[14] Standing order refers to the rules relating to working time, classification of workers, disciplinary and grievance procedures, and other related areas.

work to any worker at the establishment. These protections and benefits are provided to those recognised as 'workmen' under the IDA. The definition of 'workmen' does not include supervisors earning above a certain threshold minimum nor those working in managerial and administrative positions within the enterprise. Social security benefits in the form of social insurance were introduced by legislation such as the Employees' State Insurance Act 1948 and the Employees' Provident Fund & Miscellaneous Provisions Act 1952 and other related laws which, like the IDA, mainly apply to the formal sector of the workforce. Workers in the formal sector thus obtain a variety of benefits such as medical, maternity, disablement, death, provident fund, pension and gratuity benefits.

The IDA and SOA, with their robust provisions for employment protection and stringent requirements of prior government permission for retrenchment or notice prior to redeployment of workers, have been criticised for reducing the flexibility available to enterprises to determine employment decisions. Labour law rigidities have been used to justify the greater use of contract labour in recent years.

It is this normative framework that has been assailed as constituting a hurdle in ensuring flexibility. In the following discussion, I focus on some aspects of the legal framework and connected judicial decisions to examine if this is indeed the case, or whether they have, in fact, contributed to flexibility within India. In particular, this covers the provisions relating to retrenchment, the increased use of contract labour, and the newer response of product outsourcing as measures to reduce costs and overheads. I examine whether these measures have further reduced the capacity of labour law to provide workers with protection against vulnerability.

EMPLOYMENT FLEXIBILITY

The growing integration of Indian industry with the global economy has seen several enterprises downsize or close. There is a complex set of provisions governing retrenchment within India. The need for prior permission to retrench in the case of establishments employing 100 or more workers has been one of the most controversial provisions in recent times. This requirement is seen to constitute a rigidity but for which enterprises could down-size and respond to changing economic realities in an unhindered manner. The grounds and procedure of this requirement have been assailed as too restrictive. Under the IDA, retrenchment can take place for 'any reason whatsoever' but termination for reasons of ill-health, disciplinary reasons, retirement or expiry of the period of a fixed-term contract do not fall within this category.[15] Judicial interpretation of the expression 'for any

---

[15] IDA s 2(oo).

reason whatsoever' has held that termination for any reason other than the excluded categories would amount to retrenchment, thereby requiring the procedure laid down in the IDA to be followed, and payment of retrenchment compensation to the retrenched workers.[16] According to this broad interpretation, it is not merely the cases of termination of surplus staff (as is ordinarily understood) that are treated as cases of retrenchment, but all cases of termination of employment (other than the categories of termination excluded by the definition) have come to be treated as retrenchment under the law. This expansive interpretation of the retrenchment requirement is one reason why the law is considered to be so rigid.

This judicially created rigidity combines with the procedure required to be followed in the case of retrenchment to further restrict employers' ability to dismiss employees. Under Chapter V-B IDA, establishments employing 100 persons or more are required to seek the prior permission of the appropriate government in the case of retrenchment, lay-off or closure. Such permission is required only in the case of those employees falling within the term 'workman' under the IDA. Thus, managerial and administrative staff, supervisory workers earning above a certain amount, and workers who have not yet completed one year of 'continuous service' do not have this safeguard prior to their retrenchment. Seasonal establishments are also exempt from this requirement. The power of the government to grant permission to retrench is treated as a quasi-judicial power and the right to a hearing is granted to the affected parties, and this exercise of power is subject to the writ jurisdiction of the high courts.[17] The decision to grant permission is based upon the reasonableness of the proposed retrenchment. According to the government: 'Wherever permission is granted, it is ensured that workers' interests are protected, as far as possible'.[18] Aggrieved workmen who are retrenched consequent to the grant of permission by the government can also raise an industrial dispute pertaining to their termination before the industrial tribunal. The tribunal examines whether there has been compliance with the procedures under the IDA. The tribunal can examine the genuineness of the evidence before it and determine whether the permission to grant retrenchment was legal or not.[19]

Despite the perceived rigidity of the law or its overreach in covering all cases of termination as retrenchment (bar the excluded cases discussed

---

[16] *State Bank of India v N Sundara Money* (1976) 3 SCR 160; *Santosh Gupta v State Bank of Patiala* (1980) 2 LLJ 72 (SC); *Mohan Lal v Bharat Electronics Ltd* (1981) 2 LLJ 70 (SC). See also *Punjab Land Development and Reclamation Corporation Ltd v Presiding Officer* (1990) 2 LLJ 70 (SC).

[17] *Workmen of Meenakshi Mills Ltd v Meenakshi Mills* (1992) 2 LLJ 294 (SC).

[18] Ministry of Labour and Employment, *Annual Report 2005–06* (New Delhi, Government of India, 2006) 35.

[19] *Cable Corporation of India v Additional Commissioner of Labour* (2005) 3 LLJ 691; *Orissa Textile and Steel Mills v State of Orissa* (2002) 1 LLJ 858.

above), in practice, the law does not affect every enterprise in the formal sector employing workers. Since the law restricts the need for prior permission to those enterprises employing over 100 workmen, the number of enterprises covered is not so large. For instance, in 2003, 74 establishments applied for permission to retrench, affecting 2,911 workers, while in 2004 this number was down to 38 establishments affecting a larger number of workers—2,944.[20] Studies also indicate that permission to retrench has been liberally granted in the recent past.[21]

Early studies, such as that by Fallon and Lucas,[22] had taken the position that regulations such as those dealing with prior permissions for retrenchment imposed rigidity on business in achieving 'numerical flexibility'. Fallon and Lucas noticed a drop in labour demand following the 1976 amendment that imposed the prior permission requirement, and concluded that employment in the formal sector would have been 17.5 per cent higher in India had such job security provisions not been in place. However, subsequent studies have traced the rigidities in employment levels to other characteristics of the industries studied and not to the job security provisions regulating the manufacturing sector.[23]

Despite the possibility of job security provisions being a bottleneck in achieving flexibility in employment levels, the National Commission for Enterprises in the Unorganized Sector (NCEUS) concluded, 'the argument that the restrictions on retrenchment have negatively influenced expansion of industry or employment does not bear theoretical and empirical scrutiny'.[24]

While for a long time employers and industry chambers and the media had been very vocal about the rigidity in the law that did not permit retrenchment as a sole managerial prerogative, in recent years the ability of employers to engage contract labour who work alongside regular workers on their premises has afforded a great deal of flexibility. Attention is now increasingly upon the manner in which labour law deals with workers employed via an intermediary.

[20] Ministry of Labour and Employment, above, n 18.
[21] NCEUS, *The Challenge of Employment in India*, above n 3, at 175. It must be borne in mind that retrenchment among enterprises that employ fewer workers goes unreported since these do not require permission. Further, seasonal establishments are also exempt from the requirement to seek prior permission.
[22] Fallon, PR and Lucas, REB, 'The Impact of Changes in Job Security Regulations in India and Zimbabwe' (1993) 40 *Journal of Development Economics* 241. For a good overview of such studies see D'Souza, E, *Labour Market Institutions in India: Their Impact on Growth and Employment* (New Delhi, International Labour Organization, 2008), available at: http://www.ilo.org/asia/whatwedo/publications/lang--en/docName--WCMS_098850/index.htm.
[23] See D'Souza, above n 22 (quoting Dutta Roy, S, 'Employment Dynamics in Indian Industry: Adjustment Lags and the Impact of Job Security Regulations' (2004) 73 *Journal of Development Economics* 233), and Kannan, KP and Raveendran, G, 'Growth Sans Employment: A Quarter Century of Jobless Growth in India's Organised Manufacturing' (2009) 44(10) *Economic and Political Weekly* 80.
[24] NCEUS, *The Challenge of Employment in India*, above n 3, at 175.

CONTRACTUALISATION

Contractualisation, in the Indian context, is the employment of workers through a contractor (who are then referred to as contract labour) to work on the premises of the principal employer or user enterprise, on work connected with the work of the establishment of such principal employer.[25] Contractualisation is a specific form of commercialisation, which, as explained in Chapter 1 of this collection, is the process by which workers are removed from the scope of labour protection.[26] Though employed within formal sector enterprises covered by labour laws, contract labour constitutes a significant group of workers in informal employment in the formal sector, and is an important example of the process of informalisation taking place in India today.

The Contract Labour (Regulation and Abolition) Act 1970 (CLA) regulates the practice, which is prevalent in India, of engaging contract labour via a contractor for carrying out work connected with the work of an establishment. The enterprise that engages such contract workers is designated as the principal employer according to the terminology used in the Act. The primary liability for providing wages and social security benefits is cast upon the contractor who employs the contract labour directly.

This form of engaging contract workers has a long pedigree in India. Contractors, known as *sirdars, sattedars, thekedars* and other local names, would recruit workers from rural areas to work as contract labourers. This form of recruitment was common in tea plantations and spread to mines, textile mills and factories over the past two centuries. It was used by the British in plantations, public works and the railways, and also by private employers in the textile and coal industries in colonial times. Gangs of workers recruited by a contractor would perform work under the seemingly indirect supervision of the principal employer. This form of engaging workers who are not subject to the benefits provided to the regular, permanent workers of the principal employer is a flexibility device that cannot be termed a 'new' one, at least in the Indian context. Trade unions that organise regular workers had always struggled against this form of discrimination within the workplace and have often tried to raise industrial disputes on behalf of contract workers. The courts had ruled that workers directly employed by the employer had to establish that they had a 'direct and substantial interest', a 'community of interest' in the employment, non-employment or the terms of employment or the conditions of labour of the

---

[25] The International Labour Organization prefers the term 'triangular relationship' for such mediated employment contracts in its documents since the expression 'contract labour' does not convey this feature adequately.

[26] Fudge, J, 'Blurring Legal Boundaries: Regulating for Decent Work', in this collection.

person concerned in order to take lawful industrial action.[27] This term was given a broad interpretation by the courts, one that covered employees of a contractor.[28] As a result, workers of the principal employer could raise a demand for the abolition of contract labour.

In recent years, there has been significant pressure from trade unions demanding the absorption of contract labourers as employees of the principal employer. However, in the absence of a fraud or sham contract, contract labourers are not deemed to be employees of the principal employer and the route of raising an industrial dispute with the principal employer under the IDA is not open to such workers. The possibility of the principal employer's regular workers raising an industrial dispute on behalf of contract labour is also ruled out, since early cases have held, notwithstanding industrial solidarity, that there is no 'community of interests' between these two categories of persons working within the same establishment.[29]

With the enactment of the CLA in 1970, the ability of contract labourers to raise a dispute directly with the principal employer for abolition of the contract labour system was ruled out and the protection of the IDA was denied to them since they were not deemed to be direct employees of the principal employer.[30] Following the CLA, industrial tribunals no longer had jurisdiction to examine such disputes. However, when the appropriate government issues a notification abolishing contract labour, the contract labour can raise a dispute before the industrial tribunal contending that the contract of employment between them and the contractor is a sham and that they are direct employees of the principal employer.[31]

In rare cases, looking at several factors, the courts have lifted the corporate veil separating the principal employer from the contractor to hold that the principal employer is indeed the employer of the contract labourer.[32] However, it is very difficult to establish a sham transaction. The courts increasingly disregard actions taken by the principal employer to extend health benefits or safety equipment to contract labour as evidence of such fraud, and treat these as merely attempts to achieve homogenous working conditions in terms of health and hygiene or measures taken to retain some control over contract labour.[33] Moreover, the courts now require proof of

---

[27] *Workmen of Dimakutchi Tea Estate v Dimakutchi Tea Estate* (1958) 1 LLJ 500 (SC).

[28] *Standard Vacuum Refining Company of India v Their Workmen* (1960) 2 LLJ 233 (SC).

[29] *Workmen of Dimakuchi Tea Estate v Management of Dimakuchi Tea Estate* AIR (1958) SC 353.

[30] *Vegoils Pvt Ltd v The Workmen* (1971) 2 LLJ 567 (SC).

[31] *Gujarat Electricity Board, Thermal Power Station, Ukai, Gujarat v Hind Mazdoor Sabha* AIR (1995) SC 1893; *Steel Authority of India Ltd v National Union Waterfront Workers* (2001) 2 LLJ 1087 (SC).

[32] *Hussainbhai, Calicut v Alath Factory Thozhilali Union, Kozhikode* (1978) 2 LLJ 397(SC).

[33] *Cement Corporation of India Ltd v Presiding Officer, Labour Court cum Industrial Tribunal, Hissar* (2010) 2 LLJ 548 (P&H).

a clear intention to establish that use of contract labour was a sham or that a fraud was committed on the statute by the management before they set aside such a contract and declare the contract labourers to be direct employees of the principal employers.[34]

While the contract labourer and contractor are indeed covered by the CLA, contract labourers are employees of the contractor and not the principal employer. Contractors usually recruit workers for a particular job and have no fixed place of work, and consequently, contract labourers are often unable to enforce their rights against the contractors.[35] This is the reason that contract labourers are treated as falling within informal employment relationships in India.

There is strong support for the demand that contract labourers be granted the status of employees of the principal employer in India. The principal employer is often a large enterprise with a stable existence, often in the public sector, and is seen to have the capacity to pay various benefits.

Historically, the establishment/firm/enterprise has been seen as a monolithic unit operating as a single employer for all those working within its premises. Contractualisation fragments this monolithic conception of the employer and permits two or more employers to operate within the same enterprise. The CLA also recognises that the two employers—the principal employer and the contractor—have a hierarchical relationship between themselves. Under the CLA, ultimate liability for wage payments, working conditions and social security benefits falls upon the principal employer, should the contractor fail to provide these to the contract labour, with the proviso that the principal employer can pursue recovery of these amounts from the contractor.

Although the principal employer is liable for wages and benefits, there is the separate question of its status as an employer of contract labour. The CLA defines a contractor in relation to an establishment as a person who undertakes to produce a given result for the establishment, other than a mere supply of goods or articles of manufacture to such establishment, through contract labour or who supplies contract labour for any work of the establishment and includes a sub-contractor. The right of supervision and control by the principal employer is an important consideration for deciding whether a particular contract amounts to employment of 'contract labour'.[36] A transporter engaged in transporting finished goods is a contractor under the Act, although a supplier of goods is excluded from the definition.[37] The question whether a person is a mere supplier of goods and services or is a

---

[34] *Ibid.* See also ONGC v ONGC *Workers Union* (2008) 2 LLJ 1071 (SC).
[35] Rajeev, M, 'Contract Labour in Karnataka: Emerging Issues and Options' (2006) 21 *Economic and Political Weekly* 2086.
[36] *Gammon India Ltd v Union of India* AIR (1974) SC 960.
[37] *Keni Transports v State of Karnataka* (1994) 3 LLJ Supp 632 (Kant).

contractor must be determined by looking at the terms of the contract and the purpose of the services provided. Thus, an agreement to provide catering services in the premises of the principal employer, and which provided that the principal employer could inspect the premises, receive complaints and stipulate medical fitness requirements for contract labour, could be interpreted to indicate that the establishment, contract labour, contractor and principal employer are covered by the scope of the CLA.[38]

The CLA empowers the appropriate government, after consultation with the Central Advisory Contract Labour Board or, as the case may be, a State Board, to prohibit employment of contract labour in any process, operation or other work in any establishment. Contract labour can be abolished where the work performed is of a perennial nature which should be carried out by regular workers of the principal employer. The appropriate government takes into consideration the conditions of work and benefits provided for the contract labour in that establishment and other relevant factors namely:

1. whether the process, operation or other work is incidental to or necessary for the industry, trade, business, manufacture or occupation that is carried on in the establishment;
2. whether it is of a perennial nature, that is to say, it is of sufficient duration having regard to the nature of industry, trade, business, manufacture or occupation carried on in that establishment;
3. whether it is done ordinarily through regular workmen in that establishment or an establishment similar thereto; and
4. whether it is sufficient to employ a considerable number of whole-time workmen.[39]

Since there is no mechanism for contract labour to initiate the abolition of contract labour procedure under the CLA, the workers often file petitions in the high courts for a direction to the state government to examine the feasibility of abolishing contract labour in a particular job/department.

While initially the courts had taken a view that upon abolition of contract labour the principal employer would absorb such workers,[40] the Supreme Court has reversed its view and held that there can be no automatic absorption of contract labour upon the issuance of a notification prohibiting the employment of contract labour in any process or establishment. The principal employer is free to engage newly recruited workers for the same job.[41] As a result, trade unions' attempts to abolish contract labour systems has considerably weakened, which, in turn, has contributed to the large

---

[38] *JR Prabhu v State* (2001) 2 LLJ 1469 (Bom).
[39] CLA s 10.
[40] *Air India Statutory Corporation and others v United Labour Union and others* (1997) 9 SCC 377.
[41] *Steel Authority*, above n 30.

increase in the employment of contract labour within the formal sector. The courts have been involved in a form of 'de facto regulation', reinterpreting labour law to introduce greater flexibility without the need for a legislative amendment of labour laws to remove 'rigidities' in the labour market.[42]

The incentives to contractualise on the part of an enterprise are manifold. Contractualisation relieves the principal employer of concerns relating to recruitment and supervision, even though the principal employer usually maintains some level of supervision. The real advantage is that the regular wage scales are not payable to such contract labour whatever the duration of their employment by the contractor. They get paid lower wages since allowances and increments for experience do not get factored in, and they also obtain very few of the benefits and allowances available to regular employees.[43] Of course, licensed contractors are obliged to pay for provident fund and social insurance but since contract labourers are usually migrant workers and frequently change employers, and contractors are difficult to trace because of the poor enforcement of the CLA, contract labourers rarely obtain their social security benefits, in contrast to regular workers employed by the principal employer. This wage discrimination continues to be an important incentive to 'contractualise' notwithstanding that CLA and accompanying rules stipulate that equal wages are payable to contract labour and regular workmen performing the same or similar jobs. Other reasons for increased contractualisation include the flexibility it offers employers, higher efficiency and lower dispute propensity.[44]

The share of contract workers rose from 12 per cent in 1985 to 23 per cent in 2002.[45] Certain sectors have very high levels of contractualisation, including industries such as stone quarrying, beedi-rolling, rice shelling, brick kilns and construction. The construction industry is estimated to employ 10.7 million workers through contractors and this number represents 83 per cent of all contract workers.[46] Some sectors such as manufacturing have increases in the use of contract labour from 7 per cent in 1984

[42] Ahsan, A, *Labor Regulations in India: Impact and Policy Reform Options*, available at: http:// siteresources.worldbank.org/SOCIALPROTECTION/Resources/280558-1138289492561/2158434-1138289513224/2158436-1163806331938/LaborRegulationsIndia.pdf. The newly enacted Unorganised Workers Social Security Act 2008 seeks to provide limited social protection to such unorganised/informal workers who are currently unprotected, but does not grant them other forms of employment protection.

[43] Rajeev, above n 35. Also see Bhandari, AK and Heshmati, A, *Wage Inequality and Job Insecurity Among Permanent and Contract Workers in India: Evidence from Organized Manufacturing Industries* (Discussion Paper No 2097, Bonn, Institute for the Study of Labor, April 2006).

[44] Ahsan, A, Pages, C and Roy, T, 'Legislation, Enforcement and Adjudication in Indian Labor Markets: Origins, Consequences and the Way Forward' in Mazumdar and Sarkar, above n 7, at 262 citing other studies.

[45] NCEUS, *The Challenge of Employment in India*, above n 3, at 177.

[46] *Ibid*, at 143.

to 21.6 per cent in 1998.[47] The increase is greatest in the public sector, which is the largest employer of contract labour.[48]

The levels of contractualisation are greatest in states such as Andhra Pradesh where the use of contract labour in manufacturing rose from 33.8 per cent in 1985 to 49.2 per cent in 1995 and to 62.08 per cent in 2002.[49] The increased use of contract labour in this state is related to the state-level amendment to the CLA, which permits the use of contract labour in non-core areas (such as security, cleaning, gardening and other activities) of the enterprise even if such work is perennial in nature.

The increased use of contract labour has had tremendous effects on trade unionisation rates within large-scale enterprises. The strongest trade unions have historically been within public sector enterprises, and these have emerged as the largest employers of contract labour.[50] This practice has resulted in declining union density rates since contract labour is often not unionised. In sectors such as security, housekeeping, catering, or gardening, the principal employer tenders contracts frequently and the contractor is free to recruit his/her own employees, which makes it very difficult to unionise the workers employed by contractors. Resort to contract labour has also been a strategy to curb worker militancy in some states of India.[51]

Recent policy changes have also contributed to the increase in the use of contract labour. The bifurcation of the work of an enterprise on the lines of what is core and non-core (a move recommended by the 2002 Second National Commission on Labour) allows manufacturing industries to contractualise services such as cleaning, catering and gardening. The shift from the earlier bifurcation of perennial/non-perennial work to one of core/non-core work in states such as Andhra Pradesh has meant that perennial work in ancillary functions of a manufacturing unit can now be performed by contract labour. As a result, trade unions can no longer apply to the contract labour advisory board under the CLA for abolition of the contract labour system on the ground that the work these workers perform is perennial. Security services, catering and housekeeping are some of the services that have been almost completely contractualised and this form of work is no longer considered for abolition under the CLA.

---

[47] *Ibid*, at 177.

[48] After the initial judgment of the Supreme Court permitting absorption of contract labour, their numbers fell in public sector enterprises, but this situation has now reversed after the judgment in *Steel Authority*, above n 29.

[49] Ahsan, Pages and Roy, above n 44, at 261.

[50] For instance, the Bharat Sanchar Nigam Limited is one of the biggest public sector enterprises in the country. It employs 300,000 regular and over 100,000 casual and contract labourers. See also Sankaran, K and Madhav, R, *Gender Equality and Social Dialogue in India* (Working Paper No 1, International Labour Organization, Geneva, January 2011).

[51] Chakravarty, D, 'Trade Unions and Business Firms: Unorganised Manufacturing in West Bengal' (2010) 65(6) *Economic and Political Weekly* 45.

In many instances, the categorisation of core/non-core functions also constitutes a division in the kind of work that is performed within an enterprise. In manufacturing concerns, production-related activities are termed 'core' and it is services of various kinds that are performed by contract labour. The NCEUS reported in 2009 that the data reveals an unbundling of employment leading to 'outsourcing of various services earlier enumerated in the manufacturing sector and hence tertiarisation of employment'.[52]

'UNBUNDLING' OF MANUFACTURING/SUB-CONTRACTING

While the CLA deals with the employment of contract labour within the premises of the principal employer and who are employed 'in connection with the work of the establishment', the definition of contract labour under the CLA specifically excludes an 'outworker' who does not work in the premises of the principal employer.[53] All persons performing work connected with the work of the principal establishment, hired via intermediaries but working on other premises, are excluded from the CLA. The result is that home workers, who are employed extensively in the garment, paper products, packaging, and industrial components sectors, do not come within the purview of the CLA.

The exclusion of workers who are not employed on the principal's premises from the CLA has implications for another form of work production that is widespread in the manufacturing sector in India—the system of subcontracting where production is outsourced to other firms, with the main enterprise focused on marketing the final product. This form of contract manufacturing or product sub-contracting (as it is referred to in the literature in India, and which broadly could be classified as one *form* of *commercialisation* used in several other jurisdictions, and in this collection) has increased in India in recent years.[54]

There are two principal types of subcontracting in India. Product subcontracting involves subcontracting of production by larger enterprises to smaller enterprises (in some instances the two enterprises may be of the

---

[52] NCEUS, *The Challenge of Employment in India*, above n 3, at 14.

[53] An outworker is defined in s 2(1)(i)(C) of the CLA as a person to whom any articles and materials are given out by or on behalf of the principal employer to be made up, cleaned, washed, altered, ornamented, finished, repaired, adapted or otherwise processed for sale for the purposes of the trade or business of the principal employer, and the process is to be carried out either in the house of the outworker, or in some other premises, not being premises under the control and management of the principal employer.

[54] Ramaswamy, KV, 'The Search for Flexibility in Indian Manufacturing: New Evidence on Outsourcing Activities' (1999) 34 *Economic and Political Weekly* 363. I continue to use the expression sub-contracting because, as I show below, there are examples in India where some kinds of sub-contracting have been covered by employment relationships instead of being merely treated as forms of commercial relationships between two parties.

same size, but the sub-contracting firm may offer cost advantages due to its location or the flexibility it offers in determining production decisions). Goods produced by the subcontracted firm are sold in the same condition as purchased by the contracting firm with no value contributed by the purchasing enterprise.

This form of product sub-contracting is distinguishable from another form of sub-contracting where contract work is done at the workers' own premises on materials supplied by the main enterprise—a form of a 'putting-out' system of production. Manufacturing industries have historically deployed the putting-out system where raw materials were handed out to persons who worked at sites other than the workplace of the employer, and returned the processed or finished goods.[55] The beedi (hand rolled cigarettes) industry continues to manufacture the bulk of its products in this way. Home-based workers are often engaged in such a putting-out system of manufacture.

Some industries manifest both kinds of sub-contracting. For instance, the garment industry in Tiruppur in Tamil Nadu, India is composed of sub-contracting units that produce finished garments, as well as 'job work' (putting-out) units which carry out specific tasks such as embroidery, printing, button-hole making and button stitching. Both kinds of units produce/finish goods in the name of the exporter who engages them, and who also checks for the required quality. The former 'sub-contracting arrangement minimises the capital investment costs for the out-sourcing manufacturer, the latter arrangement minimises the need for vertical integration within the firm'.[56] Merchant exporters may sometimes own no production facilities and work may be contracted out to a trusted group of sub-contractors.

Putting-out production for work to be done by outworkers is estimated to be around 7 per cent of registered manufacturing in India.[57] It is less prevalent than product sub-contracting. The government has encouraged measures such as out-sourcing the manufacture of ancillary products, vendor development programmes and sub-contracting exchanges to facilitate sub-contracting. It is estimated that 25 to 30 percent of enterprises in the informal sector operate contracts with large enterprises under some system of sub-contracting. About a quarter of these smaller enterprises work solely for the master unit and do not sell independently in the market.[58]

---

[55] Maiti, D, 'The Organizational Morphology of Rural Industries and its Dynamics in Liberalised India: A Study of West Bengal' (2008) 32 *Cambridge Journal of Economics* 577, 578.

[56] Singh, N and Sapra, MK, 'Liberalization in Trade and Finance: India's Garment Sector' in B Harriss-White and A Sinha (eds), *Trade Liberalization and India's Informal Economy* (New Delhi, Oxford University Press, 2007) 83.

[57] Ramaswamy, above n 54, at 365.

[58] NCEUS, *The Challenge of Employment in India*, above n 3, at 272.

Workers employed through putting-out forms of sub-contracting arrangement are not covered by the CLA. Nor are such outworkers brought within the scope of the employment relationship with the principal employer, and there is no evidence in the case law of any attempts to establish employer–employee relationships down this production chain.

Thus, the two forms of product sub-contracting and putting-out sub-contracting, which are increasingly prevalent means for employers to achieve greater flexibility, fall outside the scope of the CLA. In the first case, the main enterprise and the second enterprise, which is the site of production, are characterised as engaging in a purely commercial arrangement. In the latter case of putting-out sub-contracting, the place of production is not the site of the main enterprise and thus is excluded from the scope of the CLA. Once again, the relationship is seen as a commercial relationship between the two entities. Workers employed by the smaller firm are viewed as employed *solely* by the smaller firm while the larger firm merely supplies material to the smaller firm.

Can these arrangements, which are means of achieving greater flexibility by employers, be brought within the scope of labour law? Can liability under labour law be attributed to the firm that puts out production?

The beedi industry (hand-rolled cigarettes) is an important example where workers have successfully brought such putting-out production within the employment relationship. The Beedi and Cigar Workers (Conditions of Employment) Act 1966 includes in its definition of an employee a person employed directly or through any agency who is given raw materials by an employer or a contractor for making into beedi or cigars (or both) at home (a home worker). Outworkers and home workers who work outside the constant control and supervision of the employer and whose place of work is their own dwelling home are also included within this definition of employee. The supply of raw materials to be worked on in some other premises has not been a bar to bringing such home workers with the employment relationship and the scope of labour law.

However, the example of the beedi industry, where legislation deemed such persons to be part of an employment relationship, is unusual since it was legislation that conferred employee status on such persons. The legislation was justified at that time on the ground that the so-called commercial arrangement between the contractor and the home worker was a smoke screen to disguise an employment relationship. Despite this early start, there have not been other instances where putting out systems of sub-contracting have been brought within the fold of employment relationships. Home workers in the garment industry or workers employed by putting-out (job work) units working on performing specific tasks for the main manufacturer have not been able to establish themselves as employees of that main enterprise.

Similarly, employees of a sub-contracting unit which makes goods for the product label of the eventual exporter or the enterprise that owns the brand name and that markets the products, are not treated as employees of that main enterprise in India.[59] It is only when the courts determine that there is a 'functional integrality' of the units/enterprises (despite there being two separate holding companies that own the two enterprises) that the main enterprise becomes liable, under labour law for the workers in the sub-contracting unit. The courts have examined the facts of each case to determine if there was unity of ownership, management and control between these two units to determine if they could, indeed, be treated functionally as a single unit and for liability as an employer to be imposed on the main enterprise.[60] Thus, while it is possible in theory to bring some forms of commercialisation back within the scope of labour law, in practice such instances are very rare since the two units normally maintain arm's-length relationships in terms of management and control, even where the second unit may have been hived off from the first.

The de-linking of the chain of employment through product sub-contracting/commercialisation and putting-out sub-contracting provides for greater flexibility and economic efficiency in managerial decisions. Yet, it has also led to a reduction in wages and corresponding benefits for those workers excluded from formal sector employment relationships or the opportunity to be treated as employees of larger/resource-rich enterprises. In India, this form of commercialisation has resulted in regular struggles and legal attempts by contract labourers seeking to obtain the status of employee under the principal employer; workers in sub-contracted enterprises seeking parity of wages with the workers in the main enterprise that markets their products, and workers in job-work units seeking to improve their lot. While such workers are, no doubt, employed by the sub-contracting or putting-out/job work enterprises, they seek to not only obtain parity with workers in the main enterprise but also in certain situations obtain the status of employees of the main enterprise that markets the product. The feasibility of granting such parity or even the status of employees lies at the core of the debate over informalisation and commercialisation across the world, and the attempt by labour lawyers to extend their reach in what is presented as a commercial relationship.

---

[59] See, eg, *Zheng v Liberty Apparel Co*, 355 F3d 61 (2d Cir 2003) where the appeals court took the view that the district court had erred in holding that the manufacturer was not jointly liable along with the 'jobber' contractor who employed workers to finish the garments for the manufacturer under the Fair Labor Standards Act 1938. This is not the position under Indian law, as the CLA, with its principle of eventual liability of the principal employer, extends only to work performed *within* the establishment of the principal employer as pointed out above. I am grateful to Alan Hyde for pointing this case to me. *Zheng* is discussed further in Hyde, A, 'Legal Responsibility for Labour Conditions Down the Production Chain' in this collection.

[60] *Associated Cement Companies Ltd v Workmen* (1960) 1 LLJ 1 (SC); *Workmen of Straw Board Manufacturing Co Ltd v Straw Board Manufacturing Co Ltd* (1974) 1 LLJ 499 (SC).

CONCLUSION: THE WAY FORWARD?

The case of beedi workers in India shows that it is possible to recognise that economic dependence coupled with vulnerability are factors that transform a commercial relationship into an employment relationship. However, since beedi workers were deemed to be employed in 1966, there has been little legislative extension of the scope of labour protection. Thus, increasingly, the courts have staked out the boundaries of labour protection.

One important resource that labour lawyers can turn to in their attempt to expand the scope of labour protection to include workers, who through processes of informalisation and commercialisation have been located outside its boundaries, is the International Labour Organization's *Employment Relationship Recommendation* 2006 (ILO R198). The Recommendation acknowledges the difficulties in establishing whether or not an employment relationship exists in certain situations, and it seeks to draw bright lines around who is considered to be a worker in an employment relationship, what rights the worker has and who the employer is. The Recommendation calls for a national policy to be formulated which should provide guidance on how to effectively establish an employment relationship and on the distinction between employed and self-employed workers. According to the Recommendation, the determination of an employment relationship should primarily be guided by *facts* relating to the performance of work and the remuneration of the worker, notwithstanding how the relationship is characterised in any contrary arrangement, contractual or otherwise, that the parties may have agreed upon.[61] It also declares that 'National Policy for protection of workers in an employment relationship should not interfere with *true* civil and commercial relationships, while at the same time ensuring that individuals in an employment relationship have the protection they are due'.[62] Thus, the Recommendation appears to recognise that the veil could be lifted from commercial relationships that disguise or prevent an employment relationship from being legally noticed.

The cases of product outsourcing and sub-contracting discussed in this Chapter are examples crying out to be examined to determine if they are, at their heart, commercial arrangements or a mere disguise to camouflage an employment relationship. Such an approach would greatly increase the extent of scrutiny by the courts to determine if a commercial relationship is a proxy for an employment relationship. Under such an approach, courts would have to examine not only the work performed, its supervision and control, the

---

[61] Art 9. Consideration should be given to the facts and context within which the work is carried out, the manner in which wages are provided, the extent to which the employer benefits from the work performed, the place of work, working hours, provision of tools, availability of leave periods, etc.

[62] Art 8 (emphasis supplied).

place of work, or its economic reality (some of the standard tests to determine if a person is an employee or an independent contractor), but such matters as the structure of economic production and the commercial arrangements between two parties to determine the true nature of the arrangement.

Developing an approach within labour law and policy, guided by the ILO's *Employment Relationship Recommendation* 2006, which seeks to bring a larger number of workers within the purview of an employment relationship, and thus within the category of an 'employee', holds great attraction for those currently outside the labour laws which continue to be premised on an employer–employee relationships. Given the trend towards informalisation of formal sector jobs that we see in the labour market, such an extension of the protective mantle of labour law is necessary.

3

Transform or Perish: Changing Conceptions of Work in Recycling

POORNIMA CHIKARMANE AND LAKSHMI NARAYANAN

WASTE PICKERS ARE workers who earn their livelihoods from the manual extraction, recovery and collection of recyclable scrap materials from urban solid waste for sale as raw material to industry for recycling. A variety of terms such as rag and bone men, *chiffoniers*, rag pickers, *recuperars*, binners, reclaimers, junk collectors and scavengers have been used to refer to waste pickers in different geographical, linguistic and temporal contexts. The terms are as disparaging as the demeaning nature of waste picking which involves, quite literally, handling rubbish or what is euphemistically called 'co-mingled waste', with bare hands. Waste pickers are located at the lowest level in the urban occupational hierarchy even within the informal economy. In any city waste picking is often carried out by the most economically marginalised, socially excluded or disadvantaged communities. That said, waste picking is also an occupational 'choice' that is made by workers from within a set of occupations circumscribed by their circumstances.

Waste pickers are a sub-group of what are referred to as scrap collectors, the other sub-group being itinerant waste buyers. Itinerant waste buyers use small amounts of capital to purchase, from the generators of waste, metals, newspapers, bottles, plastic containers, boxes, e-waste and other items that would decline in value if they were mixed with rubbish. The materials that are collected by waste pickers include bones, wood, types of paper and corrugated board, rags and cloth, plastics, metals, bottles, tins and types of glass. The types of materials collected by scrap collectors are linked to the demand from industry that is, in turn, based on the technology available to process specific materials in a financially viable manner. The prices of recovered scrap materials are determined on the basis of demand by industrial consumers, commodity markets and the price that consumers will pay for the end product.

Urban solid waste management in India is usually carried out by municipal governments or their agents or contractors. Historically it has been considered to be part of public health and has included the collection, transport and disposal of waste. Work carried out by municipalities takes place in the formal realm. However, scrap material recovery and trading for the most part, and processing for some part, are carried out by workers and enterprises in the informal waste recycling economy. Scrap material recovery can take place at one or more points, such as the point of generation, collection from municipal rubbish skips and open streets, during transport, at transfer stations and material recovery facilities and landfills, depending upon the collection, transport and processing methods adopted by the respective municipality. The formal and the informal systems intersect at various points, complementing and conflicting with each other. The skimming of recyclables from generation point to landfill progressively leaves behind residual, lower quality materials. The work carried out by waste pickers subsidises municipal solid waste handling and management costs. It is unlikely to be acknowledged or valued, much less recognised and quantified, in the formal solid waste management system.

Informal waste recycling provides employment to large numbers of workers but usually does not conform to standards of decent work. Waste recycling is important to the industrial economy, particularly given low carbon goals. The changes in urban solid waste management practices are driven in part by societal aspirations, business interests, government policy and legal diktat. Carbon markets have made the waste management business attractive enough to attract investment. Technology providers and waste management businesses are tapping bottom-of-the-pyramid municipal governments in India. Outsourcing, privatisation, public–private partnerships, mechanisation and waste-to-energy have entered the municipal lexicon. They seek to make short shrift of rubbish, either carting it out of sight or burning it beyond recognition, with scant regard for millions of dispossessed and newly impoverished waste pickers and other informal recyclers. There is no doubt that the informal waste recycling sector is poised on the threshold of change. The challenge lies in enabling informal waste workers to drive this change and negotiate its complexities in ways that will upgrade their livelihoods.

We use the framework of decent work and draw upon the experience of Kagad Kach Patra Kashtakari Panchayat (KKPKP) in Pune to reflect on a working model for the integration of waste pickers into integrated sustainable waste management and the accompanying challenges. KKPKP is the trade union of waste pickers and itinerant waste buyers established in 1993 in Pune, India. It means Democratic Collective of Paper, Glass, Tin Workers. Interestingly, relative to informalisation in the global north, this Chapter examines the modalities of moving away from informalisation to state regulation, and protection of workers in the informal waste economy which is the reality in India. It comprises four parts. The geo-socio-eco-political context is set out first. The Chapter then examines employment in the informal waste recycling sector in Pune, before describing the process of organising waste pickers. The issue of social security is then explored before the Chapter examines the challenges and obstacles raised by the discussion.

SETTING THE CONTEXT

Pune is the ninth-largest city in India with a population of 3.76 million.[1] It is located 170 km from India's financial capital, Mumbai, in western India. The decadal growth in population has been in excess of 40 per cent over the past four decades. It is estimated that about 50 per cent of the population increase is on account of immigration. Pune is a 'young' city—62 per cent of its population is aged less than 30 years.

The Pune Urban Agglomeration comprises the municipal corporations of Pune, Pimpri-Chinchwad and the Cantonment Boards of Pune, Dehu and Khadki. With growing economic activity in Pune, the slum population has been increasing at the rate of 6 per cent compared to 4 per cent for the rest of the city.[2]

The main drivers of the Pune economy are the car and car accessories industries, institutions of higher education (accounting for the high student population), information technology and IT-enabled services, bio-technology and agro- and food-processing industries. In 2007 Pune's GDP was estimated at US$13 billion.[3] Average daily earnings in the informal sector are highly variable. While there is a minimum wage rate specified by the government, it varies across occupations and sectors. There is almost no enforcement of the minimum wage rate in the informal sector. The average daily earnings of workers in the informal economy are approximately US$6 for head loaders,[4] US$3 for domestic workers and waste pickers, US$4 for itinerant waste buyers, US$11 for auto-rickshaw drivers, US$7 for hawkers and vendors, and US$2.5 for casual labourers.[5]

Culturally, Pune is considered to be a progressive city. It is home to many social movements. Among them are the first school for education of the Scheduled Castes,[6] the first school for girls in the state, the opening up of wells to the Scheduled Castes, widow remarriage, the first women's

---

[1] Ministry of Home Affairs, *Census of India 2011* (New Delhi, Government of India, 2011).

[2] Pune Municipal Corporation, *City Development Plan* (2006).

[3] Dobbs, R, Remes, J and Smit, S, 'The World's New Growth Frontier: Midsize Cities in Emerging Markets' (2011) 2 *McKinsey Quarterly* 46. This is the 2007 GDP for the Pune Urban Agglomeration with a population of 5.7 million.

[4] A head loader is a manual worker who carries sacks or packing crates on his head, back or shoulders to load and unload material from freight trains and trucks in market areas.

[5] The estimation of daily earnings has been provided by local organisations of unorganised workers.

[6] Erstwhile untouchable social groupings that have been listed in a schedule of the Indian constitution as being discriminated against and disadvantaged.

university in India and organisations of unorganised workers such as head loaders, waste pickers, auto-rickshaw drivers, hawkers and vendors and domestic workers. Politically, the organisation of unorganised workers is significant, and not easily dismissed by the municipal government.

EMPLOYMENT IN THE INFORMAL WASTE
RECYCLING SECTOR IN PUNE[7]

The pyramidal informal waste recycling sector is layered, having several levels of workers and trader entrepreneurs operating firms, small businesses and enterprises within a variety of exchange relationships that are quite complex. The labour market is segmented along lines of gender (90 per cent of the waste pickers are women and 70 per cent of the itinerant waste buyers are men) and caste (almost all scrap collectors belong to the Scheduled Castes). The segmentation applies in the trade as well, which shows the almost exclusive presence of trading castes at the middle and higher level. The trade is closely held and competition at all levels is intense.

Waste pickers at the base of the pyramid are numerically the largest group engaging in free scavenging of scrap from municipal rubbish skips and landfills. Waste picking is not recognised as an occupation. There is no licensing system for waste pickers. Waste pickers are usually peripatetic. They collect generic scrap including varieties of paper, plastic, metal and glass along their regular collection beats, which they guard zealously. They then congregate at fixed spots to sort their collected scrap, after which they sell the scrap to fixed traders. They earn higher than minimum wages but can be considered subsistence earners in the value chain. Itinerant waste buyers buy small quantities of scrap from homes, shops and offices, moving around on foot with push carts or bicycles. Itinerant waste buyers purchase high-value cleaner scrap and sometimes specialise in single items or a combination of items like corrugated board, plastics, ferrous metals, tins, bottles or newspapers on account of which their earnings are higher than those of waste pickers. Itinerant waste buyers also enjoy higher status and greater bargaining power with traders. The licensing system for street vendors through the municipal government does not apply to itinerant waste buyers who engage in buying rather than selling.

The registered dealers, re-processors and remanufacturers are perched at the top of the pyramid. Scrap commodities transit to formal factories and sometimes even multinationals at this point. The seeming lack of structure and regulation is deceptive because it is quite organised, even at the level of

---

[7] The information in this section is taken from Chikarmane, P, Deshpande, M and Narayan, L, *Report of Scrap Collectors, Scrap Traders and Recycling Enterprises in Pune* (Geneva, International Labour Organization, 2001).

the scrap collector. Barriers to entry and exit get progressively higher from the base to the apex. The scrap trading enterprises are usually entities registered under the Shops and Establishments Act. The smaller establishments and firms operate in slum areas by encroaching on vacant land or renting or occupying land on payment to a slum lord or political patron. All scrap traders operate with tacit or overt political patronage. The larger traders often have some space occupied legally from which they operate.

The entire pyramid consists for the most part of own-account workers. Trading margins hinge on volumes, and traders use every trick in the book to consolidate and maintain volumes. Scrap traders provide carts, weighing scales and daily capital to itinerant waste buyers. The credit market is tied to the product market all the way between layers of the pyramid. Channels of upward mobility between layers are few and tight, and easily reversed. Mortality of smaller scrap establishments is quite high.

Patron–client relations between waste pickers and their scrap dealers are best described through an illustration which is taken from unpublished KKPKP documentation:

> 'He's a good man. Seth [boss] paid for my mother's "mayat" [funeral rites]. He's the one who got me married. I agree that he doesn't give any bonus, but maybe his business is not doing so well. What can he do? You know that all fingers of the hand are not alike. Some of the waste pickers get all kinds of rubbish and dump it on him.' (Waste picker Shantabai Waghmare in defence of Raju, a scrap trader who reneged on payment of her annual bonus.)

> Waste-pickers had never brought up the scrap trader as Villain No 1. If anything at the time he was de facto Hero No 1 because he interacted with them daily and it was to him they turned in times of need despite their squabbles. The scrap traders were after all 'Pandu mama' [uncle] and 'Nangre seth' [boss], often from the same caste, sometimes from the same slums, sometimes someone who had grown up playing marbles with their own children, had taken up for them when they had been harassed. Waste pickers had known them for ages, certainly for much longer than they had known us. In some cases, three consecutive generations of waste pickers had sold scrap to three consecutive generations of the scrap dealer's family.

Market exchange in the scrap commodities market in Pune is a classic example of what Harriss-White refers to as more socially regulated, rather than regulated by the state.[8] Regulation is through a complex system of mostly oral business contracts transacted in cash, structured by tight persistent networks of repeated transactions that are regulated by reputation where reneging on commitments spells doom. This kind of network trade is efficient, cuts transaction costs and screens out large numbers of possible

---

[8] Harriss-White, B, *Informal Economic Order: Shadow States, Private Status States, States of Last Resort and Spinning States* (Working Paper No 6, Queen Elizabeth House, University of Oxford, 2006).

competitors. Enforcement is carried out by overt and covert threat, arson and, on occasion, the use of extra-legal force.[9]

ORGANISING WORKERS IN THE INFORMAL WASTE ECONOMY IN PUNE

Diminutive 50-year-old Shanta Kadam recalls that she started waste picking to feed her family when her husband, a wage labourer in a scrap enterprise, fell ill. She accompanied her relatives on their beats and suffered abuse and ignominy like the rest of them. Sometimes they were even beaten or stoned. Both husband and wife joined the KKPKP when it was formed by which time her husband Shiva had also taken to scrap collection. Harassment from law enforcers reduced after unionisation and the administrative machinery became more receptive and responsive because the functionaries knew they could not get away with what they had been doing. Society also became more accepting. Shanta actively participates in all union activities and has been to other cities to attend protests and marches. She has medical insurance cover and is a member of the savings-linked credit cooperative of the union from where she has taken a loan of US$1100 to repair her house. It's her third loan and she has given usurious moneylenders, a boot. 'My village household was decimated. I rebuilt it from waste scrap', is how she describes her work and life.

Hausa Sonavne who has been a waste picker for 22 years says pretty much the same thing but has something to add as well. A member of SWaCH Co-op,[10] she has graduated to collecting waste door to door from apartment blocks populated by middle class citizens after which she works as a domestic worker in the same building. 'The union has demonstrated the value of the work done by waste pickers,' she says, 'so people are more "sympathetic" and also wary that we will protest and agitate, if they abuse us. They would not let us enter the gates but now ask if we would like a cup of tea.' Hausa and her husband work together earning about US$200 between them. They have bought a motorised three wheeler to transport their scrap. Their daughter is an undergraduate at a local college. (As recounted by Shanta and Hausa to student-activist, Bharat Kamble, in June 2010.)

Two brief stories of union members whose lives have changed somewhat in trajectory because of having become part of a collective. What comes through very clearly is the fact that Shanta and Hausa experience greater dignity and less harassment, feel more empowered and respected relative to the rest of society, accompanied by material changes in their lives. These changes are directly related to economic gains on account of being union members such as access to credit at reasonable interest rates, medical

---

[9] *Ibid.*
[10] SWaCH Co-Op (solid waste collection handling) 'Seva Sahakari Sanstha Maryadit' is a wholly owned co-operative of waste pickers, itinerant waste buyers and other urban poor that provides front-end waste management services in Pune.

insurance cover and education assistance. For Hausa it also extends to a degree of upward mobility within the occupation as a member of SWaCH Co-op as well as her transition to an allied informal occupation (domestic work) that is considered marginally higher in the hierarchy of informal occupations. Added to which is the probable shift of occupation for the next generation, through the educated daughter. The stories also hint at the strategies of mobilisation, agitation and creation of alternative institutional structures that are adopted by the union.

KKPKP was established in 1993 as the consequence of a project titled the 'Project for the Empowerment of Waste Pickers' undertaken by project staff of the Department of Continuing and Adult Education and Extension Work at SNDT Women's University in 1990. This project, itself an offshoot of an adult education programme, issued identity cards to waste pickers, promoted source segregation of waste and advocated for waste pickers' direct access to source segregated waste in door to door collection services. The project activists allied with a veteran leader of unorganised workers and the social activist son of a waste picker to establish KKPKP. The tripartite partnership has endured for almost two decades to enable and support KKPKP to stand strong in its own right to represent the interests of waste pickers.

Occupational identity was the basis of collectivisation and the organisation is an independent, sector-specific trade union of waste pickers and itinerant waste buyers. Legally, KKPKP is a trade union registered under the Trade Unions Act 1926. Structurally it is a membership-based organisation. Membership is open to men and women who are required to renew their membership through payment of an annual membership fee. Women comprise the bulk of the membership, mirroring the gender composition within the occupation. The Representatives Council is the main decision-making body. It has 60 representatives (80 per cent women), nominated by member constituencies. The council has three non-waste picker activists.

KKPKP undertook to register members and issue identity cards soon after its inception. KKPKP members collectively articulated their position that scrap collection (and allied processes)[11] is the *work* carried out by waste pickers and itinerant waste buyers, after which the collected scrap is supplied to processing and reprocessing industries as raw material for recycling. KKPKP argued that waste pickers engaged in material recovery activities for recycling and were therefore key service providers in the waste economy, and not 'scavengers' freeloading on the surplus of the relatively wealthy. KKPKP argued that material recovery reduced municipal waste

---

[11] Scrap collection *work* includes *activities/operations* such as collection, sorting, segregation, grading, cutting, breaking, stripping, washing, carrying, shredding, loading, unloading, packing and any other related work.

handling costs;[12] was economically productive, generating jobs and income downstream; and reduced environmental degradation and costs. KKPKP systematically quantified the contribution of scrap collectors to solid waste management, the economy and the environment to substantiate *claims to municipal and state recognition and resources.*

Members participated in collective public assertions of identity in mass programmes, rallies, protests and demonstrations in large numbers to voice their demand for recognition and dignity as workers. In 1995–96 Pune and Pimpri Chinchwad Municipal Corporations (PCMC) endorsed the identity cards of scrap collectors *recognising scrap collection as work and scrap collectors as workers.* The identity card authorises the bearer to collect scrap.

The claims included financial resources by way of special schemes for medical insurance and livelihoods or infrastructure resources such as constructed space and waste collection equipment. KKPKP lobbied for and secured medical insurance with the premium paid from the municipal budget, on the basis of a study that established savings in municipal waste transport costs amounting to US$912,500, at the cost of the waste pickers' own health.[13] At an organisational level, KKPKP members are covered for life and disability under the Janashree Bima Yojana, a government-approved social insurance scheme for the poor. Members pay US$1 as an annual premium, the rest being subsidised by state and national governments. Members are also covered under the Jan Arogya Yojana, for which the premium is paid by the PMC.

A study on the economic aspects of the waste informal sector in Pune quantified the reduction in waste handling costs at US$2,400,000 per annum.[14] It became the basis for municipal support for a co-operative that integrates waste pickers in door-to-door collection of source-segregated waste. The experience has been analysed in the following section.

Green Jobs, Clean Jobs Strategy

Until 2007, Pune Municipal Corporation (PMC) was not in compliance with the Municipal Solid Waste (Management and Handling) Rules (2000) that required municipalities to *organise* (not undertake) door-to-door collection of segregated waste.

---

[12] Reduces waste transport costs and diverts waste from landfills.
[13] Chikarmane *et al*, above n 7. Estimation based on current PMC expenditure.
[14] *Ibid.* At 2007 rates.

Municipal solid waste in Pune is mostly deposited in street receptacles from where it is transported to an RDF[15] plant since July 2010. Open dumping at the landfill was stopped following a court case and protests by villagers living around the landfill.

Strategically the KKPKP chose to counter the threat of displacement of workers from landfill sites by using its critical mass to propose an alternative model of waste collection that would provide solid waste collection services to the city. The alternative model incorporated waste pickers as service providers and was designed to transform their working conditions, so as to become a demonstrable model of integration of informal waste workers at city level. The alternative model allowed the waste picker the freedom that she was accustomed to, protected her right to access recyclables, kept space for citizens' participation and helped the PMC comply with legal requirements. A pilot project carried out on the basis of a letter of authority issued by the Municipal Commissioner at the time led to a city-wide proposal by the municipal administration in 2006. The General Body (highest municipal body vested with decision-making powers under municipal law) of the PMC approved the Commissioner's proposal to set up a co-operative of waste pickers and resolved to support the management, equipment and welfare costs of the new entity for a period of five years.

The resolution was subsequently rescinded by the municipal body and reinstated by the state government at the behest of the subsequent municipal commissioner. Politicians and other interest groups, including the municipal workers' union, were quick to see the employment potential of the initiative. Each wanted a share of the pie until the Municipal Commissioner intervened to suggest an umbrella co-operative with members drawn from all the contending organisations. Political and bureaucratic uncertainties about continued support for the model for the duration of the agreement persist.

SWaCH Co-op came into existence in 2007 as a hybrid public–private partnership promoted jointly by the PMC and the KKPKP to provide daily door-to-door waste collection and front-end waste management services in Pune. SWaCH Seva Sahakari Sanstha is a wholly owned co-operative of waste pickers and other urban poor with two members each of the PMC and KKPKP on its Governing Board. There is a formal Memorandum of Understanding between PMC and SWaCH that sets out the terms of financial and operational engagement and assessment. To date PMC has fulfilled many of its commitments, if not all, but the threat of cessation of support is ever present. In 2010 SWaCH entered into an MOU with the neighbouring

---

[15] Refuse Derived Fuel—briquettes of dried and compacted co-mingled waste that are used as fuel.

municipality, the Pimpri Chinchwad Municipal Corporation for motorised door-to-door collection.

SWaCH means 'clean' in the regional language and is the acronym of 'solid waste collection handling'. SWaCH is a social enterprise. At the present time SWaCH undertakes door-to-door waste collection from 280,000 households, shops, offices and establishments through a network of 1,700 SWaCH Sathis (comrades) who are paid a monthly fee by service users in Pune. Waste pickers collect monthly fees from service users. Their earnings consist of user fees and proceeds from the sale of scrap. In PCMC 200,000 households are being serviced by SWaCH using vehicles provided by the municipality. PCMC has underwritten the collection costs for a period of two years after which user fee recovery is expected.

The most notable impacts of the transition of waste pickers into SWaCH from the members' perspective are, reduction in the hours of work, access to waste collection equipment and change in public image. Many of the other changes are location-specific and variable. Some members started getting source-segregated waste, some had access to enclosed spaces for sorting, and some members reported higher earnings, others more regular earnings and some were able to take up allied occupations. At another level there are members who have found it difficult to adjust to having to be accountable, keep regular hours and timings, and to accommodate what they perceive to be unreasonable demands from service users. The waste picker had almost no direct contact with citizens. That has changed. The SWaCH member is answerable to the citizen who pays her and is a worker aware of her rights. So if a citizen asks the SWaCH collector to return the next day to collect the user fee, the collector is likely to plonk the rubbish bin on the floor and say *'In that case I will collect your waste tomorrow'*. The relationship with the user has also had positive outcomes of overcoming or reducing caste and class barriers. There is some level of attrition among SWaCH members; some return to waste picking because the earnings are higher. Some waste pickers prefer to work outside and choose not to get integrated. Some discontent exists on account of SWaCH having to negotiate relationships with member owners and the municipality in its role as regulator and accountability to service users. The tripartite tightrope walk is challenging.

Another observable SWaCH impact has been on the relationship with the PMC. Prior to integration, waste pickers were able to take the high moral ground with respect to the work carried out. They were not paid employees and were doing the municipality a favour by reducing costs. While SWaCH collectors are not paid by the municipality, financial support to SWaCH from the PMC has changed the equation where the municipal administration holds the whip and demands accountability. This has somewhat reduced the ability to engage in collective bargaining. Nonetheless, it is also the same mid-level municipal administration that values the output of SWaCH members on account of which it is pushing the model.

SWaCH is constituted as a cooperative of waste pickers and other urban poor, the latter having been added by the PMC. KKPKP did not object because it was one way of opening up the occupation to free it from perpetuating the caste-occupation link. Structurally, 75 per cent of the membership must consist of women and representation of women on the governing body is two-thirds. Nonetheless, KKPKP added a proviso that registered waste pickers would be given priority over other groups. As it stands, most members of SWaCH are also KKPKP members and KKPKP continues to be the only organisation actually investing in SWaCH. The other opportunistic players are more or less dormant or function nominally outside the ambit of SWaCH.

The numbers of men evincing interest in becoming members of SWaCH has increased. This is consistent with the fact that when conditions of work in a sector improve, men begin to displace women, and social barriers to entry become less rigid. Members also find it easier to get their unemployed husbands to start working with them to contribute to the household kitty. There is evidence of a slight increase in the number of workers belonging to the Other Backward Classes indicating a chink in the caste occupational link. However, the majority of the new entrants share the same social background as waste pickers. Many waste pickers choose to stay clear of 'employment' relationships and are used to negotiating their own arrangements to their advantage or disadvantage. SWaCH members, for example, negotiated a hike in user fees with service users after a year or two of providing the service. Non-waste picker members in SWaCH look upon it as a stepping stone to employment in the PMC or at the very least salaried employment.

KKPKP embraced a Green Jobs Strategy as a way of securing the future of the waste pickers. The SWaCH Co-op is one initiative. The imperatives of climate change have introduced the concept of green jobs.[16] Green jobs are defined as jobs in agriculture, manufacturing, administration and services that contribute substantially to preserving or restoring environmental quality. These include jobs that reduce extraction of natural resources, material use, energy use, waste and pollution. Scrap material recovery and collection, as well as recycling, qualify as green jobs. The former, however, do not qualify as decent work because they often expose workers to unclean and difficult conditions of work. Further, some of the processes in recycling are not green because the ways in which they are carried out are polluting. The downside of recycling activities notwithstanding, its significance lies in providing employment, reducing energy use and diverting waste from landfill. Secondary steel production using scrap as raw material reduces energy

[16] United Nations Environment Program (UNEP), *Green Jobs: Towards Decent Work in a Sustainable, Low Carbon World* (Nairobi, UNEP, 2008), available at: www.unep.org/labour_environment/PDFs/Greenjobs/UNEP-Green-Jobs-Report.pdf.

requirements by 40–75 per cent. In the case of aluminium the reduction is as high as 95 per cent.

Estimation of workers engaged in the informal economy has always been a challenge and it is no different in the case of informal scrap and waste collectors. Nevertheless, the estimates on the numbers of workers engaged in scrap collection by the United Nations Environment Programme (UNEP), the ILO and the World Bank can be taken to be indicative. The ILO estimates that there are 2.5 million such workers in China,[17] 70,000 in Cairo and 500,000 in Brazil.[18] World Bank estimates put it at 1–2 per cent of the urban population. The estimate for India is 1.5 million. If other processes are added, the global estimate for Brazil, the US[19] and China is 12 million. The short-term and long-term outlook for greening recycling is reported by UNEP-ILO to be excellent.[20]

In suggesting a road map for greening jobs, the UNEP report suggests that the approach should begin with mapping the 'low-hanging fruit' or jobs in which low-cost measures can be taken immediately.[21] It also directs attention to gender dimensions and social inclusion of disadvantaged groups and regions.[22] Scrap and waste collectors qualify on all counts. KKPKP has seized upon a green job strategy for Pune and the SWaCH Co-op is evidence of its operationalisation. Estimations of the environmental contribution of informal scrap and waste collectors in Pune indicate reduction in Greenhouse Gas Emissions amounting to 294,316 in metric tonnes of carbon dioxide equivalent ($mtCO_2$-eq) per annum.[23] The corresponding figure for Delhi stands at an estimated 900,000 tons of CO_2 equivalent.[24] Informal scrap collectors and waste recyclers mitigate climate change.

[17] World Bank, *Waste Management in China: Issues and Recommendations* (Working Paper No 9, East Asia Infrastructure Department, Washington DC, May 2005).
[18] 'Brazil's Recycling Map Shows Close to 2,500 Firms Working in the Sector', *Brazzil Magazine* (4 October, 2005), available at: www.brazzilmag.com/home/29/4138-brazils-recycling-map-shows-close-to-2500-firms-working-in-the-sector.html.
[19] Environmental Protection Agency (US), 'Recycling is Working in the United States' (January 2002), available at: www.epa.gov/jtr/econ/rei-rw/charttx.htm.
[20] UNEP, *Global Environment Outlook 4* (Nairobi, UNEP, 2007) 225.
[21] *Ibid*, at 304.
[22] *Ibid*, at 293–5.
[23] Chikarmane, P and Narayan, L, *Study of the Economic Aspects of the Waste Informal Sector in Pune* (Kagad Kach Patra Kashatakari Panchayat under contract to WASTE/Skat, GTZ, 2006).
[24] Chintan and The Advocacy Project, *Cooling Agents: An Analysis of Climate Change Mitigation by the Informal Recycling Sector in India* (New Delhi, Chintan and The Advocacy Project, 2009), available at: www.advocacynet.org/files/Cooling%20Agents%20full.pdf.

CHALLENGES AND OBSTACLES

Ownership of Waste?

Waste is a misnomer for resources that are by-products of human activity or man-made resources, for want of a better term. Waste pickers use their labour to recover, collect and sort materials that have zero value, having been discarded as rubbish or waste, and sell them as tradable commodities in the market. Resources have claimants and competing claims have to be negotiated. Historically waste lay on the streets, its real value was not known and it was treated as a common property resource by waste pickers who earned their livelihood from it. What comes into municipal collection systems is primarily domestic waste, which is mixed and relatively difficult to segregate, so resource recovery was carried out manually. Under the Bombay Provincial Municipal Corporations Act 1949, the PMC is the owner of waste that is deposited in the municipal system. Today the technology that aids and enables segregation and recovery exists, but it is beyond the financial capital and technical ability of the waste pickers to install it. A proposal that the PMC set up such a facility has been stalled by the municipal administration.

Let us examine the case of Hanjer Biotech, a waste-to-energy manufacturing company that has entered into a concession agreement that is valid for 30 years. Some 20 hectares of land has been handed over to the company by the PMC for installing a RDF plant. The PMC bears the transport costs of the waste to the landfill and will be paying a tipping fee per ton from the fifth year onwards. The PMC has retained the rights to carbon credits. As per the agreement, the company has the right to sell scrap that it gets and to retain the proceeds. Hanjer installed the machinery that segregates scrap which is further manually sorted. As a result 150 waste pickers at the landfill are each losing income of US$6–8 per day. Instead, only a few of them are now permitted to carry out the same activity within the factory for no payment except the right to purchase the salvaged scrap at the rate determined by the company.

We argue that the situation of waste pickers is similar to that of privatisation of the commons and negating the customary rights of waste pickers to scrap. This could be considered to be a case of what Harvey calls accumulation by dispossession.[25] The struggle of the waste pickers is the struggle for resources rather than the struggle for higher earnings or wages. Whether it is waste, or land acquisition, or mining leases, or water or forest produce, the mass struggles of marginalised labouring populations in India

---

[25] Harvey, D, 'The "New" Imperialism: On Spatio Temporal Fixes and Accumulation by Dispossession' (2004) 40 *Socialist Register* 63.

are all about access to, and control over, resources rather than earnings or wages.[26]

Social Protection: Through the Scrap Commodities Market?

The absence of employer–employee relations is characteristic of the scrap trade. Sale purchase transactions apply in the case of commodities or labour and are determined on a piece-rate basis. Many years ago KKPKP made repeated demands for extension of the Maharashtra Hamal Mathadi and Other Unprotected Manual Workers (Regulation of Employment and Welfare) Act of 1969 to scrap markets after suitable amendments. The Act had been instrumental in radically changing the lives of head loaders and other manual workers in wood, iron and steel, grains, fruits and vegetables and other markets and railway goods yards, and also to salt workers and fishing industry workers. The Act applies to workers carrying out a range of operations in geographical areas and designated markets.

In arguing for the extension of the Act to scrap markets, KKPKP emphasised the fact that the operations carried out including collecting, sorting, grading, baling, weighing, cleaning, washing, packing, loading and unloading in the scrap markets were similar to those carried out in other commodities markets. It also argued that the relationship between the waste picker and the scrap trader was reduced to that of buyer and seller in a fragmented labour market when actually the links between the traders and the waste pickers had many similarities with employment, or at the very least a contractual relationship. This was particularly true in the case of itinerant waste buyers to whom the scrap traders provided both capital and the tools of trade. The arguments did not receive any support because head loaders operate with the permission of the traders in the market even though they are not paid wages by the trader. Scrap collectors are seen to operate individually in a 'free' market.

Integration of Waste Pickers into Solid Waste Management

The role played by waste pickers in solid waste management has been documented in successive government reports and policy documents pertaining to the environment, labour and urban development over the past decade and a half.[27] States such as Maharashtra have also issued government

---

[26] We thank Dr Abhay Shukla for drawing our attention to the fact that current labour struggles in India are over resources rather than wages.

[27] See generally Bajaj, JS, *Report of The High Power Committee: Urban Solid Waste Management in India*, (New Delhi, Government of India, 1995); Supreme Court Committee, *Report of the Committee on Solid Waste Management in Class I Cities in India* (March

resolutions, directives and guidelines based on precedents established by KKPKP and PMC. Despite the enabling policy environment, the integration of waste pickers has not moved at the desired pace for two reasons. The first is the poor organisation or unionisation of workers leading to a demand from below. The second is the absence of convergence between different government ministries.

Solid waste management falls within the ambit of the Ministry of Environment and Forests for regulation and the Ministry of Urban Development for implementation by municipal governments. There is no single legal instrument that pulls together everything related to solid waste management and recycling as in some other countries (such as the Philippines).

In some ways the absence of a unified policy instrument allows space to manoeuvre and accommodate the informal waste sector. On the other hand, given that there are so many parallel processes, institutionalisation of initiatives and mandatory compliance becomes difficult in the absence of a unified instrument.

Worker: Blurring Legal Boundaries

In the course of this Chapter we have seen that the path towards some degree of 'formalisation' that would accord social protection to recycling workers is not straight and narrow. The legal boundaries of who constitutes a worker and the status of the worker in legal terms is sufficiently obscure to merit some discussion.[28] KKPKP is the organisation of waste pickers and itinerant waste buyers. They are self-employed entrepreneurs, as distinct from *waged* municipal workers, irrespective of whether the latter are employees or contract workers, even within the ambit of solid waste management.[29] The entire value chain consists of collection—trading—intermediate processing—processing. The forward linkages in the labour market would be informal workers in scrap shops and intermediate waste

1999); Ministry of Labour and Employment, *Report of the Second National Labour Commission* (New Delhi, Government of India, 2002); Ministry of Environment and Forests, *National Environment Policy* (New Delhi, Government of India, 2006); Maharashtra Non-Biodegradable Garbage (Control) Ordinance (2006); Government of Maharashtra, Urban Development Department, Resolution No SWM 1006/CR53/UD-16 (25 October 2006); Government of Maharashtra, Water Supply and Sanitation Department, Government Resolution No Ghakavya 1001/ Pra Kra 546/ Papu-22 (5 January 2002); Ministry of Urban Development, *Report of the Parliamentary Standing Committee on Urban Development, 2009–10* (New Delhi, Government of India, 2010).

[28] As to these issues in India more generally see Sankaran, K, 'Flexibility and Informalisation of Employment Relationships' in this collection.

[29] For definitions of employee and contract workers in India see *ibid*.

processing units. The sector-specific policy and legal framework in this case would be drawn from micro-small-medium enterprises in the broad area of materials recovery and trading, and therefore commerce and industry would be the legitimate 'home'.

SWaCH, on the other hand, by intent and design, has made some waste pickers into service providers who are paid user fees for their services. So the 'home' of SWaCH is actually service provision with member owners having to be treated as service workers, irrespective of whether they are paid on the basis of piece rate (per household) or daily wages. The forward linkages in the labour market would be service workers, waste collection and allied cleaning services.

As Fudge notes, there is a tremendous amount of heterogeneity in the informal economy and different types of paid work trespass traditional economic and legal boundaries.[30] The challenge then is to bring both streams of self-employed entrepreneurial workers and service workers, both of whom sell their labour as well as commodities, into a single regulatory and social protection framework.

CONCLUSION

The journey from rag picker to recycling worker has been one of evolving and systematically constructing alternative identities of waste picker, scrap collector, and perhaps in the near future, recycling worker. The construction of alternative identities for waste pickers has evolved concomitant to changing conditions of work. The average waste picker's conception of what constituted 'work' was radically different from the reality at her workplace. She understood 'work' as being salaried employment that was nowhere near what she did and which she called '*kachra chivadne*' (rummaging through rubbish). Arguing that collection, sorting and sale of recyclable scrap constitute economically productive work, the KKPKP systematically constructed collection, sorting and other value addition activities (grading, washing, shredding and baling) as 'work' within the recycling industry. The construction of the waste pickers as raw material suppliers was within the context of the recycling industry as consumers of collected scrap. At the waste collection end waste pickers sought to quantify their unpaid contribution to reducing municipal solid waste management and environmental costs.

For the waste picker, the consciousness of what it meant to be a 'worker' in the context of the informal economy emerged during the process of collectivisation. In a sense she was the quintessential entrepreneur,

[30] Fudge J, 'Blurring Legal Boundaries: Regulating for Decent Work' in this collection.

self-employed and therefore relatively less encumbered by 'employer' demands. The construction of her identity as a worker has been accompanied by benefits such as an identity card as proof of her worker status; decrease in harassment; group life insurance; group medical insurance; access to credit at competitive rates of interest; access to sorting space, better work opportunities and agency.

4

Informal Sectors and New Industries: The Complexities of Regulating Occupational Health and Safety in Developing Countries

RICHARD JOHNSTONE[*]

INTRODUCTION

DESPITE MAJOR ADVANCES in occupational medicine and safety technology, the level of world-wide work-related illness, injury and death remains excessive, and far greater than the harm arising from sources such as armed conflicts. ILO figures estimate that approximately 2.2 million workers die every year as a result of work-related ill-health and injury.[1] Of these, 350,000 deaths are attributable to work-related incidents, and the remainder to occupational ill-health. The ILO further estimates that there are an additional 264 million non-fatal work-related injuries each year and 160 million people with work-related illnesses. It calculates the economic cost of this loss to be 4 per cent of the global GDP or $1.25 trillion US dollars.[2] The ILO also acknowledges that the vast majority of these deaths are avoidable and preventable. Most of this work-related death, ill-health and injury occurs in developing[3] and newly industrialising countries which, in recent times, have made significant developments in industrialisation, economic reform,

[*] Thanks to Igor Nossar and Judy Fudge for reading and commenting on an earlier draft, to Marius Olivier for help with research sources, and to Paul Harpur for research assistance.
[1] Hämäläinen, P, Takala, J and Saarela, KL, *Global Estimates of Fatal Work-related Diseases and Occupational Accidents* (Amsterdam, Elsevier, 2005). See also Walters, D, Johnstone, R, Frick, K, Quinlan M, Baril-Gingras, G and Thébaud-Mony, A, *Regulating Workplace Risks: A Comparative Study of Inspection Regimes in Times of Change* (Cheltenham, Edward Elgar, 2011) 1.
[2] See Hämäläinen *et al*, above n 1, and Walters *et al*, above n 1, 1. See also Alli, BO, *Fundamental Principles of Occupational Health and Safety* (Geneva, International Labour Office, 2008) 3–9.
[3] The term 'developing country' is used in this chapter to cover countries with a low standard of material well-being and an emerging and developing economy.

and the development of economic markets for their goods and services, but at the cost of the health and safety of their workers.[4] Improving all measures (including occupational health and safety (OHS) regulation) to prevent illness, injury and death at work is, therefore, an important and urgent policy issue.

Workers in developing countries on the whole experience greater risks at work than their counterparts in developed countries because of limited capital available for investment in more modern production technology coupled with insufficient job and OHS training in a context of inadequate resourcing and support at both the local and international levels. Much manual work is extremely demanding physically, causing high levels of stress and ill-health. Further, the effects of poor working conditions upon workers are exacerbated by poverty, illiteracy, low nutrition, poor social status, unhygienic living conditions, and tropical disease.[5]

While much progress has been made in regulating OHS in developing countries, OHS and the regulation of OHS in African, South and Central American, Asian and Pacific island countries faces many obstacles not found in developed countries,[6] and there are many factors which inhibit the regulatory response to OHS in developing countries. This Chapter examines some of these challenges, many of which are detailed by Judy Fudge in Chapter 1 of this collection.[7] The challenges include the rapid expansion of the informal economy, where economic activity is not recognised or protected by state authorities; new industries in developing countries, some of which are difficult to regulate; and the outsourcing of production by the use of transnational supply chains enabling firms based in developed countries to exploit labour in developing countries from a distance. The Chapter will suggest that many of the approaches to OHS regulation adopted in North America, Europe and Australia do not immediately address the issues facing OHS regulators in developing countries, and, consistent with the goal of this collection to explore the capacity of different legal approaches and techniques to protect the dignity and well-being of workers, this Chapter will begin to map out some of the possible regulatory approaches that might be taken to effectively regulate OHS in developing countries.

---

[4] Ahasan, MR and Partanen, T, 'Occupational Health and Safety in the Least Developed Countries—A Simple Case of Neglect' (2001) 11 *Journal of Epidemiology* 74, 74.

[5] *Ibid*, at 75.

[6] World Health Organization (WHO), Implementation of the Resolution of Occupational Health and Safety in the African Region, Meeting Report (Brazzaville, WHO, Regional Office for Africa, 2005) 20.

[7] Fudge, J, 'Blurring Legal Boundaries: Regulating for Decent Work' in this collection.

OHS REGULATION IN DEVELOPED COUNTRIES

Since the early 1970s, there have been significant developments in OHS regulation in most developed countries, and particularly in Europe, Australia and New Zealand, and North America (although it should be said that OHS regulation in the United States of America has not adopted some of the developments in Europe, Canada and Australasia). The major OHS regulatory developments in developed countries include a shift from technical, prescriptive 'specification standards' (which specified the safeguard required for each identified hazard)[8] to a mix of performance standards (where the outcome is specified but the means is left to the regulated firm) and process standards (where it is difficult to set a target, but instead regulated firms are required to follow a process or series of steps). This shift has required firms to take a more holistic and systematic approach to managing OHS (which is now broadly defined to include health—including psycho-social health—issues), and to do so in a manner that is integrated with the overall management of the firm.[9] In some countries, notably the UK and Australia, the general duty imposed on the employer (or, in Australia, upon the 'person conducting the business or undertaking') is now owed to all kinds of workers engaged or directed by a firm (not just 'employees') and includes 'the public',[10] an important development given the major shifts in the types of working relationships now found in modern labour forces. Most OHS statutes in developed countries also impose standards on designers, manufacturers and suppliers of plant and substances for use at work, and on designers and constructors of structures at workplaces.

Most developed countries now make provision for worker representation and participation in OHS, and some (notably Australia and Sweden) empower worker representatives with powers to require contraventions of OHS statutes to be remedied, or to stop dangerous work. In many European countries

---

[8] It is now widely acknowledged that this approach frequently resulted in a mass of detailed and technical rules, often difficult to understand, and difficult to keep up to date. Standards were developed ad hoc to resolve problems as they arose, and concentrated mainly on factory-based physical hazards, resulting in uneven coverage across workplaces. Specification standards did not enable employers to be innovative and to look for cost-efficient solutions, and ignored the now well-accepted view that many hazards do not arise from the static features of the workplace, but from the way work is organised: see Johnstone, R, *Occupational Health and Safety Law and Policy*, 2nd edn (Sydney, Thompson Law Book, 2004) 63.

[9] For further discussion of this trend, see Walters *et al*, above n 1.

[10] Johnstone, R, 'Paradigm Crossed? The Statutory Occupational Health and Safety Obligations of the Business Undertaking' (1999) 12 *Australian Journal of Labour Law* 73; James, P, Johnstone, R, Quinlan, M and Walters, D, 'Regulating Supply Chains to Improve Health and Safety' (2007) 36 *Industrial law Journal* 163. See also the 'primary duty' in section 19 of the proposed Australian Model Work Health and Safety Act (2009) available at: http://safeworkaustralia.gov.au/AboutSafeWorkAustralia/WhatWeDo/Publications/Documents/598/Model_Work_Health_and_Safety_Bill_23_June_2011.pdf.

(but not the UK), there has been a tradition of requiring firms to engage occupational health services to assist those firms to manage OHS effectively.

State OHS inspectorates in developed countries have been vested with a wider range of enforcement powers, including administrative sanctions—such as improvement and prohibition notices, and in some countries, on-the-spot fines or citations, as well as, in Australia, enforceable undertakings. In some countries there have been attempts to strengthen the role of prosecution in OHS enforcement, by increasing the level of fines, and by introducing non-pecuniary sanctions (such as court-ordered publicity, corporate probation and similar sanctions). Many OHS inspectorates are grappling with the implementation of regulatory concepts such as 'risk-based regulation' (where inspection and enforcement resources are focused on firms and industries posing the highest levels of risk to worker health and safety), and 'responsive enforcement' (where the regulator selects the appropriate enforcement method from a hierarchy of sanctions in response to the regulator's judgment about the nature of the firm's OHS compliance and its compliance history).

This contemporary approach to OHS regulation in developed countries demands significant resources from firms, unions and regulators.[11] Firms can only manage OHS systematically and effectively if management and workers are trained both in the range of OHS hazards, and the means of their identification, assessment and control. Such demands often require firms to engage experts in OHS. OHS inspectorates need to be able to identify the wide range of OHS hazards, be alert to emerging hazards, provide general OHS education and advice, and develop sophisticated ways of identifying and reaching those firms most in need of inspection. The role of a modern OHS inspector is complex, requiring not only technical OHS expertise, but also communication (especially negotiation) skills, and the ability to understand how organisations, and approaches to management, work. The complexity and cost of these demands upon OHS regulation are less likely to be feasible in developing countries, where there are significant competing public health issues in the context of fewer resources available to regulators, unions and small business operators.

STRUCTURAL OBSTACLES TO OHS REGULATION
IN DEVELOPING COUNTRIES

Resource Constraints

At a broad level, OHS in developing countries is often competing with other priorities, such as poverty alleviation, HIV/AIDS and water and

---

[11] See Walters *et al*, above n 1.

sanitation issues.[12] OHS regulatory measures are sometimes undermined by inadequate levels of education and the consequences of globalisation in the form of more deeply entrenched social and gender inequality, persistent poverty, threats to peace and security, and deregulation and reduced state intervention in the economy.[13] A particularly pernicious OHS issue for developing countries is the practice of dangerous (often second-hand) plant and substances being shifted from developed to developing countries,[14] often without adequate information as to the hazards created by the plant or substance, and possible controls.[15]

One consequence of this more acute competition between regulatory priorities is that OHS regulatory regimes in developing countries are often focused on more immediately obvious hazards like dangerous machinery, so that more complex and less immediately obvious issues arising from work organisation, such as stress and other psycho-social hazards, receive little, if any, attention.[16] Another consequence is that governments do not, or simply cannot afford to, introduce strong OHS legal standards, or devote sufficient resources (particularly numbers of inspectors and training) to inspection, or to the kind of research which enables regulators to understand local hazards and develop appropriate controls.[17] Consequently, OHS inspectors are not trained in the more complex OHS issues such as hazardous substances, ergonomics, and psycho-social hazards. The difficulty of the inspectorates' task is exacerbated by extremely low levels of reporting by workers and workplaces of the OHS problems that they face, and the incidents that occur.[18] Inadequate OHS training for mainstream health professionals often reduces their ability to relate a patient's illness to their work conditions. Further, inspectors may have difficulty getting to remote workplaces (especially rural enterprises or small-scale industries) because of inadequate transport infrastructure.

---

[12] Gutierrez, E, 'Workers' Health in Latin America and the Caribbean: Looking to the Future' (2000) 5 *Perspectives in Health* available at: www.paho.org/English/DPI/Number10_article1.htm.

[13] WHO, above n 6.

[14] *Ibid.*

[15] LaDou, J and Jeyaratnam, J, 'Transfer of Hazardous Industries: Issues and Solutions' in J Jeyaratnam and KS Chia (eds), *Occupational Health in National Development* (Singapore, World Scientific Publishing Co, 1994) 227; Ahasan and Partanen, above n 4, at 96.

[16] Kortum, E, 'Work-related Stress and Psychosocial Risks: Trends in Developing and Newly Industrialized Countries' (2007) *Global Occupational Health Network (GOHNET) Newsletter: July Special Issue* 3, available at: www.who.int/occupational_health/publications/newsletter/gohnetspecial072007.pdf.

[17] Ahasan and Partanen, above n 4, at 45.

[18] *Ibid.*

The Rapid Expansion of the Informal Sector

A further complication faced by OHS regulation in developing countries is the rapid expansion in those countries of informal sectors (including informal enterprises, informal work or informal employment)[19] where economic activity is not recognised or protected by state authorities. As Judy Fudge in this collection notes, a wide range of activities and occupations can be found in informal sectors, depending on the region and country.[20] The process of informalisation in developing countries is pervasive, as Kamala Sankaran shows in Chapter 2 in relation to India,[21] and Charles Woolfson has demonstrated in his study of the informalisation of labour in the post-communist Baltic state of Lithuania, which has resulted in deteriorating working conditions, including poor health and safety conditions.[22]

The ILO's *International Symposium on Trade Unions and the Informal Sector* identified three main segments in the informal sector workforce:

> The first segment corresponds to the owners or employers of micro-enterprises including farmers who may employ a few workers and/or apprentices. ... The second segment comprises own-account workers, which is comprised of the nominally self-employed and street vendors and small farmers. It is the largest and most visible segment in the informal sector. Despite being nominally self-employed many workers in this segment are economically dependent on a single enterprise or a middleman for their survival. The third segment encompasses employees engaged in full-time or casual employment. It includes wage labourers working in micro-enterprises on a regular, casual or contract basis, unpaid workers, including family members and apprentices, homeworkers and paid domestic workers. The workforce in this segment is often physically hidden and therefore more difficult to locate, contact and organize.[23]

Many factors contribute to this expansion of informal sectors, including globalisation and the associated search for lower labour costs, and privatisation and the contracting out of services and activities.[24] Current estimates suggest that the informal economy both in South America and in India represent 60 per cent of national income, and in some parts of Africa it is as high as 95 per cent; and of the 88 million women workers in India, only 4.5 million work in the organised sector.[25]

---

[19] International Labour Office, *International Symposium on Trade Unions and the Informal Sector: Conclusions and Recommendations* (Geneva, International Labour Office, 1999).

[20] Fudge, above n 7, and see the definition of the informal economy in this Chapter.

[21] Sankaran, K, 'Flexibility and Informalisation of Employment Relationships' in this collection.

[22] Woolfson, C, 'Pushing the Envelope: the "Informalization" of Labour in Post-Communist New EU Member States' (2007) 21 *Work, Employment and Society* 551, 555.

[23] ILO, above n 19. See Carr and Chen's hierarchy of employment statuses in the informal economy, discussed by Judy Fudge in Chapter 1 of this collection (above n 7).

[24] *Ibid.*

[25] Kortum, above n 16, at 5.

Women represent a high proportion of informal sector workers, and their working conditions (particular hours and type of work, and remuneration) differ from the conditions experienced by men.[26] Child labour is common, with children as young as four years of age engaged in work. 'The vast majority of people do not work in the informal sector by choice and it is certainly not for them a stepping stone to improvement. Rather it represents a means of survival.'[27]

Working conditions in informal sectors are dangerous, and workers' rights are largely ignored.[28] Workers in these informal sectors are generally not protected by OHS standards and social protection programmes such as unemployment benefits, health insurance coverage[29] or state-provided training and social services—even though these informal sector workers are often the outsourced workers of large international and local enterprises.[30] Trade unions have found it difficult to organise in informal sectors because workers are difficult to contact, and their needs differ from those of workers in the formal sector.[31]

The Global Economy: New Industries in Special Industrial Zones and the Impact of Transnational Supply Chains

Globalisation has also spawned the development of new industries often located in special industrial zones within developing countries, which often either are under-regulated or difficult to regulate. One example involves the 'export-processing zones' (or 'maliquiladora') representing the assembly industry in Central America.[32] Approximately 90 per cent of workers in this industry are women or children. Work conditions include job instability, temporary contracts and subcontracting, long working hours, unrealistic production quotas and incentives, inadequate restrictions on overtime, low wages and a high incidence of sexual harassment. These conditions lead both to excessive injuries to workers resulting from dangerous machinery, and also to ill-health resulting from dust, noise, inadequate ventilation, exposure to dangerous chemicals and very intense and stressful work.[33]

[26] ILO, above n 19.
[27] *Ibid.*
[28] See, eg, Woolfson, above n 22, 554–7.
[29] Gutierrez, above n 12.
[30] Kortum, above n 16.
[31] International Labour Office, above n 19.
[32] Gutierrez, above n 12; Lowenson, R, 'Women's Occupational Health in Globalization and Development' (1999) 36 *American Journal of Industrial Medicine* 34; Kortum, above n 16, at 4.
[33] Kortum, above n 16, at 4.

Another example involves the demarcation of special economic zones (SEZs) in China.[34] SEZs are areas designated by the Chinese government, which has reduced legal regulation and corporate taxes in those zones in order to encourage corporations to invest. All of the goods manufactured in SEZs must be exported outside China in order to avoid the imposition of special taxes.[35] China has consistently been the world's largest manufacturing exporter—in 2005 Chinese trade in manufactured goods made up 24 per cent of the world market.[36]

Factories in the SEZs are required by law to comply with Chinese labour laws,[37] but these OHS regulatory provisions are weak when compared with OHS standards in developed countries like Australia, the UK, and most continental European countries. Reports from international and non-government organisations indicate that labour rights in Chinese factories are often not recognised or enforced by regional enforcement agencies, with most concern focused upon factories in SEZs.

Taking up two themes introduced by Judy Fudge in Chapter 1 of this collection, the need to examine changes at the level of the firm, and the linkages of firms in the informal economy with firms in the formal economy through complex networks of intermediaries and firms, many factories in the SEZs are linked to corporations in developed countries through supply chains in which general retailers (or other major brand names) in developed countries outsource production to intermediaries and ultimately to Chinese factories in SEZs, seeking high-quality products at low cost.

Supply chains are a good example of 'the commercialisation of employment' discussed in Chapter 1, and seek to integrate separate legal entities to decrease the expense of manufacturing, supply and retail marketing of products.[38] At the top of the supply chain is usually a large retailer or brand name, which outsources, through contract, the supply of products to unrelated corporate entities. These unrelated corporate entities often act as suppliers and further outsource the production of products to factories until

---

[34] Harpur, P, *Labour Rights as Human Rights: Workers' Safety at Work in Australian-Based Supply Chains* (Queensland University of Technology, PhD Thesis, 2009) ch 4.

[35] Madani, D, *A Review of the Role and Impact of Export Processing Zones* (Washington DC, World Bank, 1999); Regulations on Special Economic Zones in Guangdong Province 1980 (PRC), Art 9, available at: www.novexcn.com/guangdong_regs_on_sez.html.

[36] China Textile and Apparel Industry, *Annual Report on Social Responsibility 2006* (2007) 11, available at: http://info.worldbank.org/etools/antic/docs/Resources/InitiativeType/AntiCorruption%20Declarations/China_Declaration.pdf.

[37] See, eg, Regulations on Special Economic Zones in Guangdong Province 1980 (PRC), above n 30, Art 2.

[38] Fudge, above n 7; Frazelle, E, *Supply Chain Strategy: The Logistics of Supply Chain Management* (New York, McGraw Hill, 2002); Beamon, E, 'Measuring Supply Chain Performance' (1999) 19 *International Journal of Operations and Production Management* 275; Simchi-Levi, D, Kaminsky, S and Simchi-Levi, E, *Designing and Managing the Supply Chain: Concepts, Strategies and Case Studies* (Irwin, McGraw Hill, 2000); Harpur, above n 34.

finally workers toil to make the products.[39] Even though supply chains may consist of a number of separate entities, the entire chain may be practically controlled or owned by the one corporate entity: the 'effective business controller',[40] which is often intent upon outsourcing production to states with lower labour costs.[41]

Supply chains in manufacturing have become increasingly globalised, a process encouraged by the World Bank and the International Monetary Fund, which have encouraged developing countries to utilise their comparative labour cost advantage.[42] The primary motive for corporations to develop supply chains is profit,[43] and globalised supply chains enable corporations to access cheap labour markets with low regulation, to increase organisational flexibility through outsourcing, and to transfer business risk down the chain, to smaller firms and ultimately to individual workers.[44] While an effective business controller can often exert substantial economic pressure over parties lower in their supply chains, the operation of the corporate veil means that the effective business controller is most often not legally liable for the conduct of parties lower in the supply chain. This creates a significant legal distance between the effective business controller and labour abuses, permitting the effective business controller to reap the benefits of lower costs and greater flexibility. The net effect of this use of supply chains is to exploit vulnerable workers in developing countries and to 'off-shore' jobs into lower cost jurisdictions in order to evade labour regulation in the effective business controller's home jurisdiction.[45]

---

[39] Gillen, M, 'The Apparel Industry Partnership's Free Labor Association: a Solution to the Overseas Sweatshop Problem or the Emperor's New Clothes?' (2007) 32 *New York University Journal of International Law and Politics* 1059; Newell, P and Wheeler, J (eds), *Rights, Resources and the Politics of Accountability* (London, Zed Books, 2006) 36–58.

[40] Nossar, I, Johnstone, R and Quinlan, M, 'Regulating Supply Chains to Address the Occupational Health and Safety Problems Associated with Precarious Employment: the Case of Home-Based Clothing Workers in Australia' (2004) 17 *Australian Journal of Labour Law* 137.

[41] Arnold, D and Hartman, L, 'Moral Imagination and the Future of Sweatshops' (2003) 108 *Business and Society Review* 4.

[42] *Ibid.*

[43] Jenkins, R, Pearson, R and Seyfang, G (eds), *Corporate Responsibility and Labor Rights: Codes of Conduct in a Global Economy* (London, Earthscan, 2002); Merino, F and Rodríguez, D, 'Business Services Outsourcing by Manufacturing Firms' (2007) 16 *Industrial and Corporate Change* 1147, 1147; Cohen, S and Roussel, J, *Strategic Supply Chain Management* (New York, McGraw Hill, 2005) 9.

[44] Weller, S, *Fashion's Influence on Garment Mass Production: Knowledge, Commodities and the Capture of Value*' (Victoria University, PhD Thesis, 2004) 27; Peck, J, 'Outwork and Restructuring Processes in the Australian Clothing Industry' (1990) 3 *Labor and Industry* 302, 306; Pfohl, H and Buse, H, 'Inter-organizational Logistics Systems in Flexible Production Networks: an Organizational Capabilities Perspective' (2000) 30 *International Journal of Physical Distribution & Logistics Management* 388; Spekman, R, Kamauff, J and Myhr, N, 'An Empirical Investigation into Supply Chain Management: A Perspective on Partnerships' (1998) 28 *Internal Journal of Physical Distribution & Logistics Management* 630.

[45] Rawling, M, Supply Chain Regulation: Work and Regulation Beyond the Employment Relationship (University of Sydney, PhD Thesis, 2010) 324.

WHAT CAN BE DONE?

Many of the issues identified in this Chapter are a result of intensified globalisation, and in particular the ability of capital to shift production to developing countries by direct investment in plant in developing countries, through supply chains or through purchasing contracts. The protection of workers' health is consequently a global issue, and needs global solutions built on co-operation between developed and developing countries.

The link between work-related ill-health and ill-health due to poverty and underdevelopment is so significant in developing countries that progress in improved health at work needs to be linked to national health strategies, and depends on further economic development, the alleviation of poverty and progress with general health systems. Within this context, OHS regulators in developing countries need to be better resourced (financially, but also through more training and education) so as to develop the capacity of their regulatory regimes to address OHS—taking into account local conditions. Certainly, OHS regulation in developing countries can be improved by adopting some of the OHS regulatory innovations of developed countries, particularly those that seek to broaden the definition of work health: provide equal protection to all kinds of workers, rather than just employees, to overcome the traditional boundaries between categories of workers; address hazards at their source; enable the participation in OHS activities of all kinds of workers (again, overcoming the traditional boundaries between categories of workers); and provide regulators with strong sanctions for breaches. The most useful provisions will be the new Australian statutory duty of care imposed, not just on 'employers', but on all persons conducting a business or undertaking (PCBUs) and owed to *all* kinds of workers (not just 'employees') engaged, directed or influenced by the PCBU,[46] and to 'others'; the Australian, UK and European duties on designers, manufacturers, suppliers, importers and installers of plant, manufacturers, suppliers and importers of substances, and designers and constructors of structures at workplaces; clarification that OHS regulatory protection extends to health (including psychological health) at work; the introduction of process standards requiring systematic OHS management across the firm; provisions enabling worker representation and participation that extend to all kinds of workers engaged in or by the firm; and a range of administrative sanctions for OHS inspectorates and high maximum penalties for successful prosecutions.

It is difficult to see how progress will be made without significant international collaboration between government departments with responsibility for labour, and particularly OHS regulatory agencies, in developed

---

[46] Model Work Health and Safety Act 2009, above n 10, at s 19; see also s 7, which defines a 'worker' as a person carrying out 'work in any capacity' for a PCBU.

countries and developing countries. Indeed, many of the problems identified in this Chapter (for example inattention to psycho-social issues, problems of supply chains, the supply of hazardous plant and machinery etc) were issues faced by OHS regulators in developed countries in the recent past. In recent years various international and regional programmes have been initiated in order to address OHS in developing countries. Examples include the World Health Organization (WHO)/International Labour Organization (ILO) Joint Effort on Occupational Health and Safety in Africa, the WHO Global Strategy for Occupational Health for All, the WHO Global Plan of Action on Occupational Health 2008–2017, and the Global Network of WHO Collaborating Centres in Occupational Health.

A core principle should be to encourage and assist developing countries to erase the distinction between formal and informal sectors and working conditions. An obvious strategy to improve labour rights, including OHS, in informal sectors is to persuade international organisations (such as the World Bank, World Trade Organization (WTO) and International Monetary Fund (IMF)) to require governments to 'formalise' informal sectors, to ensure that informal businesses become socially responsible and productive organisations, complying with their full range of legal responsibilities, including labour law obligations.[47] The World Bank, WTO and IMF should require governments to implement core ILO standards (including the key OHS conventions and the Decent Work Agenda discussed by Judy Fudge in Chapter 1 of this collection). As discussed above, a key aspect of this is to focus OHS regulatory provisions on protecting all kinds of workers, regardless of whether they work under a contract with a firm, or simply 'at the direction' of the firm, and regardless of whether they are employees.

Trade unions have an important role to play in improving OHS in developing countries. In countries with informal sectors, unions will need to develop strategies to gather information about informal workers, and ways of organising that are attractive to, and accommodate the needs of, women and child workers.[48] These strategies should include international co-ordination of support for workers in the informal sector, and international trade union co-operation focusing on areas such as:

> [P]romoting a link between labour standards and trade matters; the negotiation and implementation of codes of conduct; the development and implementation of framework agreements between international trade union organizations and multinational companies; and social labelling schemes.[49]

---

[47] International Labour Office, above n 19.
[48] See *ibid* for possible strategies.
[49] *Ibid.*

Finally, there are a range of possible approaches to addressing the issues of poor OHS conditions for workers at the bottom of international supply chains. As James *et al* note:

> There would seem to be good grounds for suggesting that supply chains can be used to promote higher levels of legal compliance among the parties within them and hence combat the adverse health and safety effects of externalisation and poor enforcement already mentioned. In many cases those at the head of supply chains are likely to be larger than the organisations undertaking work for them and hence, as the evidence presented earlier suggests, possess more sophisticated health and safety knowledge and expertise and therefore the capacity to support improved health and safety management in them. In addition, in the context of the asymmetrical power relationships that often exist between those engaged in supply chains, larger organisations at the top of them will often possess the ability to influence the 'compliance-non compliance' decision-making of those lower down by raising the possibility of their incurring financial losses, or opportunity costs, through the ability they have to terminate or withhold contracts.[50]

Further, those large organisations at the head of supply chains are more easily reached by OHS inspectorates than those further down the supply chain, and so inspectorates can influence the OHS of many down the chain by focusing on the measures taken by those at the top.

Voluntary codes seeking to regulate the behaviour of multinationals, and in particular to improve labour standards, have been produced by both the ILO[51] and the Organisation for Economic Co-operation and Development,[52] and at the international level, codes covering a similar ground, including OHS, have been developed by NGOs and trade unions.[53] Many multinationals have developed their own codes or signed up to already promulgated international or national codes. For example, in Australia, high-profile transnational corporations involved in textile, clothing and footwear production have entered into enforceable arrangements under which all sites of production must be revealed to the Textile, Clothing and Footwear Union and the union is given the contractual authority to inspect all such sites without prior notification, as well as to receive supply contract details (including pricing) and work records, and to interview both on- and off-site workers.[54] Of course, a weakness of these voluntary codes

---

[50] James *et al*, above n 10.

[51] International Labour Organisation, *Tripartite Declaration of Principles Concerning Multinational Enterprises and Social Policy* (Geneva, International Labour Office, 1977).

[52] Organisation for Economic Co-operation and Development (OECD), *Guidelines for Multinational Enterprises* (New York, OECD, 2000).

[53] See, eg, Clean Clothes Campaign, *Clean Clothes Campaign Codes of Conduct for Transnational Corporations: An Overview* (Amsterdam, Clean Clothes Campaign, 1998).

[54] See generally James *et al*, above n 10, at 176–7; Nossar, I, *The Scope for Appropriate Cross-Jurisdictional Regulation of International Contract Networks (Such as Supply Chains): Recent Developments in Australia and their Supra-National Implications'* (Keynote Presentation to ILO Workshop, Toronto, 17 April 2007), an edited version of this presentation

is that they are not enforced or enforceable, either by labour inspectorates or third parties. It is also likely that they have been accepted by transnational firms to pre-empt tougher forms of regulation.[55]

There are good examples of legally enforceable regulation of supply chains in the USA and in Australia. Weil's research shows how from 1996, the Work and Hours Division (WHD) of the US Department of Labor invoked section 15(A) of the Fair Labour Standards Act 1938 which empowered it to embargo goods that had been manufactured in violation of the Act.[56] The WHD made the release of any embargoed goods contingent on the manufacturer concerned signing two types of agreement: one with the Department of Labor itself, stipulating the basic components of a monitoring system to be used to monitor subcontractors compliance with the Act's minimum wage provisions; and another with its contractors, setting out how they will comply with these requirements. Weil shows that violations of the minimum wage provisions were significantly lower among contractors producing goods for manufacturers who were monitoring their compliance (and who were subject to significant penalties under section 15A).

Recent Australian legislation in both the clothing, textile and footwear industry and in the long-haul transport industry has sought to regulate the working conditions (including OHS) of workers in supply chains. For example, the Mandatory Apparel Retailer Codes currently operative in two Australian states impose (upon retailers and suppliers) record-keeping and (reactive and proactive) disclosure obligations, and also import standardised, enforceable provisions into retailer contracts requiring suppliers further down the chain to inform retailers about all locations where apparel production is conducted. These mandatory code obligations complement other legislative provisions which provide outworkers with rights to recover wages from any party in the supply chain, and which also ensure the effective inspection of the actual conduct of work at each location. The Occupational Health and Safety Amendment (Long Distance Truck Driver Fatigue) Regulation 2005 (NSW) (repealed at the beginning of 2012) was an extension of and an elaboration on OHS statutory general duties which made these duties specific to certain parties at the apex (and throughout) road transport supply chains, including the major retailers which act as effective business controllers of these supply chains.[57]

---

is available at: www.nationalohsreview.gov.au/NR/rdonlyres/7754B182-CA90-4DAF-B8CE-CC6A9E19B9AE/0/211TextilesClothingandFootwearUnionofAustralia.pdf.

[55] James *et al*, above n 10, at 176–7. See also Madhav, R, 'Corporate Codes of Conduct in the Garment Sector in Bangalore' in this collection.

[56] Weil, D, 'Public Enforcement/Private Monitoring: Evaluating a New Approach to Regulating the Minimum Wage' (2005) 58 *Industrial and Labour Relations Review* 238. See also James *et al*, above n 10.

[57] Nossar, above n 54.

In principle, there is no reason why these provisions could not operate across jurisdictions, so that, for example, an Australian retailer can be required by statute to require suppliers in China to inform the Australian retailer where apparel production is located, and under what conditions the apparel is produced, and to nominate trade unions to act as the inspection agent of the retailer in China. The retailer could be required to invoke commercial sanctions where the suppliers' working conditions are unsatisfactory.[58] The Textile, Clothing and Footwear Union of Australia argued, in its 2008 submission to the Australian National Review into Model Occupational Health and Safety Laws, that Australia should enhance cross-jurisdictional co-operation between regulatory agencies within Australia (between State and Territory jurisdictions) and internationally (between Australian OHS regulatory agencies and their overseas counterparts), particularly in relation to supply chains.[59]

CONCLUSION

The improvement of OHS in developing countries is an urgent policy issue. This Chapter has outlined some of the structural barriers preventing recent advances in OHS regulation in developed countries from being extended to developing countries. These barriers include competing public health priorities and inadequate public health and OHS regulatory resources in developing countries; the rapidly increasing incidence of un- or under-regulated informal sectors and new industries in special industrial zones; and the impact of transnational supply chains in developing countries. Before these barriers can be effectively dismantled and overcome, more research is needed to understand the political, social and economic dynamics leading to poor OHS in developing countries; how informal sectors might be effectively 'formalised' and properly regulated; how OHS regulatory strategies in developed countries might be used in developing countries, and areas in which novel approaches are required; how legally enforceable supply chain regulation might be extended globally and greater cross-jurisdictional co-operation be encouraged; and how the major international institutions, and international collaboration between developing and developed countries, can address the underlying factors leading to poor OHS in developing countries and improve resources for OHS (including regulation) in those countries.

---

[58] Nossar, I, 'Cross-Jurisdictional Regulation of Commercial Contracts for Work Beyond the Traditional Relationship' in C Arup, Gahan, P, Howe, J, Johnstone, R, Mitchell, R, and O'Donnell, A (eds), *Labour Law and Labour Market Regulation* (Sydney, Federation Press, 2006) 202, 221; Rawling, above n 45, at ch 10.

[59] TFCUA, *Submission for the National Review into Model Occupational Health and Safety Laws In Relation to Occupational Health and Safety Within the Context of Contract Networks (Such as Supply Chains)* (Textile, Clothing and Footwear Union of Australia, NSW/SA/Tas Branch, 2008) paras [15]–[17], available at: www.nationalohsreview.gov.au/NR/rdonlyres/7754B182-CA90-4DAF-B8CE-CC6A9E19B9AE/0/211TextilesClothingand FootwearUnion ofAustralia.pdf.

II

Between the Borders of Employment and Commercial Law

5

Legal Responsibility for Labour Conditions Down the Production Chain

ALAN HYDE

I
T IS COMMONPLACE that a purchaser of services may select from
a menu of contractual relations that economists often equate but that
lawyers distinguish. One form of commercialisation of work is the shift
from contracting for 'labour' to contracting for 'services'. For example, a
firm that needs computer programmers for a particular project, perhaps
the launch of a new website, may easily hire programmers as employees;
or as independent contractors; or deal with a consultant or agency (at
worst derisively known as a 'body shop') that will refer programmers who
will either be employed by the agency or work for it, or for the ultimate
consumer, as independent contractors. The consultant or contractor, or the
programmers, may be located anywhere on earth. Perhaps some or all of
the programming may be done by student interns, or even volunteers, creating difficult issues of coverage of labour law.

This commercialisation of work is complex and arises for many reasons,
not all well-understood. It is clear, however, that at least one reason, of
greater or lesser force in particular situations, is the desire of the ultimate
purchaser of labour services to avoid liability under labour and employment
law.[1] If this were the only reason for commercialisation, there could hardly
be a case for it. The starting point for this Chapter, however, is the assumption that it is not feasible to restore—create, really—a legal regime without

---

[1] Autor, DH, 'Outsourcing at Will: The Contribution of Unjust Dismissal Doctrine to the
Growth of Employment Outsourcing' (2003) 21 *Journal of Labour Economics* 1; Autor, DH,
'Why Do Temporary Help Firms Provide Free General Skills Training?' (2001) 116 *Quarterly
Journal of Economics* 1409; Miles, TJ, 'Common Law Exceptions to Employment-at-Will and
US Labour Markets' (2000) 16 *Journal of Law, Economics, and Organization* 74.

labour market intermediaries or self-employment. The most dynamic sectors of the US economy make heavy use of both these institutions.[2]

I want to argue in this Chapter that friends of labour need instead to develop a workable and appealing concept of the legal responsibility of consumers of services for the worst labour conditions down their particular chains of production. One might term this a kind of revised *respondeat superior*, or vicarious liability, for the twenty-first century. There is no global law-making authority that could impose such liability. The idea is that, if legal scholars could develop such an attractive and workable concept of responsibility—by no means easy or obvious—it might gradually become normative through incorporation into domestic labour codes, trade agreements, international framework agreements and corporate codes of conduct.

I put forward this suggestion in the belief that two alternative regulatory approaches, each of which has received enormous attention from legal scholars, have become dead ends, though both are well-represented in the literature. One is to restrict the ability of businesses to hire services through any means other than the conventional contract of employment. Another is to fiddle with the classification of workers in labour codes, perhaps by creating new categories like 'dependent contractor', an approach discussed by Davidov in this collection, or to redistribute workers among existing categories, by changing the criteria of classification.[3] Of course there are potential advances to be made in these analyses, and legal systems, not including that of my own country, that might respond to regulatory initiatives along these lines.[4] In my opinion, however, there are diminishing returns to these projects, and some value in considering a more direct

---

[2] Hyde, A, *Working in Silicon Valley: Economic and Legal Analysis of a High-Velocity Labour Market* (Armonk, NY, ME Sharpe, 2003) 93–124.

[3] See, eg, Davidov, G, 'Freelancers: An Intermediate Group in Labour Law?' in this collection; G Davidov and B Langille (eds), *Boundaries and Frontiers of Labour Law* (Oxford, Hart Publishing, 2006).

[4] In the US the only federal legislative reform of independent contracting that has attracted significant support, though not, yet, a majority, are Republican proposals to grant employers carte blanche to designate hiring as an employee, or hiring as an independent contractor, essentially by checking a box. Local legislation to phase out self-employed truck drivers at the Port of Los Angeles, in order to make sure that drivers were employed by fleets sufficiently capitalized to invest in emissions controls, was largely struck down as preempted by federal law, *American Trucking Associations Inc v City of Los Angeles*, 559 F3d 1046 (9th Cir 2009), though other portions of the legislation, more directly related to safety, were held to be within local regulatory competence, 596 F3d 602 (9th Cir 2010). Federal statutes that apply to 'employees' must be interpreted to apply common-law definitions, unless an alternative definition is provided, and may not be construed to incorporate elements of purposive or policy interpretation, *Nationwide Mutual Insurance Co v Darden*, 503 US 318 (1992). In theory, then, proposals to push the boundary of the legal concept of 'employee' are non-starters in the US; neither courts nor state nor local government can, and Congress won't. As we shall see, courts and state legislatures have nevertheless slightly expanded protection in recent years, but there are severe limits to this process.

approach, under which purchasers of services may structure those relations in any way that is efficient, but may not, thereby, relieve themselves entirely of responsibility for the worst labour conditions.

Part I of this Chapter discusses what we do and do not know about the commercialisation of work. Part II reviews the economic literature that treats all forms of obtaining services as substitutes for each other. While this conclusion is oversimplified from the legal scholar's point of view, the economic literature may embolden the legal scholar into more forceful equating of different modalities of contract. Part III reviews some recent legal devices which, in the perspective of this Chapter, may all be understood as preliminary approaches to fixing legal liability on ultimate consumers of services. I have in mind such legal concepts as joint employment, nondelegable duties, vicarious liability, and international framework agreements and corporate codes. Part IV attempts to synthesise a workable concept of responsibility for labour conditions, under which purchasers of those services could realise the efficiency gains from freedom of contract, while remaining legally responsible for especially bad violations of labour standards or human rights.

WHY DO WE OBSERVE COMMERCIALISATION OF WORK?

Before considering legal strategies for commercialised work, one should consider why we observe it and what functions it performs. The answer to this question is not fully understood, but there is no doubt that commercialisation of work performs important functions even in domestic labour markets. Moreover, it is so integral to economic globalisation as to make it infeasible to restrict.

National Labour Markets

As used in this collection: 'The commercialisation of employment refers to the breakdown of the boundary between commercial activities and employment.'[5] For present purposes, it is desirable to keep this concept broad, the better to capture the spectrum of contemporary modalities for contracting for services. There is probably little value in attempting a more rigorous definition of 'commercialisation' of work, or in argument whether particular legal modalities do or do not exemplify it. Definitions are probably endogenous to legal systems. In most legal systems in which contracts of employment are heavily regulated, with substantial minimum terms and

---

[5] Fudge, J, 'Blurring Legal Boundaries: Regulating for Decent Work' in this collection.

default rules, 'commercialisation' of work might mean any contract to provide services structured as something other than a contract of employment. In the US, 'contract of employment' has little technical meaning except to mark the boundaries of some regulatory and tax legislation. Most Americans who hold really bad jobs—poorly paid, highly contingent, unsafe, unaccompanied by the health or retirement benefits that Americans get either at work or not at all—are statutory employees, holding contracts of employment in which their federal income taxes are deducted by the employer and reported to the government as employment earnings.

American social scientists tend rather to observe either 'self-employment', or 'employment in the temporary help sector', because we can measure these, unlike 'commercialised' or even 'contingent' work, which we can't. A great deal of effort went into constructing an index for 'contingent' work in the 1990s and failed. At two-year intervals, beginning in 1995, the official Current Population Survey asked people whether their jobs were 'temporary' or whether they could 'continue to work for your employer as long as you wish'.[6] Under the broadest definitions, no more than 4.1 per cent of the US workforce describes itself as contingent under this definition.[7] Since about 15 per cent of the US workforce saw their jobs disappear forever just between the boom years 1993 and 1995,[8] the Current Population Survey questions on 'contingent' work tell us more about cognitive dissonance than about labour markets.[9]

Little could be said to defend any contract for services that did no more than permit employers to exempt themselves from employment regulation. Both independent contracting, and employment through temporary help agencies, sometimes serve this function in the US. However, this is only a small part of the motivation for these institutions.

Self-employment in the US is not growing. The percentage of the workforce working as unincorporated self-employed independent contractors has been steady for years at around 6.4 per cent or 7.5 per cent (depending on data series) of the US workforce, the historic low point.[10] As US self-employment is not growing (unlike, say, in Canada), it contributed nothing to the US jobs boom of the 1990s nor any special vulnerability to the job losses of the last few years. As a group, the US self-employed are older, whiter, richer,

    [6] Cohany, SR *et al*, 'Counting the Workers: Results of a First Survey' in K Barker and K Christensen (eds), *Contingent Work: American Employment Relations in Transition* (Ithaca, ILR Press, 1998) 42.

    [7] US Bureau of Labour Statistics, *Contingent and Alternative Employment Arrangements* (USDL 05-1433, 2005), available at: www.bls.gov/news.release/pdf/conemp.pdf.

    [8] Farber, HS, 'The Changing Face of Job Loss in the United States: 1981–1995' (1997) *Brookings Papers on Economic Activity: Microeconomics* 55.

    [9] Hyde, above n 2, at 99.

    [10] Hipple, S, 'Self-Employment in the United States' (2010) 9 *Monthly Labour Review* 17, 19 (Table 1).

more likely to be men, better educated, and more satisfied with their job status than statutory employees.[11] One sometimes sees employers strategically converting their workforce from employee to self-employed status, perhaps to avoid union organisation, but this is relatively rare and certainly not the major force driving self-employment. Similarly, some self-employed individuals are exploited, for example the notionally 'self-employed' truck drivers hauling cargo at the Port of Los Angeles who are unable to maintain trucks with acceptable emissions.[12] This is the group that the city tried, but failed, to have reclassified as employees. But as a group, the self-employed in the US are not exploited, and are not self-employed in order to evade regulation. Interviews suggest that many prefer self-employment because it lets them pursue technical challenges free of organisational politics, and also because they make more money that way.[13]

Similarly, temporary help agencies in the US employ only between 2 and 3 per cent of the workforce and refer both well-paid and poorly paid employees. It is true that this temporary help sector has grown rapidly, though it is still small. The reasons for this growth are not well understood and definitely include some aspect of avoiding anti-discrimination law and laws restricting employee dismissal.[14] Temporary help agencies employ a disproportionate percentage of women, African-American, and Latino/Latina workers who might plausibly raise claims of illegal discrimination if dismissed, and employers freely tell researchers how much they value the ability to call a temporary help agency and ask them to remove someone who is not working out.[15] If this were all there were to the temporary help story, it would be obvious that the customer of the agency should be either the legal employer, or joint employer, of the individual referred. However, employment through temporary help agencies performs other, valuable economic functions. Such jobs are often way-stations from welfare, or unemployment, into labour force participation.[16] They often train and screen workers more efficiently than do their customers.[17] They fit with current corporate strategies to concentrate on core competence and

---

[11] *Ibid*; Hyde, above n 2, at 112–19.

[12] Patel, S, *From Clean to Clunker: The Economics of Emissions Control* (Sierra Club, LAANE, Blue-Green Alliance and Teamsters, 2010) available at: www.cleanandsafeports.org/fileadmin/files_editor/FromCleantoClunker.pdf.

[13] Barley, SR and Kunda, G, *Gurus, Hired Guns, and Warm Bodies: Itinerant Experts in a Knowledge Economy* (Princeton, Princeton University Press, 2004).

[14] Autor, 'Outsourcing at Will: The Contribution of Unjust Dismissal Doctrine to the Growth of Employment Outsourcing', above n 1; Miles, above n 1.

[15] Autor, 'Outsourcing at Will: The Contribution of Unjust Dismissal Doctrine to the Growth of Employment Outsourcing', above n 1.

[16] Farber, above n 7; Heinrich, CJ, Mueser, PR and Troske, KR, 'The Role of Temporary Help Employment in Low-Wage Worker Advancement' in DH Autor (ed), *Studies of Labour Market Intermediation* (Chicago, University of Chicago Press, 2009).

[17] Autor, DH, *Why Do Temporary Help Firms Provide Free General Skills Training?*, above n 1; Smith, V and Neuwirth, EB, *The Good Temp* (Ithaca, Cornell ILR Press, 2008).

outsource other functions. The heaviest users of temporary help agencies are employers who provide generous benefits to a core workforce,[18] that is, the typical customer is not the most cut-throat employer. The typical employee of a temporary help agency does not remain in that status forever. Rapidly growing industries in uncertain customer markets, such as information technology, also make heavy use of temporary help agencies.[19]

They also can be vehicles for lower wages, though exactly how this works is unclear. On balance, janitors and guards hired through intermediaries are more poorly compensated than similar individuals hired directly by employers.[20] The reasons for this disparity are not obvious and are poorly understood. Why don't the employers just realise the same savings by hiring directly? The answer must have something to do with the fact that customers of temporary help agencies tend to be generous employers for their core workforce. There is no general requirement of US employment law that all payroll employees participate in benefit plans, and thus no legal impediment to an employer directly hiring janitors and guards as its employees, then excluding them from benefits plans. However, it is possible that this solution would be psychologically unsettling to that core labour force, and that it is easier for them to accept inequality at the workplace if the losers are notionally employed by a different employer. I am unaware, however, of any research establishing this conjecture.

My point is, simply, that, in my country at least, limiting employment by intermediaries is neither politically feasible nor obviously desirable. Further, in 1997, the International Labour Organization's adoption of the Private Employment Agencies Convention shifted the international approach to such agencies from prohibition to regulation.[21] One can imagine a hypothetical statute making all customers of temporary help agencies the statutory employer of all individuals referred. It is not clear what the impact of such a statute would be, but it is most unlikely that all or most individuals now working in the temporary help sector would find themselves on the customers' payrolls tomorrow. It is far more likely that most would not work at all. More feasible, then, might be a narrower concept of responsibility, to which we turn later in this Chapter.

---

[18] Houseman, SN, *Flexible Staffing Arrangements: A Report on Temporary Help, On-Call, Direct-Hire Temporary, Leased, Contract Company, and Independent Contractor Employment in the United States* (1999) vii, available at: www.dol.gov/oasam/programs/history/herman/reports/futurework/conference/staffing.htm.

[19] Hyde, above n 2, at 93–111.

[20] Dube, A and Kaplan, E, *Does Outsourcing Reduce Wages in the Low-Wage Service Occupations? Evidence from Janitors and Guards* (Working Paper No 171-08, University of California at Berkeley, Institute for Research on Labour and Employment, August 2008).

[21] *Private Employment Agencies Convention* 1997 (ILO C181). For discussion see Vosko, L, *Temporary Work: The Gendered Rise of a Precarious Employment Relationship* (University of Toronto Press, Toronto, 2000).

Globalised Labour Markets

It is in the most globalised sectors of the labour market that work is now commercialised in a way that makes 'ending commercialisation' completely infeasible, and has already given rise to emerging institutions to establish the alternative project of 'responsibility' for labour conditions in remote locations. The problem of commercialisation looks intractable when seen from a global angle of vision.

The two principal vehicles of global commercialisation of work are the globalised chain of production and migration of personnel.[22] Behind every shirt on the counter at the department store is an enormous web of contracts spanning several continents. The production of the garment, the designer or store label that lends it aura, the networks of transportation and distribution, involve numerous entities linked by commercial contracts. While an ordinary T-shirt takes on increased sales value from the aura of an Abercrombie and Fitch label, that does not mean, under current ways of thinking, that Abercrombie takes any responsibility for the working conditions of garment or transport workers, or cotton farmers, along the global supply chain.

Patterns of labour migration similarly strain the boundaries of 'commercialisation of work'. People have left their native country, looking for work, since before history was recorded. But the speed with which this fact has become the most salient fact about labour markets in modern, developed, non-frontier economies is breathtaking. Some 86 million people are working in countries other than the one in which they were born. Australia, Canada and the United States are each at their modern (postcolonial) peak in percentage of foreign-born people in the workforce. We do not all yet live in a truly global labour market, but some of us do. The global market for computer programmers is extraordinarily organised, reaching into remote villages in India to disperse knowledge workers throughout the globe.[23] Other genuinely global labour markets include doctors and nurses[24] and 'maids, nannies, and sex workers'.[25]

Compared with the sleek power of these global labour markets, legal thought is rickety and confused. As a co-author and I have shown

---

[22] As to these issues see further Fudge, above n 4; Johnstone R, 'Informal Sectors and New Industries: The Complexities of Regulating Occupational Health and Safety in Developing Countries' in this collection.

[23] Xiang, B, *Global 'Body Shopping': An Indian Labour System in the Information Technology Industry* (Princeton, Princeton University Press, 2007).

[24] Bach, S, *International Migration of Health Workers: Labour and Social Issues* (Working Paper No 209, Sectoral Activities Programme, International Labour Office, Geneva, July 2003); J Connell (ed), *The International Migration of Health Workers* (New York, Routledge, 2008).

[25] B Ehrenreich and AR Hochschild (eds), *Global Woman: Nannies, Maids and Sex Workers in the New Economy* (New York, Metropolitan, 2003).

elsewhere,[26] migrant workers may be legal subjects of the home (sending) country, or of the destination (receiving) country, or both, in no particular pattern or order. The labour law applicable to them may be set in either of these countries, or in bilateral or multilateral treaties that may supplant domestic labour law. Truly international law, such as ILO Standards or the UN Convention on the Rights of Migrant Workers, is ineffectual and would not be interesting even if successful on its own terms.[27] Labour unions in the destination country may be required to represent, or prohibited from representing, migrants working in that country, perhaps both simultaneously. Migrants may be represented by networks, formal or informal, linking unions and non-union labour rights organisations, normally without any legal status and often in the teeth of hostile legal regulation.[28]

In the rhetoric of labour movements, both global trade and, formerly, migration, are sometimes characterised as little more than capital's evasion of labour contracts, but this is far too simple. Most labour movements today in the developed world accept that productivity gains may be achieved through global trade, foreign direct investment, and migration, and seek rather to distribute such gains equitably, lest all the costs fall on small groups of developed-world production workers who cannot insure against, or spread, these costs. For this global project, commercialisation of work is inevitable, and the need, rather, is for a concept of legal responsibility.

ECONOMIC ANALYSIS OF COMMERCIALISED WORK: ON LABOUR AS 'FACTOR MOBILITY'

As we have seen throughout this collection, legal scholars struggle with the issues raised by the different contracts used to procure services (employment, independent contracting, outsourcing, hiring through an intermediary etc). It is therefore surprising that economists often treat these as complete substitutes. While this is an oversimplified view of the world, like many economic assumptions, perhaps legal scholars may take inspiration from its very simplicity, and use it to guide our efforts to blur the boundaries among these contracts, in the service of expanding the concept of legal responsibility for labour conditions.

---

[26] Hyde, A and Ressaissi, M, 'Unions Without Borders: Recent Developments in the Theory, Practice, and Law of Transnational Unionism' (2008) 14 *Canadian Labour & Employment Law Journal* 271.

[27] See, eg, *Migration for Employment (Revised) Convention* 1949 (ILO C97); *Migrant Workers (Supplementary Provisions) Convention* 1975 (ILO C143); *Migration for Employment Recommendation (Revised)* 1949 (ILO R86); UN, *International Convention on the Protection of the Rights of All Migrant Workers and Members of their Families*, which came into effect on 1 July 2003.

[28] Hyde and Ressaissi, above n 26.

The economic point is particularly clear in trade economics, particularly when trade economists address transnational migration. It is conventional in trade economics to treat human migration like any other factor mobility.[29] Indeed, a recent analysis of the economics of off-shoring solves the conceptual problem precisely by analysing outsourcing production to a developing country as if the developed country were instead importing labour.[30] On this view, there is no economic difference among: (1) importing goods and services made in India; (2) outsourcing production to an Indian firm in India that will hire Indians; (3) foreign direct investment to that Indian firm; and (4) maintaining production in the developed world, importing Indian labour. And, since Mundell,[31] trade economists have regarded as proven the proposition that equilibrium will be reached whichever factors of production are fixed or mobile, that is, in other words, that factor mobility and trade are perfect substitutes.

Some readers will reject this assumption of substitutability of factors of production as one of those economic articles of faith that is maintained, not because it is empirically demonstrable, but because it facilitates elegant analysis. This would be correct. There is no evidence that human migration substitutes for trade (and precious little that capital mobility does).[32]

However, I am willing to accept the economists' starting point because I have been investing a lot of time in developing a version of global labour rights that is compatible with the economics of trade and the theory of comparative advantage. So, like the man with a hammer in his hand who sees a world full of nails, I am inclined to see the problem of the boundaries between contracting for labour and commercialisation of work as calling for a similar conception of labour rights that are compatible with both forms of contracting and do not use labour rights to destroy legitimate gains from trade. The idea, briefly, is that some, but not all, global regulation of labour

---

[29] See, eg, Chang, HF, 'Liberalized Immigration as Free Trade: Economic Welfare and the Optimal Immigration Policy' (1997) 145 *University of Pennsylvania Law Review* 1147; Dixit, A and Norman, V, *Theory of International Trade* (Cambridge, Cambridge University Press, 1980); Hazari, BR and Sgro, PM, *Migration, Unemployment and Trade* (Norwell, MA, Kluwer, 2001).

[30] Baldwin, R and Robert-Nicoud, F, *Trade-in-Goods and Trade-in-Tasks: An Integrating Framework* (Working Paper No 15882, National Bureau of Economic Research, Cambridge, MA, April 2010).

[31] Mundell, RA, 'International Trade and Factor Mobility' (1957) 47 *American Economic Review* 321.

[32] For both propositions, see Collins, WJ, O'Rourke, KH and Williamson, JG, *Were Trade and Factor Mobility Substitutes in History?* (Working Paper No 6059, National Bureau of Economic Research, Cambridge, MA, June 1997). See also Peri, G, *Immigrants' Complementarities and Native Wages: Evidence from California* (Working Paper No 12956, National Bureau of Economic Research, Cambridge MA, March 2007) and Peri, G and Sparber, C, *Task Specialisation, Immigration and Wages* (Working Paper No 252, Centro Studi Luca d'Agliano, Milan, March 2008): immigrants as complements to, not substitutes for, other factors of production.

standards is compatible with maintaining the gains from global trade. Global labour regulation should focus on labour conditions that are not the source of national comparative advantage (such as child labour and very unsafe work practices), which persist because collective action problems impede their eradication, and should not focus on labour conditions that are legitimate sources of comparative advantage, since such regulation will be ineffective and destroy the trust necessary for regulation to function in the absence of meaningful sanctions.[33] Much contemporary global regulation of labour standards implicitly adopts this approach.

The problem of commercialisation of work is analogous. Given the ubiquity of commercialisation, and the productivity gains that it enables, regulatory efforts to limit commercialisation will predictably fail and cast doubt on the entire regulatory enterprise. What is needed instead is a blurring of the boundaries, so that commercialising work is not understood as total relief from legal liability, and a targeted approach to make the ultimate consumer of labour responsible for some, but not all, of the worst labour conditions.

APPROACHES TO REGULATING COMMERCIALISATION OF WORK

Legal concepts and devices already exist to establish the legal responsibility of an economic actor for labour conditions applying at another economic actor: vicarious liability, nondelegable duties, and joint employment, to name three. Recent developments in these concepts suggest that, even in the US, they might be part of a regulatory strategy to make ultimate consumers of labour responsible for the worst labour conditions down the production chain.

By contrast, I will not address alternative strategies, that of classifying, reclassifying and creating new categories for different types of workers (such as 'dependent contractor', semi-autonomous worker, and the like). Such strategies are canvassed within the Chapters by Davidov and Landa Zapirain in this collection.[34] This may simply reflect my location in a country whose labour legislation rarely employs classification devices more refined than 'employee' and 'self-employed'.[35] No doubt there are

---

[33] Hyde, A, 'A Game-Theory Account and Defence of Transnational Labour Standards—A Preliminary Look at the Problem' in JDR Craig and SM Lynk (eds), *Globalization and the Future of Labour Law* (Cambridge, Cambridge University Press, 2006) 143. Later version available at: http://ssrn.com/abstract=896362.

[34] See Davidov, above n 3; Landa Zapirain, JP, 'Regulation of Self-Employed Workers in Spain: A Regulatory Framework for Informal Work?' in this collection.

[35] Ruben Garcia criticises the frequent federal judicial tendency in the US to resolve difficult problems of labour regulation by creating classifications of protection and non-protection not created by Congress. He shows convincingly that such line-drawing never resolves the underlying question but can leave large numbers of workers without legal protection: Garcia, RJ, *Marginal Workers: How Legal Fault Lines Divide Workers and Leave Them Without Protection* (New York, New York University Press, 2012).

other legal systems with more invested in classification of working people, in which getting the classifications right matters. Even in such countries, however, as I have argued elsewhere, the limit to the reclassification and boundary strategy is that, wherever the boundary is drawn, it will immediately become the site of strategic behaviour both by employers and by labour organisations:

> If law pins different status to the boundaries of employment—wherever, and however broadly, it draws those boundaries—it invites employers, workers, and their organizations ... to treat that boundary strategically. Which they do. When labour market regulation is followed by increased informalisation or self-employment, this is not a regrettable and unforeseeable by-product of regulation. Rather, it demonstrates the rationality of employers and employees.[36]

In short, we need to worry far less about classifying workers. One might say that labour rights are human rights that belong to everyone who works simply in virtue of their being human,[37] or instead devices for solving particular kinds of market failure.[38] Either way, labour rights presumptively belong to all workers. The difficult issue, rather, is: against *which* economic entities may all these workers enforce their basic human rights? Every legal system attempts to answer this question, and while comparing those results should be the subject of another volume, we may briefly discuss three common answers. Purchasers of labour are responsible for labour standards violations down the production chain when they are vicariously liable under common law *respondeat superior*; when they are joint employers with the more immediate employer; and when they voluntarily assume such responsibility, for example under an international framework agreement or code of conduct.

Vicarious Liability

As the name indicates, the common law developed a concept under which purchasers of labour services are legally responsible for some torts committed by those labourers. When this applies—precisely when this applies—the purchaser, because of that vicarious liability, is called an 'employer', and the worker, whose legal liability is now shared, is an 'employee'.[39] This

---

[36] Hyde, A, 'What is Labour Law?' in G Davidov and B Langille (eds), *Boundaries and Frontiers of Labour Law* (Oxford, Hart Publishing, 2006) 48.

[37] Garcia, above n 35. For discussion see P Alston (ed), *Labour Rights as Human Rights* (Oxford, Oxford University Press, 2005).

[38] Hyde, above n 36. See also Deakin, S and Wilkinson, F, 'Labour Law and Economic Theory: A Reappraisal' in H Collins, P Davies and R Rideout (eds), *The Legal Regulation of the Employment Relation* (London, Kluwer Law International, 2000).

[39] Simon Deakin has challenged this story for Britain. He has shown with care in a series of articles that the British concept of employment is as much the creature of labour

raises the question of whether this or an analogous doctrine might similarly make those purchasers liable for the 'labour torts' of others because of the contractual relation between the two employers, even though that relationship itself is not one of common law 'employment'.

The history of the common law test for employment is not uncontroversial but fortunately need not be repeated here. I wish to make only a simple point. Inquiring whether the master had the 'right to control' his negligent servant is, at bottom, a pragmatic approach to avoiding accidents by allocating liability to the cheapest cost avoider; this allocation of legal responsibility reduces accidents, because the responsible party will now do so, and simultaneously compensates victims.[40] This may seem banal but is not how labour law scholars usually think of the common law 'right to control' test. We encounter it as a rather formalistic way of thinking about the scope of employment statutes, where it blocks recourse to more purposive or policy-oriented modes of statutory interpretation. When courts are disabled from applying pension regulation on the basis of regulatory fit, and forced to employ common law tests of right to control, the test is indeed formalistic.[41] But, applied to the problem it was meant to solve— vicarious liability for the torts of one 'working for' another—it is pragmatic and purposive, identifying the party that can control the situation, prevent future harms, and compensate victims.

This is precisely the kind of concept we need now in the contemporary world of labour regulation. Just like the master in early-nineteenth-century tort law, the contemporary garment manufacturer, or firm contracting with a temporary help or janitorial service firm, should probably be held liable for some, but not all, of the latter's labour violations. Just as in the common law analysis, deciding which those are is, at least in part, a function of the ultimate consumer's right to control labour conditions, efficiency at remedying violations, and ability to compensate victims.

Put this way, it appears that the contemporary purchaser of labour services should be liable under our new, twenty-first-century version of *respondeat superior*, for most labour rights violations down the supply chain. It has the whip hand in structuring employment, the power to insist on better standards, and the pockets to compensate victims. This follows from its control over remote labour conditions.[42]

---

legislation as of common law: Deakin, S and Wilkinson, F, *The Law of the Labour Market: Industrialization, Employment and Legal Evolution* (Oxford, Oxford University Press, 2005). While I defer to this analysis of Britain, in the US the common law understanding of employment as a relationship of subordination and control was well established before there was any relevant legislation.

[40] *Cf* Calabresi, G, *The Costs of Accidents: a Legal and Economic Analysis* (New Haven, Yale University Press, 1970).

[41] *Nationwide Mutual Insurance Co v Darden*, 503 US 318 (1992).

[42] *Cf* Sykes, AO, 'The Economics of Vicarious Liability' (1984) 93 *Yale Law Journal* 1321.

Scattered state and federal statutes in the US transcend the common law concept of employment to impose liability on those who deal with the most immediate employer. In some cases, such liability is imposed without a formal finding of 'joint employment'. The federal Fair Labor Standards Act of 1938 has, since its adoption, permitted seizure of 'hot goods' produced without complying with its standards; the effect is to enlist retailers into responsibility for ensuring compliance with labour standards.[43] Federal district courts have power to enforce this section by enjoining such shipment or sale.[44] The US Department of Labor has successfully enjoined retail sales of 'hot goods' under this provision.[45] This under-used statute is of great potential importance because clothing retailing in the US is highly-concentrated—over 70 per cent of retail sales are at the three chains Wal-Mart, K-Mart/Sears, and Dayton Hudson/Target—unlike clothing manufacture which is globalised and impossible to monitor effectively.[46] Similar statutes in California and New York have been used to establish retailer liability for labour standards in the garments they sell.[47] New York has long maintained statutes imposing on property owners 'nondelegable duties' to comply with statutory safety standards when work is done on their land; these apply even when the property has been rented out and the landowner was not capable of remedying conditions.[48] In 2003 California enacted a 'brother's keeper' law that makes liable for labour code violations anyone who enters 'into a contract or agreement for labor or services with a construction, farm labor, garment, janitorial, or security guard contractor, where the person or entity knows or should know that the contract or agreement does not include funds sufficient to allow the contractor to comply with all applicable local, state, and federal laws or regulations

---

[43] 29 USC §215(a)(1): '...it shall be unlawful for any person to transport, offer for transportation, ship, deliver, or sell in commerce, or to ship, deliver, or sell with knowledge that shipment or delivery or sale thereof in commerce is intended any goods in the production of which any employee was employed in violation of section 206 or 207 of this title [statutory minimum wage or maximum hours provisions]...'

[44] 29 USC §217. However, suit must be brought by the federal Department of Labor. There is no private right of action.

[45] Analysis and review are found in Rogers, B, 'Toward Third-Party Liability for Wage Theft' (2010) 31 *Berkeley Journal of Employment and Labour Law* 1; Goldstein, B, Linder, M, Norton, LE, and Ruckelshaus, CK, 'Enforcing Fair Labor Standards in the Modern American Sweatshop: Rediscovering the Statutory Definition of Employment' (1999) 46 *University of California at Los Angeles Law Review* 983.

[46] Pollin, R, Burns, J, and Heintz, J, 'Global Apparel Production and Sweatshop Labour: Can Raising Retail Prices Finance Living Wages?' (2004) 28 *Cambridge Journal of Economics* 153–71.

[47] New York Labor Law §345-a; *People ex rel Spitzer v 14 West Garment Factory Corp*, 697 NYS2d 458 (Sup.Ct.1999); California Labor Code §2673.1; *Fashion 21 v Coalition for Humane Immigrant Rights*, 117 CalApp4th 1138, 1151-53, 12 CalRptr3d 493, 502–04 (2004).

[48] New York Labor Law §§240; 241-a; and 241(6).

governing the labor or services to be provided.'[49] State-level statutes of this kind are entirely under-theorised and plainly reflect the political strength of garment, or building and construction unions, in the relevant state.

Outside of the US, developments in transnational supply chain regulation are aiming to have the same effect, allowing workers labouring at the bottom of supply chains to pursue their rights and entitlements up through contract networks.[50] Further, as shown by Kamala Sankaran in this collection, in India joint and several liability between direct employers and host employers for the wages and conditions of contracted labour has been implemented through legislation.[51]

Joint Employment

US labour law has produced little to praise recently, but potentially very important is the recent holding of the intermediate US Court of Appeals that workers in a garment factory in New York City's Chinatown were jointly employed by the owner of the factory, and by the customer that delivered partly finished goods there for finishing.[52] The result was that, on the disappearance of the factory owner, the customer was liable for over half a million dollars in unpaid wages and overtime. The finding of joint employment rested on three factors: plaintiffs performed a line job integral to the customer's production process; plaintiffs worked predominantly, though far from exclusively, for the customer; and the customer supervised their work.[53]

This is a very common fact pattern for what we have been calling the commercialisation of work: manufacturer or other employer outsources a portion of the production process to another independent entity whose output it supervises and purchases. Consequently, one can predict a large

---

[49] California Labor Code §2810(a). Proving that the customer knew, or should have known, that the contractor was undercapitalized will obviously be difficult. These issues are discussed in *Castillo v Toll Brothers, Inc*, 197 CalApp4th 1172, 130 CalRptr3d 150 (2011).

[50] See Fudge, J, 'The Legal Boundaries of the Employer, Precarious Workers, and Labour Protection' in G Davidov and B Langille (eds), *Boundaries and Frontiers of Labour Law* (Oxford, Hart Publishing, 2006) 295; Johnstone, above n 22; Marshall, S, 'Australian Textile Clothing and Footwear Supply Chain Regulation' in C Fenwick and T Novitz, *Human Rights at Work: Perspectives on Law and Regulation* (Oxford, Hart Publishing, 2010) 555.

[51] Sankaran, K, 'Flexibility and Informalisation of Employment Relationships' in this collection.

[52] *Zheng v Liberty Apparel Co*, 355 F3d 61 (2d Cir 2003) (remanding for jury trial, stating legal standard), 617 F3d 182 (2d Cir 2010) (affirming jury verdict for plaintiffs).

[53] The Court of Appeals identified three other potentially relevant factors, but in this case they all favoured the defendant: the customer's facilities were not used; the factory performed work for other customers; and the factory's supervision of employees was actual not notional, that is, the factory was a genuinely independent legal entity, not a subterfuge: *Zheng*, above n 52, at 71–6.

quantity of litigation seeking to apply joint employment to other common scenarios of commercialisation of work, and, no doubt, a search by less friendly US courts for limiting principles. For example, typical outsourcing of janitorial services to a contractor is an even more obvious example of joint employment. The typical building owner probably supervises the cleaning contractor even more than the garment manufacturer supervises the needle shop. At least, I do not think building owners normally hire cleaning contractors and tell them to maintain the building as they see fit, in their professional discretion. The janitors may work exclusively for one building owner, and a clean building is integral to any production process. The US Department of Labor has provided by regulation that 'joint employment will ordinarily be found to exist when a temporary placement agency supplies employees to a second employer'.[54]

I predict that the litigation action in the US over the next few years on establishing responsibility for labour conditions will explore the boundaries of this decision, and of the concept of 'joint employment'. Nevertheless, joint employment should not be the only legal device, or the outer limit, for thinking about responsibility for labour conditions. One has the sense that the number of labour customers who properly should bear responsibility for really bad labour conditions is larger than the number that will properly be found actual employers, or joint employers.

Contractual Assumption of Responsibility: Codes of Conduct and International Framework Agreements

An entirely different strategy for locating responsibility up the production chain is the corporate code of conduct, which, when formally negotiated with a global union federation, becomes known as an international framework agreement. I have recently reviewed the limited accomplishments of the latter with a co-author[55] and do not need to do so here. Roopa Madhav in this collection is sceptical that corporate codes have contributed much to garment workers in Bangalore[56] and I do not question that conclusion. I do think corporate codes and framework agreements are potentially interesting as attempts to establish the norm of responsibility, and as such are valuable, although their enforcement mechanisms leave much to be desired.[57]

---

[54] 29 CFR Sec 825.106(b)(1).

[55] Hyde and Ressaissi, above n 26.

[56] Madhav, R, 'Corporate Codes of Conduct in the Garment Sector in Bangalore' in this collection.

[57] Locke, RM, Qin, F and Brause, A, 'Does Monitoring Improve Labour Standards? Lessons from Nike' (2007) 61 *Industrial and Labour Relations Review* 3. For discussion of these issues in the context of transnational supply chain regulation in the context of the Australian clothing, textile and footwear industry see Marshall, above n 50.

TOWARDS A NEW CONCEPT OF LEGAL RESPONSIBILITY
FOR LABOUR CONDITIONS DOWN THE PRODUCTION CHAIN

Legal scholars can begin to construct a new concept of legal responsibility for abusive labour conditions down the production chain from elements of everything we have discussed. The exact boundaries of this responsibility are less important at this stage than the advancement of the basic concept: entities that purchase labour services have moral, ethical, and legal responsibility for abusive labour conditions, responsibility that cannot be evaded by structuring contracts so as to make another entity the statutory employer.[58] Since there is no global law-making authority that could really impose such legal liability, it will have to grow separately as part of the discourse of labour rights organisations, unions, trade negotiations, and domestic labour law. At some point in the future, endorsement of the basic idea by the ILO might be helpful, though this needs to await consensus among the other actors mentioned above.[59] Given this legal pluralism, it is to be expected that the precise contours of the emerging concept of legal responsibility will respond to particular legal traditions and the facts of particular problems.

However, to get a discussion going, let me suggest a few possible starting points:

(1) The right to be free of abusive labour conditions is a human right that belongs to everyone who works, irrespective of how the domestic labour regulation of her or his country classifies her work for regulatory or tax purposes.

(2) No public or private entity should be permitted to profit from violations of the four core labour rights in the ILO's 1998 Declaration of Fundamental Principles and Rights at Work: forced labour, child labour, discrimination; or denial of freedom of association. The last two present difficult issues in any legal system, so for purposes of legal responsibility up the production chain, it would be a worthy achievement to establish the slightly narrower norm that no private entity could profit from the complete suppression of labour organisation, or the complete exclusion of racial, ethnic, or gendered group from economic participation. These are fundamental rights that bind everyone who hires labour, directly or indirectly, and which every such hirer has a responsibility to combat.

---

[58] See further Fudge, above n 50.

[59] The ILO's contribution to the debate so far has been negative. A lengthy study of modalities of contracting for labour resulted in the *Employment Relationship Recommendation* 2006 (ILO R198), pinning various legal privileges precisely to the existence of an 'employment relationship'. This is a regressive move, given the explosion in competing contractual forms, outside the traditional 'employment relationship', to which this collection attests.

(3) Entities that supervise or control workers who contribute to their production are joint employers of those workers even if they are carried on the payroll of a contractor or temporary help agency.

(4) Finally, entities that indirectly hire labour that they do not directly supervise are nevertheless liable for those contractors' labour standards under a variation on *respondeat superior*, that is, when the indirect hirer dominates the relationship so as to make them the efficient actor to end abusive labour conditions, and compensate victims.

Inclusion of such a statement of legal and moral responsibility should be part of corporate codes of conduct and framework agreements.

6

A Blurred Boundary between Entrepreneurship and Servitude: Regulating Business Format Franchising in Australia

JOELLEN RILEY

THE WORKER AS 'ENTREPRENEUR'

LATE NIGHT PROGRAMMES on Australian commercial television stations frequently screen advertisements promising escape from the routine of employed work. Typically, these commercials will portray an overborne clerical worker, in drab office garb, transforming into a beaming, vibrantly dressed salesperson, while a voice-over says something to the effect: 'Sick and tired of working like a drone for other people, in a boring desk job? Wake up and smell the coffee! Become your own boss! Call now to find out more about this lucrative business opportunity.' Often the business opportunity will involve buying a van and working a territory as a mobile vendor of some product or service: domestic house cleaning, dog-grooming, mobile coffee vending, for example. A Google search of 'coffee franchise' turns up an astonishing number of business systems for mobile coffee vending: Cappuccino Xpress, Van Go, Café 2U, Espresso Mobile Café, Xpress Delight, and more. There are also numerous store-based coffee franchises: Hudson's, Gloria Jeans, and dozens of less familiar names.

A common feature of the advertising campaigns for franchised businesses, on television and in world-wide-web postings, is the seductive language of escape from servitude: 'Be your own boss', 'Become an entrepreneur'. The very word 'franchise' derives from the French 'franchir', meaning 'freedom, exemption from servitude'.[1] If the findings of a regular survey into franchising are an indication, this language has proved to have considerable appeal

---

[1] See Pengilley, W, 'The Franchising Code of Conduct: Does Its Coverage Address the Need?' (1999) 3 *Newcastle Law Review* 1, 9.

in the Australian labour market, particularly for people who wish to escape the inflexible hours of full-time employment.[2] Franchising has become big business Downunder, more so even than in the United States. According to Frazer, Weaven and Wright, there were approximately 1,100 business format franchises in 2008 (up from 960 in 2006), with an estimated 63,500 franchisees (plus a further 7,900 company-owned business units), employing a total of more than 400,000 people, and turning over sales of around $A61 billion in 2007. This revenue figure does not include a further $A69 billion in the vehicle sales and fuel franchising sector, excluded from the survey on business format franchising.[3] The number of Australian franchises represents approximately one franchise for every 20,000 citizens, which is about five times the level of density in the United States.[4]

Many franchisees are individuals, couples or family groups working from home or from a mobile van. Of the franchisors surveyed in 2008, 29 per cent indicated that they had franchisees operating from mobile units, and 27 had home-based franchisees.[5] Of the mobile and home-based franchisees, 81 per cent operated non-retail, service-based businesses, including lawn-mowing, domestic cleaning and book-keeping.[6] In other words, a significant number of franchisees are individual workers, selling their labour and little else. A rising proportion of these franchisees are women (although franchisees are still predominantly men). In 2006, 11 per cent of franchise units were operated by female sole-owners, and by 2008 this had risen to 17 per cent. When female participation in franchises operated by couples is counted, women participate in 28 per cent of franchised businesses.[7] The rising participation of women in franchising has coincided with a growing trend for franchisees to work part-time (less than 40 hours per week).[8]

Although the appeal of becoming one's 'own boss' is clearly a factor encouraging growth in this sector, in truth, there is very little opportunity for genuine entrepreneurship in a franchise relationship, particularly in sole-operated, service-based franchises. Franchising represents a clear example of the commercialisation of work relationships described by Judy Fudge

---

[2] Frazer, L, Weaven, S and Wright, O, *Franchising in Australia 2008* (Brisbane, Asia Pacific Centre for Franchising Excellence, Griffith University, 2008).

[3] *Ibid*, at 2.

[4] Parliamentary Joint Committee on Corporations and Financial Services, *Opportunity Not Opportunism: Improving Conduct in Australian Franchising* (Canberra, Commonwealth of Australia, 2008) para [3.5], available at: www.aph.gov.au/Senate/committee/corporations_ctte/franchising/report/index.htm. According to PricewaterhouseCoopers, *2010 Franchise Business Economic Outlook prepared for the International Franchise Association Educational Foundation* (2009) para [E-1], there were forecast to be 901,093 franchise establishments in the United States in 2010, representing employment of more than 9 million people, and an output of some $US863 billion.

[5] See Frazer, Weaven and Wright, above n 2, at 27.

[6] *Ibid*.

[7] *Ibid*, at 31.

[8] *Ibid*, at 33.

in Chapter 1 of this collection. The 'fragmentation and reconfiguration of production'[9] into an integrated hierarchy of formally separate but economically interdependent entities exempts the enterprise initiator (the franchisor) at the apex of the hierarchy from legal responsibility under labour protection laws for the economically dependent worker (the franchisee) who is construed as an independent, self-employed contractor. This is achieved by a highly detailed commercial contract, under which the franchisee agrees to operate an outlet of the franchisor's business according to the strict prescription of the franchisor.[10] The franchisor owns all intellectual property associated with the business concept, including trademarks, product designs and 'get-up', meaning the appearance and packaging of products, equipment, uniforms and any other business paraphernalia. This means that any business goodwill built up by successfully running the outlet accrues to the franchisor, as the owner of all the indicia of the business. The franchisee is consequently vulnerable should the franchisor decide to terminate the franchise, or fail to renew it on expiry of an initial term. A franchisee who wants to continue running a similar business will have to abandon earlier investments and begin afresh, being scrupulous not to infringe any of the restrictive covenants in the franchise agreement.

The franchisee's investments can be very substantial. Frazer, Weaven and Wright found that in 2008 the initial fees paid by a franchisee to the franchisor could be as high as $A200,000 and the median initial fee was $A30,000.[11] In addition, franchisees typically invest in inventories, fit-out of businesses and training costs. Even in a non-retail franchise, involving the provision of services only, the median fit-out and training costs were $A4,000 and $A2,000 respectively.[12] (A median initial investment of close to $A40,000 represents a substantial investment for the typical Australian worker who earns an average weekly wage of $A1,158.40 if male, and $967,90 if female.[13])

The franchisor also wields considerable control over aspects of the business that determine its profitability. The franchisor dictates sources of all business supplies (in some cases the franchisor *is* the source of all

---

[9] See Fudge, J, 'Blurring Legal Boundaries: Regulating for Decent Work' in this collection.

[10] For a thorough picture of the typical franchise arrangement in Australia see Parliamentary Joint Committee on Corporations and Financial Services, above n 4. For the United States perspective, see Pitegoff, T and Garner, WM, 'Franchise Relationship Laws' in RM Barkoff and AC Selden, *Fundamentals of Franchising*, 3rd edn (Chicago, American Bar Association, 2008) 174 and for a critical perspective of the field, see Steinberg, P and Lescatre, G, 'Beguiling Heresy: Regulating the Franchise Relationship' (2004) 109 *Penn State Law Review* 105.

[11] Above n 2, at 29.

[12] *Ibid.*

[13] For statistics on Australian earnings, see Australian Bureau of Statistics, 'Earnings', *2008 Year Book Australia* (Cat No 1301.0, 2008), available at: www.abs.gov.au/ausstats/abs@.nsf/ 2f762f95845417aeca25706c00834efa/0796FAC7CDEEA671CA2573D20010F2DD?open document.

supplies[14]), fixes pricing structures and sets out obligatory operating systems and procedures.[15] Often the agreement will contain 'collective action clauses' or 'agreements to agree' which bind franchisees to accept the franchisor's unilaterally imposed changes to these operating systems.[16] So franchisees can effectively be obliged to obey periodic orders from franchisors. Franchisors generally assert an entitlement to restrict the geographical territory in which a particular franchisee may operate, so franchisees have limited opportunities to increase their revenue by expanding the business of the outlet.[17]

Of course, many of these features of business format franchising are potentially extremely beneficial to new small-business owners. One of the main attractions of running a franchised business outlet is that it is generally less risky than establishing a completely new autonomous business, because many of the operating and marketing systems have already been established and tested. This Chapter does not criticise franchising per se. It seeks only to investigate the power relationships between franchisor and franchisees, and how the potential for exploitation of that power is best regulated. All of the constraints on franchisees mean that they have very little opportunity to make the kinds of creative business decisions generally associated with 'entrepreneurship'. In fact, in many respects, franchisees enjoy no greater liberty than the traditional servant or employee. In this pyramid business structure (where the franchisor sits at the apex, controlling a network of franchisees below) we see a clear example of the way in which the reconfiguration of production trespasses the traditional boundary between employment and commercial law.[18] The detailed franchise contract constitutes an instrument through which the master/franchisor asserts control over the franchisee's operation of the business outlet, commands the franchisees' ongoing obedience to evolving instructions, and captures the entire value of any goodwill generated by the franchisee's service. To adopt Davidov's terminology, this kind of franchising exhibits both markers of traditional employment: subordination and dependency.[19]

So in franchising, we have a paradox: the franchisee as indentured entrepreneur. Despite all the rhetoric, franchisees are investing in businesses that are only notionally their own. If the franchisee (possibly along with family

---

[14] See, eg, *ACCC v Simply No-Knead (Franchising) Pty Ltd* (2000) 178 ALR 304, where a franchisor was found to have refused to continue supply of essential ingredients to the franchisee.

[15] See, eg, *Far Horizons Pty Ltd and Hackett v McDonald's Australia Ltd* [2000] VSC 310 for an illustration of highly particularised standards of 'quality, service and cleanliness' demanded by the operating policy manual of a noted fast food chain.

[16] Steinberg and Lecastre, above n 10, at 115.

[17] Territorial restrictions can, of course, benefit the franchisee, if they prevent other franchisees from expanding into their territory.

[18] See Fudge, above n 9.

[19] See Davidov, G, 'Freelancers: An Intermediate Group in Labour Law?' in this collection.

members) is the only worker in the business, this kind of relationship is very similar to standard employment—except that the franchisee is required to purchase their entitlement to work, and accepts the risks of ownership of the depreciating assets of the business (but not the more valuable intellectual property). The fact that remuneration is by way of sharing business profits makes the franchisee something like a servant paid on commission.

Although franchisees have much in common with employees, in terms of their economic relationship with the enterprise that 'hires' their labour, regulation of franchising relationships is quite distinct from employment regulation. This may not be entirely a consequence of pressures from capital owners seeking exemption from protective employment regulation. It may also result from the appeal that the notion of entrepreneurship holds for the workers themselves. Regulators and industry participants have consistently treated these workers as small business people, and have adopted forms of regulation suited to arm's length relationships between autonomous economic actors. In more recent times Australian law has developed a protective regulatory regime to recognise the vulnerability of franchisees, but that regime has been built mainly on the assumption that improving market efficiency by removing information asymmetry will enable franchisees to help themselves.

Despite this regulation (described more fully below), there remains a relatively high level of disputes between franchisors and franchisees. According to Frazer, Weaven and Wright, 17 per cent of franchisors had been involved in a 'substantial dispute' with at least one franchisee during the 12 months previous to the survey.[20] Arguably, the kind of regulation adopted has not addressed the whole problem of vulnerability in franchise relationships, because it has focused only on the initiation and termination of franchise relationships, and not on any measures to regulate franchises as continuing relationships. This Chapter examines the regulation of business format franchising in Australia, and argues in support of the institution of an explicit statutory obligation to perform franchise obligations in 'good faith', as a further measure (additional to existing regulation) which may assist in reconciling the paradox of entrepreneurial servitude.

Good faith as a concept has developed in the context of commercial relational contracts, to enable parties to undertake open-ended commitments to mutually beneficial relationships, without bearing undue risk that their contract partners will grasp an opportunity to exploit that flexibility.[21] There is a growing acceptance of good faith obligations in certain kinds of

---

[20] Above n 2, at 40.
[21] Campbell, D and Harris, D, 'Flexibility in Long Term Contractual Relationships: The Role of Co-operation' (1993) 20 *Journal of Law and Society* 166.

commercial relationships in Australian commercial law,[22] although good faith sceptics abound, particularly in relation to the adoption of a good faith obligation in franchising.[23] Presently the Franchising Code of Conduct contains s 23A, which states: 'Nothing in this code limits any obligation imposed by the common law, applicable in a State or Territory, on the parties to a franchise agreement to act in good faith.'[24] This Chapter argues that simply *not excluding* the unsettled common law obligation to perform contracts in good faith is not sufficient: an explicit statutory good faith obligation, which articulates particular obligations (such as obligations to meet, consult and consider proposals), may assist in clarifying the mutual obligations of parties to a franchise relationship as they negotiate their day-to-day working relationship.

FOCUS ON THE FRANCHISEE

Often the franchisee is also an employer.[25] This means that the franchisee also carries the legal risks and responsibilities of employing workers, and so relieves the franchisor of much of the regulatory burden of complying with labour laws. In this respect, business format franchising is an example of the phenomenon described by Hugh Collins as the 'vertical disintegration' of industrial organisation, and it manifests the very challenges to labour law that Collins identifies.[26] In particular, it demonstrates the 'capital boundary' problem.[27] The franchisor firm determines its own size, and thereby limits its own legal responsibilities, by using standard form contracts that outsource many of the risks and responsibilities of running the business, while maintaining an entitlement to share profits and maintain ownership of the most valuable business assets (goodwill and intellectual property rights).

A chapter on franchising may easily have examined this business structure from the perspective of the especially weak workers employed by franchisees, and the influence of this form of commercialisation on declining

---

[22] Peden, E, *Good Faith in the Performance of Contract* (Sydney, LexisNexis Butterworths, 2003).

[23] Terry, A and Di Lernia, C, 'Franchising and the Quest for the Holy Grail: Good Faith or Good Intentions?' (2009) 33 *Melbourne University Law Review* 542.

[24] Trade Practices (Industry Codes—Franchising) Regulations 1998 as amended by SLI 2010 No 125.

[25] See, eg, the vast armies of employees of McDonald's franchisees in Australia. According to *McDonald's Australia Pty Ltd on behalf of Operators of McDonald's Outlets* [2010] FWA 1347, McDonald's retail food outlets in Australia engage approximately 80,000 employees.

[26] Collins, H, 'Independent Contractors and the Challenge of Vertical Disintegration to Employment Protection Laws' (1990) 10 *Oxford Journal of Legal Studies* 35.

[27] Collins, H, 'Ascription of Legal Responsibility to Groups in Complex Patterns of Economic Integration' (1990) 53 *Modern Law Review* 731.

labour standards. The franchise business structure allows a many-tentacled organisation to fragment its workforce. In labour law systems based on single business enterprise bargaining—such as the federal bargaining system under the Workplace Relations Act 1996 (Cth) in Australia from 1996 until the enactment of the Fair Work Act 2009 (Cth)—it can be difficult if not impossible for employees in small franchise outlets to organise, and bargain effectively for wages and working conditions.[28] Even after the passage of the Fair Work Act 2009 (Cth),[29] the availability of legislative provisions allowing multi-employer bargaining does not overcome many of the practical hurdles facing workers and their unions seeking to establish labour standards covering all franchisees of a single franchisor.[30] Franchisees are an example of the labour intermediaries aptly described by Weil that promote labour market vulnerability:

> Conditions leading to workforce vulnerability arise because employment policies for the millions of workers in these sectors reflect the interdependent decisions of relatively small, local employers facing significant product market competition yet having a lower stake in reputation than the multinational brands of which they are a part.[31]

Nevertheless, the albeit extremely important story of franchisees' employees remains for others to tell. This Chapter reflects upon the relationship between the franchisor and franchisees and the ways in which the assumption that the franchisee is a self-employed entrepreneur has influenced the choice of forms of state regulation of the relationship.[32]

As noted above, many enquiries into franchising, and the introduction of a mandatory Franchising Code of Conduct, have not eliminated a high level of disputation between franchisors and franchisees. According to the most

---

[28] See, eg, *Re Bakers Delight Holdings* (2002) 119 IR 20, where franchisees in a bakery chain were denied permission to bargain collectively with employees because they were held to lack the essential requirement of a 'common enterprise'.

[29] The Fair Work Act 2009 (Cth) s 249(2) expressly permits franchisees of a common franchisor to bargain together.

[30] See, eg, the obstacles faced by the Shop Distributive and Allied Union in seeking to establish the first Australia-wide multi-employer enterprise agreement in the *McDonald's* decision, above n 25. A well-meaning Fair Work Commissioner rejected the agreement for failing to meet the nuanced requirements of the 'better off overall test' applied to enterprise agreements (it did not have the most beneficial maternity and long-service leave provisions available, for example), but in doing so effectively thwarted pay rises, and the opportunity for a future of organised negotiations, for many junior casual workers on minimum wages. This decision was overturned by a full bench of Fair Work Australia in *McDonald's Australia Pty Ltd* [2010] FWAFB 4602 (21 July 2010).

[31] Weil, D, 'Rethinking the Regulation of Vulnerable Work in the USA: A Sector-based Approach' (2009) 51 *Journal of Industrial Relations* 411, 419.

[32] The celebration of entrepreneurial spirit was a dominating theme in the former Howard government's workplace relations agenda: see *The Howard Government Election 2004 Policy: Protecting and Supporting Independent Contractors* (printed and authorised by B Loughnane, Barton, ACT, 2004).

recent industry survey, 17 per cent of the 224 franchisors surveyed had been involved in 'substantial disputes' (ie, those requiring referral to an external advisor) in a 12-month period.[33] There is a high level of human and social cost in these disputes. The Reid Committee found that franchise disputes had created stress, marriage breakdown, poor health and suicide of small-business-owning citizens.[34]

Research to date is not sufficiently extensive to offer any reliable views on the reasons why these disputes continue to occur. Frazer, Weaven and Wright note that 66 per cent of disputes concern 'compliance with the system', 37 per cent involve some dispute over profitability, 21 per cent involve territorial issues, 18 per cent communication problems, and 16 per cent franchise fees.[35] The numbers do not, however, reveal why these matters are not resolved between the parties before being referred for mediation or litigation. One reason nominated by franchisors who were surveyed was 'unrealistic franchisee expectations'.[36] This suggests a mismatch between the rhetoric of entrepreneurship and the reality of the franchising business structure. Franchisees enter into these relationships expecting to run their own business and control their own economic destinies. Franchisors, on the other hand, expect that franchisees will be compliant and obedient, and expect to be able to cut off any franchisee who fails to conform with the programme, rather than negotiate a solution to disagreements. Franchisees whose enthusiastic entrepreneurship leads them to detour from the strict franchise instruction manual risk punishment by exclusion—and if that happens, the franchisees risk losing everything they have invested in the business.

The case of *Thorne v Literacy Circle Pty Ltd*[37] provides a telling illustration of mismatched expectations. A young couple became enthused by the prospect of joining a newly established franchise of tutoring colleges. The young woman in particular had her own views on how best to advertise and promote the establishment of the business and the best teaching materials to use—but these views clashed with those of the franchisors who initiated the scheme. After a series of disagreements the franchisors unilaterally decided that the best solution would be simply to terminate the relationship forthwith. This decision left the franchisees out of pocket to the tune of about $A73,523. Even though no franchise fees had been levied, the franchisees had borne the cost of leasing and fitting out suitable premises to conduct

[33] See above n 2, at 40.
[34] Explanatory Memorandum to the Trade Practices Amendment (Fair Trading) Bill 1997 at 2, referring to the Reid Committee Report, *Finding a Balance towards Fair Trading in Australia, Report by the House of Representatives Standing Committee on Industry, Science and Technology* (Canberra, Commonwealth of Australia, 1997).
[35] See above n 2, at 40.
[36] *Ibid.*
[37] *Thorne v Literacy Circle Pty Ltd* [2009] FMCA 507.

the business. The court deciding the dispute also awarded the franchisee some compensation for opportunity costs for the period during which she had attempted to run the franchise business.

The record of evidence in the case is a testimony to the parties' conflicting conceptions of their relationship. The Thornes took the promise of running their 'own' business quite literally, and asserted an entitlement to negotiate arrangements for running the business. The principals of Literary Circle Pty Ltd, however, were affronted by the regular challenges to their decision-making authority, and reacted by purporting to dismiss the franchisees. In the end, the Thornes were able to succeed (at least partially) in their claim for compensation on the basis that Literary Circle had repudiated the franchise contract by treating it as a nullity. The essential dispute at the heart of the case, however, was left unresolved, because the law had no answer to it: did the Thornes enjoy the entrepreneur's entitlement to participate in decision-making? Or must they, like servants, merely obey instructions? Ought the parties have been obliged to take deliberate steps to negotiate these matters between them, in good faith?

REGULATING THE RISKS OF OPPORTUNISM

As in any relationship between human beings that manifests an imbalance of power, there is great opportunity in the franchising relationship for exploitation of the more vulnerable party. As the report of the most recent government-initiated inquiry into franchising in Australia has noted: 'The imbalance of power within the relationship means that scope exists for rogue franchisors to use their control opportunistically for financial gain at the expense of franchisees'.[38] The potential for abuse—indeed, actual evidence of abuse—has been recognised in this field since the earliest days of franchising in the 1950s and 1960s, and legislatures have responded. Pitegoff and Garner provide examples of State-based legislation in the United States, dating back to the 1970s.[39] These laws regulate franchising as a special kind of commercial relationship, with a view to managing the risks of abuse and exploitation.

Two essential kinds of regulation have been introduced in this field. One regulatory technique—based on the assumption that people who enter dealings with open eyes and full knowledge must be trusted to make their own deals—is mandatory disclosure. Franchisors can be required to disclose a range of matters relevant to a prospective franchisee's decision to invest in the system. The other kind of regulation has been described as 'relationship

---

[38] Parliamentary Joint Committee on Corporations and Financial Services, above n 4, at 9.
[39] Above n 10, at 185.

provisions'. Relationship laws have been directed towards several kinds of abuses:

— unjust terminations of the franchise relationship which deprived the franchisee of their investment and rewards from work;
— refusals to renew franchises, so that the franchisor could capture all goodwill from the enterprise;
— refusals of requests to assign franchise agreements, so that franchisees could not realise any benefit from their work in building the business by selling out to another. Other abuses, including 'cannibalising' franchise territories by allowing another outlet to operate in the same territory (possibly an outlet owned directly by the franchisor); and
— forbidding or restricting franchisees from forming associations.[40]

DEVELOPMENT OF AUSTRALIA'S FRANCHISING
CODE OF CONDUCT

Notwithstanding that there have been precedents for disclosure and relationship laws in franchising in various United States jurisdictions since the 1970s, a mandatory Franchising Code of Conduct was not introduced in Australia until 1998, following the Reid Committee Report in 1997.[41]

Before the Reid Committee Report, the Swanson Committee review of the Trade Practices Act 1974 (Cth) in 1976 recognised a problem for franchisees in losing the value of their investments in the event of termination or non-renewal of their franchises, and recommended rights to fair compensation.[42] The Blunt Committee in 1979 made similar findings. Draft Bills following these reports did not progress.[43] Likewise, the Beddall Committee inquiry into small business regulation more generally recommended franchise-specific regulation to deal with the disclosure and relationship problems that were by now notorious.[44]

In 1993 a voluntary code of conduct was made and administered by the Franchising Code Administration Council Ltd, a tripartite body representing the interests of both sides of the industry (franchisors and

---

[40] *Ibid.*
[41] Above n 34.
[42] Swanson Committee Trade Practices Act Review Committee, *Report to the Minister for Business and Consumer Affairs* (Canberra, Commonwealth of Australia, 1976) Ch 5. See also Parliamentary Joint Committee on Corporations and Financial Services, above n 4, at 24.
[43] Trade Practices Consultative Committee, *Small Business and the Trade Practices Act Vol 1* (Canberra, Commonwealth of Australia, 1979).
[44] House of Representatives Standing Committee on Industry, Science and Technology, *Small Business in Australia: Challenges, Problems and Opportunities* (Canberra, Commonwealth of Australia, 1990).

franchisees) and also government. It was clear following the Gardini Report[45] in 1994 that this attempt at self-regulation had largely failed. In the four months from January to April 1996 no less than 41 disputes between franchisors and franchisees were listed in Australian courts.[46] Following a change in government in 1996 a new Minister commissioned a further review—resulting in the Reid Committee Report—and eventually Commonwealth Parliament enacted the Trade Practices (Fair Trading) Act 1998 (Cth) and the government instituted the Trade Practices (Industry Codes—Franchising) Regulations, which have operated since 1 July 1998 with some amendments. In 2006, the Matthews Review resulted in further amendments to strengthen the Code's disclosure provisions from 1 March 2008.[47] Most recently, the Trade Practices (Industry Codes—Franchising) Amendment Regulations 2010 (No 1) commencing in July 2010 increased the disclosure and notice obligations of franchisors, introduced specific obligations upon parties to attempt mediation of disputes, and added a provision stating that the Code did not limit any common law obligation upon the parties to act in good faith.[48] It is useful to set out the essential framework of the Franchising Code of Conduct (FCC), to illustrate the way in which it seeks to deal with the risk of franchisee vulnerability principally by mandating disclosure.

FEATURES OF THE FRANCHISING CODE OF CONDUCT

The FCC prescribes a number of obligations for franchisors, designed to ensure that franchisees have full and frank information about the business venture upon which they are entering, and have adequate opportunity to consider their decision to join. The Code also ensures that franchisees are able to exercise freedom of association without interference from franchisors, and are protected from capricious and arbitrary termination of their contracts. These last two protections recognise franchisees as workers with an interest in collective representation, 'job' tenure and income security.

The Competition and Consumer Act 2010 (Cth) ('CC Act')[49] s 51AD obliges corporations to comply with industry codes and brings into play

---

[45] Gardini, R, *Review of the Franchising Code of Practice: Report to the Minister for Small Business, Customs and Construction* (Canberra, Commonwealth of Australia, 1994).

[46] See Franchising Policy Council, *Review of the Franchising Code of Conduct* (Canberra, Department of Employment Workplace Relations and Small Business, 2000) para [1.11].

[47] Franchising Code Review Committee, *Review of the Disclosure Provisions in the Franchising Code of Conduct: Report to the Minister for Small Business and Tourism* (Canberra, Office for Small Business, 2006), available at: www.innovation.gov.au/Section/SmallBusiness/Documents/Franchising_Code_Review_Report_2006_FINAL_06120720070205134250.pdf.

[48] FCC cl 23A.

[49] Formerly the Trade Practices Act 1974 (Cth), renamed by the Trade Practices Amendment (Australian Consumer Law) Act (No 2) 2010 (Cth) from January 1, 2011.

the remedial provisions of the Act, including rights to seek damages and injunctions for contraventions.

Disclosure

Franchisors are required to make disclosures to prospective and existing franchisees, before entering into a franchise agreement, and annually after the conclusion of each financial year. The required disclosures are extensive and are prescribed in annexures to the code. Franchises with an expected annual turnover of more than $A50,000 must meet the full-form disclosure requirements in Annexure 1. A short-form version (in Annexure 2) may be used for franchises with an annual turnover of less than $A50,000. Franchisors are required to disclose (in addition to pertinent business information and information about the franchise contract terms) the business experience and qualifications of the officers of the franchisor,[50] and details of any litigation taken against the franchisor for breach of contract, competition laws, corporation laws or unfair contract review laws in the past five years, or any criminal prosecutions in the past 10 years.[51] If the franchisor provides earnings projections, they must be given on 'reasonable grounds' and must reveal the assumptions upon which they are based.[52]

Franchisors must also disclose any 'materially relevant facts', including matters concerning changes in ownership of the franchisor, pending judgments against the franchisor and changes in ownership of the intellectual property of the franchisor.[53] All these disclosures are intended to ensure that the franchisee is able to make an informed calculation of the risks of entering into the franchise agreement, including the risk of joining up with a franchisor who has a poor record of compliance with obligations to other franchisees.

The franchisor must also give potential franchisees a copy of the Code, and must receive from franchisees a written statement that the franchisee has received independent advice on the documents from a lawyer, an accountant or a business adviser, not only about their anticipated legal obligations, but on the commercial wisdom of entering the franchise agreement.[54]

Cooling-off Period

Franchisees must be given the disclosure documents at least 14 days before entering the agreement or making a non-refundable payment, and must be

---

[50] FCC Annexure 1, cl 3.
[51] *Ibid*, at Annexure 1, cl 4.
[52] *Ibid*, at Annexure 1, cl 19.
[53] *Ibid*, at cl 18.
[54] *Ibid*, at cls 10 and 11.

allowed a seven-day 'cooling-off' period after signing up or paying money, to change their mind.[55] Franchisors may deduct 'reasonable expenses' from any franchise payments before making a refund, so long as they disclosed those expenses in the agreement.[56] Cooling-off periods protect more naïve investors from decisions made in the heat of their own enthusiasm, or from the pressure of a heavy sales pitch.

Rights to Freedom of Association

Franchisors must not prevent franchisees from forming or joining associations. This provision recognises the value to vulnerable people in joining together for mutual support. The FCC is silent, however, on the actions franchisees may legitimately take in pursuit of their freedom of association. There is no explicit entitlement to withdraw their co-operation (in a form of strike action) for any particular purpose or in pursuit of particular interests. As separate business entities, franchisees are subject to the same restrictions on anti-competitive conduct as any other business entity, so there are restrictions on their ability to act collectively especially if the joint action involves boycotting a franchisor. (See the discussion of collective action for independent contractors by Shae McCrystal in this collection.[57]) Investigation of the extent to which franchisees in particular have taken advantage of their freedom of association to negotiate collectively with franchisors would be a fruitful field for further research.

Termination Rights

Summary termination of a franchise agreement is permitted only in special and serious circumstances, such as the bankruptcy or criminal conviction of the franchisee, or if the franchisee abandons the franchise, or commits

---

[55] *Ibid*, at cl 13.

[56] *Ibid*, at cl 13(4).

[57] McCrystal, S, 'Organising Independent Contractors: The Impact of Competition Law' in this collection. See also McCrystal, S, 'Regulating Collective Rights in Bargaining: Employees, Self-Employed Persons and Small Businesses' in C Arup, P Gahan, J Howe, R Johnstone, R Mitchell and A O'Donnell (eds), *Labour Law and Labour Market Regulation* (Sydney, Federation Press, 2006) 597; McCrystal, S, 'Collective Bargaining by Independent Contractors: Challenges from Labour Law' (2007) 20 *Australian Journal of Labour Law* 1; McCrystal, S, 'Collective Bargaining and the Trade Practices Act: the Trade Practices Legislation Amendment Act (No 1) 2006 (Cth)' (2007) 20 *Australian Journal of Labour Law* 207; and McCrystal, S, 'Is there a "Public Benefit" in Improving Working Conditions for Independent Contractors? Collective Bargaining and the Trade Practices Act 1974 (Cth)' (2009) 37 *Federal Law Review* 263.

fraud or some serious breach of health and safety laws.[58] If a franchisor wishes to terminate the franchise for the franchisee's breach of the franchise agreement, notice must be given under FCC cl 21. This notice must specify the breach, identify what the franchisor requires to remedy the breach, and afford the franchisee a reasonable time (not more than 30 days) to make amends. If the franchisee complies, the franchisor may not terminate the franchise for that breach. Other than that, termination can only occur according to the agreed terms of the franchise agreement, and this must include an entitlement to reasonable written notice.[59]

If a franchisee wishes to leave the franchise, the franchisor has an obligation to consider proposals for transferring the franchise agreement, and must not unreasonably withhold consent to a proposed transfer.[60] This enables franchisees to salvage some of their investment by assigning their franchise agreement for value.

Disputes over termination decisions can be taken to a special mediation service, mandated by Part 4 of the Code. This compels an attempt to resolve disputes by mediation.[61] Some specific behaviours such as attending and participating in meetings and continuing to operate the franchise during the dispute are mandated while mediation is proceeding; nevertheless, parties retain their right to litigate disputes if mediation fails.[62]

THE CODE AS REGULATION

The adoption of an industry code—even a mandatory one—is a form of regulation described by Ayres and Braithwaite as an example of 'tripartism'—regulation which responds to the needs of both sides of an industry and also the government (and hence, presumably, the community as a whole).[63] Representative industry bodies are consulted on the content of the code and modes of enforcement, so the rules ostensibly reflect 'best' or at least 'accepted' practices in the industry.

The elements of the FCC demonstrate the industry's conviction that a free and efficient market provides sufficient protection for participants in the industry. The implicit assumption of this system of regulation is that compliance with the disclosure obligations will prevent information asymmetry in the market. Hence, participants can and should be trusted to make their own deals, and must be held to them. The brief cooling-off period

---

[58] FCC cl 23.
[59] *Ibid*, at cl 22.
[60] *Ibid*, at cl 20.
[61] *Ibid*, at cl 29(6).
[62] *Ibid*, at cl 31.
[63] Ayres, I and Braithwaite, J, *Responsive Regulation: Transcending the Deregulation Debate* (New York, Oxford University Press, 1992).

allows sufficient protection from rash decisions. Beyond that, the parties must be held to their agreement. Capricious termination is controlled, but there is little in the Code dealing with negotiations between the franchisor and franchisee as the relationship progresses. The underlying assumption— fed by all of the 'be your own boss' marketing rhetoric—is that franchisees are robust and autonomous entrepreneurs, who must be free to make their own decisions.

Unfortunately, the franchisee's freedom to decide is often a one-off event. In reality, as we have seen above, once the franchise relationship commences, franchisors assume an entitlement to dictate rather than negotiate terms with franchisees. The prerogative reserved to franchisors to vary arrangements (described above as 'agreements to agree' clauses) means that a franchise is not a static agreement, but an evolving relationship. An agreement that may well have seemed fair, reasonable and workable on its face at inception may become onerous for one party as a consequence of changed circumstances. The franchisee who has sunk much of his or her own capital into the enterprise, and has no chance of extracting it on departure, may well become trapped in an intolerable relationship. So a truly responsive form of regulation for evolving relationships will allow parties to negotiate changes during the relationship, and will provide a means for supervising negotiation behaviour. This is where an obligation to negotiate and perform agreements in good faith can play a role.

GOOD FAITH?

A good faith obligation recognises that in fluid, relational contracts, power imbalances need to be controlled, lest one party take opportunistic advantage of ill-defined or open-ended terms. It can restrain the capricious and opportunistic exercise of contractual rights, and commit parties to negotiate change on a basis which respects parties' mutual entitlements to benefit from the relationship.

To some extent, franchisees have succeeded in establishing an obligation to perform franchise agreements in good faith under common law.[64] Although standard in many other jurisdictions,[65] the good faith doctrine

---

[64] See, eg, *ACCC v Simply No-Knead (Franchising) Pty Ltd* [2000] FCA 1365. Likewise, cases involving long-term distributorships have accepted an obligation to perform in good faith: see *Garry Rogers Motors (Aust) Pty Ltd v Subaru (Aust) Pty Ltd* (1999) ATPR ¶41-703.

[65] See Farnsworth, EA, 'Good Faith in Contract Performance' in J Beatson and D Friedman (eds), *Good Faith and Fault in Contract Law* (Oxford, Clarendon Press, 1995) 153 for a discussion of United States law, and Ebke, WF and Steinhauer, BM, 'The Doctrine of Good Faith in German Contract Law' in J Beatson and D Friedman (eds), *Good Faith and Fault in Contract Law* (Oxford, Clarendon Press, 1995) 171, for a discussion of German law. See also O'Byrne SK, 'The Implied Term of Good Faith and Fair Dealing: Recent Developments' (2007) 86 *Canadian Bar Review* 193.

has not been universally accepted in Australian courts, nor by Australian academics.[66] Much of this debate, however, concerns how obligations of good faith arise in commercial relationships (whether as a term implied by law into all relational contracts, or as a general principle of construction[67]), and whether the good faith obligation exists independently of the general equitable prohibition on unconscionable dealing.[68]

Notwithstanding a lack of complete consensus on these issues, it is argued here that there is substantial support (in case law and in scholarly commentary) for the view that the common law encompasses an obligation upon parties to long-term relational contracts to perform their contractual obligations in a way that permits the other party to enjoy the mutually agreed benefits of their arrangement. This obligation is not a fiduciary obligation to prefer the interests of the other over one's own, nor is it merely a prohibition on taking unconscionable advantage of the known special weakness of the other. It is a reciprocal obligation to respect the legitimate interest of the other in enjoying the benefits of the contract.[69] It encompasses an obligation of fair dealing, and a prohibition on capricious and opportunistic conduct, when undertaking the day-to-day negotiations necessary in managing a continuing relationship in a fluid business environment.

The need to institute such an obligation in the FCC was recognised in 2008 when the FCC was reviewed, yet again, by a Parliamentary Joint Committee.[70] This review made 11 recommendations for strengthening the FCC, particularly by increasing the disclosure obligations of franchisors, requiring registration of franchisors, addressing the risks to franchisees of franchisor failure (a problem no doubt emerging out of the recent economic recession) and—most important for this discussion—instituting an obligation to act in good faith in franchise relationships.[71] In recognising that despite the implementation of the FCC, the industry continued to experience problems, the Parliamentary Joint Committee said:

> There remains concern in the sector at the continuing absence of an explicit overarching standard of conduct for parties entering a franchise agreement. The interdependent nature of the franchise contract leaves the parties to the agreement vulnerable to opportunistic conduct. The committee is of the opinion that the optimal way to provide a deterrent against opportunistic conduct in the

---

[66] See, eg, Carlin, T, 'The Rise (and Fall?) of Implied Duties of Good Faith in Contractual Performance in Australia' (2002) 25 *University of New South Wales Law Journal* 99.

[67] See Peden, above n 22, ch 2.

[68] See Bigwood, R, 'Conscience and the Liberal Conception of Contract: Observing Basic Distinctions Part 1' (2000) 16 *Journal of Contract Law* 1.

[69] This understanding of good faith, and its distinction from the fiduciary principle on the one hand and unconscionable dealing on the other, has been elaborated in Riley, J, *Employee Protection at Common Law* (Sydney, Federation Press, 2005) 59–65.

[70] Parliamentary Joint Committee on Corporations and Financial Services, above n 4.

[71] *Ibid*, at xiii–xvii, 'Recommendation 8'.

franchising sector is to explicitly incorporate, in its simplest form, the existing and widely accepted implied duty of parties to a franchise agreement to act in good faith.[72]

In making this recommendation, the Parliamentary Joint Committee impliedly recognised that the existing unconscionable dealing provisions of the CC Act (ss 20 and s 22[73]) have proved to be of limited use in addressing franchisee complaints. Cases brought under these provisions have had minimal success, often because courts have permitted reliance on these provisions only after finding particularly egregious, even fraudulent conduct.[74] There is still a strong resistance in Australian courts to extending the scope of the statutory prohibitions on unconscionable dealing beyond the restrictive doctrines of the equitable jurisdiction.[75] Conduct which merely exploits a power imbalance is rarely considered to be unconscionable.

Presently, it appears that this recommendation has resulted in nothing more than a weak acknowledgment in the Code that parties will continue to be bound by any common law obligations of good faith.[76] The initial government response (issued on 5 November 2009) was that Recommendation 8 ought not to be adopted because 'the law on good faith is still evolving', so the inclusion of a general good faith obligation would 'increase uncertainty in franchising'.[77] With respect, this is a short-sighted view. One of the reasons for the current uncertainty in the law is that judges (perhaps shy of being insulted as 'judicial activists') are reluctant to articulate and develop a good faith standard in the absence of legislative permission. An express statutory obligation would justify judicial development of a good faith standard. Refusal to adopt a good faith obligation is also contrary to developments instigated by the same government in the field of labour negotiations. The Fair Work Act 2009 (Cth) enacted an express obligation upon industrial parties to bargain 'in good faith' to reach enterprise agreements.[78] This obligation to bargain in good faith stipulated a number

---

[72] *Ibid*, at xvi.

[73] Formerly Trade Practices Act 1974 (Cth) ss 51AA and 51AC respectively.

[74] Strickland, P, 'Rethinking Unconscionable Conduct under the Trade Practices Act' (2009) 37 *Australian Business Law Review* 105.

[75] See, eg, *ACCC v Berbatis Holdings Pty Ltd* (2003) 197 ALR 153 and *ACCC v Samton Holdings Pty Ltd* (2002) 189 ALR 76. For commentary on former s 51AC and its interpretation by the courts, see Tucker, P, 'Too Much Concern Too Soon? Rationalising Elements of s 51AC of the Trade Practices Act' (2001) 17 *Journal of Contract Law* 1; Horrigan, B, 'The Expansion of Fairness-based Business Regulation: Unconscionability, Good Faith and the Law's Informed Conscience' (2004) 32 *Australian Business Law Review* 159, and Strickland, above n 74.

[76] FCC cl 23A.

[77] Commonwealth of Australia, *Response to the Report of the Parliamentary Joint Committee on Corporations and Financial Services—Opportunity not Opportunism: Improving Conduct in Australian Franchising* (Canberra, Commonwealth of Australia, 2009), available at: www.innovation.gov.au/Section/SmallBusiness/Pages/FranchisingCodeofConduct.aspx.

[78] See Fair Work Act 2009 (Cth) s 228.

of kinds of required behaviours, such as meeting at reasonable times, and considering offers and counter-offers. The FCC could articulate similar particularised requirements to promote good faith conduct, such as obligations upon the franchise parties to meet and consider objections before mandating changes in operations manuals.

Fear that a good faith obligation would create too much uncertainty misunderstands the concept of good faith. A commitment to fair dealing does not necessarily release unbounded and idiosyncratic judicial orders requiring self-interested parties to act charitably. Objective fairness can sit comfortably within a legal system committed to individual liberty and autonomy.[79]

Of course, there are already important measures in the FCC designed to manage the expectations of franchisees and limit opportunities for their exploitation, including the disclosure and termination provisions described above. However, these measures stop short of recognising that franchises are ongoing relationships and parties will regularly need to negotiate change. Articulation of a good faith obligation, so that it is incumbent upon both sides to take account of the other's interests in negotiations, may go some way to addressing the risk that franchisors will resort to the master's prerogative to command obedience instead of respecting the franchisee's expectation of having a voice in the running of what they (perhaps mistakenly, but genuinely) believe is their 'own business'.

CONCLUSION

One response to the commercialisation of labour relationships is to resist the trend and revert to forms of protective legislation, such as provisions 'deeming' all vulnerable workers to be employees for the purposes of certain kinds of protection. Another response—the one recommended in this Chapter as most appropriate to franchise relationships—is to develop new forms of regulation that respond appropriately to the workers' needs and expectations. In the case of franchisees—these 'indentured entrepreneurs'— responsive regulation needs to recognise their expectations of some autonomy as 'business owners', while also addressing the serious risks they face as a consequence of their economic dependence upon the franchisor/master and their vulnerability during the franchise relationship. Contemporary

---

[79] See Atiyah, PS, 'Contract and Fair Exchange' in *Essays on Contract* (Oxford, Clarendon Press, 1986) 331; Mason, A, 'Contract, Good Faith and Equitable Standards in Fair Dealing' (2000) 116 *Law Quarterly Review* 66, 72; Collins, H, *Regulating Contracts* (New York, Oxford University Press, 1999) 8. See also Johnson, B, 'Developing Legislative Protection for Owner Drivers in Australia: The Long Road to Regulatory Best Practice' in this collection for a discussion of the appropriate regulation of another commercial relationship (trucking contracting) in the interests of comparative fairness.

franchising regulation (exemplified in the Australian FCC) adopts this responsive approach.

Notwithstanding the institution of the FCC, weaknesses still remain in the regulation of franchising in Australia. The high level of disputes in the industry is a testimony to those weaknesses. Presently, the form of regulation adopted presumes that markets will operate efficiently and fairly with sufficient disclosure, on the basis that individual economic actors are best placed to make their own decisions. However, the deceptive language of entrepreneurship disguises the real economic dependence of many of the small business people who decide to enter into franchise agreements. They are encouraged to imagine themselves to be independent entrepreneurs and the law treats them as such, by resisting requests to review their treatment by franchisors purely on the grounds of 'unfairness'. In reality, the provisions in typical franchise contracts often reserve to franchisors what can only be described as a prerogative to command. If franchise relationships are to be treated at law as genuinely equal commercial relationships, there needs to be some regulatory measure to remind the parties to these relationships that they have an obligation to negotiate their ongoing dealings fairly, with a view to enabling each to benefit mutually from the relationship. This presents a real challenge. A statutory good faith obligation may go some way to articulating a standard of conduct for these negotiations. Encouragement of good faith negotiations may, hopefully, reduce the high level of disputes in the industry, and so address some of the concerns that the commercialisation of this form of labour provision has compromised labour standards.

7

Developing Legislative Protection for Owner Drivers in Australia: The Long Road to Regulatory Best Practice

BRENDAN JOHNSON

INTRODUCTION

HISTORICALLY, THE LEGAL characterisation of truck owner drivers in Australia has been determined by the indicia of employment versus independent contracting. This distinction significantly affects the relative bargaining power and legislative protection afforded to each category of work because of the extent of legislative protections afforded to employees that are not afforded to owner drivers. An analysis of the situation of owner drivers reveals the limited capacity of commercial law to remedy their inequality of bargaining power across the federal and State jurisdictions in Australia. The experience of the heavy vehicle industry in Australia has been that the structure of the transport market has led to exploitation of both owner drivers and employees with consequent effects on remuneration and safety levels.

In 2008, a review commissioned by the National Transport Commission into remuneration and safety in the heavy vehicle industry in Australia comprehensively examined the relationship between systems of remuneration and unsafe work practices. Its recommendation was for the federal government to establish a national scheme for setting mandatory safe rates covering both employees and owner drivers in the heavy vehicle industry.[1] A Safe Rates Advisory Group was established, and a subsequent Directions

---

[1] Quinlan, M and Wright, L, *Remuneration and Safety in the Australian Heavy Vehicle Industry: A Review Undertaken for the National Transport Commission (NTC)* (Melbourne, NTC, 2008) 61.

Paper released by the federal government in response to the review canvassed a range of regulatory options.

This Chapter will analyse the bargaining power of owner drivers and employees in the Australian heavy vehicle industry in the context of commercial pressures, the result of which is a diminished focus on safety. This parallels the high degree of vulnerability of informal workers and entrepreneurs as discussed by Judy Fudge in Chapter 1 of this collection, and the associated deterioration of working conditions and labour standards which flows from an unchecked pursuit of labour market flexibility and deregulation.[2] The Chapter also discusses the competing arguments for and against the regulation of commercial relations and the debate surrounding the best methods of regulating owner drivers and employees in Australia. Regulation of owner drivers and employees in the heavy vehicle industry presents a challenge to government as it necessarily requires it to grapple with work arrangements that don't neatly fit into existing labour law models of regulation. Collins' development of comparative fairness standards in multi-segmented workforces and networks justifies the regulatory approach recommended by the National Transport Commission in relation to owner drivers and employees.[3]

Regulation of owner drivers has been implemented in the Australian States of Victoria and Western Australia through the use of 'light-touch' legislation drawing on the doctrine of unconscionable conduct and fair trading laws which have regard to the operation of vehicles on a cost recovery basis. Whilst remedial and educative legislation has a useful role, it does not have a sufficient deterrent effect so as to provide the economic structural reform required to ensure safety in the systems of remuneration adopted in the Australian transport industry. The lessons learned from the long road towards regulatory best practice in the transport industry may have application for other areas where the social and economic costs of vertical disintegration outweigh the benefits.

OWNER DRIVERS IN THE AUSTRALIAN TRANSPORT INDUSTRY

The unequal bargaining positions of individuals (or smaller companies) and larger organisations invariably leads to unequal and often unfair outcomes in the contractual terms and conditions agreed upon. The experience of owner drivers provides a useful illustration of unequal bargaining power as, in Australia, these workers are not generally subject to the statutory

---

[2] Fudge, J, 'Blurring Legal Boundaries: Regulating for Decent Work' in this collection.
[3] Collins, H, 'Multi-segmented Workforces, Comparative Fairness, and the Capital Boundary Obstacle' in G Davidov and B Langille (eds), *Boundaries and Frontiers of Labour Law: Goals and Means in the Regulation of Work* (Oxford, Hart Publishing, 2006) 327.

'safety net' provisions or tests of 'unfairness' that apply to employees. The disadvantages experienced by owner drivers are significant in certain areas, and result in a wide range of exploitative and unfair practices in agreement making with unfair and unreasonable terms and conditions being 'agreed' to by owner drivers. Examples of the issues confronting owner drivers include: bargaining on a 'take it or leave it' basis; termination of an owner driver's services without notice and for any reason; the imposition of low and unsustainable rates when examined against fixed and variable costs; unauthorised deduction of monies from payments; late payment of invoices; and labour rates which are less than the award or agreement rate otherwise applicable to employees. Clients of transport companies play a fundamental role in the creation of these issues, but where parties to a commercial contract may be characterised as being in an 'employment-like' relationship, a reliance on traditional contractual principles or traditional labour law regulation often fails to adequately address the imbalance in bargaining strength between respective parties.[4] In this sense, these owner drivers (who often structure their affairs as limited liability companies) represent subordinate or dependent labour and fall outside regulatory systems that would ordinarily apply to employees engaged in identical work.[5]

Despite an overall decline in the Australian road toll, the annual number of fatalities resulting from crashes involving articulated trucks did not shift significantly between the early 1990s and 2007. In 2007, 235 people died in accidents involving articulated and heavy rigid trucks, representing about 10 per cent of all fatal crashes in Australia.[6] This points to a systemic failure to address safety issues in the transport industry. Following the election of a federal Labor government in 2007, lobbying by the Transport Workers' Union of Australia (TWU) persuaded the then Minister for Industrial Relations, Julia Gillard, to announce an inquiry to be conducted by the National Transport Commission (NTC) to investigate driver remuneration and payment methods in the Australian trucking industry, and their effect on safety outcomes. The Terms of Reference required the NTC to review existing regulatory models and their capacity to deal concurrently with payment methods and remuneration of owner drivers and employees. The NTC was to make recommendations on the means by which federal legislation applying to employees and independent contractors could/ should accommodate a system of 'safe payments' for employees and owner drivers.[7] Professor Michael Quinlan and the Honourable Lance Wright

---

[4] Owens, R, 'Decent Work for the Contingent Workforce in the New Economy' (2002) 15 *Australian Journal of Labour Law* 1, 13.

[5] O'Donnell, A, 'Non-Standard' Workers in Australia: Counts and Controversies' (2004) 17 *Australian Journal of Labour Law* 1, 26.

[6] Quinlan and Wright, above n 1, at 8–9.

[7] *Ibid*, at 4.

QC conducted the review and made recommendations for fundamental legislative change (the 'Review'). The most important recommendation was:

> The Review recommends that a national scheme for setting mandatory safe rates covering both employees and owner/drivers be established in the heavy vehicle industry. This is the only viable and direct mechanism for addressing the imbalance in bargaining power confronting owner/drivers that affects safety in the road freight industry.[8]

This recommendation was based on evidence that the authors said had '... been accepted and indeed confirmed by government inquiries, coronial inquests, courts and industrial tribunal hearings in Australia over a number of years'.[9] Following the inquiry, the NTC made recommendations to the Australian Transport Council (ATC), which is constituted by federal and State transport and roads ministers, for the implementation of a framework for the establishment and maintenance of safe payments for employees and owner drivers, incorporating amendments to model transport laws concerning chain of responsibility obligations for safe payments.[10]

It is worth exploring in detail some of the findings of the Review in order to properly understand the backdrop to the recommended regulatory reforms. The Review found that 'the overwhelming weight of evidence indicates that commercial/industrial practices affecting road transport play a direct and significant role in causing hazardous practices'.[11] The association between remuneration and safety was found to apply to both employee drivers and owner drivers, and the authors found the use of extensive multi-tiered contracting caused a price reduction at each subcontracting point in order to provide a return to those higher in the chain.[12] The Review cited extensive research and analysis of the link between commercial practices, rewards and safety outcomes in the trucking industry including research which established a link between scheduling pressures, unpaid waiting time, insecure rewards and access to work, and hazardous practices such as speeding, excessive hours and drug use by drivers.[13] The Review found, '[t]here is solid survey evidence linking payment levels and systems to crashes,

---

[8] *Ibid*, at 6.

[9] *Ibid*, at 49.

[10] NTC, *Safe Payments: Addressing the Underlying Cause of Unsafe Practices in the Road Transport Industry*, (Melbourne, NTC, 2008) 46.

[11] Quinlan and Wright, above n 1, at 49.

[12] *Ibid*, at 10.

[13] Golob, T and Hensher, D, *Driving Behaviour of Long Distance Truck Drivers: The Effects of Schedule Compliance on Drug Use and Speeding Citations* (Working Paper ITS-WP-94-1, Institute of Transportation Studies, University of California, Irvine, May 1994); Hensher, D and Battellino, H, *Long-Distance Trucking: Why Do Truckies Speed?* (Working Paper No 90-4, Graduate School of Management and Public Policy, University of Sydney, 1990); Hensher, D *et al*, *Long Distance Truck Drivers on Road Performance and Economic Reward* (Canberra, Federal Office of Road Safety, December 1991).

speeding, driving while fatigued and drug use'.[14] The work of Williamson *et al*[15] and witness evidence was also discussed, which established the link between driver remuneration, payment methods and safety, and notably the association between payment by results and the use of stimulant drugs to cope with work demands.

The Review adopted the research of Quinlan in his report *Inquiry into the Long Distance Trucking Industry*, which was accepted as demonstrating a relationship between commercial pressures, and practices and safety in the long-haul trucking industry.[16] Quinlan reported that '[l]ow freight rates were widely seen as a direct threat to safe operations because they encouraged pushing the margins (cuts to maintenance, more trips in given period, speeding etc)'.[17] Quinlan attributed low rates to a range of reasons including:

(a) the pressure of customers in a strong bargaining position, without accompanying OHS responsibilities;
(b) intense competition amongst transport operators with heavy debts and an eagerness to undercut rates to win work, along with the use of pyramid subcontracting by firms for capture work at reduced rates;
(c) poor business practices and limited bargaining power of many operators;
(d) a regulatory environment that allows economic advantage to be gained by a failure to abide by safety standards;
(e) the use of performance-based payment systems (including industrial agreements) and widespread evasion of minimum award entitlements for drivers that effectively encouraged illegal driving practices and enabled cost savings to be made;
(f) job insecurity fears leading to employees and owner drivers undertaking dangerous work practices; and
(g) the association between tight schedules, delivery time bonus/penalties, performance-based payment systems, chronic injury and propensity to engage in dangerous practices such as speeding and excessive hours.[18]

---

[14] Quinlan and Wright, above n 1, at 49.
[15] Williamson, A, 'Predictors of Psychostimulant Use by Long Distance Truck Drivers' (2007) 166 *American Journal of Epidemiology* 1320; Williamson, A, Cooley, M, Hayes, L and O'Neil, L, *Final Report of Stimulant Use by Long Distance Road Transport Drivers Project* (Sydney, University of New South Wales Injury Risk Management Research Centre, 2006); Williamson, A *et al*, *Driver Fatigue: A Survey of Professional Heavy Drivers in Australia* (Melbourne, NTC, 2000); Williamson, A, Friswell, R and Feyer, A, *Fatigue and Performance in Heavy Truck Drivers Working Day Shift, Night Shift or Rotating Shifts* (Melbourne, NTC, 2004).
[16] Quinlan, M, *Report of Inquiry into Safety in the Long Haul Trucking Industry* (Sydney, Motor Accidents Authority of New South Wales, 2001) 22–3.
[17] *Ibid*, at 21.
[18] *Ibid*, at 22–3.

The Review also noted that the evidence suggested that the capacity to recover increases in operating costs by owner drivers and operators was inhibited by a combination of the power exercised by clients, intense competition for work, the use of multi-tiered subcontracting, imbalances in freight movements and individualised and trip/incentive-based payment levels.[19] In terms of the impact the market system has on work arrangements and safety levels in the transport industry, the Review found that the failure to pay legally mandated entitlements is a direct consequence of commercial pressures that compromise safety.[20] Whilst the Review did not make an explicit finding regarding market failure in the transport industry, the conclusions drawn by the Review indicate that the existence of market failure justified the recommended approach to reform in this industry. The linkage between payment levels and systems to crashes, speeding, driving while fatigued and drug use was found to be caused in large part by the use of multi-tiered subcontracting and the associated undercutting of rates to unsafe and unsustainable levels in a competitive market. The Review found that this in turn caused owner drivers to cut back on costs relating to the maintenance and repair of their vehicles.[21]

The Review was groundbreaking in terms of the depth and strength of its recommendations. The Review canvassed three options for recommendation including:

(1) the deeming of owner drivers as employees resulting in their regulation by industrial tribunals;
(2) conferral of powers on the Australian Industrial Relations Commission (now known as Fair Work Australia); or
(3) the creation of a specialised body under federal transport legislation with wide powers to fix rates of remuneration and related matters which ensure industry safety.[22]

The Review recommended option 3 and found that specific transport legislation and a specialised tribunal should be established, with necessary amendments made to other federal legislation. This recommendation was in turn adopted by the NTC in its Report and recommendation to the ATC in which it summarised the role of the proposed body as follows:

— to establish and maintain enforceable safe payments for employees;
— to establish and maintain enforceable safe payments for owner drivers;
— to settle disputes in a low-cost, accessible manner;

---

[19] Quinlan and Wright, above n 1, at 50.
[20] *Ibid*, at 64.
[21] *Ibid*, at 50.
[22] *Ibid*, at 61.

— to consider and, if necessary, bestow rights and impose obligations regarding safe payments on other parties in the transport supply chain; and

— to consider and, if necessary, bestow rights and impose obligations with respect to enforcement of safe payments.[23]

However, these Recommendations do not go as far as the Review suggested. The Review recommended that to ensure compliance and the effective implementation of a safe rate regime, adequate resourcing of enforcement measures is required. Such measures would make it mandatory for every heavy vehicle to carry information pertaining to payment level and rate for the trip or trips being undertaken demonstrating compliance with the safe rate, and requiring such information to be provided to accredited authorities or officials upon demand. Further, the Review recommended that where a driver did not receive their payment, a rebuttable presumption should apply that the principal contractor in any multi-tiered subcontracting arrangement is responsible for payment. Finally, the Review suggested the creation of penalties on an escalating basis for failure to pay safe rates or evade legal requirements. The Review authors considered it 'would not only be unacceptable but perverse to fail to recommend appropriate rectification' having identified the clear relationship between remuneration and safety, and the failure to adequately address it.[24] The ATC issued a communiqué following its May 2008 meeting which noted the 'potential flow-on effects from payment rates and methods on unsafe 'road behaviours' and poor safety outcomes in the trucking industry', and agreed that there is a case for investigating a whole-of-government regulatory approach to address this issue.[25]

In December 2009 the federal government established the Safe Rates Advisory Group (SRAG), which was requested to advise the federal government on the implementation of the recommendations of the Review. In November 2010 a Directions Paper titled 'Safe Rates, Safe Roads' was issued by the federal government and input from industry stakeholders was sought. The Directions Paper builds on the findings contained in the Report, noting that any tribunal established in line with the recommendations of the Report must: provide national consistency; have competence for both employees and owner drivers, as they compete for, and perform, the same tasks; review pay rates and related conditions alongside safety; include supply chains, which apply economic pressure, and have the resources to adjust the way supply chains operate to deal with safety issues; and be the

---

[23] NTC, above n 10, at 40.
[24] Quinlan and Wright, above n 1, at 55.
[25] ATC, 'Joint Communique' (7 November, 2008), available at: www.ntc.gov.au/filemedia/News/28thATCMeetingJointCommuniqNov08.pdf.

single decision-maker on pay/payment methodologies and safety in the road transport industry.[26]

Three options are proposed in the Directions Paper for the establishment of a tribunal:

(a) a new specialist tribunal with power to make orders regarding safe rates and related terms in the road transport industry (Specialist Tribunal);
(b) a safe rates panel within Fair Work Australia with power to make orders regarding safe rates and related terms in the road transport industry (Safe Rates Panel);
(c) extending the Fair Work Act 2009 to owner drivers, with Fair Work Australia empowered to make orders regarding safe rates and related terms in the road transport industry (Outworker Model).[27]

To date, no model of regulation has been announced by the government. However, the attempt to regulate complex hierarchic organisational and supply-chain structures such as exist in the transport industry represents an innovative and significant step away from labour market flexibility and deregulation. The role of governments at both State and federal levels is to provide adequate regulation in order to encourage safe and sustainable systems of work. This becomes challenging when traditional concepts of labour regulation fail to capture quasi-commercial arrangements. As demonstrated by the Review findings and the proposals in the Directions Paper, a solution to this regulatory dilemma does exist and it is worth exploring the theoretical foundation to both the problem and the solution.

REGULATING COMMERCIAL RELATIONS IN A COMPETITIVE ECONOMY

Commercial Law and Owner Drivers

Joellen Riley notes that the law of contract has long regulated commercial market transactions, and is as much a form of regulation as any other law making.[28] She notes that the liberal philosophy advocating trust in market forces to regulate voluntary dealings between autonomous actors is disingenuous if not dishonest, and that liberation of the 'entrepreneurial worker'

---

[26] Department of Education, Employment and Workplace Relations, *Safe Rates, Safe Roads: Directions Paper* (Canberra, Commonwealth of Australia, 2010) 11, available at: www.deewr. gov.au/WorkplaceRelations/Policies/SafeRatesSafeRoads/Documents/DirectionsPaper.pdf.

[27] *Ibid*, at 11–12.

[28] Riley, J, 'A Fair Deal for the Entrepreneurial Worker? Self-employment and Independent Contracting Post Work Choices' (2006) 19 *Australian Journal of Labour Law* 247.

from the strictures of employment law has involved considerable explicit legislative regulation.[29]

Regulation of independent contractors is not new, and as noted by Judy Fudge, the courts and the legal system approach the ascribing of employment-related obligations in triangular employment relationships and integrated enterprises from the perspective that employers are free to structure their enterprises in order to contract out the responsibilities of employment.[30] Fudge notes that it is up to the legislature to remedy the gaps created by triangular relationships which limit the effectiveness of remedial labour law legislation to address disputes involving parties in multi-tiered subcontracting relationships.[31] This is an important recognition of the limits of labour law in addressing fundamental imbalances in power relationships that affect individuals and small firms, and the influence of strong third parties such as clients of prime contractors in the transport industry. This dynamic establishes the preconditions for market failure which can have devastating consequences, and perhaps the regulatory proposals contained in the Directions Paper represent the type of legislative gap-filling proposed by Fudge.

Addressing the Regulatory Dilemma of Owner Drivers

In its purest form, neo-liberal theory perceives government regulation of contractual freedom to be an illegitimate intrusion into the rights of individuals. According to market-oriented utilitarians, when individual preferences are summed the result is representative of the optimal outcome for the public. Conflicting individual interests are resolved by the aggregation of individual interests, and the actions of fully informed individuals in the market are assumed to be based on individuals' rational decision making.[32] This is, of course, rarely the case as the assumptions underlying individuals' decision making are almost never fully informed, often irrational, and not always made free from economic, contractual or managerial influence. PS Atiyah contends that when people make important decisions the chance that they will act in their own long-term interest is often quite low.[33] His approach challenges the classical liberal model of contract theory derived from utilitarianism. The utilitarian model is often related to

---

[29] *Ibid*, at 247.

[30] Fudge, J, 'The Legal Boundaries of Labour Protection' in G Davidov and B Langille (eds), *Boundaries and Frontiers of Labour Law: Goals and Means in the Regulation of Work* (Oxford, Hart Publishing, 2006) 310.

[31] *Ibid*, at 313.

[32] Bottomley, S and Parker, C, *Law in Context* (Sydney, Federation Press, 1997) 34–5.

[33] Atiyah PS, 'Executory, Contracts, Expectation Damages, and the Economic Analysis of Contract' in *Essays on Contract* (Oxford, Clarendon Press, 1986) 155.

labour regulation by reference to Coase's economic model of the firm which described the relationship between employer and employee as one of the 'right of control or interference'.[34] This may be juxtaposed with a relationship between independent contractors and their hirers where such a right arguably does not exist in theory, but in practice control and interference in decision making is all too common.

Fudge neatly analyses Coase's theorem and its application to vertically integrated firms, and notes that vertical integration substitutes hierarchy for the price mechanism, and authority for market incentives.[35] Conversely, Hugh Collins describes the way in which core firms use vertical disintegration to outsource employment obligations and responsibility for labour standards to subcontractors, thereby undermining the application of the principle of group responsibility.[36] This problem is also noted by Shelley Marshall, who identifies the problem of supply chain regulation providing varied outcomes for workers depending on whether or not they are engaged by a 'core business'.[37] Collins defines group responsibility as the legal responsibility of a person or representative of a group for its members through the principles of agency and vicarious liability.[38] He discusses the establishment of complex economic organisations through the bonds of ownership, contract and authority, and posits that the legal separation of companies and independent contractors undermines the application of group responsibility.

The transport industry represents a prime example of this situation where the sub-contracting of work to owner drivers and the supreme market power of clients creates 'economic dependence of one party upon the other effectively requiring compliance with the dominant party's wishes'.[39] This may occur through a range of multi-tiered subcontracting arrangements, some of which involve freight forwarders and agents who play no functional role in service delivery. In his work *On Liberty*, John Stuart Mill identified that the only basis for governments dealing with individuals by way of compulsion and control (whether by way of legal penalties or the moral coercion of public opinion) is self-protection. He wrote: *'The only purpose for which power can be rightfully exercised over any member of a civilized community, against his will, is to prevent harm to others. His*

---

[34] Coase, RH, *The Firm, the Market, and the Law* (Chicago, University of Chicago Press, 1988).

[35] Fudge, above n 30, at 300.

[36] Collins, H, 'Ascription of Legal Responsibility to Groups in Complex Patterns of Economic Integration' (1990) 53 *The Modern Law Review* 733, 733–4.

[37] Marshall S, 'An Exploration of Control in the Context of Vertical Disintegration' in C Arup *et al* (eds), *Labour Law and Labour Market Regulation* (Sydney, Federation Press, 2006) 559.

[38] Collins, above n 36, at 733–4.

[39] *Ibid.*

own good, either physical or moral, is not a sufficient warrant.'[40] When extrapolated to the realm of multi-tiered subcontracting and vertical disintegration, Mill's approach provides the fundamental philosophical basis for legislative intervention where the conduct of contracting parties may cause harm to others. The problem of the increasing complexity of patterns of vertical disintegration within employer entities was raised as a critical issue for labour law by Collins, who saw it as undermining the justification for regulatory intervention unless there was an evolution in legal doctrine towards a concept of comparative fairness standards.[41] When applied to the experiences of owner drivers and employees engaged in the heavy vehicle industry in Australia, Mill's 'harm principle' and Collins' comparative fairness standards highlight deficiencies in existing regulatory structures which require more specific legislative action.

THE LIMITS OF COMMERCIAL LAW IN REGULATING SUPPLY CHAIN CONTRACTING ARRANGEMENTS

An Analysis of Existing Regulatory Structures

Legislative intervention by governments at federal and State levels in Australia, specifically in areas such as private transport, has been designed to bring some form of equality to bargaining processes, developing over time in both form and substance. Such legislation has included the federal Competition and Consumer Act 2010, and Fair Trading Acts in all States and Territories. There has been a push recently towards the regulation of independent contractors by commercial rather than industrial laws, and as noted by Riley this begs the question of which commercial laws will in fact regulate the dealings between larger enterprises and self-employed individuals, and whether existing commercial laws offer any promise of a legal guarantee of fairness and equality at work.[42] At the federal level, the Independent Contractors Act 2006 (IC Act) was intended to override State laws containing 'deeming' provisions, and contract review or unfair contract provisions. The application of State laws that deem independent contractors to be employees or that allow courts to review the substantive fairness of a contractual bargain struck by an independent contractor were largely excluded by the IC Act. However, the operation of both the NSW Industrial Relations Act 1996 Chapter 6 (covering the transport industry) and the Victorian Owner Drivers and Forestry Contractors Act 2005 (and subsequently the Owner-Drivers (Contracts and Disputes) Act 1997) was

---

[40] Cited in Bottomley and Parker, above n 32, at 19 (emphasis added).
[41] Collins, above n 3, at 327–35.
[42] Riley, above n 28, at 260.

maintained by the IC Act and these regulatory schemes still apply. Just like other legislation regulating this area, the IC Act fails to address the supply-chain issues of dominance and multi-tiered subcontracting arrangements referred to by the Review; however, it is worth identifying the existing regulatory structures and their relationship to commercial law vis-à-vis labour law. The main focus of the discussion will be on the Victorian Owner Drivers and Forestry Contractors Act 2005 (ODFCA) as this Act represents the most innovative attempt to regulate the work and relationships of truck owner drivers in Australia to date.

The purpose of the ODFCA is to 'regulate the relationship between persons who contract to transport goods ...' by:

(a) requiring information to be given;
(b) providing requirements for contracts;
(c) allowing negotiating agents to be appointed;
(d) providing a dispute-resolution mechanism;
(e) conferring functions on the Small Business Commissioner;
(f) establishing a Transport Industry Council;
(g) providing for codes of practice to be made;
(h) prohibiting unconscionable conduct;
(i) providing certain authorisations for the purposes of competition laws; and
(j) amending the Victorian Civil and Administrative Tribunal Act 1998.

The ODFCA was designed to eliminate unconscionable conduct, unjust contract terms and unfair dealing in particular contractual relationships. To this end, the Act contains a mixture of procedural and substantive unconscionability tests. The use and expansion of unconscionable conduct and unjust contract provisions in the ODFCA represents an extension of the jurisprudence in the regulation of commercial contracts. However, as noted by the Review:

> [I]t does not address the often fundamental bargaining power imbalance between owner/drivers and those engaging them. As such, it fails to address the problem at the centre of this Review; nor was any evidence presented to the review that indicated it had resulted in substantial changes in rates paid to owner/drivers.[43]

Other aspects of the ODFCA seek to deal with market failures and collective action problems by correcting information asymmetries, mandating contract terms and providing access to collective bargaining. Section 20 of the ODFCA requires that terms and conditions of contracting parties engaging in work regulated by the ODFCA must be recorded in writing, state the guaranteed minimum number of hours or income level, and set out the rates to be paid and the minimum notice period. Another significant

---

[43] Quinlan and Wright, above n 1, at 54.

feature of the ODFCA is the requirement under s 21 for the provision of a notice period, or payment in lieu of notice, for the termination of a regulated contract. This notice period differs depending on the size of the vehicle involved. The requirement for information booklets and 'rates and cost schedules' to be distributed to owner drivers by hirers intending to engage them was intended to change the dynamic of the information asymmetry, and place obligations on hirers to ensure fairness in the bargaining process. The 'rates and cost schedules' take account of fixed and variable overhead costs that owner drivers may not otherwise factor into costings, such as registration, maintenance, running costs, administration costs, workcover premiums, self-funding of superannuation, finance, labour and depreciation. A potential problem with this aspect of the ODFCA is that individuals, corporations and other entities are prohibited from colluding in the setting of prices for goods or services by the federal Competition and Consumer Act 2010. However, this Act also allows for authorisations to be made which effectively legalises otherwise prohibited activity, provided it is within the scope of the authorisation.[44] The ODFCA creates an authorisation under the Competition and Consumer Act 2010 for conduct undertaken in accordance with the ODFCA including the making of a code of practice and conduct in relation to collective bargaining with target businesses (called joint negotiations under the Act).

This capacity for owner drivers to negotiate collectively by way of an authorisation for the purposes of the CC Act represents a move towards hybrid legislation based on a combination of commercial law and labour law, and implicit recognition that the National Competition Code supports legislative intervention in commercial contracts where market failure may otherwise occur. Shae McCrystal, in this collection and elsewhere, provides a thorough analysis of collective bargaining, its implications and potential under the CC Act.[45]

The ODFCA was never intended to operate in the same manner as the 'contract determinations' that set minimum terms and conditions in New South Wales,[46] and upon its introduction was described as 'light-touch' regulation. The TWU submission to the Review noted that the ODFCA had 'brought some improvements (in terms of a cost model and unconscionable contracts dispute mechanism) [but] it did not establish a minimum rates

---

[44] See further McCrystal, S, 'Organising Independent Contractors: The Impact of Competition Law' in this collection.

[45] McCrystal S, 'Collective Bargaining by Independent Contractors: Challenges from Labour Law' (2007) 20 *Australian Journal of Labour Law* 1, 11–14; McCrystal, S, 'Is there a "Public Benefit" in Improving Working Conditions for Independent Contractors? Collective Bargaining and the Trade Practices Act 1974 (Cth)' (2009) 37 *Federal Law Review* 263; McCrystal, above n 44.

[46] The NSW Contract determination system is discussed below.

structure—and this was what was required at national level'.[47] The Review observed that the mechanisms for disputing contracts places the onus on individual owner drivers, and that this may lead to an unknown number deciding not to pursue complaints due to time and resources, or due to a fear of blacklisting and loss of future work.[48] The Annual Report of the Office of the Small Business Commissioner states that during 2008/2009 only 37 owner drivers and forestry contractor disputes were referred to it, of which 30 were completed with an 86.7 per cent success rate.[49] In terms of dispute resolution, this small number indicates either a successful deterrent value in the legislation, or more likely, leakage resulting from the types of reasons cited by the Review. It may also reflect the failure of aggrieved individuals to pursue rights where they exist, a problem discussed by Anna Pollert in this collection.[50] In assessing the effectiveness and limits of the ODFCA, the Review stated that the ODFCA addresses the issue of what is an acceptable minimum rate in an individual and voluntary/non-mandatory fashion, but that providing better information does not address the fundamental power imbalance between owner drivers and those engaging them.[51]

New South Wales has regulated the work of owner drivers involved in short-haul transportation through contract determinations which set minimum rates and conditions to which contracting parties must adhere, as well as through provisions relating to unconscionable conduct in the NSW Industrial Relations Act 1996. The Act also contains unfair contract provisions whose application was largely excluded by the IC Act, while the contract determination provisions for the short-haul transport industry were specifically preserved.[52] The Act allows the NSW Industrial Relations Commission to inquire into matters arising under certain short-haul contracts of bailment or carriage, and make a 'contract determination' with respect to the remuneration.[53] Such determinations may include allowances in lieu of leave entitlements, and other regulation of working conditions.[54] At the time of writing there were approximately 35 current contract determinations in effect in NSW.[55] This probably represents the most

---

[47] Quinlan and Wright, above n 1, at 31.

[48] *Ibid.*

[49] Office of the Victorian Small Business Commissioner (OVSBC), *Annual Report* (Melbourne, OVSBC, 2009) 25.

[50] Anna Pollert, 'How Britain's Low Paid Non-Unionised Employees Deal with Workplace Problems' in this collection.

[51] Quinlan and Wright, above n 1, at 44–5. See also Riley, J, 'A Blurred Boundary between Entrepreneurship and Servitude: Regulating Business Format Franchising in Australia' in this collection for a discussion of a similar problem in the context of the regulation of business format franchising in Australia.

[52] Independent Contractors Act 2006 (Cth) s 7.

[53] Industrial Relations Act 1996 (NSW) ss 312–13.

[54] *Ibid.*

[55] The list of current determinations is available at www.lawlink.nsw.gov.au/irc.

prescriptive model for regulation of transport industry participants amongst the Australian States, but is limited in application and does not cover owner drivers working in the long-haul transport sector. Despite this, submissions by the TWU and other transport industry participants to the Review indicated that the mandatory setting of minimum rates in the short-haul transport sector in NSW had operated effectively to 'protect their interests in terms of safety'.[56]

In Western Australia ss 9 and 13 of the Owner-Drivers (Contracts and Disputes) Act 2007 includes provisions implying terms requiring payment within prescribed time limits if no written contract exists, and which ban terms delaying payment to contractors until payment is received from a third party. Just as with the ODFCA, this legislation establishes a Road Freight Transport Industry Council to (amongst other things): advise the Minister on the development and review a Code of Conduct; prepare and review guidelines rates; and develop, publish and review model owner driver contracts. Part 6 of the Act largely replicates the ODFCA provisions concerning unconscionable conduct and s 35 gives the owner driver or their agent the right to inspect premises and records of businesses.

The Recommendations of the NTC

The development in the transport industry of the types of practices highlighted in the Review demonstrates that existing regulatory intervention adopted by federal and State authorities has failed to address the imbalance of bargaining power that is created by vertical disintegration within employer entities. As noted by the Review, 'attempts to set minimum rates for owner drivers on a voluntary or consensual basis, while they may exert some influence, have repeatedly failed since the late 1970s because they lacked the capacity to ensure meaningful coverage and compliance (inevitably breaking down under competitive pressure)'.[57] One is therefore inevitably drawn to the logic of the recommendation of the Review (adopted by the NTC) that 'a national scheme for setting mandatory safe rates covering both employee and owner/drivers ... is the only viable and direct mechanism for addressing the imbalance in bargaining power confronting owner/drivers'.[58] This corresponds with Roopa Madhav's conclusion in this collection that 'soft law' such as voluntary codes of conduct struggle to provide any substantial benefits to workers.[59] The endorsement by the NTC of

---

[56] Quinlan and Wright, above n 1, at 29.
[57] *Ibid*, at 45.
[58] Quinlan and Wright, above n 1, at 61.
[59] Madhav, R, 'Corporate Codes of Conduct in the Garment Sector in Bangalore' in this collection.

the establishment of a new regulatory framework for the establishment and maintenance of safe payments for employees and owner drivers arguably represents a move towards a regulatory regime which approaches the issues surrounding vertical disintegration from a network approach, encouraging the establishment of effective comparative fairness standards in the industry as well as effective cross-jurisdictional regulation of commercial contracts.[60] Further, the approach proposed in the Directions Paper suggests decisions made by a tribunal would have a binding effect on employers, employees, owner drivers, clients and other industry participants across the Australian road transport industry, and would bind industry participants across the supply chain.

Opponents of the NTC proposals cite the possible negative effects on competition and resultant increases in prices to the consumer as grounds for rejecting regulatory intervention. In their submission to the Review, the Australian Trucking Association (ATA) stated (amongst other things) that the implementation of a 'safe rates' regime would:[61]

(a) impose substantial additional costs;
(b) adversely impact on the wider economy due to the price sensitivity of customers to transport costs;
(c) not account for the highly variable nature of the freight task;
(d) impinge on commercial operations' freedom and flexibility to innovate and evolve and set rates accordingly;
(e) lead to many non-complying operators possibly discounting from the 'Safe Rate' to win or retain business; and
(f) possibly act as an incentive for drivers to drive longer, faster and heavier.

The ATA argued that existing safety and regulatory mechanisms adequately protect the interests of owner drivers, and that government should only interfere in commercial operations where there has been a clear and significant market failure, and where there is a clear and demonstrable requirement to do so.[62] The Review rejected these arguments, and found that 'the evidence indicates that the transport industry will remain intensely competitive even following the setting of minimum rates for owner/drivers and more vigorous implementation of employee driver entitlements'.[63] Any increase in the

---

[60] See, eg, Nossar, I, 'Cross Jurisdictional Regulation of Commercial Contracts for Work Beyond the Traditional Relationship' in C Arup *et al* (eds), *Labour Law and Labour Market Regulation* (Sydney, Federation Press, 2006) 203–9.

[61] ATA, *Submission to the National Transport Commission in Regards to the Safe Payments Inquiry 2008* (Canberra, ATA, 2008) 3–11, available at: www.atatruck.net.au/policies_submissions.html.

[62] *Ibid*, at 10.

[63] Quinlan and Wright, above n 1, at 51.

price of transport services would necessarily reflect a functioning market rate and therefore promote healthy competition by eliminating economic rewards and incentives to operators and clients gaining a competitive advantage through illegal and unsafe work practices. Proper regulatory measures would prevent the type of non-compliance envisaged by the ATA, and promote sustainable prices for transport services.

The reliance of transport companies on utilitarian free-market arguments to oppose regulation is perhaps predictable, but a notable submission made by the ATA pointed to wider supply-chain problems underlying the 'competitive' reduction of rates, or 'race to the bottom'. The ATA submitted that customers assess the going market rate and use this as a ceiling from which they demand substantial discounts.[64] Collins' desire for a 'network' concept to determine comparative fairness standards is based on the existence of 'intense co-ordination and cooperation between employing entities without the need to demonstrate that one effectively dominates the other'.[65] The ATA's submission justifies the approach adopted by the Review to remove the competitive advantage for customers of transport companies and owner drivers which is maintained by the cutting of labour costs and adoption of unsafe work practices. In regulating commercial arrangements involving the use of heavy vehicles by all contracting parties in the transport and retail supply chains, the government is inevitably confronted with the allegation that it is creating distortions in the market, thereby negatively affecting the competitive movement of prices. Perhaps this freely functioning movement in price is the exact root of the problems identified in the Review? The NTC Report to the ATC noted the submission of the TWU which stated that 'the power accrued by the mass amount of transport movements creates a hyper-competitive market for transport services. Major transport users no longer maintain their own fleets. They contract out the transport function on a cost-competitive basis'.[66] Neo-liberal economists would argue that the market should be allowed to achieve equilibrium through the movement in price and the balancing of demand and supply, without regulatory barriers. However, they would also recognise that where market failure occurs through the inability of prices to move to a sustainable rate, regulatory intervention is not only justified but required. According to Collins, comparative fairness standards do not rely on market failure or some kind of imperfect information to exist in order to justify intervention.[67]

---

[64] ATA, above n 61, at 10.
[65] Collins, above n 3, at 336.
[66] NTC, above n 10, at 24.
[67] Collins, above n 3, at 322.

CONCLUSION

The significant difference between the Review recommendation of a mandatory minimum rate for owner drivers and employees and the ODFCA model is that by recommending a mandatory structure with minimum prescribed remuneration, the Review has recognised the limited capacity of commercial law to remedy inequality of bargaining power for owner drivers across federal and State jurisdictions in Australia. Whilst remedial legislation has a useful role, it does not have a sufficient deterrent effect to provide the economic structural reform required to ensure safety in the systems of remuneration adopted in the transport industry. The adoption of a mandatory minimum safe rates scheme for employees and owner drivers would establish a comparative fairness standard based on a network principle as envisaged by Collins. This approach may be usefully adopted in other areas where multi-tiered subcontracting has detrimental effects on labour standards.

POSTSCRIPT

The Road Safety Remuneration Act 2011 was passed into law by the Australian Parliament on 20 March 2012 and will come into effect on 1 July 2012.

8

Organising Independent Contractors: The Impact of Competition Law

SHAE MCCRYSTAL

INTRODUCTION

IN THE INTRODUCTORY chapter to this collection, Judy Fudge defines commercialisation as the breakdown of the boundary between commercial activities and employment.[1] Across the developed world, the vertical disintegration of firms and the breakdown of internal labour markets have impacted on production processes and the manner in which workers are engaged. Work tasks that were once core activities performed by insider employees are increasingly being constructed as peripheral; the work is offered instead on the services market to outsider enterprises, not uncommonly self-employed workers. The engagement of such workers in a commercial rather than employment context challenges the traditional divide between labour and commercial regulation.

In common with many countries, the Australian legal system has struggled with the task of distinguishing between genuinely self-employed 'entrepreneurial' workers (independent contractors) and workers engaged predominantly in pursuing the business interests of others (employees). Workers who are characterised as employees in Australia fall within mainstream labour law regulation, while independent contractors are generally regulated in the commercial realm. The tests for distinguishing between employees and independent contractors remain relatively easy to manipulate,[2] facilitating the capacity of large businesses to shift many of the costs and risks associated with doing business onto external independent contractors. These workers often bear the hallmarks of those in the middle group identified

---

[1] Fudge, J, 'Blurring Legal Boundaries: Regulating for Decent Work' in this collection.

[2] Stewart, A, 'Redefining Employment? Meeting the Challenge of Contract and Agency Labour' (2002) 15 *Australian Journal of Labour Law* 235. As to the problem generally, see Davidov, G, 'Freelancers: An Intermediate Group in Labour Law?' in this collection.

by Judy Fudge.[3] They own some capital and have some control over their work processes. However, their working arrangements are characterised by risk: of illness, lack of work and lack of bargaining power.

A group of workers in Australia who fit this pattern are mail transport and delivery workers contracted to the national postal provider, Australia Post (AP). They own their own transportation, competitively tender for mail contracts and enjoy limited autonomy in their work on a daily basis. However, they are placed under onerous contractual obligations, bear considerable risk and may receive remuneration rates that are substantially below those received by equivalent employed workers. As independent contractors they are denied the protections available under Australian labour laws, but they have limited opportunities to enjoy the benefits of entrepreneurship.

The focus of this Chapter is to explore the capacity of collective bargaining frameworks in Australia 'to protect the dignity of these workers, promote their self-determination, and protect them against social risks'.[4] There are two frameworks to consider for this purpose: employee bargaining under the federal Fair Work Act 2009 (FW Act) and independent contractor bargaining under the federal Competition and Consumer Act 2010 (CC Act). This second option involves Australian competition law and provides a useful illustration of the pitfalls of using a competition-based regulatory approach to govern access to collective bargaining.

The discussion will briefly review the use of independent contractors at AP, before examining the circumstances of a particular AP independent contractor. The discussion will then consider whether or not employee collective bargaining has any role to play in protecting working conditions of independent contractors, before examining the process under the CC Act which may permit collective action by independent contractors who are otherwise treated as competitors under the Act.

INDEPENDENT CONTRACTORS AT AUSTRALIA POST

Australia Post (AP) is a government business enterprise established under the Australian Postal Corporation Act 1989 (Cth) as a body corporate wholly owned by the Australian Government. Its principal function is to supply postal services within Australia, and between Australia and other countries, and it has a limited monopoly on the collection, carriage and delivery of standard letters within Australia.[5]

[3] Fudge, above n 1.
[4] *Ibid.*
[5] Australian Postal Corporation Act 1989 (Cth) (Cth refers to the Commonwealth or federal jurisdiction in Australia as opposed to the States and Territories) ss 14–19, 27, 29–30.

'Self-employed' mail delivery workers (independent contractors) have been a continuous feature of the postal service workforce in Australia. In colonial Australia, post offices used independent contractors to assist with a range of activities including the laying of telegraph cables and the transportation of mail.[6] After Federation (1901), independent contractors were used for the management of non-official post offices and for mail transportation, particularly in rural and remote areas where the amount of business transacted did not justify the use of full-time employees.[7]

In 1975 the corporatisation of mail services in Australia began when the Postmaster-General's Department was disbanded and the employees and independent contractors engaged by the former department were split between the newly formed Australian Postal Commission and the Australian Telecommunications Commission. AP subsequently came under political pressure to operate on a commercial basis by reducing costs, returning a profit to its government owners and increasing the use of independent contractors.[8]

The degree of engagement of independent contractors by AP since 1975 in connection with mail transportation and delivery has been varied.[9] Statistics can be gleaned from AP Annual Reports from 1975 to 2010.[10] After 1975, the use of independent contractors for mail transportation and delivery declined from 4,441 independent contractors in 1976 to a low of 3,269 in 1991. However, by 2002, the use of independent contractors had increased to 5,613 mail contracts. From 2002 to the present day, the number of mail contracts has remained steady, fluctuating between 5,462 contracts in 2003 and 5,086 in 2010. It is difficult to ascertain exactly what proportion of the total AP workforce (including independent contractors) is represented by these figures. The method of reporting the use of independent contractors in connection with mail transport and delivery changed in the 1997–1998 Annual Report. Previously, the Reports had simply listed numbers of independent contractors. In 1998 (and in all later reports), the statistics listed the number of contracts in place, rather than the number of individual contractors. However, the change may not have been all that significant in practice, as the 1996–1997 Report listed 4,741 independent contractors and the 1997–1998 Report, using the new method, listed 4,924 contracts.

---

[6] McIntosh, K, Shauness, J and Wettenhall, R, *Contracting Out in Australia: An Indicative History* (Canberra, Centre for Research in Public Sector Management, University of Canberra, 1997).

[7] *Ibid.*

[8] Gerritson, R, *Deregulating Australia Post: Another Attack on Regional Australia*, ACRLGS Monographs in Applied Policy No 1 (Canberra, University of Canberra, 1998); Plowman, D, *Industrial Relations in an Australian Public Corporation: the Case of Australia Post* (Working Paper No 57, Department of Industrial Relations, University of New South Wales, Kensington, 1984).

[9] There are a significant number of workers in non-official post offices who are not employed by AP but they are outside the scope of this study.

[10] Australia Post, *Annual Reports* (Canberra, Commonwealth of Australia, 1976–2010).

On the numbers provided within AP Annual Reports we can roughly estimate that mail transport and delivery independent contractors represented about 8–9 per cent of the total AP workforce from 1975 until the early 1990s, and since then has represented around 12–13 percent of the workforce. This has coincided with a substantial increase in part-time employment. While total numbers employed by AP have remained steady, the part-time workforce has increased from approximately 7 per cent in 1976 to 29 per cent in 2010. This means that the relative amount of work independent contractors carry out at AP compared with the employed labour force appears to have significantly increased.

These increases in numbers of independent contractors and the extent of work that they are responsible for have attracted the attention of trade unions which represent AP employees. The industrial tactics undertaken in response to the increased engagement of independent contractors will be discussed below. However, first it is helpful to examine the circumstances under which individual AP independent contractors are engaged in order to identify the degree to which these workers are in need of regulatory assistance. In a study of rural mail delivery contractors in Canada, Cranford *et al* demonstrated that Canada Post delivery contractors had almost no bargaining power, tended to rely on mail delivery contracts as their primary source of income and were subject to Canada Post's power to dictate terms.[11] While I was unable to locate information of this kind with respect to the bulk of AP mail transport and delivery independent contractors, the following case study suggests that AP independent contractors' experiences are similar to their Canadian counterparts.

CASE STUDY: CONTRACTED MAIL SERVICES
IN BALLINA, NEW SOUTH WALES (NSW)

In the limited literature available concerning industrial relations at AP, the working conditions of mail transport and delivery contractors are not discussed.[12] However, a decision of the NSW Industrial Court in *Cartaar v Australia Post* (*Cartaar*),[13] which examined an allegation that certain contracts issued by AP were unfair, provides a useful case study of the position of an individual AP independent contractor. This information has been

---

[11] Cranford, C *et al*, *Self-Employed Workers Organize: Law Policy and Unions* (Montreal, McGill-Queen's University Press, 2005) ch 2.

[12] See generally Baird, M and Lansbury, R, 'Workplace Change and Enterprise Bargaining at Australia Post' in D Mortimer, P Leece and R Morris (eds), *Readings in Contemporary Employment Relations* (Nepean, Centre for Employment Relations, University of Western Sydney, 1997) 427; Plowman, above n 8; Preiss, B, 'Enterprise Bargaining in the Public Sector' (1994) 53 *Australian Journal of Public Administration* 348.

[13] *Cartaar v Australia Post* [2009] NSWIRComm 186 (*Cartaar*).

supplemented by reference to publicly available AP tender documents which include a sample standard form contract and lengthy information on tender preparation including costing, equipment requirements and work rules.

In early 2001, AP called for tenders for three five-year postal service contracts in and around Ballina on the North Coast of NSW. Contract one was for clearing street post boxes (estimated at 7.5 hours weekly; costed per hour), contract two was for shuttling mail between the local mail delivery centre and the local post office (estimated at 6.75 hours weekly; costed per hour) and contract three was for sorting and delivering parcels in the Ballina area (estimated at 17 hours weekly; costed per delivery). Contracts one and three were awarded to one person and contract two was awarded to a second person. However, by August 2002, all three contracts had been assigned, with the permission of AP, to Gregory Cartaar, who had purchased the contracts from the original tenderers for a combined total of $18,500.

Since Mr Cartaar was not the original tenderer, the facts of the case do not reveal if the contracts were awarded at the tendered price or at a price set by AP after receiving the tenders. However, the price set for each contract reflected an AP costing formula which took into account the estimated number of hours of work (or deliveries), transport costs (fuel and vehicle depreciation) and labour costs. Important features of the contracts included:

— the person undertaking the work was expressly identified as an independent contractor;
— the provision by the independent contractor of a light commercial vehicle to standards approved by AP and a back-up vehicle with second driver for heavy periods (contract two);
— the ability to subcontract or assign the contract only with the permission of AP;
— goodwill generated by the performance of the contract belonged to AP;
— the capacity to delegate work;
— unilateral variation of the service and performance requirements under the contract by AP;
— adjustment of the contract fee to take into account increased labour, fuel and vehicle operating costs; and
— a dispute resolution term providing for arbitration at a cost to be shared between the parties.

The full terms of the actual contracts assigned to Mr Cartaar were not revealed in the reported case. However, the sample standard form contract provided in AP tendering documents contains extensive terms that demonstrate how difficult it is for AP independent contractors to develop their own business out of contracting to AP.[14] The standard contract removes

---

[14] *Mail Contractor Agreement*, version 1.0 (December 2009).

any obligation on AP to guarantee that any services will actually be required; shifts all costs associated with the contract onto the independent contractor; assigns to AP all intellectual property that relates to the services created by the independent contractor during the contract period; imposes 100 per cent performance requirements (breach of which gives rise to a right to terminate); allows AP to require the independent contractor to wear AP attire and display AP signage; and imposes a six-month post-contract restraint period in respect of similar services.

It is not possible to ascertain if all independent contractors accept the range of terms set out in the standard contract. The tender documents encourage tenderers to obtain legal and financial advice before submitting a tender. However, unless tendering parties are well-resourced entities, tendering for a range of contracts, it seems likely that AP exercises a considerable degree of power in the blind competitive tendering process, and would have strong capacity to dictate terms. All three contracts in *Cartaar*, although originally entered into by two different individuals, contained identical standard terms, only differing as to the service requirements under each contract.

In November 2002, Mr Cartaar raised a dispute with AP. He claimed that the amount allowed for the cost of labour under the contracts was less than an employee would receive under relevant industrial instruments for performing the same work. Further, he argued that it took longer to deliver the services under the contracts than the contract rates provided for, partially due to increases in the size of the areas serviced under the contracts. AP and Mr Cartaar remained in dispute from November 2002 to June 2006. AP recosted and relogged the contract work; however, Mr Cartaar disagreed with the revised offers made during the life of the contract. The contract dispute resolution process was activated, but no resolution was forthcoming. Mr Cartaar withdrew from the process when his half of the arbitration costs had reached $7,500. Further, when Mr Cartaar sought to reassign his contracts in February 2004 (selling the remaining terms), AP informed a prospective purchaser that if they took the contracts on, permission to reassign the contracts would be refused. This effectively denied Mr Cartaar the capacity to sell the mail contracts, even though he himself had paid $18,500 for them and AP had not objected. In June 2006 the three contracts came to an end and Mr Cartaar unsuccessfully tendered for two new amalgamated contracts providing substantially identical services.

Mr Cartaar initiated action in the NSW Industrial Court in 2005 under legislation specific to NSW that, at the time of the case, allowed any person engaged under a contract to perform work in any industry to seek review of the substantive fairness of the contract.[15] Mr Cartaar alleged that the

---

[15] Industrial Relations Act 1996 (NSW) s 106; See generally Riley, J, 'Regulating for Fair Dealing in Work Contracts: A New South Wales Approach' (2007) 36 *Industrial Law Journal* 19.

remuneration under the contract was unfair and that AP had acted unfairly in unilaterally departing from its earlier practice with respect to assignment of mail contracts. Judgment in Mr Cartaar's favour on these points was handed down in November 2009, seven years after Mr Cartaar had initially raised the dispute with AP.

The remuneration aspect of the case is illuminating. Under the three contracts, Mr Cartaar was contracted for a total of 31.25 hours per week. The court accepted (based on Mr Cartaar's evidence and evidence adduced by AP concerning the 'relogging' of the jobs) that the average time taken to perform all duties under the three contracts was 44 hours per week. In considering whether or not the remuneration Mr Cartaar received was fair, the court determined the rate of profit earned by Mr Cartaar each year calculated by assessing the amount of money actually received by Mr Cartaar, less his expenses (not including a price for his labour). The court then assessed the difference between the profit and the hourly rate a full-time employee would have been paid for the same work under relevant industrial instruments. The court determined that, compared to the amount Mr Cartaar would have received had he been employed by AP, Mr Cartaar was underpaid by an average of $15,862.50 per year over the four years he held the contracts (a total amount of $63,450). This amount was arrived at both on the basis that the contract required more hours than it was costed at, and that the rate allowed for labour under the contract was less than the rate required to be paid to a comparable employee performing the same work. To put this in context, from July 2005 to June 2006, Mr Cartaar earned an average of $446.55 per week for 44 hours. At the time the Federal minimum wage (which is less than Mr Cartaar would have received had he been employed) for a full-time 38-hour week by an unskilled employee was $484.40.[16]

If the contractual arrangements of Mr Cartaar are not atypical, this suggests that mail transport and delivery contractors engaged by AP resemble the workers discussed by Judy Fudge in Chapter 1 of this collection. They own some capital (vehicles for mail delivery) and exercise minimal control (work can be delegated), but otherwise shoulder all the risks associated with their working arrangements, have very little bargaining power and virtually no opportunity to create any form of goodwill or saleable assets in the course of their work.[17] Ultimately Mr Cartaar was able to access a

---

[16] *Safety Net Review—Wages June 2005* (2005) 142 IR 1. Notably, an award-covered employee would also have been entitled to overtime wage rates for the additional six hours per week, significantly increasing the disparity.

[17] This is also true of the workers described in this collection by Riley (franchisees) and Johnson (truck owner drivers); see Riley, J, 'A Blurred Boundary Between Entrepreneurship and Servitude: Regulating Business Format Franchising in Australia' in this collection; Johnson, B, 'Developing Legislative Protection for Owner Drivers in Australia: The Long Road to Regulatory Best Practice' in this collection.

legal remedy to address his complaints of substantive unfairness. However, this took more than seven years, involved lengthy litigation and was an individual determination which had no effect on the contracts of other AP independent contractors. Further, the legislation under which Mr Cartaar brought his action no longer applies to the great majority of independent contracts entered into in Australia.[18] Instead, the federal Independent Contractors Act 2005 (Cth) (IC Act) applies. While the IC Act has an unfair contracts jurisdiction, the assessment of fairness is expressly limited to the terms of the contract at the date of entry into the agreement.[19] In *Cartaar*, the court specifically found that the contracts created by AP were 'fair' at inception and only became unfair over the course of their operation.[20] If Mr Cartaar had commenced his action 12 months later, he would have been unlikely to obtain a remedy.

The Chapter will now consider the potential for collective bargaining frameworks to allow independent contractors like Mr Cartaar to have meaningful input into their pay and working conditions. The discussion will consider action by employees engaged by AP to improve the working conditions of mail contractors and whether or not the independent contractors themselves can collectively bargain with AP.

COLLECTIVE ACTION BY EMPLOYEES OF AUSTRALIA POST

The Cranford *et al* study of the efforts of Canadian rural route mail contractors to collectivise and bargain with Canada Post details a difficult and lengthy organising campaign which ultimately succeeded in part because of 'the resolve of a majority of the rural and suburban mail couriers to join the union combined with the union's willingness to strike over the status of those members'.[21] The involvement of Canada Post employees and the potential use of the strike weapon by those employees were critical to the campaign's success. This raises the question in the Australian context of whether the unions representing AP employees could exercise lawfully their industrial power over the status or working conditions of AP independent contractors.

Collective bargaining and industrial action by most employees in Australia is regulated by the FW Act. Employers and employees may enter into collective agreements over matters which genuinely pertain to the relationship

---

[18] In 2005, the application of State-based unfair contracts jurisdictions was almost entirely abolished by the Independent Contractors Act 2005 (Cth). See further Riley, above n 15.

[19] Independent Contractors Act 2005 (Cth) s 12(3).

[20] *Cartaar*, above n 13, at para [123]. This finding reflects the potential for bureaucratic power imbalance to develop in long-term work contracts as demonstrated by Collins; see Collins, H, 'Market Power, Bureaucratic Power, and the Contract of Employment' (1986) 15 *Industrial Law Journal* 1.

[21] Cranford *et al*, above n 11, at 95.

between the employer and employees to be covered by the agreement, and the relationship between the employer and any union to be covered by the agreement (the 'genuinely pertains' requirement).[22] Lawful strike action is permitted during negotiations, to support claims in bargaining. Unions act in this process as bargaining representatives of their members.[23]

The 'genuinely pertains' requirement restricts the matters that unions can pursue through legally enforceable agreement making and lawful strike action.[24] Matters in collective agreements that do not genuinely pertain are not enforceable and lawful strike action cannot be taken to support non-permitted matters.[25] Disputes over this issue are usually played out in the context of union applications to the federal industrial tribunal Fair Work Australia (FWA) for strike ballots, a necessary prerequisite to lawful strike action.[26] FWA will not order a ballot unless the applicant reasonably believes that the claims they are making meet the 'genuinely pertains' requirement.[27]

The use of independent contractors by AP is a concern for unions representing AP employees. Unsurprisingly, their primary focus is the potential for AP's use of independent contractors to undermine the job security and working conditions of the employed postal workforce. Postal services are labour-intensive and however automated mail-sorting services become, mail needs to be transported and delivered. Reducing the cost of labour (as opposed to the fixed costs of vehicles, petrol and maintenance) is, as the *Cartaar* case demonstrates, one of the few areas in which you can reduce the cost of delivering the mail.

From 2006 to 2010, AP was in negotiations for a new collective agreement. The preceding collective agreements had contained clauses in which AP had acknowledged that the use of independent contractors could 'impact on opportunities for employees and agree that such arrangements will not be used unless there are sound business reasons for doing so including appropriate consideration of the use of Post's employees'.[28] A major sticking point in the negotiations for a new agreement were claims by the Communications, Electrical, Electronic, Energy, Information,

---

[22] Fair Work Act 2009 (Cth) s 172.

[23] See generally Cooper, R and Ellem, B, 'Fair Work and the Re-regulation of Collective Bargaining' (2009) 22 *Australian Journal of Labour Law* 284; Creighton, B and Forsyth, A (eds), *Rediscovering Collective Bargaining: Australia's Fair Work Act in International Perspective* (forthcoming, Routledge).

[24] Unions and employers can enter into agreements outside of the collective bargaining framework but such an approach is fraught with legal difficulties; see generally Stewart, A and Riley, J, 'Working around Work Choices: Collective Bargaining and the Common Law' (2007) 31 *Melbourne University Law Review* 903.

[25] Fair Work Act 2009 (Cth) s 253.

[26] Fair Work Act 2009 (Cth) s 409(2).

[27] *Australian Postal Corporation v CEPU* [2010] FWAFB 344. See generally McCrystal, S, *The Right to Strike in Australia* (Federation Press, Sydney, 2010) ch 7.

[28] *Australia Post Enterprise Agreement 2001*, AG812967, cl 6.3; *Australia Post Enterprise Agreement 2004–2006*, cl 6.26.

Postal, Plumbing and Allied Services Union of Australia (CEPU) to include provisions imposing restrictions on the capacity of AP to engage independent contractors. Between August 2009 and January 2010, CEPU brought a number of applications to FWA seeking strike ballots, all of which were opposed by AP on the grounds that CEPU's independent contractor claims did not meet the 'genuinely pertains' requirement.

The status of union claims concerning the capacity of employers to hire independent contractors is a contentious area. The engagement of independent contractors has the capacity to undermine employee working conditions and job security and thus could arguably be a matter that 'pertains' to the employment relationship. However, the Federal Court has held that provisions which restrict or qualify an employer's right to use independent contractors are not matters that genuinely pertain to the relationship between an employer and employees because they are not sufficiently related to the employment relationship.[29] In the AP negotiations, CEPU initially sought to stop all new AP use of independent contracts during the life of the agreement, along with a guarantee that all existing independent contracts would be gradually brought in-house.[30] Over the course of negotiations these claims were whittled back to a claim for a term in the agreement acknowledging that the use of independent contractors can threaten the employment conditions of existing staff, a requirement for independent contractors to undergo similar training to employees, and a claim that where independent contractors perform work that is comparable to the work of AP employees, they will receive the same pay, conditions and working arrangements as AP employees.[31] The third claim, if permissible, may enable employees to take strike action to ensure that independent contractors receive 'at least' the same working conditions as comparable employees. While it appears to be a term which 'qualifies' an employer's capacity to engage independent contractors, these clauses have been permitted where they do not result in independent contractors costing an employer more than a comparable employee. This has been accepted by the federal tribunal on the basis that such claims seek to protect the conditions of the employed workforce.[32] In 2010 a new collective agreement was reached at AP.[33] In the agreement AP acknowledged that the use of independent contractors can impact on the employment relationship, agreed not

---

[29] *Wesfarmers Premier Coal Ltd v AMWU (No 2)* (2004) 138 IR 362.

[30] *Australian Postal Corporation v CEPU* [2009] FWAFB 599.

[31] *CEPU v Australian Postal Corporation v CEPU* [2009] FWA 998.

[32] See, eg, *Re Schefenacker Vision Systems Australia Pty Ltd, AWU, AMWU Certified Agreement 2004* (2004) AIRC PR952801, 28 October; *TWU v National Transport Operations Pty Ltd* (2003) 121 IR 399. In the dispute under discussion, a Full Bench of FWA in *Australian Postal Corporation v CEPU* (2010) FWAFB 344 found that CEPU had a 'reasonable belief' that the claim did genuinely pertain and thus was entitled to a strike ballot.

[33] *Australia Post Fair Work Agreement 2010*, AE881694.

to use independent contractors to pursue reductions in wages or conditions for employees and agreed to consult on the use of independent contractors in future.[34] However, AP did not agree to guarantee that wages and conditions of independent contractors would equal those provided for equivalent employees under the agreement.

The implication of these restrictions on union access to collective bargaining and strike action under the FW Act is that a union campaign utilising the strength of the employee workforce, similar to the campaign in Canada, would be fraught with difficulties in Australia. CEPU's campaign demonstrates the obstacles faced by any union trying to guarantee the working conditions of independent contractors by utilising employee pressure. The FW Act specifically inhibits the capacity of employees to use industrial pressure to impact on employer decisions concerning how it engages its workforce or over the status of those workers. While unions and employees may be able to use industrial pressure to seek terms in enterprise agreements which ensure that independent contractors performing comparable work are treated in a comparable manner, in practice such clauses may be relatively easily avoided by ensuring that there are no comparable employees, or that the work itself is not comparable. For example, in *Cartaar*, AP asserted that there were not, nor were there ever, any employees of AP performing the same duties as Mr Cartaar.[35] Further, such clauses would be unenforceable by the independent contractors themselves who would not be covered by the agreement.

COLLECTIVE ACTION BY AUSTRALIA POST MAIL CONTRACTORS

The preceding discussion demonstrates that in Australia it is difficult for employees to take action in support of the working conditions of independent contractors, even where they are engaged by the same entity. However, it may be possible for independent contractors, on their own or with the assistance of a union, to organise and bargain on their own behalf.

Independent contractors in Australia are subject to a variety of different legislative regimes, which, for the most part, treat them as commercial enterprises. They are guaranteed the bare right to associate (or not associate);[36] have access to protections against unconscionable, misleading and deceptive conduct in the process of making a contract;[37] and a limited unfair contracts regime to challenge the substantive fairness of a contractual bargain as originally made.[38] However, they are not protected if they engage

---

[34] *Ibid*, at cl 7.9.
[35] *Cartaar*, above n 13, at [57].
[36] This right is protected by the general protections in the Fair Work Act 2009 (Cth).
[37] Competition and Consumer Act 2010 (Cth).
[38] Independent Contractors Act 2005 (Cth).

in collective bargaining.[39] Leaving aside potential common law liability,[40] collective negotiations or action by independent contractors is likely to breach the CC Act.[41] Part IV of the CC Act governs anti-competitive conduct, rendering collusion and combination by competitors unlawful on the basis that it is 'anti-competitive' in effect. Collective conduct by competitors will be unlawful if it constitutes a collective boycott, price fixing or has the effect of 'substantially lessening competition'.[42] Collective boycotts and price fixing are outlawed; any conduct of this kind is unlawful and deemed to be inherently anti-competitive in effect. Contracts, arrangements or understandings that do not constitute a collective boycott or price fixing will only be unlawful if it is shown that they are actually anti-competitive in effect.

If AP independent contractors sought to bargain with AP as a collective over the price of their contracts or if they acted collusively in the competitive tendering process, they would almost certainly be found to have engaged in price fixing. If they collectively refuse to submit tenders or to perform their existing arrangements, they may be found to have committed a collective boycott. Attempts to engage in collective negotiations over contract terms or the tendering process where price is not involved could constitute conduct which substantially lessens competition between the members of the collective.

The CC Act allows parties to seek permission from the competition regulator, the Australian Competition and Consumer Commission (ACCC), to engage in behaviour which would otherwise breach the prohibitions where they can satisfy the public benefit test. Each application is assessed individually, which can take anywhere from 14 days to six months depending on the circumstances and type of application.[43] These provisions do not provide a right to act in association, but they allow collectives of independent contractors to act free from potential CC Act liability if they can frame their claim in an economic context which competition regulators can accept. The framework requires each specific group of independent contractors to identify market failure reasons to justify their access to collective bargaining. The potential for such arguments to assist in providing a regulatory basis for labour law intervention as a whole (not just limited to independent contractor bargaining) has been raised by scholars including Deakin

---

[39] Exceptions include the Industrial Relations Act 1996 (NSW) ch 6 (drivers of public vehicles and carriers) and the Owner Drivers and Forestry Contractors Act 2005 (Vic).

[40] See generally McCrystal, S, 'Collective Bargaining by Independent Contractors: Challenges from Labour Law' (2007) 20 *Australian Journal of Labour Law* 1.

[41] Under s 51(2)(a) of the Competition and Consumer Act 2010 (Cth), some anti-competitive conduct provisions do not apply to conduct in relation to contracts, arrangements or understandings relating to the remuneration, conditions of employment, hours of work or working conditions of employees to the extent that the provisions relate to employment conditions.

[42] Competition and Consumer Act 2010 (Cth) ss 45(2), 44ZZRD.

[43] See generally McCrystal, S, 'Collective Bargaining and the Trade Practices Act: The Trade Practices Legislation Amendment Act (No 1) 2006 (Cth)' (2007) 20 *Australian Journal of Labour Law* 207.

and Wilkinson,[44] Dickens[45] and Hyde.[46] The CC Act process provides an illustration of the application of these arguments in practice, although it is limited to a strictly competition-based regulatory regime.

The public benefit test, which is the primary legal obstacle under the CC Act to ACCC authorisation of anti-competitive conduct, requires that the applicant demonstrate that any anti-competitive detriment from allowing the proposed conduct is outweighed by the public benefit that will result from the conduct, providing a net public benefit overall.[47] In establishing whether proposed conduct will have a net public benefit, the ACCC establishes the market in which the conduct will take place and assesses the impact of the conduct on that market.[48] Collective bargaining by independent contractors who are otherwise competitors in the market for their services will reduce competitive pressures and price signals which direct resources to their most efficient use.[49] The extent of this anti-competitive detriment will be determined by reference to the degree of existing negotiations in the market, the size of the group relative to the market (density), any existing market power held by the group and the inclusion of any compulsion in the proposal.[50] Any existing market power held by the individuals in the group will produce a high degree of anti-competitive detriment.

Once the level of anti-competitive detriment is established, the ACCC will assess the public benefit that will flow from the proposed conduct. While, in theory, public benefit can be 'anything of value to the community generally', in practice the focus is on efficiency gains that can be made by allowing collective bargaining to occur.[51] Public benefits in this context include arrangements that provide parties with greater input into contracts to enable efficiency gains, transaction cost savings, greater information exchange and the facilitation of new market entrants. Improved industrial relations or increased bargaining power are not considered to be relevant public benefits.[52] Equally, while

---

[44] Deakin, S and Wilkinson, F, 'Labour Law and Economic Theory: A Reappraisal' in H Collins, P Davies and R Rideout (eds), *The Legal Regulation of the Employment Relation* (London, Kluwer Law International, 2000) 29.

[45] Dickens, L, 'Problems of Fit: Changing Employment and Labour Regulation' (2004) 42 *British Journal of Industrial Relations* 595.

[46] Hyde, A, 'What is Labour Law' in G Davidov and B Langille (eds), *Boundaries and Frontiers of Labour Law* (Oxford, Hart Publishing, 2006) 37.

[47] Competition and Consumer Act 2010 (Cth) ss 88, 93AC.

[48] Australian Competition and Consumer Commission (ACCC), *Guide to Collective Bargaining Notifications* (Canberra, Commonwealth Government, 2011).

[49] See, eg, *Draft Objection Notice in respect of a collective bargaining notification lodged by the AMA (Vic) Pty Ltd on behalf of a group of doctors at Werribee Mercy Hospital*, CB00005, Public Register Number C2007/1930, 8 November 2007, para [3.58]; *Assessment: Collective Bargaining Notification lodged by the Australian Newsagents' Federation*, CB00003, Public Register Number C2007/1612, 13 September 2007, para [3.25].

[50] ACCC, above n 48.

[51] *Re Queensland Co-Operative Milling Association* (1976) 8 ALR 481, 510–11.

[52] ACCC, above n 48.

the 'public' to whom the benefits of any efficiency gains can flow includes the proposed participants in the collective bargaining process (eg in the form of increased remuneration or better working conditions), more weight appears to accord to gains that flow to the consuming public.[53]

Where a collective bargaining group can demonstrate net public benefit they will generally be permitted to act collectively. However, the approach taken by the ACCC to requests by independent contractors seeking to engage in collective bargaining suggests that any bargaining which ultimately is authorised may be so diluted in strength that it would have little impact in practice. Requests to engage in collective boycotts will rarely, if ever, be approved. The ACCC considers that collective boycotts involve such a high level of anti-competitive detriment that it is virtually impossible to demonstrate sufficient public benefit to pass the public benefit test.[54] Further, in order to keep the degree of anti-competitive detriment sufficiently low that a net public benefit can be demonstrated, the size of the bargaining group must be kept low relative to the market, and there can be no compulsion involved in the application. This means that no member of the bargaining group, or the target, can be required to agree to, or abide by, the bargained outcome. All parties must be free to continue to negotiate individually.

Two authorisations of collective bargaining by independent contractors demonstrate the limited utility of the provisions. In February 2009 the ACCC authorised collective bargaining arrangements by a group of 24 truck owner drivers who wanted to negotiate collectively with earthmoving contractors in relation to terms, prices and conditions for the supply of earthmoving services.[55] At the time of the application, the bargaining group was subject to standard form contracting arrangements and represented a small proportion of the relevant market. The group was only able to demonstrate limited public benefit (increased input into contracting arrangements) and had to keep their proposed arrangements entirely voluntary (no compulsion of members of the group or the target) in order to gain approval. Even in these circumstances, the ACCC only granted conditional authorisation of the application, requiring the bargaining group to provide the ACCC with regular updates on the number of participating drivers in order to ensure that any bargaining remained purely voluntary and any increase in the size of the group did not allow for coercive conduct. In May 2010, the ACCC authorised proposed collective bargaining arrangements by freelance journalists (independent

---

[53] *Qantas Airways Ltd* [2004] A Comp T 9, paras [183]–[185].

[54] ACCC, above n 48; McCrystal, S, 'Is there a "Public Benefit" in Improving Working Conditions for Independent Contractors? Collective Bargaining and the *Trade Practices Act 1974* (Cth)' (2009) 37 *Federal Law Review* 264.

[55] *Determination, Application for authorisation lodged by CFMEU Qld in respect of collective negotiations by current and future owner drivers with current and future acquirers of earthmoving services in south-east Queensland*, 26 March 2009, Authorisation No A91103, Public Register No C2008/1627.

contractors) with four different media organisations.[56] The bargaining group in this instance was significantly larger (approximately 2,000 freelance journalists), but so were the targets (including Fairfax Media Limited and News Limited). The ACCC authorised collective bargaining, finding that the increased bargaining power of the journalists as a collective could provide greater input into the largely standard-form contracting arrangements used by the media outlets. Further, collective bargaining could reduce the transaction costs experienced by the journalists (but not the media outlets who had already reduced their costs through the use of standard-form contracts) in negotiating as individuals. However, in order to achieve this outcome, the process had to be entirely voluntary such that the news outlets did not have to recognise the collective for the purposes of bargaining, bargain with the collective or actually use any collectively bargained outcome that was reached. Further, the journalists could not engage in coercive conduct to try to force agreement. As the ACCC noted in the authorisation, 'individual freelance journalists will have no choice but to negotiate individually with the targets if that is each target's preference'.[57]

This process does offer AP contractors an opportunity to seek permission to act collectively. If the independent contractors demonstrate low anti-competitive detriment from their proposed conduct (little existing competition in the market, standard form contracts, low bargaining group density) and a net public benefit from increased collective input into contractual terms, a correction of information asymmetry or decreased transaction costs from individual negotiations, the ACCC could permit collective bargaining to proceed. However, given that AP provides a high level of information to contracting parties through the tender document process (reducing information asymmetries) and that the level of existing competition between individual tenderers for AP contracts over contract terms and prices is unknown (suggesting that collective bargaining may have a high anti-competitive detriment), permission to bargain may be difficult to obtain. Further, to achieve permission the proposed bargaining must be entirely voluntary for all parties concerned which means that it only offers a collective solution if AP is willing to participate.

This outcome appears odd from the perspective of labour law regulation in which collective bargaining generally offers employees both increased bargaining power and the opportunity to exercise that power. However, in the logic of competition regulation the outcome conforms to the desire of competition regulators to avoid any interference in competitive markets which increases market power. This tension is illustrated by the ACCC

---

[56] *Determination, Application for Authorisation lodged by MEAA in respect of collective negotiations of the terms of engagement of freelance journalists by Fairfax Media Limited, ACP Magazines Ltd, News Limited and Pacific Magazines*, 26 May 2010, Authorisation No A91204.
[57] *Ibid*, at [4.45].

authorisation with respect to the freelance journalists discussed above. The media outlets opposed the application, arguing that they would not bargain collectively and thus the authorisation would be futile. In response, the ACCC acknowledged that the proposed public benefits from the conduct would only result if collective bargaining actually occurred, but noted that the targets did not have to agree to bargain.[58] The anti-competitive detriment would be too high if the journalists were allowed to compel the media outlets to agree to bargain. This demonstrates the limitation of using a competition framework to empower a disempowered group. For competition regulators, market power through combination is anathema.

CONCLUSION

The case study in this Chapter is an illustration of the ability of firms to outsource and reduce the labour costs and risks of doing business while maintaining a high degree of control over the services provided by independent contractors (even retaining goodwill and public visibility) that was highlighted by Collins.[59] Labour costs represent a substantial element of providing postal services. The use of independent contractors recruited through competitive tendering operates in practice as a way of reducing these costs. Transport and fuel prices are fixed. Reductions in labour costs appear to be one of the only mechanisms available to tenderers to reduce their tender price. In the case of Mr Cartaar, this left him working for less than minimum wage.

The question posed by this Chapter was whether in Australia collective bargaining offers an opportunity for independent contractors to act collectively to improve their working conditions. The discussion demonstrated that the Australian regulatory regimes suffer from multiple failures. The FW Act mechanisms that allow for employees to bargain collectively and exercise coercive power in bargaining cannot be used either by independent contractors or by employees to support independent contractors. The CC Act mechanism that may permit collective bargaining by independent contractors does not allow the exercise of any form of collective or market power. Ultimately this leaves independent contractors in the position of Mr Cartaar without any meaningful way to act collectively in order to influence the price on which they sell their labour or the conditions that apply. This contrasts sharply with the legislative regime applicable to employee collectives. The differing treatment of AP's two labour forces starkly illustrates the contradictions that arise when the contract of employment is used to delineate access to meaningful collective bargaining.

---

[58] *Ibid* at [4.66]–[4.68].
[59] Collins, H, 'Independent Contractors and the Challenge of Vertical Disintegration to Employment Protection Laws' (1990) 10 *Oxford Journal of Legal Studies* 353.

9

Regulation of Dependent Self-employed Workers in Spain: A Regulatory Framework for Informal Work?

JUAN-PABLO LANDA ZAPIRAIN*

INTRODUCTION

S INCE THE BEGINNING of the employment contract in Spain, other regulatory techniques have contributed to the expansion and success of labour law by allowing for a nuanced application of general labour law, which was designed for the worker of the Fordist industrial age, to other employment relations that are different but also in need of protection. It was through this process that special contracts for home-based workers, merchant seamen and domestic workers were born. For example, the special contract for home-based workers has been regulated in Spain since 1926, and has functioned with virtually no changes. This special contract is the regulatory framework for new forms of home-based work, and, specifically, for Spain's many teleworkers.

Until quite recently, Parliament did not see the need for regulatory intervention in the field of independent contractors or self-employed workers, except to guarantee their social protection via a special regime of social security law.[1] These workers were considered to be professionals or artisans who freely contracted with their clients on a balanced and equal footing. Moreover, since there was no legal subordination in their relations, it was not considered appropriate to extend the application of labour law, which applied to subordinate employees.

---

* This chapter was translated into English by Maria Aragón Castiella.
[1] Self-employed workers are covered by the Spanish Social Security Act ('LSS 1994') and the Occupational Health and Safety Rights Act ('LPRL 1995').

In common with other developed countries, Spanish employment relations in the post-Fordist age have involved the rise of new occupations, mainly in the services sector, and of many small businesses (individual enterprises, co-operatives, micro-entrepreneurs or entrepreneurial workers) that do not correspond to liberal professions or traditional jobs. These new occupations are not specifically regulated, and these workers are rarely members of professional associations such as those for traditional workers, which helps explain the move of some of these new workers towards the informal economy.

Another important development in the Spanish labour market is the fragmentation of entrepreneurial activity facilitated by economic globalisation. Often, 'firms pursue flexible forms of labour, as outsourcing and *other forms of subcontracting that offer the prospect of minimising fixed non-wage costs*'.[2] Spanish labour law's answer has been to establish a legal system to determine which entity bears responsibility for the legal obligations owed to employees in the event of outsourcing and subcontracting in order to guarantee workers' rights, and especially to co-ordinate employers' obligations on health and safety at work. The approach taken by Spanish regulators has never been to attempt to regulate subcontracting, and even less to limit it.

The 'informal sector' exists in Spain (an estimated 17 per cent of Spanish GDP),[3] increasing in size during recessionary times such as the present (recent 2011 estimates have put it as high as 21.5 per cent).[4] I believe that the informal sector is the key to understanding why marginalisation and poverty do not appear to have grown exponentially in Spain despite 20.8 per cent unemployment.[5] It is, however, too soon to assert this claim categorically, because local and family networks, public subsidies and social assistance are still effective at preventing generalised social exclusion in some areas. The informal sector in Spain feeds undeclared work, multi-jobs, moonlighting or its co-existence with unemployment subsidies, and social assistance incomes. But its existence is decisive in the functioning of an economic model that needs the informal sector to cushion the social effects of a labour market that is loosely structured and poorly governed.

---

[2] Fudge, J, 'Blurring Legal Boundaries: Regulating for Decent Work' in this collection (emphasis added).
[3] According to the OECD, Spain takes third place after Greece and Italy in the ranking of first-world countries with a shadow economy of 22% of its GDP; see Katsios, S, 'The Shadow Economy and Corruption in Greece' (2006) 1 *South-Eastern Europe Journal of Economics* 61.
[4] Arrazola, M, de Hevia, J, Mauleón, I and Sánchez, R, *Dos ensayos de actualidad sobre la economía española* (Madrid, Fundación de Cajas de Ahorros, 2011), available at: www.funcas.es/Publicaciones/InformacionArticulos/Publicaciones.asp?Id=1697.
[5] Dirección de Coyuntura Estadistica de la Fundación de Cajas de Ahorros (data as at 8 July 2011), available at: www.funcas.es/descargarArchivo.asp?Id=2.

In many cases, the informal economy has grown as a result of the marginalisation of self-employed workers in the face of the lack of a regulatory framework suitable for new paid work, particularly in the services sector. In the absence of clear-cut rules, clients may take advantage of self-employed workers. However, in 2007 the Spanish Parliament passed the Self-Employed Workers Act ('LETA') to regulate economically dependent self-employed workers ('TRADE' in the Spanish acronym, Trabajador Autónomo Económicamente Dependiente).[6] This was complemented in 2009 by a set of Regulations ('RETA').[7]

The passage of the LETA, aimed specifically at regulating economically dependent self-employed workers, provides an opportunity to examine how this form of regulation 'blurs traditional legal boundaries', and, in line with the objectives set by Judy Fudge in Chapter 1 of this collection, it allows us to assess 'the challenge this poses to traditional forms of labour regulation'.[8] Specifically, the question posed in this Chapter is whether the legal approach taken under the LETA and RETA adequately protects the dignity, employment security and social risks of dependent self-employed workers regardless of their especial employment status. The Chapter also stresses the linkages that exist between formal and informal activities. It begins by examining the political and economic context of regulation of economically dependent self-employed workers in Spain, before examining the LETA and RETA in detail. The coverage and scope of the legislation will be explored, as will the underlying justifications for the implementation of the new regulatory scheme. The Chapter will then consider whether or not the legislation has been a success in securing legal protection for economically dependent self-employed workers before concluding with observations on whether or not the Spanish model of regulation offers a template for regulating other forms of informal work in the global economy.

THE POLITICAL AND ECONOMIC CONTEXT OF
REGULATION OF ECONOMICALLY DEPENDENT
SELF-EMPLOYED WORKERS IN SPAIN

The LETA and RETA fall within the legal model of 'sheltering intervention' in the Spanish regulatory framework, which is a form of legal intervention designed to guarantee protection of the weakest party to a labour relationship. To this end, the Spanish Parliament has followed the model enshrined in the Spanish Constitution which provides for Parliament to regulate a set of rights for salaried employees and state employees. These rights are

[6] Law 20/2007 (11 July 2007).
[7] RD 197/2009 (23 February 2009).
[8] Fudge, above n 2.

presently enacted in the Workers' Rights Act 1995 (hereafter referred to as the Workers' Statute), and the State Employees Rights Act 2007.[9]

There are 3,200,000 self-employed workers registered as such in Spain (more than the number of state employees) representing approximately 12 per cent of the total workforce.[10] The LETA mirrors the original mandate of the Spanish Constitution model by establishing a specific set of statutory rights for the self-employed. It represents a comprehensive approach to regulating self-employment, separate and distinct from the regulation of salaried and state employees, enhancing the regulatory autonomy of the self-employed and its particular subgroup, the economically dependent self-employed (hereafter referred to as TRADE).

As discussed by Esther Sánchez Torres,[11] paraphrasing Alain Supiot, there are four concentric circles of labour and social protection, from the smallest circle, labour law for salaried employees which provides the highest degree of protection, to the largest circle of universal and constitutional social rights for all kinds of workers. In Spain, the smallest circle coincides with the protections guaranteed for salaried employees under the Workers' Statute. However, the largest circle applies only partially to the self-employed: it includes the rights to dignity, equality and non-discrimination, together with individual rights to work, but does not include constitutional workers' rights such as collective action and collective bargaining.[12]

From the perspective of the subject of protection, the largest circle is constituted by the system of social protection contained in the Social Security Act 1994, even above the social rights of the Constitution. The Social Security Act covers all workers, and some of its social security benefits cover Spanish citizens and foreign residents irrespective of their employment status. Secondly, the Occupational Health and Safety Rights Act 1995 applies to state employees, salaried employees, and self-employed workers. Thirdly, the Labour Procedure Act 1995 applies to all salaried employees, some state employees (those who have an employment contract with the public administration) and some self-employed (TRADE). Fourthly, the

---

[9] Both Acts have been discussed at length elsewhere: see, eg, Ninet, G and Palacio, V, *Derecho del Trabajo* (Madrid, Aranzadi, 2010); Valverde, M, Sañudo, R and Murcia, G, *Derecho del Trabajo* (Madrid, Tecnos, 2010).

[10] Data from the Spanish Self-Employed Association (ATA), available at: www.autonomos-ata.es.

[11] Sanchez Torres, E, 'The Spanish Law on Dependent Self-Employed Workers: A New Evolution in Labor Law' (2010) 31 *Comparative Labour Law & Policy Journal* 231, 234.

[12] The Spanish Constitution contains the following rights for all kinds of workers: dignity of persons (s 10), equality and no discrimination (s 14), personal and moral integrity and the right to life (s 15), privacy, honour and identity (s 18), freedom of expression and right to truthful information (s 20), assembly (s 21), association (s 22), judicial protection (s 24), education and training (s 27), unionisation (s 28), rights to job search, job security, choice of profession or occupation, to be promoted, to an adequate remuneration (s 35) and the rights to be protected by the public powers against social risks, to health security, to limitation of the working day and to vacations (ss 40, 41, 43, 49, 50).

Act on Trade Union Freedom applies to salaried employees and state employees (with some exceptions, such as the army and the judiciary), but only recognises the freedom to join a trade union for those self-employed workers who do not engage any of their own employees (section 3.1). The self-employed do not enjoy any other union rights, even though the LETA includes collective rights for the self-employed, and the TRADE in particular (freedom of association; 'agreements of professional interest' between unions and employers concerning self-employed workers) and access to the out-of-court institutions of mediation and employment conciliation. Lastly, the Workers' Statute regulates all types of salaried employees and those assimilated to them through special contracts (artists, lawyers practising in legal firms, sportsmen, doctors in training, etc).

Prior to the passage of the LETA through Parliament, the Spanish Government commissioned a report by a group of experts to recommend the best way to regulate self-employment.[13] The LETA is largely based upon the recommendations in this report. The inspiration for the Spanish model came from other European countries, in particular Germany and Italy. It also appears to have been based on European Directives concerning anti-discrimination, health and safety, working days and time off.[14] The Spanish law is closer to the German law than to the Italian law, which is generally credited with being the source of inspiration.[15]

The Spanish regulation mostly mirrors the definition of dependent self-employed found in section 12 of the German Collective Agreement Act of 1974. Two characteristics of the Spanish regulation stem from the German concept of the dependent self-employed: first, economic dependence; and second, being in need of social protection in the manner of a salaried employee. Economic dependence means that the dependent self-employed must provide services to one main client from whom most income is received, even while working for other clients. The essential element in the German regulation that has directly influenced Spanish regulation is the requirement (which has become a condition for the TRADE under the LETA) that a high percentage of the self-employed person's entire income comes from the main client. However, the LETA does not adopt the

---

[13] Valdés Dal-Re F (Dtor) ('Committee of Experts'), 'Un Estatuto para la promoción y tutela del trabajador autónomo', Informe de la Comisión de Expertos (2005) 75 *Documentación Laboral* 117.

[14] *Ibid*.

[15] 'Lavoro Para-Subordinato': Law Vigorelli of 14 July 1959 and the Law of 11 August 1973 reforming the Civil Code, that extends its protection to agents and commercial representatives, among others, and defines the para-subordinate worker as a non-subordinate collaborator that carries out his activity in a personal manner, and in a coordinated and continued form; see Reyna Fernández, S, 'El trabajo autónomo en el modelo social europeo y en el ordenamiento jurídico de la UE en la Estrategia de Lisboa después de 2010: especial referencia al trabjador autónomo dependiente' (2010) 1 *Revista del Ministerio de Trabajo e Inmigración* 109, 116.

second element of the German definition: that whenever the self-employed experience low levels of income, because of lack of empowerment, they need some kind of protection.[16] Indeed, in my opinion, the LETA should also have included this element of 'contractual weakness' in the definition of the concept of TRADE so as to better delimit its scope of application. In this way, the courts would have a clear sign to identify and classify as TRADE many workers that will now depend exclusively on the fulfilment of the formal requirements of the written contract (with all the clauses that the RETA requires, as we will see next), and in particular, on the will of the client to sign it.

Other regulatory characteristics that have also been imported from the German model are the adjudication by employment courts of disputes concerning the relationship with the client, and the requirement that the TRADE does not employ salaried employees or subcontract part of the activity.

ESSENTIAL ELEMENTS OF THE LEGAL CONCEPT OF TRADE

Under s 1 of the LETA, a self-employed worker is any natural person who habitually and personally carries out a for-profit economic or professional activity on their own account and is not managed and organised by another person, regardless of whether or not the self-employed worker hires a third party.[17]

An economically dependent self-employed worker (TRADE) refers to self-employed workers who habitually and personally carry out for-profit economic or professional activities directly and predominantly for a physical or legal person, called a client, on whom they depend economically, with at least 75 per cent of their income deriving from their economic and professional services (s 11 LETA).

Moreover, the TRADE must meet all of the following conditions set by the LETA:

(a) not have any salaried workers in their charge, nor contract out or subcontract the activity to third parties;
(b) not carry out work that is identical to the services rendered by salaried workers contracted by the client;
(c) have their own productive infrastructure and the materials needed to carry out their activities independently of the client's infrastructure and materials;

---

[16] Sorge, S, 'German Law on Dependent Self-Employed Workers: A Comparison to the Current Situation Under Spanish Law' (2010) 31 *Comparative Labour Law & Policy Journal* 249, at 249.
[17] Sánchez Torres, above n 11, at 235.

(d) carry out their activity using their own organisational criteria without prejudice to the technical indications they may receive from their client; and

(e) receive valuable consideration depending on the result of their activity in accordance with the contract with the client and at their own risk (s 11.2 LETA).[18]

From a formal point of view, to fall within the definition of TRADE it is necessary for the worker to have a written contract with the main client, whereby both parties agree to abide by the above conditions, and to file a copy of the contract with the National Public Service of Employment. Section 5 of the RETA sets out a long list of 10 specific clauses that must be contained in the written contract. Some must be jointly signed by the parties; others can be declared to have been met by the TRADE. The rigidity of this written contract has the purpose of ensuring its fair use and limiting it to those who are truly economically dependent self-employed, in order to avoid fraud and abuse by the client. However, this requirement may also be the reason for the lack of use of this model in practice. I will expand on these considerations at the end of the Chapter.

One difficulty dealt with in the RETA is the method for calculating the requirement that 75 per cent of income must derive from the main client. Section 2 of RETA states that: 'income from the client with whom the self-employed has a relationship will include all types of income, monetary or in kind, deriving from the economic or professional activity carried out for profit on his own account'. The problem lies in quantifying the 75 per cent of the total income of the TRADE. The RETA attempts to clarify this by stating that: 'said income will be calculated exclusively in relation to the total income derived from economic or professional activities carried out on his own account for all clients ... as well as income derived from salaried employment ... excluding capital income or capital gains, and income derived from the sale of assets employed in its economic activities' (s 2.1 RETA).

Calculating income is left to the TRADE, who swears to its truth when signing a contract with a client. However, as Sánchez argues, the formula to establish economic dependence cannot always be used by the TRADE, since many such workers do not have regular contact with the Inland Revenue.[19] Indeed, the only method of proof mentioned by the RETA (although it does not exclude other methods, it does not specify which) and considered valid is 'the last income tax return, or an income statement from the State Tax Office' (s 2.4 RETA).

---

[18] *Ibid* at 236–7.
[19] *Ibid* at 237.

Transitional sections 2 and 3 of the LETA set out fixed time periods for existing TRADE to sign written contracts with their clients, unless the client chooses to terminate the contract. These transitional provisions were, effectively, an invitation for clients not to assume the obligations of the LETA. Indeed, the transitional time period gave clients the option to try to avoid the application of the LETA, by terminating existing civil, commercial or administrative contracts.[20] If they did not terminate their existing arrangements, clients became bound by the new obligations set out in the LETA at the end of the transitional period (especially by s 15 on termination causes). The LETA has been fully in force since September 2009, except with respect to commercial and transport agents for whom entry into force was August 2010.

The transitional provisions were predicated on freedom of contract as the ruling principle, which raises doubt over the application of the LETA in the future, given the problem of express or implied consent, not just on the part of the TRADE, but also on the part of the client. At the end of the transitional period, the LETA took effect and clients became subject to the obligations under the LETA with respect to salary, working time, time off and damages upon termination. In return, clients now enjoy more legal certainty in their contractual relationships with the TRADE. This is because they can avoid a finding that the worker is in fact engaged under an employment contract under the legal presumption in section 8.1 of the Workers' Statute which otherwise applies whenever the supposedly autonomous nature of the self-employed worker is proved to be false.

THE SCOPE OF LEGAL PROTECTION UNDER THE LETA

The new written contract between the TRADE and the main client regulated by the LETA does not alter the civil, commercial, or administrative nature of the relationship, which depends on the type of activity carried out, or on the type of contracting parties (public or private). The LETA imposes a set of protective measures, inspired by the guarantees found in the Workers' Statute for salaried employees, which are automatically applicable to the new contract between the TRADE and the main client. It also allows for the negotiation of 'agreements of professional interest' between representative organisations and employer's associations to apply to contracts entered into by relevant clients and any TRADE represented by the organisation.

Briefly, the protection measures for the TRADE set out in Chapter III of the LETA are:

(a) vacation rights (18 working days), as well as time off due to illness, maternity or paternity leave, among other reasons;

---

[20] This interpretation has been confirmed by Decision of the Tribunal Superior de Justicia of Castille and Leon of 12 May 2010 (AS/2010/1732).

(b) the right to weekly rest and holiday days, maximum hours of work and their even weekly distribution if the total amount is calculated on a monthly or annual basis (to be established in their contract or in the agreement of professional interest);

(c) a payment guarantee in the event of insolvency, to be provided for by reform of the Civil Code;

(d) if the TRADE is affiliated to a trade union or professional association, they will have the right to enjoy the advantages provided for in any agreement of professional interest that the association has negotiated. If they are not, they will have to affiliate to get such benefits when entering into an agreement with a client;

(e) the right to notice of termination and, if terminated by their main client, to a justified cause, failing which they may ask for damages. The client may also ask for damages if the reverse takes place and harm is caused. Damages will be calculated depending on the notice given or the absence of justified cause if the agreement is unilaterally terminated. The criteria for determining damages are set out in section 15.4 of LETA; and

(f) the right to adjudication by the employment courts if any of the above rights are not recognised.

In reality, the new regulation does not depart from the general framework of civil law and the principles of freedom of contract. Consider, for example, the collective rights of the TRADE, which are also regulated in Chapter III of the LETA:

(a) the right to affiliate to a trade union or, alternatively, to join a professional association of the self-employed that does not have the nature of a trade union;[21]

(b) the right of trade unions or professional associations to enter into agreements of professional interest with employers' associations that represent the clients for whom they work; and

(c) the right to resort to alternative dispute resolution, whether collectively agreed or not, through mediation, conciliation and arbitration.

Not only is the right to strike not recognised (which is arguably legal from a constitutional point of view[22]), but agreements of professional interest are not true collective agreements. Some commentators consider these

---

[21] Valdés Alonso, A, 'Asociaciones Empresariales, asociaciones de trabajadores autónomos y organizaciones sindicales ... (A propósito de la Sentencia del Tribunal Supremo de 1/6/2009)' (2009) 87 *Documentación Laboral* 137, 149.

[22] Fernández López, MF, 'Los derechos fundamentales de los trabajadores autónomos dependientes' (2008) 42 *Revista de Derecho Social* 13, 21; Arozamena Laso, A and González Alonso, A, 'Aspectos Constitucionales de la Ley del Estatuto del Trabajo Autónomo' (2009) 85 *Documentación Laboral* 13, 26.

agreements to be 'improper collective agreements', which maintain a link with standard labour law and the protections afforded to standard collective agreements.[23] However, in my opinion, Parliament has conceived of these agreements as collective civil agreements regulated by private law, whose content is transferable to the individual contract depending on the affiliation of the TRADE to the association signatory to the agreement. Otherwise, their application depends on the TRADE's claim for the client to comply with them and the opposite pressure from the client to keep or terminate their contract, which is not the type of juridical general efficacy granted to collective agreements by Spanish labour law. On the other hand, this interpretation means that agreements of professional interest are subject to less protection than collective agreements against the application of Community Regulations that develop the old section 81.3 of the EC Treaty (s 101.3 *Treaty on the Functioning of the European Union*, 2007).[24]

This special regulation for the TRADE (which allows them to join professional associations) must co-exist with the right recognised by the Act on Trade Union Freedom for the self-employed to join trade unions whose association rules contemplate membership of the TRADE, or other self-employed workers. It will be interesting to see how trade unions representing the TRADE will act, and whether they will, in good faith, renounce use of their traditional instruments of conflict and collective negotiation.

By contrast, the LETA has extended to the self-employed certain social benefits from the social security system of salaried employees. This extension covers benefits for temporary incapacity or benefits for work accidents and work-related illnesses for occupations with a higher risk. In addition, the last great novelty of legal regulation of the TRADE is new social security legislation passed in 2010 that provides protection in the form of unemployment benefits for self-employed workers at the end of their work activity.[25]

JUSTIFICATIONS FOR LEGAL INTERVENTION

The main justification for Spanish regulation of the TRADE is the need to provide protection for independent contractors who either carry out qualified activities in sectors which are not covered by traditional firms,

---

[23] Trillo Párraga, FJ, 'Derechos colectivos del trabajador autónomo económicamente dependiente' (2009) 85 *Documentación Laboral* 89, 99.

[24] Mercader Uguina, JR and de la Puebla Pinilla, A, 'Comentario a la Ley 20/2007, de 11 de julio, del Estatuto del Trabajo Autónomo' (2007) 2 *Relaciones Laborales* 1129, 1144; Cabeza Pereiro, J, 'El Estatuto del trabajador autónomo español' (2008) 127 *Revista Internacional de Trabajo* 99, 103.

[25] Act 32/2010, of 5 August, establishing a specific system of protection for unemployed self-employed workers (BOE 6-8-2010). Commentary by Garcia Viña, J, 'Primeras Notas Sobre la L.32/2010. de 5 de agosto' (2011) 23 *Rev General de Derecho del Trabajo y de la Seguridad Social*, available at: www.Iustel.com/v2/revistas/detalle_revista.asp?id=1.

or who work in subcontracting and outsourcing (telework, etc) where economic dependence generates a contractual imbalance. In the Spanish regulatory model, we would say (with no caveats) that protection is given 'by default'.

According to the ILO's Report on Decent Work and the Informal Economy, 'informal workers and entrepreneurs are characterized by a high degree of vulnerability'.[26] The Spanish Parliament has constructed its own system of protection, adapted to the reality of the economically dependent self-employed, with the goal of granting protection to a substantial part of the informal economy.

The question is whether it would have been preferable to bring all economically dependent workers into the scope of labour law by extending the definition of the dependent worker in section 1 of the Workers' Statute. The answer given in the Group of Experts' Report was a technical one: if there is no dependence in the legal sense (contractual) it would be a contradiction in terms to extend the definition to this type of work.[27] For the same reason, it was decided to stress the graduation or intensity of the guarantees specific to the salaried worker when transposing them onto the TRADE, and this is why their collective rights have been limited.[28] This answer is similar to the one given by Harry Arthurs when he recommended a third category of employment status, the dependent contractor worker who would be entitled to some, but not all, basic employment standards.[29]

Another justification for the separate regulation of the self-employed from labour law is the difficulty of regulating salaried and self-employed workers together. The creation of a unitary regime would be likely to result in an exodus of workers and businesses out of the labour law regime and an increase of the informal sector.[30]

By contrast, other authors consider that this regulation commercialises what should have been a labour relationship in the strict sense.[31] Many commentators consider that the TRADE would have benefited from the labour provisions for special employment contracts.[32] This is certainly

---

[26] International Labour Conference, 90th Session, *Decent Work and the Informal Economy: Report VI* (Geneva, International Labour Office, 2002) 2.

[27] See Committee of Experts, above n 13.

[28] Cruz Villalón, J, 'Propuestas para una regulación del trabajo autónomo' (2005) 73 *Documentación Laboral* 9, 19.

[29] Fudge, J, 'A Canadian Perspective on the Scope of Employment Standards, Labour Rights and Social Protection: The Good, the Bad, and the Ugly' (2010) 31 *Comparative Labour Law & Policy Journal* 253, 254.

[30] Cruz Villalón, above n 28, at 26.

[31] Rivas Vallejo, P, 'Aspectos estructural es y primeras reflexiones sobre el Estatuto del Trabajo Autónomo' (2007) 136 *Revista Española del Derecho del Trabajo* 763, 781.

[32] Sagardoy Bengoechea, J, *Los trabajadores autónomos. Hacia un nuevo Derecho del Trabajo*, 1st edn (Madrid, ed Cinca, 2004) 110; Gutiérrez Solar, B, 'El autónomo económicamente dependiente: problemática y método' (2002) 18 *Aranzadi Social* 1, 11.

the case for some trades or professions linked to sectors such as building or retail. However, some of the special employment contracts currently in force offer even fewer guarantees than the TRADE regulation. Other commentators doubt the consistency of the LETA. If it is not labour law, why does it use techniques which are typical of labour law without, at the same time, acknowledging powers of organisation and management (if only at a technical level) that the client will logically employ to determine the job or activity to be carried out by the self-employed worker?[33] As such, the regulation facilitates the continuation of disguised self-employment.[34] In practice, it is true that there is some difficulty delimiting the boundaries between the dependent self-employed and the disguised self-employed and it will be up to the employment courts to establish these boundaries on a case-by-case basis, as they have already done with salaried employees and the self-employed.

But there is little that employment courts can do if the main difficulty lies in having a 'written contract', as the client may refuse to sign one. In the face of this refusal, or of the termination of the contract by the client, there is the possibility of adjudication by the employment courts. The court will determine whether there exists a TRADE contract or, in the alternative, a labour contract.[35] In doing so, the court will base its decision on the classical four-fold test to verify the existence of an employment contract, as well as on a new set of criteria to be developed in relation to section 11 of the LETA. Some court judgments on the application of section 11 of the LETA confirm the difficulty of fitting the facts within the legal definition, above all the difficulty in proving the 75 per cent figure, given the burden of proof placed on the claimant, who is generally the worker.[36] The courts have, for instance, rejected the use of invoices to the client as proof of economic dependence.[37] The Spanish courts have yet to develop the case law on the application of the criteria for determining the existence of a TRADE contract.

---

[33] Garcia Murcia, J, 'El Estatuto del Trabajador Autónomo: algunos apuntes críticos' (2007) 8 *Actualidad Laboral* 2156, 2158.

[34] Guerrrero Vizuete, E, 'La "acertada!?" regulación del trabajador autónomo dependiente ...' (2010) 20 *Aranzadi Social* 149, 153.

[35] The debate as to whether the written contract is a constituting element of the legal relationship between the main client and the TRADE, or just a mere presumption of its existence divides the Spanish regional courts. In favour of the first thesis are: Tribunal Superior de Justicia of Andalucia-Granada of 25 March 2009 (AS 2009/1593) and of Madrid of 2 December 2010 (AS/2011/297). In favour of the second thesis: Tribunal Superior de Justicia of Catalonia of 17 September 2010 (AS/2010/1929) and of Castille and Leon of 12 May 2010 (AS/2010/1732).

[36] Decision 468/08 of Juzgado Social de Valencia Number 16 of 5 August 2008. Decision of the Tribunal Superior of Justicia of Castille and Leon of 12 May 2010.

[37] Ruling of the Tribunal Superior de Justicia de León of 29 October 2008 (RA3764).

MEASURING THE SUCCESS OF THE LETA

The regulation of self-employment in the LETA anticipates some of the objectives approved by the European Council of 18 and 19 June 2010, mainly the Europe 2020 Strategy.[38] Achievement of 75 per cent employment by 2020, when in 2011 there was 20.8 per cent unemployment and Spain was in a deep recession, requires a reduction of the informal economy and the regulation of non-declared work.

Given general ignorance of the law and fear of contract termination, especially during the recession, it is not surprising that out of the approximately 300,000 TRADE in the Spanish labour market, only 10,000 have registered their contracts.[39] The transitional periods have ended, and the written contracts have now been transformed, *legally* incorporating rights and obligations of the LETA. However, it will always be difficult to quantify the actual number of contracts, because the TRADE will rarely file them with the public employment office without the client's consent.

Some commentators argue that the limited success of the regulation is due to the difficulty of quantifying 75 per cent of income. They suggest an alternative way to define the TRADE: exclusive activity for a single client, which the LETA contemplates for self-employed carriers (additional s 11 LETA) and for insurance agents (s 8 RETA).[40] Some also maintain that 100 per cent of income derived from a sole client would not preclude a worker from being a TRADE.[41]

The truth is that three years after its enactment, the LETA has had only modest success. Nonetheless, it will make possible the regularisation of some types of work considered to be 'grey areas' of labour law, for example carrier owners, commercial and insurance agents, and some types of freelancers. It will also ease the transition towards becoming TRADE for some cases of outsourcing and subcontracting that were clearly abusive in sectors like building and corporation services.

The question whether the LETA extends labour rights to the independent self-employed[42] can only be partially answered in the affirmative. The extension is clear at an individual rights level, but not in relation to collective rights. Indeed, by limiting the scope of labour rights applicable to the TRADE there is a general erosion of workers' rights. This is a real danger, and this criticism can be applied to the whole European strategy of flexicurity.[43] However, this cannot detract from the fact that the LETA

---

[38] Communication of 3 March 2010, COM(2010)2020.
[39] Data from the Spanish Self-Employed Association (ATA): http//www.autonomos-ata.es/.
[40] Martínez Abascal, V, 'El Estatuto del Trabajador Autónomo: alcance protector y linderos del DT' (2008) 3 *Aranzadi Social* 1, 3.
[41] *Comentarios a la LETA* (Valencia, ed CISS, 2007) 247.
[42] Fudge, above n 29, at 254.
[43] *Ibid* at 265.

has improved conditions and security for some self-employed workers who were never part of the inner core of labour law.

In any event the real question is not the intervention of the European strategy of flexicurity, but the definition of the roles and goals of labour law. Do we reconfigure the concept of work by broadening the subjective scope of labour law and modulating degrees of legal protection depending on the varying needs of workers, a method suggested by Guy Davidov in this collection?[44] Or should we approach the emergence of new types of workers with specific regulations for their protection by emulating the techniques developed for salaried employees? I think that both approaches are compatible. From a practical point of view, it will be more useful to extend the application of labour law in some cases, and in others, to regulate workers more flexibly, depending on the level of protection required for each case.

The Spanish legislators in passing the LETA may be faulted for their lack of regulatory ambition. It appears that Parliament only intended the legislation to apply to a small group of workers. Otherwise, the LETA should have included a provision similar to section 2 of the Workers' Statute that would allow its application to other types of workers.

This regulation, while not a mirror of the European strategy of flexicurity is, however, compatible with it. Flexibility in the exercise of labour rights may be combined with security in the labour market, which always requires social protection guarantees for the professional and economic needs of workers. The improvement in social protection for the TRADE is a goal of the LETA, and is complemented by the new social security legislation discussed earlier which extends coverage for social risks of the self-employed by including unemployment benefits applicable at the end of the work activity.

The challenge for labour law in the 21st century is to protect and shelter workers during transitions in the labour market: from employee to state employee or to self-employment, through different life stages of the individual (from training, through social and political activism, to balancing work and family life) and from transitions regarding capacities, opportunities and jobs. This challenge does not mean that labour law should relinquish its traditional role of protecting workers in the first circle, the hard circle of the industrial worker and trade unionist. But labour law's importance will diminish as history progresses if it is not capable of providing efficient responses, which attend to well-being and environmental sustainability, to emerging forms of work, and within the 'other' economy.

---

[44] Davidov, G, 'Freelancers: An Intermediate Group in Labour Law?' in this collection.

DOES THE LETA REGULATION MODEL OFFER
SOLUTIONS FOR OTHER TYPES OF INFORMAL
WORK IN THE GLOBAL ECONOMY?

The main question to address when judging the validity of the new Spanish regulation of the TRADE is whether it fits into the framework of typical legal protection for workers (labour law), or rather, to a type of legal framework for commercial contracts (which mercantilises the labour force, as human capital in commercial circulation). To answer this new question we must invoke a double test: is this regulation inspired by the observation of the fundamental rights of workers? Does it include development and empowerment beyond the traditional focus of labour law?

The LETA is a legal regime designed more to compensate, rather than to guarantee rights. The loss of traditional workers' rights is compensated by an increase in social protection. Economic globalisation, with its impact on the productive economy, the change in the productive paradigm brought by the service economy, and the expansion of the post-industrial society from the developed world to developing countries have probably put an end to the expansive trend of labour law as the guarantor of labour rights based on the productive model of the industrial revolution. This model has been in constant expansion by providing new rights and by extending those rights to new kinds of workers. In this sense, the LETA is a sign of the times and should not be frowned upon as a symbol of the current segmentation of traditional labour law.

In any event, the LETA has not brought about the disappearance of labour law, because the labour market still needs to be governed and therefore regulated by labour law. However, this fact does not mean that labour law has entered the 21st century unharmed. The recognised success of systems of industrial relations built during a long 30-year period of uninterrupted growth after the Second World War could be the reason for labour law's present difficulties. Perhaps the real reason for the weakening of labour law is simply its unbounded expansive ambition.

Indeed, this expansion of labour law is accompanied by a segmentation of guarantees depending on degrees of vulnerability. The present trend is not to empower workers, but to perfect the sustainability and improvement of systems of protection (with security measures and social assistance) without reinforcing union power, the only power that workers have really ever experienced. Whilst reinforcing professional autonomy and the freedom of contract of individual workers is a symbol of these times, more individual power and less collective power belong to the model of state social protection complemented by private savings.

In the face of this major challenge for labour law, Spanish trade unions have opted for defending the first circle, that of the dependent workers who are employed and have stable professional careers. They have neglected the other circles, particularly in respect of the regulation of young and informal workers. In this situation, labour law segments its regulatory intervention by graduating its protection depending on the signals sent by the labour market. This segmentation leaves to the unions the task of defending their members and workers of the first circle, and offering to the other labour sectors social protection as wide as possible, with basic guarantees based on the recognition of human and social international rights.

Only global and homogenous answers at an international level will stop the return of labour law to the 19th century and rearrange its traditional structures so that it may continue to be an essential instrument of labour relations in the new century, protecting human progress and social justice and individuals with little or no power at all. In uneasy times like these it is not a bad thing to remember that thanks to the original impetus of the ILO, labour law may, today as yesterday, be back on that road again.

In the face of present trends towards reforming labour law at local level as a solution to regulatory dilemmas,[45] the road to take is that of international principles and regulatory standards; basic rights and guarantees for all kinds of workers. We should remind ourselves of the origins of the ILO and affirm its validity as a source of political guidance and a legal basis for economic globalisation. This has been done by Alain Supiot, recalling the five elements of the Declaration of Philadelphia, upon which the ILO is based, and the UN and the Universal Declaration of Human Rights of 1948.[46] In the first place, there is human dignity, the founding principle of the legal order and fundamental rights; and directly linked to this principle, human freedom, which cannot occur without physical or economic security. This connection between freedom and security inevitably leads to the essential idea, that of the subordination of the economic organisation to the principle of social justice, and not the other way round, which occurs when the objective of social justice is replaced by the free circulation of goods, services and capital.

---

[45] Tucker, E, 'Reforming Labour Law: Can We Escape Labour Law's Recurring Regulatory Dilemmas?' (2010) 2 *Industrial Law Journal* 99, 100–1.

[46] Supiot, A, *L'esprit de Philadelphie (La justice sociale face au marché total)* (Paris, Editions du Seuil, 2010) 24.

10

Freelancers: An Intermediate Group in Labour Law?

GUY DAVIDOV

INTRODUCTION: THREE STORIES FROM ISRAELI CASE LAW

R EUVEN SIVAN WAS a linguist and a teacher. For a number of
years during the late 1960s and early 1970s he prepared and delivered weekly broadcasts for Israeli radio. His employer/client, the
Israel Broadcasting Authority (IBA), drafted a contract, which Sivan had
signed, declaring that he shall not be considered an employee. But after
being dismissed, he applied to the Israeli Labour Court, claiming that he
was in fact an employee and should be entitled to severance pay and vacation pay—statutory employment rights. It was quite obvious that Sivan did
not have any characteristics of a business entity. But the court thought that
he did not fit the paradigm of an employee either. The court likened Sivan's
status to that of Alterman, Shlonsky and Agnon, three Israeli literary giants,
who in earlier years used to publish poems and short stories in daily newspapers, sometimes on a regular weekly basis. It is 'inconceivable', the judges
said, to view those three as if they were employees of the newspapers. As
a solution, the court invented a new legal category, 'free contributors'—or
'freelancers'—for people who do not fit the mould of employees nor have
any real characteristics of independent contractors.[1]

However, as a matter of practice, labour laws[2] apply only to 'employees'. So
for all legal purposes the 'freelancers' are just like independent contractors:
they are completely excluded from the scope of the protection of labour
laws.

In a subsequent case the court explained that authors, poets, artists and
journalists who operate as 'freelancers' are free from any organisational
obligations and free from any disciplinary rules or a duty to obey the

---

[1] *Israel Broadcasting Authority v Reuven Sivan* 4 PDA 520 (1973). The term 'freelancer' is
used to describe the same category in later cases. See, eg, *Shaul Stdaka v The State of Israel*
36 PDA 625 (2001).
[2] I use this term to include what North Americans call employment law and workplace
discrimination law as well.

employer. They contribute their work to the newspaper or an artistic
project as they see fit—only as they please.[3] Could one be a 'freelancer'
(legally speaking) in other sectors as well? The National Labour Court
answered this question in the negative.[4] But the issue was later challenged
before the Supreme Court.

Shmuel Mor was the owner and manager of a private investigations
business, who employed Gideon Angel as a 'freelancer'. The arrangement agreed upon was that Angel would be assigned specific cases, and
would get 35 per cent of the income coming from those cases. Most of the
expenses incurred for performing the investigations were covered by Mor.
However, Angel was not reimbursed for transportation (he used his own
car), nor did he receive any *per diem* payments. The workload changed
from time to time, and was reduced twice at the request of Angel, once
when he started his studies at university, and again when he moved from
an evening programme of studies to the regular day programme. After
eight years Mor decided to terminate the engagement, and Angel sued
for severance pay, vacation pay and other statutory employment rights.
The National Labour Court concluded that Angel was an employee: he
had very few characteristics of an independent contractor (and notably,
no other 'clients'), and the court refused to consider the possibility of
extending the 'freelancer' category outside of the media/arts sector.[5] The
Supreme Court affirmed the decision of the National Labour Court, but
its judgment added to the confusion.[6] Chief Justice Barak noted that,
to the extent there is indeed a separate legal category of 'freelancers', it
cannot be limited to specific sectors only. However, he implicitly doubted
whether this category is needed, given the fact that the term 'employee'
should be interpreted purposively in each and every context. In contrast,
the other two judges of the three-member panel thought that in recent
years freelancing has become common in many sectors, and courts should
acknowledge this development legally and make increased use of the 'freelancer' category.[7]

A couple of years later, when a 'freelance' journalist applied to the
labour court asking for employee rights, the National Labour Court
had to decide—in light of the different views expressed in the Supreme

---

[3] *Ozer Admon v The State of Israel* 5 PDA 169 (1974). This was obviously not the arrangement between Sivan and the IBA; as noted above, he was required to prepare and deliver
a weekly broadcast. Indeed, in *Shmuel Mor v The National Labour Court* 50(4) PD 628
(1996), Chief Justice Barak of the Supreme Court noted that he would have considered Sivan
an employee.
[4] *Gideon Angel v Shmuel Mor* judgment of May 12, 1993 (unreported).
[5] *Ibid*.
[6] *Shmuel Mor v The National Labour Court*, above n 3.
[7] In the context of the specific case, Judge Tal thought that Angel was indeed a 'free con-
tributor', but Judge Goldberg disagreed and thought he was an employee. Hence the final
judgment affirming the National Labour Court decision.

Court—whether to dispose of the 'freelancer' legal category or to revive it.[8] Shaul Tsdaka served during the 1980s as the correspondent of Ha'aretz (a major Israeli newspaper) in London. While there, he also had an arrangement with Galey Tsahal, an Israeli radio station, according to which he prepared news reports and delivered them to this station. The agreement, which defined him as a freelancer, prevented him from making similar arrangements with any other Israeli radio station. In most cases Tsdaka would choose what to report on, but on occasion he was asked by the station to cover specific events. He was paid $30 per report, and also a small fixed sum ($30 per month) to cover his phone calls to the station. There was no agreement regarding the number of reports he had to deliver, which as a matter of practice varied between several reports a day at times and only one report per week at other times—between 10 and 20 per month on average. After eight years Galey Tsahal decided to terminate the agreement, and Tsdaka sued for statutory severance pay.

The President of the National Labour Court, Judge Adler, embarked on a reconsideration of the 'freelancer' category, and came to the conclusion that it is viable and valuable and should be retained.[9] He argued, however, that 'freelancers' should not be excluded entirely from the protection of labour law. Rather, at least *some* labour regulations should apply to them—based on what he called 'the purpose test'. In the specific case he concluded that Tsdaka was indeed a 'freelancer' and he should be entitled to all the rights that he claimed (severance pay, notice before termination, wage differences). But President Adler was left in dissent on this point. The majority of the court thought that there is no need to change the law dealing with the 'freelancer' category: it should be retained as it was developed in *The Israel Broadcasting Authority v Reuven Sivan*.[10] They understood the Supreme Court comments as demanding a change in the *application* of the tests, not the tests (or categories) themselves. The majority then came to the conclusion that Tsdaka was an employee of the radio station. However, it was not entirely clear what arrangements would fall into the 'freelancer' category, which they thought should be retained. By expanding the 'employee' category to include the case of Tsdaka, the majority judges of the National Labour Court left very little room for the 'freelancer' category.

Sivan, Angel and Tsdaka had different work arrangements, but also one thing in common: they were all considered to be 'freelancers' by their employers. In other cases people also describe *themselves* as freelancers.[11]

---

[8] *Shaul Stdaka v The State of Israel* 36 PDA 625 (2001).
[9] *Ibid.*
[10] *Israel Broadcasting Authority*, above, n 1.
[11] Unfortunately there are no data available on the extent of this phenomenon in Israel. A recent report estimates the number of freelancers in the UK at between 1.4 and 4 million

Such self or imposed definitions are obviously not determinative as far as labour laws are concerned. It is highly likely that many people who are considered to be 'freelancers' in the market are in fact employees of their client as a matter of law. In such cases the problem is one of enforcement. In other cases, however, it seems that 'freelancers' share some of the characteristics of employees and independent contractors.[12] Should they be classified to one of these poles, or is there room for an intermediate 'freelancer' legal category in between independent contractors and employees? This chapter is an attempt to answer this question, in three steps. Part II confronts the idea of an intermediate category with the alternative of purposive interpretation leading to different meanings for the term 'employee' in each and every context. Part III then turns to the possibilities open for legislatures wishing to devise an intermediate category, and briefly describes what legislatures in different countries have done. I will argue (as I have done elsewhere) that it is useful to add an intermediate category of workers who are characterised by dependency on a specific employer, but not subordination. Part IV concludes by considering whether this kind of intermediate category also fits workers that are commonly described as 'freelancers' in the market, as well as those who truly 'contribute as they please'.

PURPOSIVE INTERPRETATION VERSUS INTERMEDIATE CATEGORIES

To examine whether purposive interpretation can make the addition of an intermediate category unnecessary, let me start by explaining the idea of purposive interpretation, and how it can be applied in the current context.

Laws are obviously enacted for a reason. They are meant to achieve some societal purpose. They are designed (or should be designed) to best achieve this purpose. It is generally accepted in many areas of laws and many countries that laws should be interpreted 'purposively', ie that terms in legislation should be given the meaning that best advances the *purpose* that the legislation is aimed to achieve.[13] Labour laws are no exception. The rich body of labour laws which one can find in most countries is supposed

---

people; see Kitching, J and Smallbone, D, *Defining and Estimating the Size of the UK Freelance Workforce* (Surrey, Kingston University, 2008), available at: http://eprints.kingston.ac.uk/3880/.

[12] On the blurring of boundaries see Fudge, J, 'Blurring Legal Boundaries: Regulating for Decent Work', in this collection.

[13] This is not the place to defend the purposive approach. I do so, to some extent, elsewhere. See Davidov, G, 'The Reports of My Death are Greatly Exaggerated: 'Employee' as a Viable (Though Overly-Used) Legal Concept', in G Davidov and B Langille (eds), *Boundaries and Frontiers of Labour Law: Goals and Means in the Regulation of Work* (Oxford, Hart Publishing, 2006) 133; Davidov, G, 'A Purposive Interpretation of the National Minimum Wage Act' (2009) 72 *Modern Law Review* 581. In any case, although I wholeheartedly

to achieve a number of purposes, which can be articulated at a high level of abstraction (distributive justice, protecting workers' dignity, protecting workers' autonomy, achieving workplace equality, etc) or at a more concrete level (ensuring that wages are paid on time, ensuring that workers are not required to work extreme hours, etc).[14]

In most cases, legislatures apply the entire body of labour-related laws to the same group of people ('employees'), without defining the scope of this group. It is left for the courts to give meaning to these terms by inventing tests and placing boundaries. Courts around the world have developed very similar tests, and in most cases have used them in the same way with regard to the entire body of labour laws. Thus, they have determined whether one is an 'employee' or not without limiting this decision to the context of any specific legislation. Once one is considered an 'employee', the entire body of labour laws applies (subject to specific exceptions stipulated in legislation).

This approach is sometimes based on a formalistic and simplistic application of legal concepts, in the sense that judges sometimes think that they can recognise an employee when they see one, and that the term employee necessarily has the same meaning any time it is used in common language as well as legislation. But the same approach can also be based on a more sophisticated and benign *purposive* interpretation of labour laws, if a judge takes the view—at least implicitly—that all labour laws share the same basic purposes. Thus, for example it could be said that all labour laws are designed to counteract the inequality of bargaining power that is prevalent in employment relations, or to confront the vulnerability of employees in this relationship, and so on. According to this analysis, because all labour laws share the same basic purpose, they should apply to the same group of people—those in need of this kind of protection—and accordingly the term 'employee' should have the same meaning in every labour law context.

In recent years, however, there is increased willingness in some countries (eg Israel, Canada) to consider specific purposes of specific laws, and as a result to allow a situation in which one is considered an 'employee' for one purpose but an independent contractor for other purposes.[15] Assume, for example, that the purposes behind a minimum wage law are different from the purposes explaining the passage of a working time law. If this is the case, then a truly purposive approach would mean that the scope of the term 'employee' should be different for each of these laws. Such an approach would ensure that *all* those (and *only* those) who require the protection of the minimum wage law will enjoy it; it would also ensure that

---

support the purposive approach to interpretation, the current chapter focuses on the *limits* of this approach and discusses legislative solutions.

[14] Davidov, G, 'Re-Matching Labour Laws with Their Purpose' in G Davidov and B Langille (eds), *The Idea of Labour Law* (Oxford, Oxford University Press, 2011) 179.

[15] See Davidov, 'The Reports of My Death are Greatly Exaggerated', above n 13.

all those (and *only* those) who require the protection of the working time law—not necessarily the exact same group—will enjoy it.

While this is indeed the view adopted in theory in Israel (and perhaps some other countries), in practice courts are very reluctant to actually 'break' the concept of 'employee' into multiple meanings. This is understandable, because in a reality of deficient enforcement, when many violations of labour laws never reach the courts, a high degree of determinacy is necessary. At present most people know that they are employees and therefore they are entitled to a defined set of rights. Once this can be questioned with regard to each and every right separately, indeterminacy will rise significantly, and employers will use any new 'grey areas' created to further evade their legal responsibilities.[16] Moreover, if we are interested in developing or at least maintaining group consciousness—which is necessary for organising, and probably for a decent level of enforcement as well—this is almost impossible if people do not share the same status.

So, on the one hand we would like to reach a perfect fit between the scope of each legislation and its purpose, but on the other hand we are interested in having a clear understanding of who is an 'employee', to allow workers (and all other parties involved) to know their rights. How can we balance between these two competing interests?

One solution is to develop a 'general' test for identifying who is an 'employee'—a test based on the general purposes that unite all labour laws—and allow for exceptions or extensions in specific circumstances, when this is justified based on specific purposes of specific legislation.[17] As a matter of practice, I believe that such exceptions are not likely to be common, so there is no risk that they will 'swallow the rule'. This means that there will be a clear definition for who is an 'employee' (based on some general tests), which will apply in most cases, so workers will be able to know their status and rights, but at the same time there will be variations in specific circumstances to ensure the fit to specific purposes.

In my view, this is the best solution available to courts, as long as a legislature is silent. But a balance between determinacy and precision (ie applying the law to the precise group of people who need it) is easier to reach in legislation. If we know that a group of workers has certain characteristics that justify the application of some labour laws but not others, an intermediate legal category would significantly contribute to determinacy. People would know that while 'employees' generally enjoy the entire body of labour laws (say, laws A, B, C, D and E), and independent contractors are entirely excluded, once you are seen to be within the intermediate group you are entitled only to certain employment rights (say, laws A, B and C). This does not preclude the use of purposive interpretation in any way. But it does add a significant degree of determinacy.

---

[16] *Ibid.*
[17] Davidov, G, 'The Three Axes of Employment Relationships: A Characterization of Workers in Need of Protection' (2002) 52 *University of Toronto Law Journal* 357.

DEVISING INTERMEDIATE CATEGORIES

If we are to add an intermediate category, there is obviously no point in adding a category that for all legal purposes is equivalent to one of the existing categories. The development of the 'freelancer' category in Israel, which legally speaking is simply a subset of 'independent contractors', is therefore difficult to understand. One possible explanation is that the judges mistakenly considered the two poles of 'employee' and 'independent contractor' to have a positive meaning.[18] If one should have certain characteristics to be an 'employee' (legally), and a set of other characteristics to be an 'independent contractor' (legally), then it is possible that one would not fall into either group. A third category could then be added to include those who do not fall into the other two. Nonetheless, the term 'independent contractor' (or 'self-employed', or any other similar term) does not appear in Israeli labour legislation. The laws simply say that employees are entitled to various rights, so the legal question is simply whether one is an employee or not. If you are not an employee, it does not matter what exactly you are; the term 'independent contractor' is used as a residual category for anyone who is not an employee. A different explanation for the puzzling introduction of the 'freelancer' category into Israeli law is that courts were interested in legitimising the practice of employing freelancers without employment rights, perhaps because they thought it was justified. Arguably they found it difficult to say that such workers are independent contractors, and needed the new category—however awkward legally speaking—to justify the exclusion of this group as a policy matter.

The alternative model proposed by President Adler (in dissent), which would extend *some* labour rights to 'freelancers', makes more sense. But if the main goal is to achieve determinacy, a judge-made category developed on a case-by-case basis would hardly achieve this goal. Moreover, it is doubtful if such judicial legislation is legitimate. If the legislature decided that 'employees' should enjoy certain rights, courts can interpret this term differently in different contexts, but creating a new category altogether is more appropriately a legislative task. Indeed, a number of countries have replaced the traditional binary divide between 'employees' and 'independent contractors' with a three-category system. Legislatures in Sweden, Germany and Canada introduced long ago the concept of 'dependent contractor', or 'employee-like', referring to people who have some characteristics of independent businesses, but at the same time some of the vulnerabilities of employees, especially in the sense of depending entirely or mostly on a single employer/client.[19] Other legal systems in Europe have

---

[18] This view is explicitly found in the judgment of Justice Tal in *Shmuel Mor v The National Labour Court*, above n 3.

[19] For a brief review see Langille, B and Davidov, G, 'Beyond Employees and Independent Contractors: A View from Canada' (1999) 21 *Comparative Labor Law & Policy Journal* 6.

followed suit in recent years.[20] In these cases, legislatures have chosen to apply some labour laws (eg the right to bargain collectively) but not others. Technically, this can be achieved by stating in specific laws that they apply not only to 'employees' but also to 'dependent contractors', or that for the purpose of the specific law, the term 'employee' also includes dependent contractors.[21]

The proliferation of intermediate categories in recent years is not always problem-free. The backdrop is usually vast evasion of the law through misclassification of employees as independent contractors, which courts are unable or unwilling to stop. Between 1995 and 2007 legislatures in the UK, Austria, Italy and Spain have introduced a third category in order to provide at least *some* protection for such workers. But these protections are often quite minimal (usually the focus is on social security rather than direct employer obligations), and the worrying side-effect is the legitimising of the existing order in which workers who often have *all* the characteristics of employees are excluded from full protection. The failure of courts to prevent such misclassification is surely no excuse for legislatures, who only went half way (or even less) to protect workers in need of protection, and despite good intentions have helped to perpetuate their unjustified exclusion.

But let us leave this difficulty aside. Even if courts would function perfectly and interpret the term 'employee' in the best possible way, there is

---

[20] For useful comparative information see Pedersini, R, *Economically Dependent Workers, Employment Law and Industrial Relations*, available at: www.eurofound.europa.eu/eiro/2002/05/study/index.htm; Pedersini, R and Coletto, D, *Self-Employed Workers: Industrial Relations and Working Conditions* (Dublin, European Foundation for the Improvement of Living and Working Conditions, 2010) ch 4. See also Cabeza Pereiro, J, 'The Status of Self-Employed Workers in Spain' (2008) 147 *International Labour Review* 91; Sánchez Torres, E, 'The Spanish Law on Dependent Self-Employed Workers: A New Evolution in Labor Law' (2010) 31 *Comparative Labor Law & Policy Journal* 231; Landa Zapirain, JP, 'Regulation of Dependent Self-Employed Workers in Spain: A Regulatory Framework for Informal Work?' in this collection; Fudge, J, 'A Canadian Perspective on the Scope of Employment Standards, Labor Rights, and Social Protection: The Good, the Bad, and the Ugly' (2010) 31 *Comparative Labor Law & Policy Journal* 253.

[21] A similar result can also be achieved using a slightly different structure, when a legislature introduces a new concept which is broader than the regular 'employee'. Thus, for example, in the UK some labour laws apply to all 'workers', a concept defined in legislation in much broader terms than those developed by the courts to identify employees. As a result, there is the group of 'employees' who enjoy all labour laws, and those who are 'workers' but not 'employees' who enjoy only *some* labour laws. The technique is slightly different, but the result is the same. On the UK intermediate category see Davidov, G, 'Who is a Worker?'(2005) 34 *Industrial Law Journal* 57. Another technique could be to provide some 'independent contractors' with the possibility of exemption from competition laws that generally prevent collective bargaining. This technique exists in Australia, although it appears to be difficult to employ; see McCrystal, S, 'Organising Independent Contractors: The Impact of Competition Law' in this collection. Yet another technique developed in Australia—again not without practical weaknesses—creates a special regulatory regime for franchisees, a group that has some of the characteristics of employees but not others; see Riley, J, 'A Blurred Boundary between Entrepreneurship and Servitude: Regulating Business Format Franchising in Australia' in this collection.

still room, as we have seen, for an intermediate category—assuming, of course, that in practice there is some discernible difference between different groups of workers that can justify the application of *some* labour laws but not others.

The Two Basic Characteristics of Employment

When trying to define the unique characteristics of employment relations—which in turn also point to the reasons for regulating these relations (ie the purpose of labour laws)—scholars and courts often refer to 'subordination' and 'dependency'. After a long journey of trying to find the characteristics of employment myself, I came back to the same two concepts.[22] So I think scholars and courts are correct in pointing to subordination and dependency. But a number of important clarifications and caveats must be added.

First, these concepts cannot be used interchangeably, as if they both refer to the same problem. These are two different vulnerabilities that employees face vis-à-vis their employers. Thus, for example, regulation of wages is needed when, as a result of *dependency*, the worker might agree to terms that society finds unacceptable. On the other hand, regulation intended to protect workers' privacy (for example) is needed when the worker subjects himself to a degree of *subordination* that gives the employer the power to violate his privacy.

Second, the idea of subordination that I think is relevant to identifying those in need of protection—those to whom labour laws should apply—is what I call 'democratic deficits'. When a person works for others, if she is subject to the control and command of a boss (whom she did not choose or vote for), or otherwise subject to the rules of an organisational structure (without being able to take part in setting those rules)—then the relationship is characterised by democratic deficits. This is a vulnerability that in turn justifies certain legal protections. So it is not the narrow 'legal subordination' that matters, but a broader idea of democratic deficits in the relationship.

Third, when referring to dependency, I think the relevant issue is not only economic dependency, but more generally reliance on the continuation of the relationship with a specific employer, which one can come to depend upon both in economic terms and for the fulfilment of social and psychological needs. This dependence is best understood as inability to spread risks. An independent contractor has contacts with a number of different clients, customers, suppliers etc, and thus has the ability to spread the risks,

---

[22] Davidov, 'The Three Axes', above n 17.

without relying too heavily on any single relationship. An employee, on the other hand, has to 'place all the eggs in one basket'. This is yet another vulnerability that justifies protection, and can explain the need for certain labour laws.

Finally, it is important to realise that there are no clear-cut distinctions between the existence and lack of these characteristics. Rather, it is always a matter of degree, and the question will be whether the *degree* of subordination and/or dependency in any given situation is sufficient to justify the application of labour laws.

In my own view,[23] the term 'employee' should be understood as based on both of these concepts. A worker should enjoy the protection of labour laws as an 'employee' when he is characterised by a degree of subordination vis-à-vis a specific employer as well as a degree of dependency on the relationship with this employer. To a large extent I think this is also a fair description of what courts around the world are doing. But more importantly, as a normative matter I think this is the best way to understand the term 'employee' in the broad context of labour laws as a whole. If some laws are designed to protect workers against one vulnerability (subordination) and other laws are intended to protect against another vulnerability (dependency)—and perhaps yet other laws are designed to protect against both vulnerabilities—it makes sense to look for both of them (at least to some extent) when giving a general meaning to the term 'employee'.

This approach has been criticised by Judy Fudge for (a) its insistence on understanding the employment relationship as personal and bilateral, (b) the fact that in reality independent contractors also experience similar vulnerabilities, and (c) the reliance on subordination as one of the characteristics justifying labour law.[24] Regarding (a), consider a minimum wage law, for example (the analysis is the same for any other piece of labour legislation). If our goal is to interpret the legislation (eg the concept of 'employee' setting its scope)—and the legislation requires an 'employer' to pay an 'employee' a minimum wage—I fail to see how this relationship can be understood in any way other than bilateral and personal. If we are thinking about *devising* legislation, then again the normative question we are facing is whether a person (or a company) employing another person should be subject to the legal requirement to pay at least the minimum wage—the question remains one of bilateral and personal obligations. With regard to (b), Fudge confuses her *description* of the changing reality (for example, the fact that many of those considered 'self-employed' in the market are vulnerable) with the normative question. Perhaps what she describes is simply a problem of enforcement. But even if some workers who are considered by current law

---

[23] As developed at length *ibid*.

[24] Fudge, J, 'Fragmenting Work and Fragmenting Organizations: The Contract of Employment and the Scope of Labour Regulation' (2006) 44 *Osgoode Hall Law Journal* 609.

to be independent contractors in fact suffer from democratic deficits and/or dependency, this has no bearing on the discussion of what the law *should* be: they should simply be classified as employees or as dependent contractors. Regarding (c), Fudge never explains her objection to subordination (understood as democratic deficits) as an indicator, except for noting the general difficulty of 'a lack of precision',[25] which is a necessary lesser evil in such legal distinctions. In fact, in her discussion of the goals of labour law, Fudge emphasises the idea of establishing effective institutions of counter-vailing power.[26] How would we know that legal intervention to allow or create countervailing power is needed and justified, if not by reference to workers' democratic deficits?

As a matter of practice, it seems that most of the people who are commonly considered 'employees' are indeed characterised by both subordination and dependency, so there is nothing revolutionary about this proposal. It is, however, important to remind judges, who often use long lists of indicia, not to rely too heavily on such indicia. They can sometimes be helpful in identifying the existence of subordination and dependency, but the ultimate question should be to what extent these broad vulner-abilities exist. Lists of indicia are useful aids but must remain so, and not become the ultimate tests themselves. And, more importantly for current purposes, if you accept the proposition that subordination and dependency are two different vulnerabilities, and that both of them char-acterise employment, the distinction between them becomes highly useful when we wish to add an intermediate group, in-between 'employees' and independent contractors.[27]

Dependent Contractors

Consider the following example: John is a copy editor of books. He has his own company, he issues invoices and so on. But he has no employees, he works alone. And in practice, he only has one client—he does all the editorial work for one single publisher. The publisher considers him to be a 'freelancer' and works with several other such 'freelancers'. To a large extent John has control over his own time. He is not committed to take all the work that the publisher sends him; if he wants to take a vacation or a day off, he will simply tell the publisher to send any urgent materials to other editors. He chooses when to work, where to work and how many hours per day to work. He is also not subject to any organisational rules of the publisher.

---

[25] *Ibid* at 632.
[26] *Ibid* at 629.
[27] Davidov, 'Who is a Worker?', above n 21.

What is John's legal status? We should probably not consider him an 'employee'. Although he has just one client, he does not appear to suffer from all the same vulnerabilities as internal employees of the publisher. Specifically, his relationship with the publisher is not characterised by sub-ordination. On the other hand, it is obviously characterised by dependency. He has no real ability to spread risks. He relies entirely on work provided by the specific publisher. So it would be fair to argue that he should be entitled to *some* labour law protection. For example, he should probably be allowed to bargain collectively with other 'freelance' editors, so as to improve their bargaining position vis-à-vis the publisher. Arguably, people like John should also enjoy the protection of minimum wage laws and other laws setting minimum monetary terms. On the other hand, there is obviously no justification to apply working time laws or workplace privacy laws, for example, in this case.

In such cases, when the relationship is characterised by dependency but no subordination, it is useful to call the worker a 'dependent contractor' and apply at least some labour laws. In other words, dependency alone should be sufficient to justify a floor of basic labour-related rights, with additional rights (which are tied to subordination) granted only to 'employ-ees'. I am therefore justifying an intermediate group very similar to the one that exists in some countries, but with a number of differences. First, I think the focus of the examination should be the ability or inability to spread risks, rather than the indicia currently used by courts such as risk of loss, chance of profit, ownership of tools and so on. Most of these indicia can easily be manipulated by employers trying to evade legal responsibili-ties. Second, I have argued that social/psychological dependency should be examined as well, rather than just economic dependency. Third, I think we should not demand any level of subordination for this group. This indeed appears to be the case in Germany (with regard to the 'employee-like' group), but not in Canada, for example, where the 'dependent contractor' category has been legislated to require at least *some* level of subordination as well (even if lower than that required for 'employees'). Finally, I believe that this intermediate group of workers should enjoy much broader pro-tection than what is currently common in the countries that have so far recognised such a group. In Canada, for example, the only right granted to 'dependent contractors' is the right to bargain collectively. But dependency justifies many other labour-related rights as well. Indeed, it seems that all labour laws that regulate wages and other monetary terms, for example, should apply to 'dependent contractors' as well.

If you agree that people like John (our editor) should enjoy *some* labour laws as 'dependent contractors', we will have to enter the difficult sphere of trying to set boundaries for this group. Should we consider John an 'employee' (rather than a 'dependent contractor') if, for example, he receives on-going instructions from the publisher about how to perform the work, or has agreed to co-ordinate his vacations with the publisher in advance? From the other direction, should we consider John an independent contractor—with no entitlement to labour-related rights whatsoever—if he works with two or three publishers rather than one, or if he is assisted by one or two employees of his own? These are difficult questions with no clear-cut answers. But it seems to me that the basic questions remain the same: what is the degree of subordination and what is the degree of dependency in the relationship between the two parties. It is sometimes a judgment call to decide where to put the line, and some degree of indeterminacy is inherent in this process. Yet it is wise to leave some latitude of discretion to courts, to avoid the pitfall of specific clear-cut rules that create an illusion of determinacy but bring about exacerbated levels of evasion.

I therefore disagree on this point with those who try to get rid of line-drawing altogether.[28] Line-drawing is always difficult, but it is an indispensable part of law. While we can obviously reach a higher degree of determinacy by granting all rights to everyone, it would necessarily lead to a very minimal list of rights. The more rights we want to offer as part of labour law, the higher the need to create more nuanced distinctions, to ensure that the rights are granted only to those who need and deserve them.

BETWEEN DEPENDENT CONTRACTORS AND FREELANCERS

So far I have argued that an intermediate category added in legislation would be useful, and suggested to base such a category on the distinction between subordination and dependency—with those in the intermediate category characterised only by the latter. We have also seen that at least some people considered 'freelancers' in the market could very well fall within this 'dependent contractors' category. Now let us go back to the three stories which opened this Chapter and consider whether the same intermediate category is useful for them as well.

Reuven Sivan (the linguist) was subject to a relationship of subordination vis-à-vis the IBA, even if the degree was slightly lower than that experienced by most employees. He also experienced dependency on the IBA; the fact that he probably had another job and this was a part-time engagement does not change the fact that he relied on this regular income and was not in a position to disperse risks. It seems that such cases should be classified as employment relations. Gideon Angel (the private investigator) had

---

[28] See, eg, Fudge, J, Tucker, E and Vosko, L, 'Employee or Independent Contractor? Charting the Legal Significance of the Distinction in Canada' (2003) 10 *Canadian Labour & Employment Law Journal* 287; and see, in the specific context of criticising the introduction of an intermediate group, Fudge, above n 20.

perhaps a slightly lower degree of subordination, but a stronger degree of dependency (it was his only income). It seems that the Israeli courts were right to consider him an employee. Shaul Tsdaka (the journalist reporting from London) had the lowest degree of subordination between the three, in my view. He was not subject to any control of the radio station (Galey Tsahal), and was not part of the organisation in any meaningful way. Yet Tsdaka was arguably dependent—at least for part of his income—on the specific relationship. He did not have characteristics of an independent contractor that would allow diversification of risks. So perhaps in such cases a worker should be classified as a 'dependent contractor'.

An intermediate category based on dependency appears to be useful for analysing the main cases that Israeli courts have grappled with in the context of so-called 'freelancers'. Interestingly, however, none of these cases was characterised by what the National Labour Court saw (in theory) as the hallmark of being a freelancer: a worker freely contributing as she sees fit. Imagine, for example, that Julie is a journalist writing stories independently, on topics that she chooses, in a frequency she chooses, and controlling her own time. Once an article is ready, she is free to offer it to any newspaper she likes (assume she has no contractual obligation to any newspaper). Assume also that Julie works in practice with several newspapers. In such a case it appears that she is an independent contractor. Obviously there is no subordination; and the ability to disperse risks between several clients means that there is also no dependency. As other entrepreneurs who own very small businesses, Julie is vulnerable in some respects and the law should be responsive to that. Thus, for example, perhaps assistance is needed to help such self-employed workers operating by themselves in terms of securing pensions. But the lack of an employer which could be held responsible means that a different set of laws is needed, rather than labour laws.

What if most or all of Julie's income comes from a single client? In such cases I believe she should be considered a dependent contactor, and enjoy those labour laws that were designed to counteract such dependency. Although there is difficulty in determining a worker's status based on considerations that are out of the employer's control—the employer does not necessarily know if Julie has relations with other newspapers—on balance this is a price worth paying. If all your income comes from a single employer, there is a high degree of dependency that justifies some protection, even if the employer itself is not 'responsible' for your lack of additional sources of income.

It turns out that there is no need for a special legal category of freelancers, once an intermediate category of dependent contractors is introduced (in the form I have suggested above). People who are considered freelancers in the market are sometimes in fact employees (Angel the private investigator), sometimes they are dependent contractors (Tsdaka the

London correspondent, or John the imaginary editor), and sometimes they are independent contractors (Julie the imaginary journalist working with several newspapers).

CONCLUSION

A growing number of people perform work for others as 'freelancers'. This is not a legal term. The question examined in this Chapter was whether this *should become* a legal term—whether freelancers should be classified as a unique intermediate group in labour law. When we examine each and every piece of labour legislation separately, the binary divide is necessary: one could either be subject to the specific law (eg minimum wage) or not. In other words, in the context of a specific law, one can either be an 'employee' or not. But what if some people, such as freelancers, should be subject to *some* labour laws but not others? I have started by examining whether this could be achieved by using purposive interpretation and giving the term 'employee' different meanings in different contexts. While possible, we have seen that in order to secure a higher degree of determinacy it is preferable to create an intermediate group in legislation.

I then moved to consider how an intermediate group between employees and independent contractors should be devised in legislation. There are two basic characteristics of employment relations that distinguish them from other contractual relations, and justify the application of labour laws: subordination (in a broad sense of democratic deficits) and dependency (in the sense of inability to spread risks, resulting in strong reliance on the specific relationship). These two characteristics point to different vulnerabilities that sometimes justify different labour laws. They can thus be useful in setting the boundaries of an intermediate group. I have argued in favour of maintaining a 'dependent contractor' group, characterised by dependency. Workers in this group should enjoy a floor of rights together with those classified as 'employees' (and the latter will enjoy some additional rights).

Finally, I examined a number of examples in which people are considered 'freelancers' in the market, to see whether the three-category system suggested provides suitable solutions. It turns out that some freelancers are in fact employees, some are independent contractors, and yet others should be considered dependent contractors. Once this intermediate group is added, the legal structures are suitable to provide labour law protection for those 'freelancers' who need it.

Part III

Paid Care Workers—The Significance of Institutions for Decent Work

11

The Wages of Care-workers: From Structure to Agency

GUY MUNDLAK

CARE-WORK AND CARE-WORKERS IN THE WELFARE STATE

THE NOTION OF 'care-work' can be considered an oxymoron. There is a tradition of contrasting care with work, the one being intimate and the other commercial. Seemingly, the two belong to separate spheres.[1] This theoretical tradition has also entailed an elaborate critique which points out that care is also a duty, a burden shouldered mostly by women.[2] While its nature as a type of work does not eliminate its other dimensions, it should be at least partially commodified, to highlight both the labour involved and its relationship to other partially commodified relationships, such as the employment relationship.

The scope of care-work would best be described in a functional manner as encompassing all tasks that tend to the needs of individuals who cannot (fully or partially) care for themselves. Such individuals include children, the elderly and the (permanently or temporarily) disabled. Provision of care is distinct from the provision of health and education, and it is geared to the satisfaction of basic needs—from active daily living functions (ADL) to emotional needs. The duty of care requires constant attention and engages the caregiver in full. It can be rewarding, particularly when the fruits of care are readily visible, but also simply for knowing that one has given personal attention to a person in need, provided care to one's own parents, or improved the quality of life of others. Care can also be draining, physically straining, a locus of encounter with the human body in its non-esthetic being, and a dreaded situation that elicits mixed emotions of pity, compassion and resentment.

---

[1] Roberts, DE, 'Spiritual and Menial Housework' (1997) 9 *Yale Journal of Law and Feminism* 5; Folbre, N and Nelson, J, 'For Love or Money?' (2000) 14 *The Journal of Economic Perspectives* 123.

[2] See, eg, Williams, J, *Unbending Gender* (Oxford, Oxford University Press, 2000).

Care is a central task of the welfare state, and the methods by which states arrange care-work are among the factors that distinguish between welfare regimes.[3] Traditionally care was relegated to family members, and, with the emergence of the welfare state, care was shouldered by the state to the extent that the family (nuclear or extended) was unable to provide care. Some welfare 'models have adopted a more extensive network of care provision. Public support for care was intended to relieve family members of some of the financial and emotional costs of care. Moreover, providing support for care was intended to facilitate the growing participation of family caregivers in public life and market activities, the development of their careers, and their investment in improving human and social capital. Public provision and guarantee of care arrangements has an impact on the economy as a whole and on the distribution of resources, increasing productivity and raising the gross domestic product. Public intervention in the provision of care involves the commodification of care, since the provision of care outside the framework of familial obligations creates a labour market of care providers and care institutions. In a global era, the market for care has expanded beyond any one state's borders and is tightly linked with waves of migration and the creation of transnational care-chains.[4]

Care arrangements are therefore a fundamental question at every level of analysis—from the personal to the national and the global. They also provide a lucid demonstration of changing legal boundaries on multiple frontiers (public/private, domestic/global, de/commodification, foreignness and intimacy, traditional classifications of welfare state institutions, gender relations and more). Given the fluidity of traditional boundaries, the choice of care arrangements is a field of contestation that is being shaped by the competing interests of many agents, who can generally be classified into five groups: the people in need of care (who may often be in need of representation, lacking the agency to represent themselves), family members who may provide care by default (absent an alternative arrangement they can afford or wish to afford), the state, caregivers, and their employers. The sides of the pentagon are porous. For example, recipients of care may also be the employers. Moreover, no side of this pentagon is monolithic. The interests of children are not the same as those of the elderly; the interests of familial caregivers are heavily gendered and do not apply equally to men and women; some of the state's branches seek to extend care (the legislature

---

[3] On welfare regimes see Esping-Andersen, G, *The Three Worlds of Welfare Capitalism* (Princeton, Princeton University Press, 1990); a later version incorporates some of the gendered critique of the original typology, Esping-Andersen, G, *Social Foundations of Postindustrial Economies* (Oxford, Oxford University Press, 1999).

[4] Hochschild, AR, 'Global Care Chains and Emotional Surplus Value', in W Hutton and A Giddens (eds), *On The Edge: Living with Global Capitalism* (London, Jonathan Cape, 2000) 130; Parreñas, R, *Servants of Globalization: Women, Migration, and Domestic Work* (Stanford, Stanford University Press, 2001).

and welfare authorities), while others seek to contain costs (the executive branch and the Ministry of Finance); and paid caregivers are situated in many different employment situations—in the public and private spheres, as employees or independent workers, as documented or undocumented migrants, as entrepreneurs or as hourly workers.

The complex pentagon of interests is shaped differently in different welfare regimes and states. Public guarantee of care takes various forms and can be distinguished along various axes, including the method of support (monetary support for family care or provision of care alternatives outside the family), the method of provision (benefits that are designated for care, tax incentives to use care options, and the provision of care in kind), and the mix of public and private measures (public provision of care on the one hand and encouragement of a market for care on the other, with various intermediate hybrids of public and private).[5]

The development of care institutions in Israel displays the diversity of care provision arrangements.[6] While care in the past was considered to be a matter that was predominantly a familial obligation, extra-familial alternatives have gradually emerged. These include aid in the care of infants up to the age of three, after which the public education system takes over. From the age of three until the age at which children become more independent, supplemental care is provided within the education system. Similarly, for children with disabilities, supplemental care is provided until adulthood within the educational system or in separate care institutions and includes in-house care after the end of the school day. For people with disabilities the task of care continues into adulthood and can be provided in the context of the workplace, in rehabilitation and community centres, and in health facilities. A similar mix of in-house care and care in separate institutions is available to the elderly.

Many of these arrangements are public in the sense that some state intervention is necessary. There is a segment of care-work that is wholly in the private sector, although it is limited to individuals and families who can afford the market price of aid. The state draws on various measures of public provision in order to extend care to a larger segment of the population, including direct provision of care in kind, funding or subsidising care options, providing care services for fee and for free, and recognising care expenses for the purpose of taxation. The debates over the optimal method of care provision usually focus on which role the state should assume, the public costs of care, the extent of need, and how public funds could be best distributed to match the needs for care.

---

[5] On the methods of care-work see Shamir, H, 'The State of Care: Rethinking the Distributive Effects of Familial Care Policies in Liberal Welfare States' (forthcoming, *American Journal of Comparative Law*).
[6] *Ibid.*

So far, in this discussion the care-workers have been invisible and instrumental to the general interest in providing care, which is, I argue, commonly the view of the welfare state. The lack of attention to care-workers is not because their work is deemed to be unimportant, but because they are assumed to be like all other workers in that their interests are seen as being met by the operation of the labour market, which includes employment standards and freedom of association. It is this assumption I will contest, arguing that the state actually treats care-workers as exceptional workers and it is heavily implicated in creating their disadvantage.

Care-work is low-status and low-paying, despite variations within and between welfare regimes. As will be demonstrated, there is the high-end of the care industry, provided by market players who demand reasonable market wages from affluent families for a task that is difficult to perform. They are separated from other providers in the field by status symbols and titles such as 'nannies', 'registered private nurses' and the like. Most other care-workers are clustered around the minimum wage. The relative position of care-workers in comparison to others in the low-skilled labour market is shown in Table 11.1.

As demonstrated by Table 11.1, the wages of care-workers are typical of occupations that are dominated by women, but even lower than other occupations in the same group. Drawing on several examples, I will argue that despite the difficulty attributed to care-work, private and public

Table 11.1: Comparison of wages in selected occupations

	Cashiers and clerks	Warehouse staff	Guards and conductors	Laundry, cleaning and kitchen staff	Care-workers
% Female	77	17.7	6.2	72	93.6
Mean monthly wage (NIS)[1]	8,852	8,032	4,515	3,521	3,353
Mean wage per hour (NIS)[1,2]	47	40	27	25	23

Source: Central Bureau of Statistics, Income Survey (2008)
[1] Includes both employees and independent workers. The currency is shekels.
[2] Calculated on the basis of reported monthly income, divided by reported number of hours.

measures of cost containment extend care possibilities by keeping labour costs low.[7] Hence, care-workers are not like other workers, and their wages are not merely the result of market forces, even when the market is confined by general employment standards and collective representation. Institutional factors play a significant role in determining the social position of care-workers. The wages of care-workers are the outcome of intricate institutional considerations that can only be interpreted by looking at the interests of all the agents in the pentagon. The primary focus of the analysis is therefore on the importance of labour market institutions, and their embeddedness in the political economy.

It is difficult to generalise the problems encountered by care-workers, particularly because there is a great diversity of care arrangements that are provided, guaranteed or constructed by the welfare state. In the following section I will abstain from arguing a single logic of care-work and proceed from an inductive approach, drawing on four examples to illustrate very different methods of care provision and different types of care-work. Despite these differences, the examples reveal recurring patterns in which the institutional design of care provision caps compensation and rewards for care-workers. Even in the case of care that is administered through allegedly (private) 'free-market' transactions, wages are determined by (public) institutional factors.

The focus is on the method in which the interests on most sides of the pentagon coalesce to cap the wages of care-workers. However, the four examples also reveal the agency and power of care-workers who respond to the structures that limit them. None of the examples serves as a prime demonstration of collective action, but together they display care-workers' creativity in attempting to deploy countervailing power against the public and private powers that disregard them.

SUPPRESSING THE COSTS OF CARE AND RAISING THE WAGES OF CARE-WORK

The four types of care-work chosen to illustrate the structures that determine the wages of care, as well as the attempts of care-workers and their collective agents to improve their wages and conditions are: (i) care assistants in the education system for the very young; (ii) care-workers for the elderly who are employed by sub-contractors under the umbrella of a publicly funded care programme; (iii) in-home independent care providers

---

[7] This proposition is also aptly demonstrated in Bernstein, S, 'Sector Based Collective Bargaining Regimes and Gender Segregation: A Case Study of Self-Employed Home Childcare Workers in Quebec' in this collection.

for infants; and (iv) migrant care-workers who work in the private sector of care provision. This list demonstrates the institutional heterogeneity that challenges traditional, taken-for-granted boundaries.[8] It does not exhaust the various care arrangements, but it is sufficiently diverse to map the different interests along the sides of the pentagon and to show how they interact, the manner in which legal constructs are used to structure the fundamental suppression of wages, and the methods care-workers adopt to bypass the barrier of cost containment.

Collective Bargaining for Care-assistants Employed in the Public Sector

Nothing intrinsic to care-work suggests that the workers should be employed in casual and privatised arrangements. Indeed, a few care-work arrangements can be found in the public sector, whereby workers are employed directly by the public employer. Given that the public sector is almost completely under the coverage of comprehensive collective agreements, it might be assumed that care-workers will be relatively generously compensated. I will use care-assistants to kindergarten teachers as an example of care-workers who belong to this group.[9]

The assistants are employed by the local municipalities and are represented by the General Histadrut Union (the central labour organisation in Israel), as part of its representation of all employees in local municipalities. They are part of the general bargaining unit which includes all the employees in local government throughout Israel.[10] Their wages and benefits are set by the collective agreements and they are generally at the lowest end of the wage-scale.[11]

In light of a financial crisis faced by many municipalities, the employment conditions of workers in municipalities have been in the spotlight for several years. Furthermore, there has been ongoing controversy between the central and local governments regarding the state's responsibility for aiding

---

[8] Fudge, J, 'Blurring Legal Boundaries: Regulating for Decent Work' in this collection.

[9] Unlike care-workers, kindergarten teachers are required to have a formal college education and certification as a kindergarten teacher. They are represented by the Elementary School Teachers Union and their wages are similar to those of school teachers. I do not deal with workers in education in this Chapter, assuming that care-work and educational work, while related, should be held distinct.

The information in this section of the Chapter was obtained with the help of Adv Gil Bar-Tal of the General Histadrut.

[10] The bargaining unit for the general collective agreement applies to all the municipalities (except the largest three, which conduct separate negotiations for their employees). There are also separate bargaining units in different localities for local collective agreements, which supplement the state-wide agreement. For both the state-wide and the local agreements the care assistants are not represented on an occupational basis, but rather as part of workplace-based (industrial) representation.

[11] See s104.11 of the Local Municipalities' Labour Constitution.

municipalities in crisis. In the process, workers in some municipalities were denied their wages for months. The dispute has also been waged in the courtroom and by means of industrial action.[12] Throughout the process, care assistants were never singled out as a group worthy of particular attention. They have therefore faced the general hardship of the group as a whole, aggravated as a result of their relative ranking in the represented class (although they are not the only low-waged workers in the group).

Given the recognition that they are under-compensated for their service, over the years there have been several attempts to raise the wages of the care-assistants in several municipalities. Usually, these efforts have been initiated by more prosperous municipalities. However, such attempts have run aground against section 29 of the State Budget Law, which requires that extraordinary compensation in a budgeted entity (which includes local government), over and above the common compensation for state workers, must receive prior approval by the Ministry.[13] On the basis of s29, sporadic attempts to raise the compensation of care-assistants have been thwarted, and there were instances in which the Ministry of Finance sought to retrieve unapproved compensation, even though the level of additional payments was miniscule.

In collective negotiations over the wages of municipal workers in 2009, the Histadrut secured additional payments for employees who otherwise are not awarded occupational-related fringe benefits, including the care-assistants.[14] The additional payment raised their wages by approximately 20 per cent. While still low and only slightly above minimum wage, the additional sum is significant to the care-assistants.

Prima facie this is a trivial story of negotiations in the public sector. However, it does hold an important lesson. Studies demonstrate that sector and state-wide (corporatist) bargaining is generally more egalitarian than local and occupational-based bargaining.[15] The care-assistants' membership of the broader bargaining unit of public employees in the municipalities, and the corresponding absence of a designated bargaining unit for care-assistants, has a dual effect on their compensation. On the one hand, it helps

---

[12] The dispute was documented in the National Labour Court Collective Dispute 1016-1019/04 *Chambers of Commerce and others—the General Histadrut* (7 November 2004).

[13] Section 29 of the Budget Principles Law (1985). Absent such approval, the compensation will be retrieved from the employee. Section 29 was introduced in 1985, in order to deter 'irresponsible' fiscal behaviour by entities that receive money from the state's budget, on the assumption that the state will bail them out in times of hardship. It further sought to ensure equal compensation throughout the public sector, broadly defined, so as to discourage an untamed 'race to the top'. On the rationale of s29, see Mundlak, G, *Fading Corporatism: Israel's Labour Law and Industrial Relations in Transition* (Ithaca, Cornell University Press, 2007) ch 4.

[14] General Collective Agreement 2032/2009 between the General Histadrut (Ha-Maof) and the Local Government Bureau, the Municipalities of Tel-Aviv, Jerusalem and Haifa, and the Regional Councils Bureau (25 October 2009).

[15] Kristal, T and Cohen, Y, 'Decentralization of Collective Agreements and Rising Wage Inequality in Israel' (2007) 46 *Industrial Relations* 613.

making the care-workers' problem invisible, as their cause is framed within the broader category of municipal workers. They have no standing as an occupational group, and their political clout within the broader category is rather low. On the other hand, their recent gains were only made possible because their cause was framed within the broader problem of correcting low wages for municipal workers as a whole.[16] Moreover, the general framing of the problem also eliminates other agents from the bargaining table. For example, it brackets the role of the care-work's beneficiaries (the children and their parents), whose participation, as will be demonstrated by other examples later in this Chapter, raises an obstacle to efforts to raise wages. It is difficult to guess the outcomes of a counterfactual scenario in which the care-assistants would have been represented separately. Hence, their integration in the larger bargaining unit is partially a drawback, since it ignores their relative position in the group for the sake of class-based negotiations. At the same time it is also the source of their strength, given that it is entirely uncertain that the claim of assistant care-workers would have elicited much sympathy from the central government.

Collective Representation for Care-workers who are Employed Through Private Intermediaries

Privatisation, broadly defined, includes the growing reliance on private service providers who are contracted by the state to provide public services. This is currently the form that care-work in the public sector most commonly takes. Unlike the care-assistants discussed above, this kind of worker does not have a direct employment relationship with the public employer, but a private employment relationship with the not-for-profit or commercial agency that is the direct employer. However, the subcontractors who employ them provide services that are mandated by law. To demonstrate the nature of this structure of employment, I will draw on the legal initiatives that were made on behalf of care-workers for old people who were found to be in need of care services, under the Care Program for the Old (CARE).[17]

Personal services are provided by the Israeli welfare state in lieu of monetary benefits to various populations, particularly those for whom there is a concern that they will not be able to use monetary benefits properly. These include children in risk, people with disabilities who require rehabilitation, and the disabled elderly. While the law requires the provision of personal services, it does not mandate that these will be provided directly

---

[16] On the importance of framing the group to which benefits apply, see Lester, G, 'Can Joe the Plumber Support Redistribution? Law, Social Preferences, and Sustainable Policy Design' (2011) 64 *Tax Law Review* 313.
[17] National Insurance Law (Consolidated) (1995), ss223–237.

by the state. A process of privatisation has delegated the provision of most personal services to private (not-for-profit) organisations.

The CARE programme was established in 1980 and started operating in 1988.[18] It provides elderly people who face difficulties in performing active daily living tasks with a bundle of personal services from which they can choose, including a specified number of care hours, which are provided by care companies that are licensed by the National Insurance Institute (NII). The number of hours varies according to the level of dependence and level of income. While the benefit is means-tested, its admissibility criteria are relatively generous, and do not target only the elderly who live in poverty.

The decision to provide care hours by the provision of the service in kind was driven by the goal of containing costs, on the assumption that fewer people would apply for hours in kind than for monetary benefits.[19] The decision to delegate the employment of care providers to subcontractors was made to avoid an expansion of employment in the public service, with its rules of seniority and collectively negotiated wages and working conditions. Hence, the state created the demand for the service, and at the same time created the infrastructure for a private market. The state remains in the background by establishing and applying the criteria and choosing the contractors via a tender process.[20] Those in need of care do not pay for the services, and therefore—as in the case of the care-assistants in the municipalities discussed earlier—they are not directly interested in the labour costs of care. However, an important factor in privatisation processes is the guarantee of quality, rather than merely the quantity of hours.

Consequently, the care-providers themselves are not directly employed by the state, nor are they covered by collective agreements that apply to employees in the public sector. The wages and working conditions of the care-workers are determined by the subcontractors. While the subcontractors tend to stick to the minimum level mandated by law, some engage in practices that are on the verge of legality, including the simple evasion of legal standards, or frequent dismissals and rehiring to avoid certain benefits (such as severance pay which is granted to workers terminated after one year of employment).[21] None of the benefits, limited as they may be, which are accorded to workers who are directly employed by the public service

---

[18] On the CARE programme see Schmid, H, 'The Israeli Long-Term Care Insurance Law: Selected Issues in Providing Home Care Services to the Frail Elderly' (2005) 13 *Health and Social Care in the Community* 191; Shamir, above n 5.

[19] On the rationale of the program see Eizenstadt, M and Rosenhak, Z, 'Privatization and New Modes of State Intervention: The Long Term Care Program in Israel' (2000) 29 *Journal of Social Policy* 247.

[20] *Ibid.*

[21] On the problems of employment by subcontractors generally see Davidov, G, 'The Enforcement Crisis in Labour Law and the Fallacy of Voluntarist Solutions' (2010) 26 *International Journal of Comparative Labour Law and Industrial Relations* 61.

(like the care-assistants described earlier), are accorded to those employed by the subcontractors.

Since 1995, the NII, which administers the program, has tried to raise the level of wages and protection to care-workers. Arguments in favour of this initiative were based predominantly on a presumptive causal relationship between improved compensation and job protection and the quality of care that is provided. Given the development of the CARE programme, the NII's efforts did not include the option of incorporating care providers into the state service. Instead, the NII sought to improve their wages and working conditions by changing the conditions in the procurement that is used to recruit contractors to the programme.

Starting in 1995, the Association of Care-Providing Companies filed a series of petitions to the Supreme Court, and later to the newly established District Courts on Administrative Matters, in an attempt to defeat the NII's procurement process. The first petition sought to address the limitation of the number of contractors that would be entitled to provide care-work under the CARE programme.[22] Six subsequent attempts by the NII to proceed with the procurement process encountered further legal challenges, and while the courts have always sided with the NII, the procurement process did not materialise. Following the court's approval of the process in 1995, the legal debate has centred on the NII's requirements for raising the wages and benefits to the care-workers themselves.

The challenge to the employment requirements in the procurement process was based on an argument that such requirements infringe the contractors' freedom of occupation (which in Israel is akin to the right to compete), freedom of contract and property rights. Together the three rights constitute the rights of a free market.[23] The argument was that even if the state proceeds with the process of selecting the contractors providing care-workers for the CARE programme, it is not the state's business to prescribe the workers' employment conditions. More specifically, the companies argued that given the sums awarded to them by the state, their margin of profit after raising the care-workers' wages would be inadequate. The NII defended its position on the basis of the public nature of the programme, the particular nature of the quasi-private market that has emerged, and the concern for cost-cutting and its implications for the quality of care. The NII argued that the care companies pocket considerable portions of the money that is paid for the benefit of the workers themselves (for example, money that is designated for severance pay). In a series of cases the courts upheld

---

[22] Supreme Court HCJ 7217/95 *The Care Providers Association v the National Insurance Institute* (7 July 1997).

[23] On constitutional claims and the free-market tilt, see Gross, AM, 'How Did "Free Competition" Become a Constitutional Right? Changes in the Meaning of the Right to Freedom of Occupation' (2000) 23 *Tel-Aviv University Law Review* 229.

the NII's position, holding that the conditions of the procurement are at the prerogative of the NII, and that the requirements meet the test of reasonableness.[24] The courts also approved the NII's rights to raise standards above and beyond the statutory minimum.

Throughout the decade of litigation, the administrative court held consistently that:

ensuring the quality of service, particularly when it is based on personal service and an intimate relationship between the care giver and receiver, can be promoted, inter alia, by the guarantee of fair compensation for the givers ... This link has been demonstrated and proved in court by the NII.[25]

While this position takes account only of the care-recipients, the court also gave voice to the care-workers, holding that:

[A]s part of the public interest, we should not neglect a basic rule—protecting the rights of the workers providing the service. The parties to the procurement process have an incentive to accept the lowest offer (for the administrative agency that publishes the offer) and the greatest profit (for the contractors bidding in the process). This identity in interests may obviate the public interest that concerns the protection of the workers, even if they do not have a direct relationship to the agency conducting the tender.[26]

An additional element in the saga pertains to the role of the General Histadrut. In the process of litigating one of the petitions against the NII's procurement, the Histadrut and the employers' association drafted a collective agreement that was proposed to the court as an adequate safety net that would make the NII's concerns redundant.[27] The benign explanation for this move was that protection by a collective agreement is more effective than protection by the procurement's conditions that require subsequent scrutiny, assessment and enforcement. The more sinister explanation was that the employers' association, seeking to cap the workers' rights, had allied with the trade union, which sought to expand its membership, or at least the agency fees to be paid by individuals who are covered by the collective agreement, but not members of the union.[28] Unfortunately, the content of the collective agreement supported the latter interpretation since the agreement secured the statutory standards with only a very slim increase beyond what the workers

---

[24] For the NII's position see, inter alia, Jerusalem District Administrative Court 1003/09 *The Care Providers Association et al v National Insurance Institute* (4 February 2009); Jerusalem District Administrative Court 1315/04 *The Care Providers Association et al v National Insurance Institute* (3 July 2005)—decision upheld on appeal Supreme Court 7801/05 (7 February 2006); Jerusalem District Administrative Court 201/01 and 1182/03 *The Care Providers Association et al v National Insurance Institute* (17 February 2002).

[25] Jerusalem District Administrative Court 1003/09, para [30].

[26] *Ibid* at para [36].

[27] Collective agreement between the General Histadrut—the Care Providers Union and the Care Providers Association (an employer's association) (27 December 2004).

[28] On the trade unions' reliance on agency fees see Mundlak, above n 13, at 84–5, 126–7.

were entitled to by law. The court refused to accept the collective agreement as cause for interfering in the procurement process and the collective agreement ultimately met its demise.

In the 2009 litigation on the most recent procurement (again, upheld by the court), the partners to collective bargaining entered into negotiations and once again concluded a new collective agreement.[29] Unlike the previous agreement, this agreement provides a wage hike of 4 to 6.5 per cent, as well as several other rights that improve the workers' income and rights package. While the Histadrut's interest in increasing membership and agency dues remains, its bargaining position has improved, as the procurement process is legally secured and the companies are required to provide a higher level of rights and benefits. The ambivalent role of collective negotiations is indicated by the fact that the parties to the agreement did not register the new agreement as required by law, and there are numerous obstacles for the agreement to actually come into effect.[30]

To conclude, the process described above resulted only in a potential increase in wages and rights for care-workers. The downside of this process was first and foremost the long time required to induce change (approximately 15 years). Secondly, even the procurement process sought to increase the workers' wages and rights at the expense of the contractors' profits, while at the same time respecting and accepting the public budget constraint. Hence, the state sought to raise wages, but to limit its responsibility. It did not consider directly employing the workers, or contributing higher sums to the CARE project. Unlike the relatively simple two-sided story in the first example (employers in local municipalities versus collective agents), this story features more agents with more interests: the Ministry of Finance (capping the public costs and structuring the programme as semi-privatised), the NII (accepting the public cap, but also seeking to improve the quality of care through the tender process), the workers (who have been generally passive throughout the whole process), the employers-contractors who seek to increase their margin of profit, and the trade union that infuses welfare-regarding interests of workers and its organisational self-regarding interests into the equation.

The process does not fit into a simple strategy of collective bargaining. The collective representative of the workers is detached from the workers themselves and is pursuing joint interests with the employers' association. Bargaining is conducted in the shadow of law, whereby the trade union

---

[29] Collective agreement between the General Histadrut—the Care Providers Union and the Care Providers Association (an employer's association) (2 July 2009).

[30] This information was obtained from the State's Commissioner of industrial relations. Among the obstacles it is important to note that the agreement is contingent on obtaining a state-wide extension order. The process of obtaining such a decree cannot be set in motion until the agreement is formally submitted for registration.

sells the interests of the workers at a relatively low price when the legal situation of the procurement process has yet to be determined and later gains strength as the legal legitimacy of the process increases. Procurement processes may be a useful way of collectively improving rights, as well as protecting existing rights, but they are dependent on the multiple and often conflicting motivations of the various agents in the pentagon of interests.

Collective Representation by Independent Workers who Provide Care Services in a Publicly Regulated/Private Provision Regime

While the second example demonstrated the provision of public care by private means, the welfare state also structures quasi-market arrangements when it seeks to make a service accessible to many recipients. Hence, in this category I refer to situations in which the state is not obligated by statute to provide a service, but maintains an interest in its provision by private means. To demonstrate this category, in this section I discuss the arrangement of in-family daycare facilities (IFDC).

IFDC provision generally refers to women who take charge of up to five infants (from six months to three years) for daycare in their homes. The care providers must pass a certification course provided by the Ministry of Labour. They are then licensed to operate the IFDC by the municipality. The state and municipalities establish the days of operation (vacations, for example) and the number of hours per day. They also determine the number of meals that must be provided and the menu. If the IFDC care provider is sick or must take time off, the municipality must receive advance notice and send the children to other IFDCs. The fees are determined by the state/municipality, but collected by the IFDC care provider. Some parents receive subsidies from the state or the municipality. The municipality provides a budget for purchasing items, such as toys. The care providers sign a contract stating they are independent contractors, and that no employer-employee relationship exists between them and the municipality.[31]

In the 1990s there were several attempts by care providers in IFDCs to obtain recognition of their employment status in the labour court, claiming the right to employment benefits. These attempts were rejected by the court in convoluted decisions, which noted that while the conventional test for assessing the existence of an employment relationship yields an ambivalent result, the fact that the care providers signed a contract in which they explicitly agreed to their status as independent contractors raises the level

---

[31] This description is based on the Ministry of Commerce, Trade and Labour's protocol for the operation of IFDCs, available at: www.moital.gov.il/meonot-yom.

of proof that they must demonstrate, and hence the court upheld their independent status and denied their claim.[32]

Consequently, these legally classified independent workers were relegated to the market sphere. However, their margin of profit is almost solely decided by the state. The regulator determines the fees they are allowed to collect and the costs they must bear. Whereas in the case of the workers in the CARE programme, the state sought to raise the workers' wages at the expense of the sub-contractors' margin of profit for the benefit of the people who are in need of care, the situation here is different. The care-workers in the IFDC receive the parents' payments which cover their expenses and their profits. Given the heavy regulatory hand of the state and municipalities, the only way to raise their wages/profit is by raising the level of pay by the parents (or by increasing the subsidies, which would involve increasing the budget). Unlike the NII, which sought to protect the care-workers, in this case the public institutions took the role of guaranteeing the rights of the parents and denied the claims of the IFDC care providers.

In 2008 the Knesset's (Israel's legislature) Research Department attempted to calculate the 'profit/wage' earned by the care-provider, after estimating their earned income and the regulated costs—meals, equipment, utilities and operating costs, events and miscellaneous payments. It found that their 'profit/wage' does not reach the minimum wage level and is approximately 20 per cent lower than the income of a caregiver in a kindergarten.[33]

Since 2008, over a thousand care providers in IFDCs have decided to organise and draw on their collective power to raise their income. Several other issues triggered the organising drive, including the proposal to privatise the state-regulatory body that supervises the IFDCs and problems with the collection of fees in the Arab municipalities. Their organisation was accomplished in the framework of a newly established small trade union that provides grassroots representation to employees. Its strategy is distinct from that of the General Histadrut Union, which was an active participant in the previous examples (the care assistants in public kindergartens and the care-workers in CARE). Although Israeli case law requires that a trade union, by definition, should primarily represent 'employees', the union decided to respond to their request to organise on the basis of

---

[32] See, eg, National Labour Court 95/2-5 *Varda Dabul et al—The State of Israel and the Municipality of Jerusalem* (14 March 1996). It is interesting to compare this position with the Canadian jurisprudence, where similar attempts to carve care-workers out of labour law's protective sphere resulted in similar, albeit more developed, collective organisation. Bernstein, above n 7.

[33] Schwartz, E, *IFDC Fees: Description and Analysis, Research Paper submitted to the Parliamentary Committee on the Rights of Children* (Jerusalem, Knesset Research and Information Centre, 2008). See also Committee on the Rights of Children, *Protocol No 18 of the 18th Knesset*, Second Session (20 October 2009).

three premises.[34] First, the status of care-workers as independent workers should be continuously contested and they should continue to struggle for recognition of their status as employees. Second, even if they are independent workers, their cause is sufficiently similar to that of employees to warrant collective representation. Moreover, the labour court has recognised that the status of employee is not monolithic, and therefore while these workers may not be employees for some purposes, they nonetheless may be considered employees within the domain of the right to associate in a trade union.[35] However, while their collective claim was for the purpose of improving their disposable income (akin to employees' demands), their status as independent workers makes it necessary to target the regulatory tariffs and ask to raise the level of payment to parents.

Given the nature of the claim, the union targeted the Ministry of Labour as the primary responsible agent. Hence, while it is not an 'employer', it is the most appropriate target for negotiations. Throughout 2009, negotiations were conducted by correspondence and in meetings, but after accusing the Ministry of foot-dragging, the trade union held a demonstration in front of the Ministry's main offices in June 2009. Given that the demonstration was conducted during working hours, it was effectively a short strike. A subsequent cessation of work was conducted in May 2010, in protest against a municipality's attempt to terminate the employment of two care-providers. The group's argument was that the decision was based on anti-union animosity and the desire to weaken the power of the organisation. During the last year of negotiations, slight progress was made, such as a partial adjustment of the tariff (falling short, by approximately 66 per cent, of the sum demanded by the caregivers and their union), and costly regulatory requirements were waived (for example, installing an emergency distress button in all IFDCs).[36]

The future of this collective attempt is unclear at the time of writing. However, the last two years have brought together care-workers who are dispersed in thousands of small family set-ups around the country. Of particular interest is the strong alliance between Jewish and Arab caregivers and the solidarity that has been fostered along occupational lines, leaping over ethnic and national divides.

---

[34] The information regarding the organisation drive of these workers was received from Adv Itai Svirski, Director of the Clinical Program on Law and Labour at Tel Aviv University Faculty of Law, who is representing the group.

[35] Supreme Court HCJ, Further Hearing 4601/95 *Sarusi v National Labour Court* (14 October 1998).

[36] Supervisory Warrant on Prices for Commodities and Services (Tariffs for IFDCs) (26 August 2009) 5756 Law Books 192. Further information was obtained from correspondence between the Ministry of Commerce, Trade and Labour, The Department for Day Care and IFDCs and Koach La-Ovdim—Democratic Workers Organization (the trade union representing the IFDC care providers) December 2008—December 2009 (on file with author).

The legal construct of the care-workers in IFDCs is yet another example of how wages are regulated and managed implicitly by public governance. Holding care-providers to be independent workers, like the employment of CARE staff through subcontractors in the previous example, helps to keep wages low and contain the costs of care. While this arrangement seems to guarantee that each and every care-provider must act as an individual entity, the collective organisation of caregivers challenges the boundaries of labour law. It suggests another method of collective representation, which requires overcoming the intrinsic and intentional individualisation of care provision. A complication in this example, unlike the former two, is that the Ministry of Labour must juggle its responsibility to the care-providers on one hand and its responsibility to keep care-costs low in the interest of working parents on the other hand. Care is not only an occupation and a source of income, but also a necessity to allow parents, and particularly women, the possibility of freeing their care-time for the purpose of participating in the labour market. This conflict was made clear by the Minister of Labour, who, in one of the meetings with the union, stated explicitly that he would try to help the care-providers in IFDCs, but he would not permit the added cost to be passed onto the parents.[37] Hence, in the alchemy of care-work, the only possibility of satisfying both conditions (improve income and prevent the raising of tariffs to parents) is to increase the state's subsidy. Such an option is most likely to encounter strong objection from the Ministry of Finance and is currently not feasible.

Collective Representation of Private Providers in a Private Regime—the Case of Migrant Caregivers

The final example is that of care-workers for the old and disabled in the private sector. Beyond the basic provision of care by the state (examples 1 and 2), or the semi-private/public provision of care (example 3), families still require extensive aid at home, particularly in single-parent and dual-career households. Infants who are placed in childcare may still need attention throughout the rest of the day, as the parents' work schedules are often not synchronised with those of the daycare facilities. Caring for parents raises further problems, as parents often do not live with their children, and their needs for help are not fully met by focused programmes, such as CARE. Moreover, many families find that in addition to their growing needs for care-work they have other needs for help in household and family chores, most notably cleaning and cooking.

---

[37] Protocol of meeting held in the ministry with Koach La-Ovdim, 20 July 2009 (on file with author).

There is a wholly private segment of care-work that is provided by care-providers (as well as by providers of other commodified services) and purchased by families who can afford it. Market competition secures wages that are approximately 50 per cent higher than those of the care-workers described thus far. At the same time, the segment of the population that can afford private care is limited. The state's attempt to expand care possibilities, in order to relieve parents of care duties, therefore requires one of two options: increasing the state's funding of care, or suppressing market wages for care-work. The first option does not resonate with the neo-liberalisation of the Israeli welfare state. The previous examples have already shown that the state seeks to limit its public funding. The alternative has been similarly demonstrated by the previous examples, but it would seem difficult to implement in a private market regime. However, the entry of migrant workers into Israel since 1993 has opened up the possibility of publicly intervening in the private market.

The entry of migrant workers is a relatively new phenomenon in Israel. Initially the motivating drive was to infuse the labour market with substitutes for Palestinian workers from the Occupied Palestinian Territories (OPT), who worked primarily in construction, agriculture, industry and services. Work permits and visas have been provided since 1993, in tandem with restrictions on the entry of Palestinians from the OPT. However, the opening of the gates created a new market for care-work. Like the CARE programme, the government's decision to admit care-workers considerably expanded the private market for care. However, permits were granted only for care-work for the old and disabled (and not for children, or for domestic chores). Even as it was creating the demand for care-work, the state took several measures, deliberate or unintentional, to suppress the wages of care-workers.

An important factor in the suppression of wages was the policy that bound each migrant worker to a designated employer. That is, the visa was tied to a work permit, which assigned the worker to an employer, restricting the right of migrant workers to change employers. Consequently, termination of the employment relationship resulted in the termination of the visa as well. Factoring into the equation the thriving industry of labour brokers in Israel and abroad who charge extraordinary sums for their visa and permit arrangements, workers had to preserve their jobs for a long time to secure their expected earnings after paying their debts. Wages for care-workers were therefore established de facto at the minimum wage level, but slack enforcement and the workers' vulnerability led to the widespread practice of underpaying and grossly unfair employment conditions. A growing share of care-workers opted to abandon their jobs and seek undocumented alternative care-work (for children) and domestic work in more affluent households. Hence, documented care-work for families in need was guaranteed by the binding arrangement, and market power was granted to the workers only at the price of becoming undocumented.[38]

Two complementary processes attenuated the cleavage between documented and undocumented work. First, in 2005 the Supreme Court held that the binding arrangement was unconstitutional.[39] Second, the state tightened its immigration enforcement policies, rendering the option of undocumented work more precarious.[40] The Supreme Court ruling was based on the interests of migrant workers themselves, and their right to take part freely in the labour market, rather than only for a designated employer. It also constituted an acknowledgment of the failure of the explicit justification of the binding arrangement—stronger control over the borders. Harsher immigration enforcement policies were driven primarily by the desire to maintain control over migrant workers. The combination of the two processes had the potential to undermine the suppression of wage escalation, although wages remained at the minimum wage level.

The legal drive to increase the migrant care-workers' wages moved to an ongoing series of lawsuits in which NGOs have sought to secure overtime payment for live-in migrant workers. It is noteworthy that this legal strategy was not devised by the trade unions. The General Histadrut has been almost invisible with regard to migrant workers generally and migrant care-workers in particular. Given the nature of care-work, in which workers are isolated in separate households, work around the clock, are unfamiliar with the legal and social culture of the state, and intimidated by the state's institutions, migrant care-workers have resorted mostly to representation, consultation and aid by a number of NGOs. These organisations do not represent their clientele on the basis of membership, but advance collective claims by attempting to change the basic legal infrastructure.

Starting in 2000, a few NGOs, primarily Kav-La'Oved (Workers' Hotline), have represented live-in care-workers who claimed they deserved overtime pay over and above the minimum wage they received. The Labour Court's position on this question has see-sawed several times over the last decade.[41] Certain rulings have held that live-in care-work is exempted from overtime legislation altogether, and therefore overtime pay is merely a contractual matter (and effectively non-existent). At the opposite end of the legal continuum, other rulings have decreed that the law applies to these workers, and that they can succeed by proving their general work timeframe in order

---

[38] On the binding arrangement see Mundlak, above n 13, at 201–7.

[39] Supreme Court HCJ.4542/02 *Kav La-Oved et al v The State of Israel* (30 March 2006).

[40] Mundlak, G, 'Irregular Migration in Israel', *CARIM Analytic and Synthetic Notes—Irregular Migration Series* (2008), available at: http://hdl.handle.net/1814/10104.

[41] For a survey of the case law, see Mundlak, G and Shamir, H, 'Bringing Together or Drifting Apart? Targeting Care Work as "Work Like No Other"' (2011) 23 *Canadian Journal of Women and the Law* 289.

to receive overtime. There have been some creative intermediate options, like paying minimum wages and a general estimate of overtime compensation (for example, 30 per cent of the minimum wage). The final verdict (at the time of writing) was the Supreme Court's intervention, holding that the overtime law does not apply and that *sui generis* legislation is necessary to resolve the problem.[42]

An important component in the debate on overtime has been the need to expand the market opportunities to employ care-workers. The courts, particularly when choosing not to apply the overtime law to live-in care arrangements, have emphasised that the people who are in need of care and their families are a group in need of protection themselves. Moreover, some of the families in need of care rely on state benefits for people with disabilities. These benefits are relatively low and do not fully cover a migrant's wage even without overtime pay. Raising care-workers' wages is likely to leave some of the needy without proper care. Consequently, in the process of litigation, groups representing the care companies and families who are in need of care (particularly those who are reliant on the state's disability benefits) have advocated against the application of overtime pay.

To conclude, even the private provision of care, as in this example, is found to be heavily regulated by the public regime. Only a small segment of care providers and purchasers are actually involved in a predominantly market transaction, and the price of care in that segment is considerably higher than in all other options. This private price of care is indicative of the real market wages, and the other public/private regimes of care provision channel wages and compensation to a considerably lower level.

An additional lesson to be drawn from this final example is the need to identify collective strategies for raising wages and improving employment conditions. The wages and conditions of care providers are determined by the public regime and therefore require a collective response. Where collective organisations, whether the state, trade unions, employers of care-workers or consumer groups (families in need of care), coalesce to maintain the suppression of wages, human and labour rights NGOs step in to voice the collective interest of the care-workers themselves. While the current state of the debate has been resolved against the interest of care-workers, the process was uneven and has also planted the seeds for potential future change, despite the relatively strong coalition of interests against the improvement of wages.

---

[42] Supreme Court HCJ 1678/07 *Yolanda Gloten et al v National Labour Court* (29 November 2009).

STRUCTURE AND AGENCY—SUMMARY OF
FINDINGS AND CONCLUSIONS

The four examples provide an overview of different care arrangements and
the collective strategies that were used in pursuit of change. Table 11.2
summarises the examples.

Table 11.2: Summary of cases

	Care assistants in public kindergartens	Care-workers in the CARE programme	Care providers in IFDCs	Migrant care-workers
Public/private — provision	Public	Private	Private	Private
— Funding	State	State	Parents with some state subsidies	Families
— Regulation of demand	Full—through public service appointments	Determining entitlement on the basis of ADL tests administered by the state	For working mothers and welfare recipients	Employment permits granted to people in need of care, as determined by the state
— Regulation of supply	Wages and benefits of workers are collectively negotiated	Procurement processes select several care companies to provide care hours	Registration and certification of care providers	By means of immigration law and the application of employment standards
Legal (employment) status of care providers	Public sector employees, covered by collective agreements of local municipalities	Care-workers employed by private subcontractors	Independent contractors	Employees in the private sector
'Consumers' of care-work	Disinterested, as the service is publicly provided	Mostly disinterested, as the service is publicly provided, but concerned with quality	Interested, as raising tariffs will increase their expenses for care	Interested, as higher wages will be prohibitive for some

Table 11.2: (*Continued*)

	Care assistants in public kindergartens	Care-workers in the CARE programme	Care providers in IFDCs	Migrant care-workers
Collective forms of wage suppression	Care-workers are placed at the bottom of the collectively negotiated wage scale; legal arrangements to prevent wage rises	Subcontractors limit wages to ensure their own margin of profit, given the state's fixed pay for subcontractors	Fixed tariffs for payment by parents, and regulation of expenses	Binding arrangement and denial of overtime pay
Collective measures for raising wages	An attempt to raise wages for low-waged workers in municipalities (not targeted at care-workers specifically)	An attempt to limit the profit margins of the subcontractors by the National Insurance Institute; currently, an attempt to advance a collective agreement for the entire sector of care-companies	An attempt to organise, despite the fact that the care providers are not 'employees'; collective negotiations with the state over the tariffs and expense requirements	An attempt to raise wages by litigation over regulatory barriers, initiated by NGOs
Outcomes	A 20% wage rise in 2009	A 5% wage rise in 2009	A 10% wage rise in 2009 (while the demand is for a 30% rise in income)	A significant, yet difficult to claim, right to overtime pay (10–35%); in 2009 the right was rolled back by the Supreme Court

The welfare state is responsible to both recipients of care and care providers. The debates over care-work focus on recipients and their families because it is assumed that the general concern of the welfare state for its workers is adequate to provide necessary protection to care-workers as well. However, the comparison demonstrates that the primary goal of extending care options serves as a catalyst for entrenching the low wages of care-workers. Low wages are accomplished through various measures, including the privatisation of care provision (to exclude care-workers from the coverage accorded to state employees), the segmentation of work (to render the association of workers more difficult and to put the concern for care-workers out of mind), the use of atypical employment constructs (to deny them the benefits of employees), and their exclusion from coverage because of the occupation's particular characteristics (the case of overtime exemption).[43] The assumption that the welfare state is therefore involved in the *particular* extension of care options to recipients and the *general* extension of protection to all workers alike is flawed. To attain the former, it is involved in a particular suppression of wages.

As discussed by Einat Albin in this collection, care-work can be regarded as any other occupation, or it can be held to be a distinct form of work.[44] Structures that suppress wages and collective methods of response draw on this interplay. For example, the assistant care-workers in the public kindergarten system are merely part of the diverse workforce in the municipalities. By contrast, in the case of care-workers in the CARE programme it is the particular occupation that is targeted by regulation. There is nothing 'natural' about these distinctions. The reasons why care-assistants in the municipalities are directly employed and blended into a general bargaining unit, while workers for CARE are indirectly employed and treated as a unique group, include historical conjunctures and strategic choices. In the case of both groups, other structures of employment and methods for determining wages could have been applied. It is therefore important to underscore that the question of whether care-workers can simply rely on the general protective measures extended by the welfare state to all employees or require particular protections does not capture the extent of the problem. The pentagon of interests channels and distorts general and particular protections alike. No single measure can be effective without securing power and agency to the care-workers themselves.

---

[43] While the findings focus solely on wages in Israel, the list of legal techniques matches Einat Albin's effective demonstration of labour law's role in constituting the sectoral disadvantage of care-workers; see Albin, E, 'From "Domestic Servant" to "Domestic Worker"' in this collection.

[44] *Ibid*; International Labour Conference, 99th Session, *Decent Work for Domestic Workers: Report IV(1)* (Geneva, International Labour Office, 2009) 13, available at: www.ilo.org/public/english/protection/condtrav/pdf/dw_eng.pdf. See also Blackett, A, 'Promoting Domestic Workers' Human Dignity through Specific Regulation' in A Fauve-Chamoux (ed), *Domestic Work as a Factor of European Identity: Understanding the Globalization of Domestic Work, 16th–21st Centuries* (Bern, Peter Lang SA, 2005) 211.

The many forms of engaging care-workers outside the domain of the 'typical' employment relationship weaken the care-workers agency. However, the examples demonstrate the emergence of atypical forms of response that strategically manoeuvre within the general/particular maze. Care-workers gain a wage supplement in the municipalities because their situation is presented as part of the plight of low-waged workers in general. The care providers in IFDCs claim that they have a right to associate like other workers. They turn to a trade union representing grassroots employees' collective associations and employ collective strategies like those of all others, such as a strike. At the same time, they also emphasise their difference and draw on arguments that highlight the idiosyncratic nature of care-work, the need to assure the quality of care, and the particular difficulties that emerge in this line of work.

The four examples, taken together, indicate that the fragmentation of care provision and its differentiation into multiple forms lie at the basis of the state's method for cost containment. They challenge the argument that the welfare state must focus on the market for care and not on the labour market for care-workers. The examples demonstrate that the welfare state actually places a heavy hand on the labour market. The Brazilianisation of the labour market,[45] which is characteristic of the quasi-privatised state, does not imply the removal of the state's heavy hand. At the same time, the numerous forms of employment and regulation that are used to suppress the power of care-workers are also revealed to be a source of potential power. They create leeway for care-workers to draw on shared occupational interests, particular job-related structures, shared interests with other workers, and the particularities of care provision to advance their claims.

---

[45] Beck, U, *A Brave New World of Work* (Cambridge, Polity, 2000).

12

Sector-based Collective Bargaining Regimes and Gender Segregation: A Case Study of Self-employed Home Childcare Workers in Quebec

STÉPHANIE BERNSTEIN

INTRODUCTION

TENSION BETWEEN ESTABLISHING limits to the cost of most forms of care not provided by family members and adequate remuneration for those who do provide care is neither peculiar to childcare nor to Canada.[1] Childcare policy in Canada, as elsewhere, raises the complex issue of providing affordable and accessible care to enable parents'—and particularly women's—participation in the labour market. Over the years, this policy has been predicated on the acceptance by paid childcare providers of working conditions that are considered affordable to both parents and the State. The policy, in effect, rests on a gendered construction of caring skills and the subsequent undervaluing of care work in economic terms.[2] Even within the world of childcare provision, divisions exist between paid childcare that takes place in childcare establishments, be they not-for-profit or for profit, and that which is offered by home childcare providers. As Guy Mundlak illustrates in his Chapter in this collection, the institutional context in which care is provided is crucial for determining how it is valued as well as the

---

[1] Daly, M, 'Care as a Good for Social Policy' (2002) 31 *Journal of Social Policy* 251; Knijn, T and Kremer, M, 'Gender and the Caring Dimension of Welfare States: Toward Inclusive Citizenship' (1997) 3 *Social Politics* 328, 348–52. See Mundlak, G, 'The Wages of Care-Workers: From Structure to Agency' in this collection.

[2] Findlay, P, Findlay, J and Stewart, R, 'The Consequence of Caring: Skills, Regulation and Reward Among Early Years Workers' (2009) 23 *Work, Employment and Society* 422; Hooyman, N and Gonyea, J, *Feminist Perspectives on Family Care: Politics for Gender Justice* (Thousand Oaks, Sage, 1995).

remuneration and the terms and conditions of work for the care providers. Childcare provided outside the home is formalised and employees of these establishments have been recognised as 'real' employees and benefit from the general application of labour laws and social security schemes accessed through employee status. Home childcare providers, on the other hand, have been relegated to the ill-defined category of 'self-employed worker'.

As working conditions have improved for employees of not-for-profit early childcare centres in the province of Quebec,[3] most notably through collective bargaining efforts, home childcare providers have organised as well to attain parity in working conditions. They have, however, met consistent resistance from the State which depends on these women to help contain the rising costs of childcare for parents—and the State. At the same time, over the years the State has increasingly been regulating the so-called 'private' domain of home childcare in response to parents', and in general society's, desire to ensure the health, safety and cognitive development of children.[4] There is, therefore, a constant formalisation of home childcare in terms of what providers can and cannot do as carers, but until recently there has been little formalisation—in the sense of their legal protection—with respect to their working conditions and access to social protection. As these workers have become indispensable to the viability of Quebec's family policy, their bargaining power has increased and they have undertaken collective action to counter the individualisation of social and economic risk inherent in their self-employed status.

This Chapter explores the recently created sector-based collective bargaining regime for home childcare providers in Quebec. The regime's purpose, on the one hand, is to contain the rising costs to the State of subsidised childcare, and on the other, to appease unions' demands in the political and judicial arenas for the full recognition of home childcare providers' collective bargaining rights. First, I provide a brief overview of childcare policy in Quebec and then I focus on the evolution of the recognition of collective bargaining rights for home childcare providers. This examination of the new regime is followed by some reflections on its potential pitfalls and on its effectiveness in eliminating deeply ingrained gender-based discrimination, as well as discrimination on the basis of occupational status, in relation to care work.

---

[3] Under the Canadian Constitution labour law generally falls under provincial jurisdiction, as does the regulation of childcare services: Constitution Act 1867, 30 & 31 Vict, ch 3 (UK), ss 91, 92.

[4] See the sections applicable to home childcare providers in the Educational Childcare Regulation, Revised Statutes of Quebec [RSQ], ch S-4.1.1, reg 2 ('Educational Childcare Regulation').

SITUATING CHILDCARE POLICY IN QUEBEC

In 1997, a new family policy was launched in Quebec with three main goals: universally accessible educational childcare services[5] with a reduced parental contribution; improved fiscal measures for families with children under 18 years; and provincial parental leave insurance that would be an improvement on the existing federal scheme.[6] This policy reflected an important shift from a paradigm under which families essentially have full responsibility for the well-being of their children, to one which Jane Jenson calls 'an investing-in-children paradigm' whereby this responsibility is shared outside the family, and the State plays an important role in its redistribution.[7] The centrepiece of the policy in Quebec was what would be known as '$5-dollar-a-day daycare',[8] which is a universal, heavily State-subsidised childcare programme. Under this programme, parents would only be required to pay $5 per day and the rest of the childcare cost would be borne by the State.

Although the implementation of the programme took place over three years, it was deemed urgent to create tens of thousands of childcare spots within a short time. Childcare services would continue to be offered by different service providers: not-for-profit early childhood centres, other childcare centres (for profit, workplace childcare, etc) and home childcare providers. Before the implementation of the new childcare programme, government subsidies per place per day totalled $10.79 (Cdn) in early childhood centres and $4.06 per place in home childcare facilities, whereas the parental contribution was $18.06 in the centres and $16.24 for home childcare providers. In 2002–2003, with the reduced parental contribution in place, government contributions to places in early childhood centres rose to $37.54 per day and to $21.83 for places in home childcare facilities.[9]

---

[5] On the educational specificity of Quebec childcare services, see Bigras, N and Cantin, G (eds), *Les services de garde éducatifs à la petite enfance du Québec. Recherches, réflexions et pratiques* (Quebec, Presses de l'Université du Québec, 2008).

[6] Ministère du Conseil exécutif, *Nouvelles dispositions de la Politique familiale: Les enfants au cœur de nos choix* (Quebec, Government of Quebec, 1997). Compared to elsewhere in Canada, Quebec has the most generous leave for expectant mothers and new parents with the entry into force of the Quebec parental insurance plan in 2006 and important changes to minimum employment standards legislation: *Act Respecting Parental Insurance*, RSQ, ch A-29.011 (Parental Insurance Act) and Act Respecting Labour Standards, RSQ, ch N-1.1 (Labour Standards Act), ss 81.2—81.17; Ministère du travail, *Étude comparative de la législation sur les normes minimales du travail au Canada* (Quebec, Government of Quebec, 2009); Organisation for Economic Co-operation and Development (OECD), *Babies and Bosses: Reconciling Work and Family Life: A Synthesis* (Paris, OECD, 2007).

[7] Jenson, J, 'Changing the Paradigm: Family Responsibility or Investing in Children' (2004) 29 *Canadian Journal of Sociology* 169.

[8] The parental contribution has since been increased to $7 a day, Reduced Contribution Regulation, RSQ, ch S-4.1.1, reg 1, s 5.

[9] Ministère de l'Emploi, de la Solidarité sociale et de la Famille, *Scénarios de développement et de financement pour assurer la pérennité, l'accessibilité et la qualité des services de garde: Consultation 2003* (Quebec, Government of Quebec, 2003) 19. Home childcare providers care

As parental demand increased, home childcare spots were seen as a more economical solution to the dearth of spots and, thus, home childcare was regarded as necessary to ensure the viability of the childcare policy. In 2003, 46 per cent of the childcare spots subsidised by the government in Québec were offered by home childcare providers, who, at the time, were under the control of not-for-profit early childhood centres, and the number of places between 1998 and 2003 had almost quadrupled.[10] In 2010, the ratio of home childcare spots to spots in not-for-profit early childhood centres remains about the same (44 per cent).[11]

At the same time, the cost to the State of the reduced parental contribution programme had been rising steadily since its inception in 1997.[12] Among the reasons for the increase in cost were the improved working conditions, including remuneration, of employees in early childhood centres. At the end of the 1980s and during the 1990s, not-for-profit early childhood centre employees had increasingly unionised, and engaged in intense negotiations, that included resorting to pressure tactics, with the government to improve working conditions. Increased union presence in the sector (in 2009, 40.3 per cent of educators employed by not-for-profit early childhood centres were covered by a collective agreement)[13] resulted in vastly improved conditions for these workers.[14] The differences in remuneration, access to fringe benefits and working time between early childhood centre employees and home childcare providers were and remain considerable.[15] To illustrate, in 2010 educators in early childhood centres earned between $16.06 and $21.28 per hour with various benefits, while home childcare providers often earned less than minimum wage ($9.50/hour in 2010), without benefits, while bearing the financial costs of their childcare activities.[16] This disparity in treatment led to a unionisation movement among home

---

for 1 to 9 children at a time. In 2009, 76 per cent cared for 6 to 9 children: Ministère de la Famille et des Aînés, *Situation des centres de la petite enfance, des garderies et de la garde en milieu familial au Québec: Analyse des rapports d'activités 2008–09* (Quebec, Government of Quebec, January 2011) 92.

[10] Ministère de l'Emploi, de la Solidarité sociale et de la Famille, above n 9, at 11. In 2009, 43 per cent of childcare spots were offered by home childcare providers: Ministère de la Famille et des Aînés, above n 9, at 9.

[11] Ministère de la Famille et des Aînés, 'Portrait des services de garde: Places en services de garde' (2011), available at: www.mfa.gouv.qc.ca/fr/services-de-garde/portrait/places/Pages/index.aspx.

[12] Ministère de l'Emploi, de la Solidarité sociale et de la Famille, above n 9, at 17–18.

[13] Ministère de la Famille et des Aînés, above n 9, at 73.

[14] See the evidence summarised in *Confédération des syndicats nationaux v Québec (Procureur général)*, 2008 QCCS 5076, para [156 ff] (*CSN v Quebec*).

[15] Doherty, G, Friendly, M and Beach, J, *Examen thématique de l'éducation et l'accueil des jeunes enfants de l'OCDE: Document de base sur le Canada* (Ottawa, Queen's Printer, 2003).

[16] Ministère de la Famille et des Aînés, *Rémunération du personnel salarié des services de garde et des bureaux coordonnateurs de la garde en milieu familial pour la période 2007–2012* (Quebec, Government of Quebec, 2007).

childcare providers under the Quebec Labour Code,[17] the general collective bargaining regime that applies to employees in Quebec, which resulted, nearly ten years later, in the conclusion of first collective agreements in late 2010.

THE DIFFICULT ROAD TO RECOGNITION OF COLLECTIVE BARGAINING RIGHTS FOR HOME CHILDCARE PROVIDERS

In 2003, the provincial government introduced legislation, Bill 8, to exclude home childcare providers from labour legislation by deeming them to be independent contractors.[18] Thus, these workers were, and still are, the only workers in Quebec to be deemed, by law, to be self-employed.[19] The legislation was adopted in reaction to several labour commission decisions, and eventually a Labour Court (appeals tribunal) decision, that determined, on the basis of criteria developed in previous case law, that home childcare providers were employees of not-for-profit early childhood centres for the purpose of collective bargaining.[20] While Bill 8 was implicitly directed at unionisation and collective bargaining, recognition of employee status was precluded under most labour and social security laws, since the bill stated that these workers could not enter into a contract of employment with their provider of work.[21] By resorting to a form of 'legal fiction', the legislation created an irrebuttable presumption that they were independent contractors, notwithstanding the actual level of control over the home childcare providers' work and their real ability to increase their income through the development of their 'business'. Not only did these laws eliminate all possibility of having the courts determine that the workers are 'employees' by applying the traditional tests developed by the case law, they also reversed administrative, quasi-judicial, and judicial decisions rendered before the amendments came into force at the end of 2003, and in effect cancelled the

---

[17] RSQ, ch C-27, s 1 l (Labour Code).

[18] Bill 8, An Act to Amend the Act Respecting Childcare Centres and Childcare Services, 1st Sess, 37th Leg, Quebec, 2003 (assented to 18 December 2003); Statutes of Quebec 2003, ch 13 (Bill 8). Another category of care workers, intermediate resources, was also targeted by such a deeming provision in a separate bill: Bill 7, An Act to Amend the Act Respecting Health Services and Social Services, 1st Sess, 37th Leg, Quebec, 2003 (assented to 18 December 2003); Statutes of Quebec 2003, ch 12. An intermediate resource is a resource (a person or persons) attached to a public social services institution that provides a person requiring care with a living environment appropriate to his or her needs, while maintaining this person's access to public support or assistance. Such resources are normally located in private dwellings.

[19] With the exception of intermediate resources (see *ibid*).

[20] See, eg, *Centre de la petite enfance La Rose des vents v Alliance des intervenantes en milieu familial Laval, Laurentides, Lanaudière (CSQ)* [2003] DTE 763 (Tribunal du travail).

[21] For example, on the exclusion from the workers' compensation scheme, see, eg, *Simard v Centre de réadaptation en déficience intellectuelle de Québec* (26 January 2004), Quebec 191174-32-0209, CLPE 2003LP-267 (Commission des lésions professionnelles).

certification of existing unions.[22] These workers, almost all of them women,[23] had thus become 'entrepreneurs' under the law, despite the extensive control State agencies wield over how they do their work, when they do their work, and how much they can charge.[24]

Significantly, tensions among workers in the sector regarding a preference for either independent contractor or employee status further facilitated the adoption of the bill. Some home childcare providers preferred the latitude and the fiscal advantages attached to self-employed status and did not wish to be employees, preferring to be their 'own bosses'.[25] So, on the one hand, a group of home childcare providers, grouped together with the Association des Éducatrices en Milieu Familial du Québec, demanded recognition as entrepreneurs and a loosening of some government control over their activities, while on the other hand, other providers formed the Alliance des Intervenantes en Milieu Familial and demanded recognition as employees under labour legislation.[26] The confrontation between an entrepreneurial logic embraced by some home childcare providers and a more classic trade union logic embraced by others[27] no doubt influenced the final legislative outcome, which took six years, with respect to home childcare providers status as independent contractors.[28]

Three of Quebec's main union centrals contested the constitutionality of Bill 8 as contrary to freedom of association guarantees and as sex discrimination and a violation of equality rights under the *Canadian Charter of Rights and Freedoms*[29] and under the *Quebec Charter of Human Rights and Freedoms*.[30] They relied on a 2007 decision by the Supreme Court of Canada, which held that freedom of association under the Canadian

---

[22] Bill 8 ss 1, 3.

[23] In 2009, 99.6 per cent were women, Ministère de la Famille et des Aînés, above n 9, at 92.

[24] Cox, R, *Making Family Child Care Work: Strategies for Improving the Working Conditions of Family Childcare Providers* (Ottawa, Status of Women Canada, 2005).

[25] See the brief presented by the Association des Éducatrices et Éducateurs en Milieu Familial du Québec Inc during the Parliamentary hearings on Bill 8, supporting their recognition as self-employed workers: *Mémoire de l'Association des éducatrices et éducateurs en milieu familial du Québec Inc (AÉMFQ) sur le projet de loi no 8 intitulé Loi modifiant la Loi sur les centres de la petite enfance et autres services de garde à l'enfance* (2003).

[26] D'Amours, M, 'Les logiques d'action collective d'associations regroupant des travailleurs indépendants', (2010) 65 *Relations industrielles/Industrial Relations* 257, 263–66. While most of the home childcare providers seeking recognition as employees were grouped under the umbrella of the Alliance, affiliated with a major Quebec union central—the Centrale des syndicats du Québec, others were affiliated with another major union central, the Centrale des syndicats nationaux.

[27] *Ibid*.

[28] See, eg, the brief presented by the Association des Éducatrices et Éducateurs en Milieu Familial du Québec Inc during the Parliamentary hearings on the 2009 Bill, once again strongly supporting their recognition as self-employed workers: *Consultations particulières sur le projet de loi no 51* (2 June, 2009).

[29] Part I of the Constitution Act, 1982, being Schedule B to the Canada Act 1982 (UK), 1982, ch 11, ss 2(d), 15(1).

[30] RSQ, ch C-12, ss 3, 10, 16.

Charter included collective bargaining.[31] They also filed a complaint with the International Labour Organisation's Committee on Freedom of Association, which determined that the impugned law did not respect ILO principles of freedom of association and collective bargaining.[32] The Committee's conclusions were taken into account in the Superior Court's judgment.[33] In her decision, Judge Danielle Grenier of the Superior Court determined that in effect Bill 8 violated home childcare providers' freedom of association and equality rights.[34]

While Bill 8 allowed for home childcare providers to form associations to further some of their interests, the associations had to comprise 350 members to be recognised as representative by the minister responsible for childcare services.[35] Furthermore, the agreements that could be reached between the associations and the minister did not include agreements on working conditions, but only on the services and programmes offered by home childcare providers.[36] The judge found that the legislative intention behind Bill 8 was clearly to put an end to the home childcare providers' unionisation movement, and curtail their bargaining power by deciding which associations would be considered representative and what could be negotiated.[37] The home childcare providers' freedom of association and collective bargaining rights had therefore been violated; not only was the legislature's intent clear, the State had, as the Supreme Court of Canada stated in its landmark 2007 ruling, 'substantially interfere[d] with the ability of a union to exert meaningful influence over working conditions through a process of collective bargaining conducted in accordance with the duty to bargain in good faith'.[38]

Judge Grenier also found that home childcare workers' equality rights had been violated, as the impugned legislation discriminated against them on the basis of sex because childcare is stereotypically identified as women's work,

[31] *Health Services and Support—Facilities Subsector Bargaining Assn v British Columbia* [2007] SCC 27 (*Health Services and Support*). This decision overturned 20 years of Supreme Court case law on the inclusion of collective bargaining in the guarantee of freedom of association under the Canadian Charter.

[32] Committee on Freedom of Association, 'Complaints against the Government of Canada concerning the Province of Quebec presented by the Confederation of National Trade Unions (CSN) supported by Public Services International (PSI) (Case No 2314); the Centre of Democratic Trade Unions (CSD), the Quebec Trade Union Centre (CSQ) and the Quebec Workers' Federation (FTQ) (Case No 2333)', Report No 340, Cases Nos 2314, 2333, *Official Bulletin*, Vol LXXXIX, 2006, Series B, No 1.

[33] *CSN v Quebec*, above n 14, para [302 *ff*].

[34] *Ibid.*

[35] For an analysis of the impugned legislation, see also Coiquaud, U, 'La loi et l'accès à la syndicalisation de certains travailleurs non salariés vulnérables: une relation pathologique?' (2007) 48 *Les Cahiers de Droit* 65.

[36] Bill 8 ss 73.3—73.5.

[37] *CSN v Quebec*, above n 14, para [291 *ff*].

[38] *Health Services and Support*, above n 31, at para [90]; *CSN v Quebec*, above n 14, at para [314].

as well as on the basis of their occupational status as home care workers, in opposition to early childhood centre employees who were not targeted by the legislation.[39] The judge determined that home childcare providers, as home workers, constitute a vulnerable group that must be protected against discrimination. In doing so, the judge adopted Judge Claire L'Heureux-Dubé of the Supreme Court of Canada's dissident position[40] regarding the recognition of agricultural workers as a disadvantaged and marginalised group on the basis of their occupational status and therefore deserving of the Canadian Charter's protection against discrimination. Judge Grenier's foray into the recognition of occupational status as an analogous ground of discrimination under the Canadian Charter is in itself interesting, and reflects an incipient judicial recognition of a person's precarious 'non-standard' employment status as a potential ground of discrimination.[41]

Again, the judge referred to international law for guidance in determining the normative content of the right to equality and the prohibition of discrimination.[42] In conclusion, she states that Bill 8 'creates a distinction based on an enumerated ground [of section 15 of the Canadian Charter] (sex) and an analogous ground (care work performed in the home in the majority, by women), and this distinction's effect is to perpetuate unfavourable prejudice against people who perform this work, in application of a stereotype that this type of work is not real work'.[43] The judge recognised the interrelated dual forms of legal marginalisation experienced by care workers on the basis of sex and occupational status.

The legislation was struck down and the Attorney General decided not to appeal the decision, no doubt since a provincial election had been called and an appeal was not seen as politically expedient.[44] The Quebec Government began discussions with the concerned unions and existing home childcare provider associations on a new legal framework for

---

[39] *CSN v Québec*, above n 14, at para [364 *ff*].

[40] *Dunmore v Ontario (Attorney General)* [2001] SCC 94, para [71 *ff*].

[41] Under the Quebec Charter, there have so far been two Human Rights Tribunal decisions recognising this form of discrimination under the enumerated ground of 'social condition', interpreted to include occupational status. *Commission des droits de la personne et des droits de la jeunesse v Sinatra* [1999] CanLII 52 (Tribunal des droits de la personne) (denial of access to rental accommodation on the basis of precarious employment status as a freelance journalist); *Commission des droits de la personne et des droits de la jeunesse v Syndicat des constables spéciaux* [2010] CanLII 3 (Tribunal des droits de la personne) (discrimination with respect to working conditions on the basis of casual employee status). See also Paquet, E, 'Le statut d'emploi: Un élément constitutif de la condition sociale?' (2005) 60 *Relations industrielles/Industrial Relations* 64.

[42] *CSN v Québec*, above n 14, paras [321 *ff*], [367].

[43] *Ibid* at para [388] (my translation).

[44] 'Syndicalisation des services de garde en milieu familial—Le gouvernement Charest n'ira pas en appel', *Le Devoir* (24 November, 2008).

representation and collective bargaining for these workers.[45] The result was the 'Act Respecting the Representation of Certain Home Childcare Providers and the Negotiation Process for their Group Agreements'[46] which entered into force in October 2009.

THE NEW SECTOR-BASED BARGAINING REGIME

The new regime is hybrid in the sense that it affords certain traditional guarantees with respect to unionisation and collective bargaining, while at the same time deeming a home childcare provider to be a self-employed worker. She is thus defined as 'a natural person, [...] who is an own-account self-employed worker who contracts with parents to provide childcare in a private residence, in return for payment'.[47] The only other complete collective bargaining regime for self-employed workers in Quebec is the status of the artist regime which applies to self-employed artists.[48] However, artists who are not self-employed are covered by the general regime under the Quebec Labour Code which applies to employees. The applicable collective bargaining regime for artists therefore depends on the employee status of the artist, according to traditional criteria developed in the case law. This is not the case for home childcare providers. The reality of their relationship with the home childcare co-ordinating offices[49] (which play a role similar to that played by early childhood centres before a series of legislative amendments, and, while the name has changed, many of the co-ordinating offices are in fact early childhood centres) is immaterial.[50]

The law creates a sector-based collective bargaining regime in which certification provides the bargaining agent exclusive representation on a territorial basis; there cannot be two associations representing home childcare providers with activities on the same territory and affiliated to the same home childcare co-ordinating office.[51] This provision mirrors the traditional collective bargaining regime in Quebec and Canada generally, which recognises the majority union as the sole bargaining agent of a defined group of

---

[45] Government of Québec, 'Communiqué : Dépôt des projets de loi pour les responsables de garde en milieu familial (RSG) ainsi que pour les ressources intermédiaires de type familial' (13 May, 2009).

[46] RSQ, ch R-24.0.1 (Home Childcare Providers Act).

[47] Home Childcare Providers Act s 84; Educational Childcare Act, RSQ, S-4.1.1, s 53.

[48] Act Respecting the Professional Status and Conditions of Engagement of Performing, Recording and Film Artists, RSQ, ch S-32.1; and Act Respecting the Professional Status of Artists in the Visual Arts, Arts and Crafts and Literature, and Their Contracts with Promoters, RSQ, ch S-32.01.

[49] Educational Childcare Regulation s 45 *ff.*

[50] Home Childcare Providers Act s 61.

[51] *Ibid* at ss 8, 10–11.

222 *Stéphanie Bernstein*

workers in its dealing with an employer.[52] Once the association has been certified, it has the mandate to defend and promote the 'economic, social, moral and professional interests' of its members, who, in turn, must pay the dues determined democratically by the association.[53] Dues are collected by the minister responsible for childcare services by deducting them from the grant payable to the home childcare provider, and they are then sent to the association.[54] The association can also negotiate and conclude a collective agreement—or 'group agreement' as it is called in the legislation[55]—according to the terms set out in the law.

The associations, or groups of associations, within or outside of a union central, negotiate directly with the minister, and both parties have a duty to bargain in good faith.[56] The matters that can be negotiated include, but are not limited to, the government childcare subsidy (which directly affects the providers' remuneration), leave and holidays, procedures for interpreting the group agreement, the establishment of different committees, and the compensation due to providers for lost income when their permit has been unjustly revoked.[57] The negotiation of other issues will depend on the bargaining power of the associations. Most importantly, however, contrary to Bill 8, working conditions can now be the subject of negotiation. Remuneration is specifically addressed in the law, which says that home childcare providers should, through collective bargaining, receive funding that allows them to be remunerated on a level commensurate with the salary of employees doing similar work.[58] In particular, the funding should be sufficient to also include compensation for holidays prescribed under the Labour Standards Act, parental insurance premiums, workers' compensation premiums, public health insurance premiums, and some work-related expenses, all of which are normally paid by employers.[59]

On a procedural level, the law models the dispute resolution mechanisms on those available to employees and their employers, including mediation and arbitration.[60] Home childcare providers also have the right to engage in strike action. In this case the minister can withhold financing, but a provider

---

[52] Labour Code s 21 *ff.*
[53] Home Childcare Providers Act s 18. Under the Quebec Labour Code, the employer deducts the dues from the employees' wages and remits them to the union (s 8). Under the 'Rand Formula', all employees must contribute regardless of whether or not they are union members. The home childcare provider's regime also requires that all providers affiliated with a co-ordinating office where a recognised providers association exists pay dues. Home Childcare Providers Act ss 18, 19.
[54] Home Childcare Providers Act s 19.
[55] Home Childcare Providers Act s 30 *ff.*
[56] *Ibid* at ss 30, 37.
[57] *Ibid* at s 31.
[58] *Ibid* at s 32.
[59] *Ibid* at s 32. Parental insurance premiums are paid by employers and employees.
[60] *Ibid* at ss 38 *ff*, 56–7.

cannot lose her permit or be otherwise sanctioned for having participated in this action.[61] The law also provides limited recourse in the case of reprisals for home childcare providers' participation, or non-participation, in union activities, and in the case of interference by the minister or third parties in the formation or the activities of an association.[62]

While the new regime is a notable improvement on Bill 8, it still presents serious shortcomings given the situation of home childcare providers. Several statutes that cover employees and establish a minimum floor of protection do not apply to them.[63] One of these statutes is the Labour Standards Act, which regulates minimum wages, hours of work and overtime, statutory holidays, unpaid parental and family leave, unpaid sick leave, prior notice in the case of lay-offs, protection against unjust dismissal and the prohibition of psychological harassment. The scope of this law is vast and there are very few exemptions, making it a veritable minimum threshold for collective bargaining.[64] This threshold has particular implications for women workers in the context of work–family balance, for instance, since it sets out limits on working time and determines the length of maternity, parental and family leave, and provides for job protection when taking this leave. While the provincial parental insurance scheme[65] covers self-employed workers with respect to income replacement, this scheme offers none of the guarantees of the Labour Standards Act. These guarantees will now have to be bargained. However, other provisions regulating childcare services already place potential limits on what can be bargained, since the agreement reached with the minister cannot contradict the rules set out in the law regulating childcare services.[66] For example, a home childcare provider who has to interrupt her activities by reason of the birth of a child can only suspend her activities for 12 months.[67] If she were considered to be an employee, she would be able to take up to 70 weeks of leave.[68]

Occupational health and safety legislation[69] does not apply to home childcare providers either, although the provisions on preventive reassignment for pregnant workers do apply until the government adopts a regulation

---

[61] *Ibid* at s 49 *ff.*

[62] *Ibid* at ss 5–7.

[63] *Ibid* at ss 108–10.

[64] Bernstein, S, 'Mitigating Precarious Employment in Quebec: The Role of Minimum Employment Standards Legislation' in LF Vosko (ed), *Precarious Employment: Understanding Labour Market Insecurity in Canada* (Montréal, McGill-Queen's University Press, 2006) 221. On the role of minimum employment standards legislation, see also Fudge, J, 'Reconceiving Employment Standards Legislation: Labour Law's Little Sister and the Feminisation of Labour' (1991) 7 *Journal of Law and Social Policy* 73; Blackett, A and Sheppard, C, 'Collective Bargaining and Equality: Making Connections' (2003) 142 *International Labour Review* 426, 443–4.

[65] Parental Insurance Act, SQ 2005, c 13.

[66] Home Childcare Providers Act s 33(1).

[67] Educational Childcare Regulation s 79.

[68] Labour Standards Act ss 81.4 and 81.10.

[69] Act Respecting Occupational Health and Safety, RSQ, ch S-2.1.

to create a specific programme for home childcare providers.[70] Preventive reassignment allows a pregnant worker to be assigned work or to have her schedule modified to eliminate any danger to the pregnancy or to the foetus. If reassignment is not possible she is entitled to receive income replacement through the workers' compensation scheme. It is not surprising that this exception to the exclusion from the Occupational Health and Safety Act was included in the new regime since the risks to pregnant early childhood workers are documented (viral and bacterial infections, heavy lifting, etc).[71] However, rules on protective equipment and on the right to generally refuse dangerous work, for example, do not apply. Home childcare providers can be covered by workers' compensation in the event of an occupational accident or illness, but they have to self-insure: if they have not paid the premiums they are not covered, unlike employees who are automatically covered, whether or not their employer has paid the premiums.[72] The government also contributes to a pension plan for early childhood centre employees, from which home childcare providers are expressly excluded.[73] Improvements to this situation can be bargained, but the new regime has eliminated the minimum threshold.

Finally, independent contractors are excluded from the purview of the Quebec Pay Equity Act,[74] and, despite opposition from trade unions,[75] the home childcare provider regime reiterates this exclusion.[76] In September 2006, a pay equity agreement was signed between the government and early childhood centre employees,[77] which increased the cost of childcare services for the State. Yet home childcare providers are in no less a female-dominated occupation (99.6 per cent) than employees of early childhood centres. This exclusion will no doubt hinder the elimination of disparities of treatment between those who work in their home and those who work in centres. It also poses questions of public policy aimed at the elimination of wage disparities between

---

[70] Home Childcare Providers Act s 108. At the time of writing this text, no regulation had yet been adopted.

[71] See, eg, Bright, KA and Calabro, K, 'Child Care Workers and Workplace Hazards in the United States: Overview of Research and Implications for Occupational Health Professionals' (1999) 49 *Occupational Medicine* 427.

[72] Act Respecting Industrial Accidents and Occupational Diseases, RSQ, ch A-3.001, s 18.

[73] Act to Facilitate the Establishment of a Pension Plan for Employees Working in Childcare Services, RSQ, ch E-12.011, s 2§2.

[74] RSQ, ch E-12.001, s 9. There is a limited exception to this exclusion which might have applied to some home childcare providers before the adoption of the Home Childcare Providers Act. See Cox, above n 24, at 60–1.

[75] See, eg, Confédération des syndicats nationaux, 'Mémoire de la Confédération des syndicats nationaux (CSN) sur le projet de loi 51' presented to the Commission des affaires sociales, Québec (3 June 2009).

[76] Home Childcare Providers Act s 109.

[77] Ministère de la Famille et des Aînés, *Bureaux coordonnateurs de la garde en milieu familial: Règles budgétaires pour l'année 2009–2010* (Quebec, Government of Québec, 2009) 8.

men and women in the labour market,[78] as well as concerning some of the concessions that were made to the government under the new regime.

EMBEDDED GENDER SEGREGATION OR REINFORCED BARGAINING POWER?

The regime is still young, but it is nevertheless already worthy of study. Most importantly, it is a sui generis model of sector-based bargaining targeting a category of workers—female workers—who have always operated on the margins of labour and social security regulation. After a series of court decisions confirming their employee status, this status was nevertheless relinquished in favour of that of independent operator. Recourse to a large number of self-employed home childcare providers was considered necessary by the government to fulfil the promise of the 1997 Quebec family policy; in fact, this appears to have been one of the essential premises of the policy. Its success has thus in part been predicated on home childcare providers bearing a considerable part of the economic and social risks of their work.

Indeed, the regime is founded on a continued 'legal fiction'. The situation of home childcare workers has not substantially changed since the judicial battle over Bill 8. They remain economically dependent on the government: they can only charge $7 (previously $5) to parents, although, now with the new regime, through their associations, they will be able to negotiate, to a certain extent, the amount of the government subsidy for childcare spots. Their work and the organisation of their place of work (their home) is highly regulated in the interest of the children's well-being. They must notify the co-ordinating office, which is mandated by the government, if they take leave, and inform the office of their opening hours and of the services offered.[79] Home childcare facilities offer extended opening hours with 53 per cent open in the evening, 23 per cent at night and 31 per cent at weekends, compared to early childhood centres which offer almost no services in the evening, at night or at weekends.[80] In the end, providers have relatively little control over their work. They have gone from a disguised employment relationship[81] to de jure self-employed workers. Yet, despite them being deemed 'self-employed', they remain 'employee-like' and should therefore be protected by a substantial part of protective labour legislation.[82]

---

[78] On these policies in Quebec, see Bernstein, S, Dupuis, M-J and Vallée, G, 'Au-delà de l'égalité formelle: Confronter l'écart entre les sexes sur un marché du travail en mutation', in P Auvergnon (ed), *Genre et Droit Social* (Bordeaux, Presses Universitaires de Bordeaux, 2008) 357.

[79] Educational Childcare Regulation.

[80] Ministère de la Famille et des Aînés, above n 9, at 104.

[81] International Labour Conference, 91st Session, *The Scope of the Employment Relationship: Report V* (Geneva, International Labour Office, 2003) 19.

[82] Davies, P and Freedland, M, 'Employees, Workers, and the Autonomy of Labour Law' in H Collins, P Davies and R Rideout (eds), *Legal Regulation of the Employment Relationship*

The elimination of a minimum threshold with regard to working conditions and access to several forms of social protection for home childcare providers inevitably means that bargaining on these issues will be that much more difficult. While the legislator expresses the wish that bargaining result in conditions comparable to those of employees doing this work, there are no guarantees that this will be the case. The express exclusion of home childcare providers from pay equity legislation and the government-financed complimentary pension plan for employees of childcare establishments sets, to a certain extent, the terms of bargaining with respect to remuneration. While some social risks have been collectivised in Quebec (eg health coverage), home childcare workers have shouldered a disproportionate burden of these risks in light of their level of remuneration in the form of additional premiums for most social security schemes. They also bear the cost of their work activities, which again must be undertaken according to government specifications, thereby making their level of remuneration vulnerable to fluctuations. There has been, in effect, an unequal distribution of social and economic risks[83] between home childcare providers and employees in childcare centres, although the work performed is essentially the same and part of the same family policy. An artificial status of independent contractor has thus been imposed to consolidate this difference in treatment which leaves home childcare providers in a more vulnerable position than their counterparts in early childhood centres. Yet are they any less deserving of legislative protection?

As Guy Davidov explains, employees' need for protection rests on the level of control exercised by an employer, the role played by the employer in giving importance—both socially and individually—to the work, and on the ability of workers to spread work-related risks.[84] While Davidov's aim is to re-examine the traditional criteria used to determine employee status, and thus coverage under labour law, the factors he has identified also serve more generally to explore workers' level of protection in relation to their bargaining power with the entity that defines the parameters of the work relationship. Despite their categorisation as self-employed workers, home childcare providers are subject to control over their work, albeit through

---

(The Hague, Kluwer Law International, 2000) 267, 274–8. A similar position was adopted by the Commission on the Federal Labour Standards Review, whereby it was recommended that a new category of 'autonomous worker' be established and '[t]o the extent necessary to protect their basic right to decent working conditions, and to protect the interests of employees from unfair competition, 'autonomous workers' should be eligible for limited coverage under [federal minimum labour standards legislation]'. The extent of this coverage would be sector-based. This recommendation has not been implemented. Commission on the Federal Standards Review, *Fairness at Work: Federal Labour Standards for the 21st Century* (Ottawa, Human Resources and Skills Development Canada, 2006) 64.

[83] D'Amours, M, *Le travail indépendant: Un révélateur des mutations du travail* (Quebec, Presses de l'Université Laval, 2006).

[84] Davidov, G, 'The Three Axes of Employment Relationships: A Characterisation of Workers in Need of Protection' (2002) 52 *University of Toronto Law Journal* 357.

the regulation of childcare services and not through the more traditional means of being under the direct or indirect control of an employer. They are also dependent on the State for both the financial and the social recognition of their work. Finally, they have little ability to spread their risks, since they have no control over what they can charge nor over how they can organise their work to avoid certain risks, and their low income does not generally allow them to insure against unforeseen events (eg long-term illness or destruction of their workplace by fire).

In a 2003 report to the Quebec Minister of Labour on the need for protection of particular categories of workers (employees in 'non-standard' work and own-account self-employed workers), Jean Bernier, Guylaine Vallée and Carol Jobin proposed extending coverage of labour legislation, including pay equity legislation, to workers in 'employee-like' situations.[85] They also proposed a series of measures targeting own-account self-employed workers to ensure the application of some labour laws covering only employees, which go beyond simply facilitating the uncovering of 'disguised' employment relationships. For example, the report recommended that 'real' own-account self-employed workers should be covered by occupational health and safety legislation, which includes the right to refuse to perform dangerous work and to preventive reassignment.[86] In particular, the report recommended the establishment of a general, non-sector-specific collective bargaining scheme for own-account self-employed workers enabling them to attain better working conditions and levels of social protection.[87] This regime would guarantee rights attached to unionisation, such as protection against reprisals and against domination of an association by the provider of work. It would also establish a duty for the parties to negotiate in good faith and mechanisms for dispute resolution. The recommendations in the report were not implemented, but, as we have seen, the new home childcare providers' regime has integrated many of these elements.

At the time of writing this text, over 30 home childcare provider associations had been certified, and three collective agreements had been concluded, grouping together associations affiliated with two union centrals and one independent province-wide association, and covering most

---

[85] Bernier, J, Vallée, G and Jobin, C, *Les besoins de protection sociale des personnes en situation de travail non traditionnelle. Rapport final* (Quebec, Ministère du Travail, 2003) 431. The definition of the relationship would limit itself to three factors: the person works for another person (natural or legal) in exchange for payment, the existence of an employment contract under traditional case law would not have to be proven, and the person personally works for another person and is economically dependent on this person. Judy Fudge, Eric Tucker and Leah Vosko go a step further and propose that labour law protection should be extended to persons who personally perform work for remuneration: Fudge, J, Tucker, E and Vosko, L, 'Changing Boundaries in Employment: Developing a New Platform for Labour Law' (2003) 10 *Canadian Labour and Employment Law Journal* 361.

[86] Bernier, above n 85, at 515 *ff*.

[87] *Ibid.*

providers in the province (approximately 15,000).[88] Some limited strike action was undertaken to hasten the negotiation of first group agreements, leading to the signing of an agreement in principle in November 2010.[89]

Some important gains with respect to remuneration were made: compensation for 24 days off per year including eight legal holidays (before there was no compensation) and compensation (18.6 per cent of the government grant per child) for a portion of what employers would pay for compulsory contributions to government social protection programmes (workers' compensation, public pension scheme, parental insurance, health insurance) and for contributions to private group health insurance and retirement plans. However, it should be noted that, since providers are independent contractors, they must self-insure and the payment of workers' compensation premiums remains voluntary; they also do not have access to the public unemployment insurance scheme. The group agreements also contain provisions on union leave and professional training. Finally, each of the agreements creates province-wide joint committees whose mandate is to discuss difficulties relating to their interpretation and application. In the relatively short period of time since the entry into force of the new regime, the providers have been able to organise on a province-wide level and establish sufficient bargaining power to conclude first group agreements.

CONCLUSION

Unionisation in the care work sector has enabled women workers, particularly employees in the public sector, to challenge some of the gender-based assumptions surrounding this sector and to participate more fully in setting the conditions and the limits of their work.[90] Yet, certain categories of care workers—in this case home childcare providers, but domestic workers are an even more emblematic example—have been particularly marginalised within the dominant (and, arguably, more effective in terms of the improvement of working conditions) collective bargaining regimes

[88] 'Entente collective intervenue entre la Ministre de la Famille et la Fédération de la santé et des services sociaux-CSN' (25 March, 2011), 'Entente collective intervenue entre la Ministre de la Famille et la Centrale des syndicats du Québec' (12 April, 2011), 'Entente collective intervenue entre la Ministre de la Famille et le Regroupement des travailleuses et travailleurs autonomes des centres de la petite enfance' (21 April, 2011), available at: www.mfa.gouv.qc.ca.

[89] See, eg, 'Plusieurs garderies en milieu familial intensifient leurs moyens de pression dès ce matin', *Le Devoir* (5 July, 2010); 'Les responsables de services de garde en milieu familial sont en grève mercredi', *Le Devoir* (10 November, 2010); Ministère de la Famille et des Aînés, 'Le Gouvernement du Québec conclut des ententes historiques avec près de 15 000 responsables d'un service de garde en milieu familial', press communiqué (25 November, 2010), available at: www.mfa.gouv.qc.ca.

[90] Armstrong, P and Armstrong, H, 'Public and Private: Implications for Care Work' (2006) 53 *The Sociological Review* 169, 173.

targeting employees.[91] This marginalisation with respect to collective bargaining rights is necessarily exacerbated when women workers are further pushed out of the scope of labour legislation in answer to perceived policy (ironically family policy in this case) requirements. Indeed, the situation of self-employed women workers generally also reflects existing gender segregation in the labour market, as they fare less well than self-employed men and suffer from a larger wage gap with men than women who are employees.[92] Home childcare providers are thus doubly disadvantaged as care workers and as self-employed workers.

The Quebec home childcare providers' collective bargaining regime is unique in the sense that it establishes the parties' 'terms of engagement' by razing the edifice of legislated protective norms, in order to rebuild this protection to the extent allowed by the providers' bargaining power. It is apparent that without the support of established trade unions over an extended period of time the bargaining rights of home childcare providers in Quebec would continued to have been ignored. Without a doubt, the new regime has remedied many of the democratic deficits of Bill 8, and has put home childcare providers in a better position to negotiate the terms of their work and social protection. But the establishment of a specific regime for this category of workers also contributes to confirming gender segregation in the labour market, and the continued undervaluing of care work in terms of skills recognition and remuneration. Care work, and in this case more specifically childcare, have yet to be adequately identified in public policy, including labour law, as a 'public good' deserving of the same, or even more, consideration and valuing as work in other sectors.[93] It remains to be seen whether the new regime will serve to further divide workers in the childcare sector on the basis of occupational status, with some early childhood educators enjoying recognition as 'real' workers within the fold of the traditional collective bargaining regime and labour and social security legislation, and others depending solely on the bargaining power they can establish within the institutional framework of Quebec family policy. Or, on the contrary, it is possible that the new regime will be a catalyst to level the playing field: the gains made with the first group agreements are cause for cautious optimism. Only the results of the renegotiation of these agreements over the next years will tell which of these possibilities will be realised.

---

[91] Blackett and Sheppard, above n 64. See Albin, E, 'From "Domestic Servant" to "Domestic Worker"' in this collection for a discussion of domestic workers.

[92] Hughes, K, *Gender and Self-Employment in Canada: Assessing Trends and Policy Implications* (Ottawa, Canadian Policy Research Networks, 1999) 4.

[93] Fischl, RM, 'A Woman's World: What if Care Work Were Socialized and Police/Fire Protection Left to Individual Families' in J Conaghan and K Rittich, *Labour Law, Work, and Family: Critical and Comparative Perspectives* (Oxford, Oxford University Press, 2005) 339; see also Knijn and Kremer, above n 1.

13

From 'Domestic Servant' to 'Domestic Worker'

EINAT ALBIN

INTRODUCTION

DOMESTIC WORK IS one of the most challenging forms of work for labour law. It is situated at a junction of paid labour and work in the home, triggering common conceptions of the law regarding what is seen as 'work', the forms of 'employment relationship', and the boundaries between the private sphere of the household and the labour market. This year the ILO has addressed the challenge of regulating domestic work, adopting a Convention and a Recommendation that set a baseline of labour standards for the protection of domestic workers.[1] The ILO's position is that domestic work should be seen as 'work like any other, work like no other', and this Chapter assesses that approach by taking a look at the regulation of domestic work from an historical perspective.

Although domestic work seems to be closely associated with changes that have characterised the labour market in recent years—the growing employment of women, processes of globalisation, and the increase in consumption of services in the household—it is, in fact, one of the most ancient sectors in the labour market. It is a sector that can be defined by the term 'sectoral disadvantage', meaning a situation in which the *rules* of a specific sector—its structure and culture—impact on workers in the direction of disadvantage. The notion of 'sectoral disadvantage' posits the sector as a central locus of investigation; within a sectoral context, it is claimed,

---

[1] *Domestic Workers Convention* 2011 (ILO C189); *Domestic Workers Recommendation* 2011 (ILO R201); and see also previous reports of the ILO on the subject: International Labour Conference, 99th Session, *Decent Work for Domestic Workers: Report IV(1)* (Geneva, International Labour Office, 2009) 1–2; International Labour Conference, 99th Session, *Decent Work for Domestic Workers: Report IV(2)* (Geneva, International Labour Office, 2010); International Labour Conference, 99th Session, *Committee on Domestic Workers: Draft Report* (Geneva, International Labour Office, June 2010).

insights can be gained into the complex state of disadvantage, including its embeddedness in history.[2]

For several centuries domestic work has been subject to legal regulation. Thus, in order to understand the sectoral disadvantage of domestic workers in thinking about the legal mechanisms regulating their terms and conditions of work, it is crucial to consider how the law has dealt with domestic workers in the past. The Chapter does so by focusing on the historical legal category of 'domestic servant' that existed in British labour law until the mid-twentieth century. It shows how the current legal situation of domestic workers is rooted in this past historical categorisation, emphasising that continuity extends between that historical category and the current sectoral disadvantage of domestic workers. Even though it may seem that '[t]he eighteenth-century hired domestic servant's contractual status and legal persona make her or him difficult to compare with unregulated, informal twenty-first century domestics',[3] within legal thought there is, in fact, a strong link between the two situations.

This continuity does not mean that there haven't been any transformations, but because these have drawn the attention of studies in recent years, this Chapter places more focus on continuity and its implications for the workers' legal situation. My analysis stresses that historical legal regulation took a dominant part in shaping the boundaries between different forms of work, employment relationships, and private and public. On the basis of this analysis, I shall go on to assess whether and to what extent the ILO's new Convention and recommendations may potentially be suited to address the problems encountered by domestic workers in the British field of labour law. I argue that domestic work has to be treated as 'work like no other', and that towards that end a sectoral focus makes an important contribution to thinking about its regulation. The ILO Convention and recommendations take an important step in that direction. However, several of the core causes of domestic workers' disadvantage have not been touched upon and remain to be dealt with in the future.

The Chapter is structured as follows. The first part discusses the historical legal category of 'domestic servant' from the eighteenth century until the mid-twentieth century. The Chapter then addresses the current legal situation of domestic workers under British labour law, stressing its embeddedness in historical legal thought. The third part looks at the ILO Convention and recommendations, and the last part concludes.

---

[2] On the notion of 'sectoral disadvantage' see Albin, E, *Sectoral Disadvantage: The Case of Workers in the British Hospitality Sector* (University of Oxford, DPhil dissertation, 2010) introduction and ch 1.

[3] Steedman, C, *Labours Lost: Domestic Service and the Making of Modern England* (Cambridge, Cambridge University Press, 2009) 28.

THE HISTORICAL 'DOMESTIC SERVANT' LEGAL CATEGORY

Several recent studies have focused on the historical group of domestic servants, which up until now has been quite neglected in theoretical literature on the British labour market and its regulation. Domestic servants were omitted from the writings of most of the central theorists, among them Adam Smith, Karl Marx and Edward Palmer Thompson, who concentrated so heavily on the manufacturing sector that they tended to disregard the significance of domestic work.[4] This paved the way for leaving a very central and involved group of workers—domestic servants—outside the scope of theoretical thought about the labour market, its workers, and its laws.[5] However, recent studies on the historical group of domestic servants show that during the eighteenth and nineteenth centuries domestic servants were a central and recognised group of workers within the labour force.[6]

In this Part, I will show that domestic servants constitute a legal category that was central to labour law discourse, and that court judgments and legislation have led to this category being situated as distinct from other categories of workers. Boundaries emerged between different legal categories. These boundaries benefited domestic servants during the eighteenth and nineteenth centuries, placing workers located within this category in a rather advantageous position in comparison to those included in other categories of workers. However, in due time the continued existence of this category and its distinction from other groups of paid labour were strengthened by the courts and by legislation. By the end of the nineteenth century and especially during the twentieth, this distinction placed domestic servants at a disadvantage. As will be discussed below, this process occurred at a time when collective bargaining was growing, and when the contract of employment and worker-protective legislation were being increasingly developed.

Scope of Protection for the Historical 'Domestic Servant' Legal Category

The antecedent of the term 'domestic servant' is the term 'menial servant', which existed in British legislation from the fifteenth century on. This group was the first type of servant to be introduced by Blackstone in his

---

[4] Smith, A, *The Wealth of Nations, Books I–III* (London, Penguin Books, 1986) 429–49, 133–40; Marx, K, *Capital Volume 1* (London, Penguin Books, 1990) 1043–5; and see generally Steedman, above n 3, at 16–17, ch 2.

[5] Figures show that domestic service was a central occupation in Britain. In 1911 it was the occupation with the largest number of workers (1,302,438). See 1911 census at: http://media.1911census.co.uk/census-factsheet.

[6] Steedman, above n 3; Albin, above n 2, at ch 3.

Commentaries, 'so called from being *intra moenia*, or domestics'.[7] The meaning of the Latin word *moenia* is 'walls', especially the walls of the household or encircling walls. According to Blackstone's definition, the term menial referred to those working *and* living within the household. This can be deduced from his discussion of another type of servant, the class of labourers who 'do not live *intra moenia*, as part of the household'.[8] Menial servants were seen as having a private, personal relationship with their masters. Two of Blackstone's other groups also shared personal forms of relationship, namely apprentices and labourers,[9] but domestic servants were unique in their assimilation within the family home.

Menial servants were one group of servants among others, and all were conceptualised as forming the workforce. The recognition of different groups of workers is a fundamental characteristic of that period, as Deakin and Wilkinson have shown. In their work, *The Law of the Labour Market*, Deakin and Wilkinson revealed that until the mid-twentieth century there were a few groups of workers within labour law, each with its own set of rules.[10] Although not discussed in their work, 'domestic servant' was a central category. It was one of the four categories addressed by Blackstone, and also a category to be found in various pieces of legislation and in court judgments.

From Blackstone's work we learn that when he was writing his *Commentaries*, some form of reciprocity existed in the work relationship between menials and their masters or mistresses, something that is not evident in his discussion on other groups of servants. Blackstone noted that:

> The contract between them and their masters arises upon the hiring. If the hiring be general without any particular time limited, the law construes it to be a hiring for a year; upon a principle of natural equity, that the servant shall serve, and the master maintain him, ... [but] the contract may be made for any larger or smaller term.[11]

He went on to say that all servants are entitled to wages, but that menial servants, as opposed to others, should receive this right 'according to their agreement'.[12]

At that point in time, when the employment relationship was seen as one of status and not contract,[13] recognition of some form of reciprocity

---

[7] Blackstone, W, *Commentaries on the Laws of England: A Facsimile of the 1st edn of 1765–1769* (Chicago, University of Chicago Press, 1979) 413.

[8] *Ibid*, at 414.

[9] *Ibid*, at 410–15; see also Kahn-Freund, O, 'Blackstone's Neglected Child: The Contract of Employment' (1977) 93 *Law Quarterly Review* 508, 510–12.

[10] Deakin, SF and Wilkinson, F, *The Law of the Labour Market* (Oxford, Oxford University Press, 2005) ch 2 and especially the table at 106.

[11] Blackstone, above n 7, at 413.

[12] *Ibid*, at 416.

[13] Kahn-Freund, above n 9.

for domestics was extended by the courts, continuing beyond Blackstone's period into and throughout the nineteenth century. The main means used by the courts to achieve this was to incorporate contractual terms through the use of custom. By the beginning of the nineteenth century, courts had accepted the custom of a month's notice in the employment of domestic servants.[14] Another custom was recognised in 1880 with a court's decision that the law of tacit relocation of work contracts applied specifically to domestic servants.[15] Moreover, in *George v Davies* the court accepted the claim that for domestic servants a custom existed enabling them to give notice in the first month of work, before the expiration of the first fortnight. By handing in her notice, the servant was entitled to wages for the period of that month.[16] This line of judgments not only points to a specific type of protection given by the courts to domestic servants, but also reflects the centrality of domestic servants in the labour market. Their power is indicated by the actions they took in turning to the courts with various claims and their requests for acknowledgment of contractual entitlements. It was, as Carolyn Steedman said, the legal practice that revealed the making of the labour force.[17]

The differentiation of domestic servants from other groups of servants, which also put domestic servants during that period in a rather advantageous legal position, is seen not only in court judgments, but in legislation as well, specifically the Master and Servant Acts. The body of law known as the 'Master and Servant Acts', which set criminal sanctions on those defined as 'servant', consisted of a number of Acts enacted in the course of the late eighteenth and the early to mid-nineteenth centuries. These were gathered together into, and partially reformed by, the Master and Servant Act 1867. The earlier Acts neither expressly excluded nor expressly included domestic servants, but some of them specifically referred to manufacturing sectors, or provided that they applied to specific occupations, not including domestic ones. In *Kitchen v Shaw* the court held that, even when an Act was stated to include 'any other person' in addition to the sectors listed, it was not part of its intention to include a domestic servant.[18]

Steedman has found that even though domestics were exempted from the Master and Servant Acts, magistrates dealt with cases of domestic servants.[19] Hence she claims that the practice of domestic servants to resort to the law reveals their central part in the labour force. Indeed, domestic servants were fundamental in the labour market. But it is important to stress that their

---

[14] *Turner v Mason* [1845] 2 Dow & L 898, 14 LJ Ex 311.
[15] *Lennox v Allan* cited in *Stanley Ltd v Hanway* [1911] 2 SLT 2.
[16] *George v Davies* [1911] 2 KB 445.
[17] Steedman, above n 3, at 172.
[18] *Kitchen v Shaw* [1837] 6 AD & E 729, 112 ER 280.
[19] Steedman, above n 3, at ch 6.

centrality is not evident from legal practice alone. It can also be learned from legal definitions, abstract categories and court decisions. Due to the legal framework of that time, which set different rules for distinct groups of workers, the distinctive treatment of domestic servants by law did not mean they were placed aside. On the contrary, according to Blackstone, they were more related to other groups of servants than, for example, the fourth category of servants that consisted of ministerial and clerical workers.[20]

That domestic servants were part of the workforce but at the same time a distinctive legal category is important. This is because the separation between domestics and other groups of workers—such as 'labourers', 'apprentices' and the ministerial and clerical workers—gradually increased with the adoption of later legislation, and had severe implications for the situation of domestics. Already during the nineteenth century the short-comings that went hand in hand with the protected legal state of domestics became evident. When domestics were excluded from criminal sanctions, they were also exempted from protective legislation, such as the Truck Act 1831.[21] Additionally, domestic servants were required to serve and obey their masters and mistresses around the clock—day and night—without any recognition of their own time and leisure.[22] Apprentices and labourers also suffered from similar problems, but when the situation of the latter groups changed during the end of the nineteenth century and the first half of the twentieth, placing them in a more protected state, domestic servants were left behind and became a precarious legal category.

By the end of the nineteenth century, collective bargaining was growing in tandem with the strengthening of union power. Unionised labour had become the focus of attention, not only within the market, but in political discussion and action as well. During that period the reciprocal contract of employment as we know it today began to be developed, but only for some groups of workers—first for managerial and clerical workers that Deakin and Wilkinson termed 'employees', and later on for 'workmen'.[23] Worker-protective legislation was also structured around the category of 'workman', namely the manual workers consisting of the previous cat-egories of 'labourers' and 'apprentices'. These became a protected group by law. And while these categories drew closer together, domestic servants were distanced and set apart.

---

[20] While Blackstone notes that there were four types of servants, in his discussion of the fourth group he says: 'There is yet a fourth group of servants, if they may be so called, being rather in a superior, a ministerial, capacity; such as stewards, factors and bailiffs', Blackstone, above n 7, at 415. This is a similar group to that which Deakin and Wilkinson later referred to as 'employees', Deakin and Wilkinson, above n 10, at ch 2.

[21] The Truck Act 1831 s XX.

[22] *Turner v Mason*, above n 14.

[23] Deakin and Wilkinson, above n 10, at ch 2.

In 1867 the Master and Servant Act was enacted, applying to all workers within the various categories which had been designated by the earlier Acts, but to no others.[24] It in turn was replaced by a further reforming statute, the quasi-criminal Employers and Workmen Act of 1875, which specifically excluded the category of 'domestic servant' from its scope.[25] Although this definition of 'workman' was set in a quasi-criminal piece of legislation, the same definition or similar ones were later adopted in worker-protective legislation. The notion of 'workman' in the Employers and Workmen Act 1875 referred to in the Employers Liability Act 1880 and the Truck Acts,[26] expressly left domestic servants outside the boundaries of worker-protective legislation. Similar exclusion could also be found in other legal mechanisms that did not adopt the Employers and Workmen Act's definition, such as the Shop Hours Act 1892 and the Unemployment Insurance Act 1920.[27] Moreover, additional worker-protective Acts, such as the Factory and Workshop Acts, provided aid to occupations listed in the schedules of the Acts, excluding tasks performed by domestics. Worker-protective legislation providing welfare rights to workers also exempted domestic servants. The Workmen's Compensation Acts of 1906 and 1925 excluded casual workers who were employed otherwise than for the purposes of the employer's trade or business.[28] Interpretation of this provision led to the placing of workers in household establishments or other small establishments outside legal scope.[29]

Hence, the late nineteenth and early twentieth centuries marked a shift in the status of the legal category of 'domestic servants', and the law was a central factor in that process, causing domestic servants to be disadvantaged. The development of collective regulation in some sectors and not others, the formation of the modern contract of employment for identified groups of workers, but not including domestics, as well as the structuring of worker-protective legislation around specific groups—all left domestics aside. What were the reasons for the separation of domestic servants from the category of 'servant', and later on 'workman', and for their eventual exclusion from legal scope? One explanation is the focus by the law—in its criminal stage, its quasi-criminal stage, and then in its protective period—on

---

[24] The Master and Servant Act 1867 s 3; see list of enactments referred to in sch 1.

[25] The Employers and Workmen Act 1875 s 10.

[26] The Employers' Liability Act 1880, which regulated employers' liability to compensate workmen injured during service, covered only 'workmen' as defined in the Employers and Workmen Act 1875 (in s 8 of the Act). S 2 of the Truck Amendment Act 1887 that applied the principle Truck Act 1831, which regulated the payment of wages and deductions from wages, referred to the notion of 'workman' in the Employers and Workmen Act 1875 as well.

[27] Section 10 of the Shop Hours Act 1892 excluded those 'wholly employed as a domestic servant'. Another Act exempting 'domestic servant' from its scope was the Unemployment Insurance Act 1920, 'except where the employed person is employed in any trade or business carried on for the purposes of gain' (Pt II of sch 1).

[28] The Workmen's Compensation Act 1906 s 13; The Workmen's Compensation Act 1925 s 3.

[29] See Albin, above n 2, at ch 4.

industrial workers. Such focus cannot be detached from the social location of industrial workers who were mainly men and not women. As the literature demonstrates, in the eighteenth century women worked in 'female' occupations, were seen as secondary labourers, were barred from specific occupations and rarely took part in unionisation processes. This situation resulted from their engagement with household chores and traditional women's work, from conceptions regarding what women could properly and honourably do, and from limitations set by unions and employers themselves.[30] Women's main occupations, domestic service being one of them, were not part of the general movement that focused on industrialism.

Another explanation that should be noted for the exclusion of domestic servants is the specific relationships that domestic servants were believed to have with their masters and mistresses within the household, or in household-like establishments. This is *a work-related* aspect that distinguishes specific types of work relations from others. The belief in the existence of such special relationships between domestic servants and their masters and mistresses meant that magistrates were inclined to refrain from interfering. This explanation, too, cannot be detached from the social location of those who perform domestic work—primarily women—but it results from the way labour law approached regulating distinctive work relations. As will be seen in the following section, the distinctive character of domestic work became *the legal reasoning* for the rather advantaged position of domestics during the eighteenth and nineteenth centuries, and subsequently for their precarious legal situation by the end of the nineteenth century and the beginning of the twentieth.

Personal Relationships in Households or Household-like Establishments

In labour law discourse, the specific relationship between the domestic servant and her master and mistress within the household, or in household-like establishments, was mentioned as the cause for the specific legal approach towards this group of workers. In the case of *Turner v Mason*,

---

[30] See Lewis, J, *Women in England 1870–1950: Sexual Divisions and Social Change* (Brighton Bloomington, Indiana University Press, 1984) chs 4–5; Rubery, J, 'Pay-Equity, Minimum Wage and Equality at Work: Theoretical Framework and Empirical Evidence' (Working Paper No 19/2003, International Labour Office, November 2003) 2–16; Steinbach, S, *Women in England 1760–1914* (London, Weidenfeld & Nicolson, 2004) 9–12, 26–27; Fredman, S, *Women and the Law* (Oxford, Oxford University Press, 1997) 74, 107, 111–12; Webb, S and Webb, BP, *Industrial Democracy* (London, Printed by the Authors Especially for the Trade Unions of the United Kingdom, 1898) 495–507; Bird, MM, *Women at Work, A Study of Different Ways of Earning a Living Open to Women* (London, Chapman & Hall, 1911) 105.

the court mentioned that it is the domestic's role to obey her master throughout the entire year of her service, day and night, due to the type of service work that is demanded within the household.[31] The type of service provided—personal—and the location of the work were major factors in the judgment.

In *Nicoll v Greaves*, the court was faced with the question whether a huntsman was a 'domestic servant' or a 'servant'.[32] In deciding he was a domestic the court noted that 'there are some contracts for service which bring the parties into such close proximity and frequency of intercourse',[33] and the service can be 'of such a domestic nature as to require the servant to be frequently about his master's person'.[34] A few years later, in the case of *Pearce v Lansdowne*, the court stated, as the reason for the exclusion of 'domestic servants' from the protection of the Employers' Liability Act 1880, that they were 'persons whose personal relations in the household or retinue of their masters made it inconvenient that the disputes between them and their masters should be settled before magistrates'.[35] According to the court, the *type of relationship or work in a household* legitimised such exclusion. This was a very similar approach to that adopted in *Nicoll*.

However, in *Pearce* the court took the close proximity test set in *Nicoll* a step further, strengthening the divisions and boundaries between the 'domestic servant' category and those located within it, and other legal categories. This was accomplished by defining paid service work performed for the leisure of others as being distinct from other forms of paid labour, by viewing the personal relationship as differing from other employment relationships, and by conceptualising the household or household-like establishments as different from other work establishments.

Justice Collins observed that 'menial servant' denotes 'those persons whose main duty is to do actually bodily work as servants for the personal comfort, convenience or luxury of the master, his family and his guests, and who for this purpose become part of the master's residential or *quasi*-residential establishment'.[36] This line of thought continued in the case *Junior Carlton Club*,[37] in which the court dealt with the issue of whether club servants fell into the excluded category of 'domestic servant'. The court found that 'domestic servants are servants, whose main or general function is to be about their employers' persons, or establishments, residential or quasi-residential, for the purposes of ministering to their employers' needs or wants, or to the needs or wants of those who are members

---

[31] *Turner v Mason*, above n 14.
[32] *Nicoll v Greaves* [1864] 17 CB NS 27, 141 ER 11.
[33] *Ibid*, at 14.
[34] *Ibid*.
[35] *Pearce v Lansdowne* [1893] 69 LT 316.
[36] *Ibid*, at 319.
[37] *Junior Carlton Club, Re* [1922] 1 KB 166.

of such establishments, or of those resorting to such establishments, including guests',[38] thus stretching Collins J's test even more. The focus was on the 'main or general' functions of the workers, and the new test included relationships between workers and 'members' of the establishments and with those resorting to such establishments, including guests. Once again the court emphasised the provision of service, or as the court said, the need 'to be about their employers' persons, or establishments, residential or quasi-residential',[39] as a central reason for the decision that all workers in the club were domestic servants and excluded from the Act's protection.

Expanding the test for defining a 'domestic servant' to include all those performing personal service in a residential or quasi-residential establishment paved the way for placing within this category various sorts of workers, including workers in hospitals, hotels, boarding houses, colleges, homes for the elderly, etc.[40] The law was put into confusion by the increasingly blurring boundaries between the private and the commercial, paid labour and work in the house, and different types of employment relationship. Eventually, the distinction between 'workman' and 'domestic servant' was not dictated by the commercial activity of the establishment, but rather by the two pillars of personal service and type of establishment—residential or quasi-residential—placing domestic workers outside the boundaries that regulated the industrial world.

It was at this period of time that two worlds of labour relations emerged in labour law thought.[41] The first was structured around the industrial worker, which was gradually situated closer to workers in high managerial positions—defined as 'employees'. The second applied to the group of domestic servants, whose laws continued to be those set in the pre-industrial and pre-bureaucratic stage. This latter group was left outside legal scope and outside the thought of labour law. At this time, then, the legal consciousness of labour law emerged only in respect of the first group, ignoring the second in the belief that personal work relationships in household-like establishments should be left unregulated.

---

[38] *Ibid*, at 170.
[39] *Ibid*.
[40] See *London County Council v Perry* [1915] 2 KB 193; *Cameron v Royal London Ophthalmic Hospital* [1941] 1 KB 350; *Vellacott, Re* [1922] 1KB 466.
[41] I would like to thank Mark Freedland for helping me clarify and formulate the notion of two worlds of employment relations. This idea is related to a suggestion he offered with Paul Davies to shift the emphasis in labour law thought from employment patterns and their evolution towards systems of organisation and management of personal work relations. See Davies, PL and Freedland, MR, *Towards a Flexible Labour Market: Labour Legislation and Regulation Since the 1990s* (Oxford, Oxford University Press, 2007) 17.

BRITISH LABOUR LAW AND DOMESTIC WORKERS: TODAY

This division into two worlds, as described above, is very much evident in today's British labour laws that are embedded in the way the courts addressed the legal category of 'domestic servant' until the first half of the twentieth century. This, of course, does not mean that there have not been any shifts in the legal approach. One central transformation is the move from a rather selective regime that typified British labour law until the mid-twentieth century to a more unitary regime from the 1960s onwards. This unitary regime supposedly brought together the previously distinctive groups of 'workmen', 'employees' and 'domestic servants', within the modern contract of employment, into one category of 'employees'.[42] The move from a selective to a unitary framework was believed to be socially progressive in reducing or even eliminating distinctions between groups of workers, and factually accurate for employment relationships that were seen as converging more systematically upon the secure, permanent, full-time employment pattern.[43] However, in recent years studies have begun to reveal the shortcomings of this unity.[44] In the domestic service sector, workers are still in a highly precarious state, and, as will be seen below, for reasons similar to those of the past. Therefore, the conversion of labour law to a more unitary regime since the mid-twentieth century has been almost entirely ineffective for this group of workers.

Under current British labour laws, domestic workers are seen as 'employees', but are entitled to only a very limited set of worker-protective rights. One central reason for the problems of domestic workers is that they work in or are associated with households. This problem is reflected in the regulation of working time and of minimum wages. Regulation 19 of the Working Time Regulations excludes domestic servants in private homes from the majority of Regulations 4–8, which cover maximum weekly working time (Reg 4), maximum working time for young workers (Reg 5A), length of night work (Reg 6), night work by young workers (Reg 6A), and restrictions on the patterns of work that can be set by employers when there is risk to the health and safety of a worker (Regs 7 and 8). This is a more restrictive exclusion than Britain could have adopted according to the framework

---

[42] The first pieces of legislation structured around the modern contract of employment were the Contracts of Employment Act 1963 and the Redundancy Payments Act 1965. The Redundancy Payments Act 1965 s 19 specifically provided that domestic servants are included within its scope. This was no new entitlement, for the right to redundancy payments was already recognised in case law during the nineteenth century. However, it made a statement that domestics are included in the category of 'employee' defined in s 25 as an individual who 'entered into or works under a contract with an employer'.

[43] Freedland, MR, *The Personal Employment Contract* (Oxford, Oxford University Press, 2003) 16–17.

[44] See Mark Freedland's discussion on the false unity and false duality in *ibid*, at 15–22.

Directive,[45] but it is still comprehensive. Similarly, Regulations 2(2) and 2(3) of the Minimum Wage Regulations 1999 exempt family members and those living within the family household who are not family, but work in the household or for the family business, from the scope of protection. The courts have interpreted this exclusion to include only domestic workers that are treated as family members, such as an au pair that is provided with accommodation and meals and shares the tasks and leisure activities of the family.[46] In addition to these exemptions domestic workers are located outside the scope of health and safety laws, one reason being the problem of conducting inspections in the private sphere of the household.[47]

In these legislative norms, living-in households and being associated with the family are reasons for exclusion, thus reflecting an understanding of the non-regulatory situation of those associated with the household establishment and the boundaries between private and public, closeness to the family and more distant work relationships. Such a conceptualisation— which, as seen in the discussion held above, was established during the eighteenth century—creates divisions between the home and other spheres, even when the home is a work establishment in itself.

A crucial point in this respect is that even if workers in these establishments were to be brought within legal scope, in many circumstances they would still be left with very low degrees of protection. An example of this sort is the situation of domestics under equality and anti-discrimination laws. The Equal Pay Act 1970 aims to provide unitary protection for all women workers, regardless of their sector, occupations or other work differentials. As section 1(6) of the Act declares: employed means employed under a contract of service or of apprenticeship or a contract personally to execute any work or labour. This is a very broad form of categorisation that covers workers excluded from other terms found in British worker-protective legislation. However, in practice, in order to be entitled to the protection given by the Act, there is a need for a comparator working under the same single source responsible for the unequal pay,[48] one that for domestic workers does not exist. Other pieces of anti-discrimination legislation, such as the Equality Act 2010,[49] also require a comparator, but as noted above, such a comparator is usually hard to find. Moreover, the legal

---

[45] Art 3 defines a 'worker' covered by the Directive as 'any person employed by an employer, including trainees and apprentices but excluding domestic servants'.

[46] Case 2202606/2002 *G Sujatha v A Manwaring* [ET] decision, 17/7/03.

[47] Health and Safety at Work Act 1974, s 51.

[48] See generally Fredman, S, 'Reforming Equal Pay Laws' (2008) 37 *Industrial Law Journal* 193.

[49] The Equality Act 2010 s 211(2), sch 27, pt 1 repealed the previous Race Relations Act 1976 and the Sex Discrimination Act 1975, adopting a similar attitude towards direct and indirect discrimination: see ss 13, 19.

option to find a hypothetical comparator is also complicated, as is evident from the case of *Aduma*.[50]

Aduma does not concern a domestic worker in a private household, but rather a worker in a hotel, a type of establishment whose workers until the mid-twentieth century were conceptualised as domestics, as decided by the court in *Junior Carlton Club*. However, from this case much can be learned about the difficulties experienced by domestic workers. Mr Aduma, a Nigerian, was employed as a hotel manager in a small hotel, whose owner also had a dry cleaning business where his son was employed as the manager. Despite repeated requests, Mr Aduma received no contract of employment. Additionally, his wages were not recorded and thus he received no wage slip. The terms of Mr Aduma's employment were arranged in such a way that the employer was able to avoid paying the minimum wage and to require him to work hours in excess of those set by the Working Time Regulations 1998. Mr Aduma filed a race discrimination claim, in which he cited the employer's son as the comparator for determining his wage level. In its judgment, the court rejected this comparator on the grounds that he was working in another business and offered a hypothetical comparator—a worker earning at least the minimum wage. Accordingly, Mr Aduma's compensation was set at minimum-wage level, no higher.

The problems associated with finding a comparator are striking in this case. This is a true hurdle for those working in small establishments, even those who are not within the household. But it is even more challenging, if not impossible, for those working in households. Furthermore, in the case of domestic workers, a hypothetical comparator earning at least the minimum wage, or working reasonable hours, is an irrelevant issue, because, as seen, domestics are exempted from these laws. This severely limits the situations in which one can turn to relief from equality and anti-discrimination legislation, and it seems that legal intervention becomes possible only on a very basic level, when human dignity is violated.[51] Clearly evident from this perspective are the limitations of current rules that were structured according to a specific work relationship, which did not include workers in small establishments.

Another difficulty for the provision of efficient legal protection to domestic workers stems from the personal service they provide. 'Personal service' is a type of service activity found in classifications of service work and defined in the literature as the modern equivalent of servitude in the

---

[50] *Aduma v Mehmet (t/a Rose Hotel Group)* [2007] All ER (D) 04 (Jun).

[51] This is not to say that the protection of basic human dignity for domestic workers is insignificant. On the contrary, various tools are being developed to deal more effectively with forced labour and slavery, see Mantouvalou, V, 'Servitude and Forced Labour in the 21st Century: The Human Rights of Domestic Workers' (2006) 35 *Industrial Law Journal* 395; Mantouvalou, V, 'Modern Slavery: The UK Response' (2010) 39 *Industrial Law Journal* 425.

past—butlers, maids, cooks, gardeners, and other domestic help.[52] There are two dimensions to this notion: first, the service orientation of the work, and the personal aspect second. Both set limitations for achieving labour rights within today's legal regime. To start with the service orientation, while the literature in the fields of economics and geographic economics has begun discussing the special features of today's service worlds,[53] labour law has not paid enough attention to the challenges that the move to a service economy has set for it.[54] Labour law, as widely acknowledged, is based on the manufacturing model of employment, which the term 'Fordism' represents. It thus does not address the specific features of service work that affect the state of workers.

Taking into consideration the features of services, and specifically of personal service work, is highly crucial when it comes to regulating the situation of domestic workers. In personal service work, for example, the constant availability demanded of a worker, instances of sexual harassment, and issues of privacy have their specific presentations, and the current legal frameworks are less than adequate to address them.[55] One example of the manufacturing orientation of labour law is evident from the line of cases discussing the measuring of working time for on-call workers. Until 2006 the view adopted by the British courts was that sleep time was not work time.[56] This line of decisions changed under the influence of decisions emanating from the European Court of Justice.[57] However, the legal test from the recent past reflects the problems entailed for those who provide service work, whose work arrangements and specific features of their services are rarely addressed by labour law.[58]

The second aspect of personal service is the personal relationship created, which in today's world of work is closely associated with what in legal language are termed 'undocumented', 'informal' or 'illegal' relationships. Informality is tightly bound to the history of domestic service employment, which, as the court noted in *Nicoll*, brings the parties into close proximity with each other, creating something more familial and less formal. It cuts across the domestic work sector and is found in other sectors that were

---

[52] Browing, HL and Singelmann, J, *The Emergence of a Service Society: Demographic and Sociological Aspects of the Sectoral Transformation of the Labour Force in the USA* (Springfield, National Technical Information Service, 1975) 7–8.

[53] For a discussion on services, see Bryson, JR, Daniels, PN and Warf, B, *Service Worlds: People, Organizations, Technologies* (London, Routledge, 2004).

[54] Albin, E, 'Labour Law in a Service World' (2010) 73 *The Modern Law Review* 959.

[55] *Ibid*.

[56] *English v Gunter* [1957] 1 WLR 915; *Walton v Independent Living Organization* [2003] All ER (D) 373(CA).

[57] Case C-303/98 *SIMAP v Conselleria de Sanidad y Consumo de la Generalidad Valenciana* [2000] IRLR 845 (ECJ); Case C-151/02 *Landeshauptstadt Kiel v Jaeger* [2003] IRLR 804 (ECJ).

[58] For a more elaborate discussion see Albin, above n 54.

traditionally tied to the domestic service category, such as hospitality. This was the situation in the case of *Aduma* discussed above. The work conditions of Mr Aduma were set in an informal way, enabling the employer to disregard the law's formalities, as happens quite often in this type of relationship. Although Mr Aduma voiced his claims in court instead of simply exiting the work relationship, the court found it difficult to grant him rights owing to his informal work relationship. In this case, informality raised hurdles to proving his claims.

There are other important consequences of informality or illegality that should be mentioned. Some workers may find themselves outside legal protection because their contract will be seen as illegal.[59] Informality also creates feelings of reliance and obedience which hamper attempts to organise, or to approach the courts where there is a breach of contract or of working conditions.[60] Indeed, a search of case laws on domestic workers in Britain revealed that there are only 10 cases discussing the labour conditions of domestic workers, all of which address domestics in hospitals or homes for the elderly, and none of them brought by domestics in private households.[61] This finding can of course be explained by the very limited rights these workers have under the current labour law regime. However, another explanation is the informal relationship or illegal situation of the workers, which deters them from approaching the courts.

To conclude this part of the Chapter, it can be said that boundaries between specific types of paid labour, between locations where work is performed, and fluctuations in the type of work relationship continue to be found in today's legal framework, affecting the work domain and those participating in it. The legal institution that has created these divisions over time has difficulty overcoming them. As the discussion has showed, it is not necessarily the inclusion of workers within legal scope that will lead to the higher degrees of protection hoped for. This is clearly illustrated by the case of anti-discrimination and equality rights. Hence, for labour law to become effective for domestic workers, it may well have to detach itself from its embedded legal thought and become attuned to the detailed sectoral disadvantage of domestics.

---

[59] See Fraser, S and Sher, A, 'The National Minimum Wage: Under Threat from an Unlikely Source?' (2006) 35 *Industrial Law Journal* 289. Specifically on domestic servants see the recent case *Allen (Nee Aboyade-Cole) v Hounga* [2011] UKEAT/0326/10/LA 31 March 2011.

[60] See discussions on these problems in respect of workers in the hospitality industry whose work relationships are also seen as close and informal in Albin, above n 2, at ch 2. See findings on feelings of belonging on the one hand and alienation on the other in Lucas, RE, *Employment Relations in the Hospitality and Tourism Industries* (London, Routledge, 2004) 227; Ram, M *et al*, '"Apprentice Entrepreneurs"? Ethnic Minority Workers in the Independent Restaurant Sector' (2001) 15 *Work, Employment & Society* 353, 362; and Evans, Y, *et al*, 'Making the City Work: Low Paid Employment in London' (London, Department of Geography Queen Mary, University of London, 2005) 26.

[61] Last checked on 28 June 2010.

Put differently, we are still confronted by two worlds of employment relationships. One is a world of pre-industrial, pre-bureaucratic, informal household employment, the other a world of highly managed and bureaucratised work. These two worlds place different demands on labour law, and there is a crucial need to delve into the challenges such a separation poses, especially with the growing extent of blurring boundaries between the private and the public and between different forms of paid labour. I propose that these boundaries, which have been created in the course of the past three centuries, can be addressed in two different ways. The first is to bring domestic workers into the public sphere by using more bureaucratic forms of employment, such as agencies. In that case, tools developed for the industrial world can be used to break down the personal relationships and household-like environment that continue to exist in the working life of domestics. Dzodzi Tsikata's discussion of Ghana in this collection is an example of using industrial techniques to improve the conditions of domestic workers.[62]

Another way is to shape regulation differently from the Fordist model of regulation, which from its outset did not take account of the specific work circumstances of domestics. The embeddedness of legal thought in the Fordist model makes it difficult to think about such regulation. But, although imagining a protective regulatory regime that differs from Fordism is not an easy task, it is something that the sectoral focus can help accomplish, as the above discussion has made clear. Once the multilayered state of disadvantage is assessed, and the institutions leading to sectoral disadvantage are more openly acknowledged, thought can be given to the tools that can best address such disadvantage.[63] This perspective, I believe, guided the drafters of the ILO's Convention—the way 'work like no other' was thought of—even though they have not taken that approach far enough, as discussed in the following part.

THE ILO CONVENTION AND RECOMMENDATIONS

In 2008 the ILO decided to place the issue of decent work for domestic workers on its agenda, and since then it has worked hard to offer a set of standards that have been recently adopted in a Convention supplemented by recommendations.[64] The ILO's general approach is to treat domestic

---

[62] Tsikata, D, 'Employment Agencies and Domestic Work in Ghana' in this collection.

[63] See Albin, above n 2, at chs 6, 7, conclusion.

[64] The International Labour Office's first report, published in 2009, above n 1, intended to facilitate the discussion of domestic work at the International Labour Conference in 2010. In 2010, on the basis of the replies received, the ILO produced a further report, above n 1, putting forward proposed conclusions for a Convention and Recommendation. In June 2010 the International Labour Conference drafted another set of proposed conclusions: ILO, *Draft*

work as 'work like any other, work like no other'.[65] Apprehensions were raised as to the difficulties associated with that approach, namely that addressing domestic work as 'work like no other' entails a risk that the standards may end up unintentionally replicating the existing tendency to exclude domestic workers from common employment standards.[66] Here I make a different argument, claiming that the 'work like no other' approach is crucially important, and that the best way to promote that approach is by means of a sectoral focus.

The discussion above has shown that domestic servants' sectoral disadvantage is embedded, among other things, in the legal treatment accorded to the category of domestic servant and stems from the main feature of this kind of work: personal relationships in households or household-like establishments. Based on that discussion, I have claimed that over time two worlds of labour relations emerged in legal thought: one located within the scope of labour law's protection and its legal structure, and the other—that of domestic service—outside those boundaries. If domestic workers' sectoral disadvantage is to be addressed, then their work has to be seen as work like no other, because it is a type of work that labour law has never dealt with before.

The ILO has taken some important steps in that direction and I believe that the strengths of its conclusions lie in the measures targeting the specific causes of domestic workers' precarious situation. For instance, work time is an important issue, as one of the defining elements of these workers' sectoral disadvantage, resulting from their work within the household establishment and the personal relationship they have with those receiving their care. The Convention and supplementary recommendations aim to limit the constant availability of workers and manage their work hours in quite a significant way.[67] The detailed treatment of work time addresses the problems that can arise from personal service work provided by domestic workers, and reflects a view of their work as 'work like no other'. Another example of this sort is found in Article 13 of the Convention where it is noted that measures in respect of health and safety should be taken, 'with due regard to the specific characteristics of domestic work'. Of course, this will require further thought of the occupational safety and health hazards that domestic workers face. Also indicative of the consideration taken of the specific sectoral disadvantage of domestic workers is Article 15, which

---

Report, above n 1. In June 2011 the ILO adopted the Convention and its supplementary recommendations, above n 1.

[65] ILO report 2009, above n 1, at 12.

[66] Mundlak, G and Shamir, H, 'Bringing Together or Drifting Apart? Targeting Domestic Work as "Work Like No Other"' (2011) 23 *Canadian Journal of Women and the Law* 289.

[67] *Domestic Workers Convention* 2011, above n 1, at Art 10; see also *Domestic Workers Recommendation*, above n 1, at recommendations 8–13.

is aimed at protecting domestics recruited or placed by private employment agencies. This is a real problem that domestic workers face, especially those who are migrant workers.[68]

At the same time, though, in some instances the Convention and its supplementary recommendations treat domestic work more like 'work like any other', and less like 'work like no other', applying the same unitary rules for all workers to domestics. This approach leads to some problems. Such is the situation in Article 6 of the Convention referring to fair terms of employment, and Articles 11 and 12 that discuss minimum wage coverage. Treating domestics like other workers avoids looking at their specific sectoral disadvantage, one example of which is the implications resulting from their living in the workplace. The price paid by domestics for living in, including isolation, lack of companionship, total devotion to the family, being on-call day and night, etc, are addressed in a limited way.[69] Adopting the general approach towards accommodation and food, which sees them as a benefit and not as a price, might be unsuitable for this type of paid labour. Another example of a unitary and highly problematic approach is Article 2 of the Convention, which says that each member should take measures to respect, promote and realise 'the elimination of discrimination in respect of employment and occupation'. The discussion in the previous part showed the problems that such a general application of equality and anti-discrimination rules entails.

The general rules within the Convention and the recommendations lead to a twofold fear. First, that they will be irrelevant to domestics, and therefore their adoption will not bring any change in the legal regime; and second, that subtle strategies will emerge to ensure that the precarious legal situation of domestic servants is perpetuated. Such fears are all the more acute due to the economic interests in leaving domestic work unregulated and cheap,[70] and also due to the social location of those performing domestic work, being today mainly women workers, either immigrants or members of disadvantaged groups. These groups are increasingly found in service work and in personal, 'undocumented', 'informal' or 'illegal' work relationships, and for all these reasons are more likely to be exploited. It seems that as long as special attention is not given to the sectoral disadvantage of domestic workers, their legal situation will remain precarious. Their work has to be treated as 'work like no other' for the rules to be effective,

---

[68] Fudge, J, 'Global Care Chains, Employment Agencies and the Conundrum of Jurisdiction: Decent Work for Domestic Workers in Canada' (2011) 23 *Canadian Journal of Women and the Law* 235.

[69] Some aspects are addressed by recommendation 14, which states that 'when a domestic worker is required to live in accommodation provided by the household, no deduction may be made from the remuneration with respect to that accommodation, unless otherwise agreed to by the worker'.

[70] On the economic interests, see Mundlak and Shamir, above n 66, at 297–99.

and a sectoral focus could provide a better understanding of their specific disadvantage and make it possible to address it properly. The Convention and recommendations have generally adopted such a focus, but there remains a tension in the instruments. However, a sectoral approach can be useful in the interpretation and implementation of these two documents in various national settings and internal legislation.

For example, attention should be devoted to the problems associated with finding a comparator in the sector of domestic workers. This problem can be dealt with either by employing workers through agencies, thus creating a larger setting for comparison, or by releasing the comparison from the requirement for a single employer, or single source, thus making it possible to compare terms and conditions of work on a larger scale, such as within a sector or other sectors with similar characteristics. Whether agencies are exploitative of domestic workers or beneficial to them depends upon the legal regimes governing the agencies.[71] Thought should also be given to the question whether deductions for accommodation and food are appropriate in this situation, even if the worker agrees to them. As mentioned above, in the domestic service sector the requirement for the worker to sleep in the employer's home is often a loss rather than a gain, and thus it might be sensible to refrain from allowing these costs to be subtracted. In sum, in order to assure the relevancy and value of the ILO measures, each and every rule should be thought of in light of the particular disadvantaged state of domestics and the primary causes of the distinction between them and other workers—the personal work they provide in household or household-like establishments.

CONCLUSION

In this Chapter I have argued that the current situation of domestic workers is one of sectoral disadvantage, embedded in the past historical category of 'domestic servants', extant in historical pieces of British legislation until the mid-twentieth century. I have shown that over a period of two centuries, from the eighteenth until the twentieth, domestic servants were separated from other groups of workers. At the beginning of that period, when labour relations were dependent upon status rather than contract, that separation had positive outcomes for domestics. However, with the increase in union power, the growth of industrialisation and bureaucratic forms of management, and the development of the modern contract of employment and worker-protective legislation, it has placed domestics in a precarious legal position. The separation produced two worlds of labour relations

---

[71] Fudge, above n 68; Tsikata, above n 62.

within legal thought: the industrialised, bureaucratic world, and that of the 'domestic servant' category. A similar separation continues to obtain in today's legal domain. Now, with domestics becoming a topic on the agenda of the ILO, and with the adoption of a new Convention, more attention should be devoted to their embedded position in order to achieve the goal of decent work for domestic workers.

14

*Employment Agencies and Domestic Work in Ghana**

DZODZI TSIKATA

INTRODUCTION

OVER THE LAST three decades, the livelihoods of the majority of workers in Ghana have been organised in the context of far-reaching economic liberalisation policies, the growing informalisation of labour relations and an exponential growth of the informal economy. While historically much of the labour force has operated within the informal economy, the particular processes of informalisation since the economic liberalisation policies of the 1980s are worthy of attention because their impact on the character, structure and quality of livelihoods have been significant. Domestic work in Ghana has been largely informal and unregulated, except in a minority of cases where domestic workers are employed by the corporate and public sectors for senior employees and in guesthouses and hotels.

The majority of domestic workers are undocumented, do not enjoy even the basic rights guaranteed by the Labour Code (under the Labour Act, Act 651 of 2003 (the Labour Act)), and face particular challenges related to the personal and secluded nature of domestic work. Some experience isolation, physical and psychological violence, the arbitrary varying of their job description and violations of their dignity.

The importance of domestic work lies in the fact that it employs a large army of younger and older women who perform some of the most vital reproductive functions for individuals and the society. A study has argued that most urban households have one or more domestic workers who are

---

* This Chapter is a revised version of the article first published by Tsikata, D, called 'Employment Agencies and the Regulation of Domestic Workers in Ghana: Institutionalizing Informality?' in (2011) 23 *Canadian Journal of Women and the Law*. Reprinted by permission from University of Toronto Press Incorporated, www.utpjournals.com.

usually female.[1] Women's predominance in this segment of the labour market is emblematic of women's paid work.

Poverty studies have argued that while a broader definition of poverty beyond income is critical, the quality of employment and livelihoods remains a central determinant of poverty.[2] In spite of these and other studies which have drawn attention to the far-reaching implications of economic liberalisation for livelihoods, there has not been much policy interest in the changes in employment regimes and labour relations. This inattention is not surprising given the wider policy neglect of employment issues since the early 1980s. There are no comprehensive employment statistics and census data does not provide important information about the labour force. The Ghana Living Standards Surveys[3] have therefore become the main source of information about employment. There is a crying need to begin to understand the impacts of economic liberalisation on the structure of the labour force, its gender composition and employment relations.

Domestic work is undergoing changes that are worthy of attention. For example, we can observe an increasing commercialisation of domestic work as a result of the entry of informal and formal recruitment agents into the sector. Employment agencies, now sanctioned by the labour laws of Ghana, are providing some predictability in the terms and conditions of service of domestic work. An examination of what formal agencies offer domestic workers suggests that they may be improving some of domestic work's more problematic aspects without tackling its fundamental characteristics. Even more significantly, the majority of domestic workers continue to be recruited through informal agents, family and friends on widely differing terms and conditions, including in kind payments.

This Chapter examines the extent to which employment agencies have changed the landscape of domestic work in Ghana, paying particular attention to how their practices differ from those of the more established informal methods of recruitment.

---

[1] There are men involved in domestic work. However, domestic work is gender-segmented, with male domestics often employed as gardeners, drivers and cooks, while female domestics work as general workers, nannies and cooks, often earning less money than the men: LAWA-Ghana (Leadership and Advocacy for Women in Africa-Ghana), *Domestic Workers in Ghana: First to Rise and Last to Sleep* (Washington DC, Georgetown University Law Centre, 2003).

[2] Whitehead, A, 'Tracking Livelihood Change: Theoretical, Methodological and Empirical Perspectives from North-East Ghana' (2002) *Journal of Southern African Studies* 575, 598; Heintz, J, *Employment, Poverty and Gender in Ghana* (Working Paper No 92, Political Economy Research Institute, University of Massachusetts Amherst, April 2005); Economic Commission for Africa (ECA), *Economic Report on Africa 2005* (Addis Ababa, ECA, 2005).

[3] The Ghana Living Standards Surveys are nation-wide surveys conducted by the Ghana Statistical Service which collect detailed information, including demographic characteristics of the population, education, health, employment and time use, migration, housing conditions and household agriculture. The Living Standards Surveys are available at: www.statsghana. gov.au.

DOMESTIC WORK AND DOMESTIC WORKERS IN GHANA

There are few studies of domestic work in Ghana,[4] despite the fact that domestic workers in Ghana constitute an important segment of the rural and urban labour force. The two main studies are 'Domestic Workers in Ghana: First to Rise and Last to Sleep' by Leadership and Advocacy for Women in Africa-Ghana ('LAWA')[5] and 'A Study of Child Domestic Work and Fosterage in Northern and Upper East Region of Ghana' by Nana Araba Apt ('Apt').[6] Domestic workers typically come from poor rural backgrounds and most of them are women. The predominance of women in domestic work is related to the fact that the tasks that domestic workers perform are seen as women's work. Domestic workers also work primarily for women, placing them in direct conflict with their female employers who come from a wide range of backgrounds.

Domestic workers are involved in a wide range of tasks—cleaning, laundry, cooking, shopping, taking care of children and attending to the elderly or infirm.[7] The location of the domestic workplace in the privacy of homes is very challenging for efforts to regulate domestic work and leaves domestic workers isolated and vulnerable to abuse.

Both the LAWA and Apt studies found that the wages of domestic workers were often below the minimum wage and in a variety of arrangements: cash, both cash and payment in kind, or in kind payments. Some were paid, whether in cash or kind, only at the end of their period of service, which could run into years, and often on the basis of oral and imprecise agreements. The nature of such informal employment contracts means that there are no proper remedies should the employers fail to honour their promises, something which happens often.[8]

The large supply of potential domestic workers has meant that although there is great demand for them, they can still be procured cheaply. As well, domestic work is considered unskilled work, although many of its elements require great skill. Domestic workers are vulnerable to injuries resulting from their work for which they rarely receive treatment. In some cases, they also suffer from malnutrition.[9]

The difficult situation of domestics is compounded by the fact that a large proportion of them are under 16. The LAWA study found that domestic workers were generally aged between 14 and 45. However, some were as young

---

[4] LAWA-Ghana, above n 1; Apt, NA, *A Study of Child Domestic Work and Fosterage in Northern and Upper East Region of Ghana* (UNICEF, 2005).
[5] LAWA-Ghana, above n 1.
[6] Apt, above n 4.
[7] LAWA-Ghana, above n 1.
[8] *Ibid*; Apt, above n 4.
[9] Apt, above n 4.

as seven and the majority of domestic workers in Ghana were adolescents. About 800,000 children were estimated to be working in Ghana.

Child domestic workers are a particular issue of concern because of their lack of bargaining power, and their particular needs as children. Often deprived of the basic necessities of life, as well as education, rest, leisure and recreation, and family life, they are also exposed to physical, sexual and psychological abuse. The majority of domestic workers who are children are not in school and the rest often go to school exhausted, hungry and without school supplies. They may be pulled out of school on account of their domestic responsibilities and many drop out due to their poor performance, their lack of the requisite school necessities or when their employers fail to pay their school fees.[10]

Social practices, such as child fostering, disguise domestic work. Apt found that the line between a young domestic worker and a fostered child had become blurred over the years.[11] As fostering is considered to provide underprivileged children with maintenance, socialisation and opportunities for self-improvement, there is very little public discussion of the situation of fostered children.[12]

THE POLICY UNDERPINNINGS OF DOMESTIC WORK

As Guy Mundlak explains in his Chapter in this collection, the conditions of domestic work have been shaped and reinforced by the policy context.[13] Ghana's Economic Recovery Programme, which was instituted in the 1980s, resulted in the reversal of a deep economic crisis and close to three decades of economic growth. However, the impacts of economic policies on employment and social security have been devastating. Economic growth did not translate into the creation of employment, while some of the policies pursued resulted in labour retrenchment. One result of these policies was the exponential growth of the informal economy in Ghana. Workers who lost their work in the formal economy, a growing population of young people who had completed their basic, secondary and tertiary education, three decades of jobless growth and the informalisation of labour relations in the formal economy have been responsible for this expansion.[14] Currently, 80 per cent of the total

---

[10] LAWA-Ghana, above n 1; Apt, above n 4.

[11] Apt, above n 4.

[12] LAWA-Ghana, above n 1.

[13] Mundlak, G, 'The Wages of Care-Workers: From Structure to Agency' in this collection; see also Bernstein, S, 'Sector-based Collective Bargaining Regimes and Gender Segregation: A Case Study of Self-employed Home Childcare Workers in Quebec' in this collection.

[14] Informalisation has been discussed in the literature as a) the growth in size of the informal economy which has accompanied the reduction in size of the formal economy, and b) the systemic changes in labour relations from formalised to more informal arrangements: Sethuraman, SV, 'Gender, Informality and Poverty: A Global Review (Washington DC and

Table 14.1: Distribution of working population by location and sex in 2003.

Category	Public	Private formal	Private informal	Semi-public	NGO/int organs	Others	Total
Location							
Urban	12.0	11.2	75.0	0.5	0.3	1.0	100.0
Rural	3.6	3.0	92.0	0.3	0.1	1.1	100.0
Gender							
Male	10.2	9.5	78.6	0.6	0.2	0.1	100.0
Female	4.4	3.7	90.5	0.2	0.1	1.1	100.0

Source: Ghana Statistical Service, 2003.

labour force of Ghana is in informal work.[15] Table 14.1 below shows the distribution of the working population by location, type of employer, and gender. Significantly, the gender composition of the private informal economy shows that a larger proportion of working women than working men are found in private informal work.

While the expansion of the informal economy has created new work opportunities, particularly in the area of services, most of these opportunities have not been at the top end of the informal economy where the most lucrative and secure jobs are found. Instead, most of the new jobs are in the part of the informal economy in which people work simply in order to survive and where conditions do not conform to ILO standards for decent work.[16]

Some of the literature on the informal economy concludes that it has long been a space in which gender inequalities are visible.[17] The majority of women

Geneva, World Bank and WIEGO, 1998); Beneria, L, *Shifting the Risk: New Employment Patterns, Informalization, and Women's Work* (Mimeo NY, Cornell University, 2001); Charmes, J, *Women Working in the Informal Sector in Africa: New Methods and Data* (Geneva, UNDP and WEIGO, 1998); Pape, J, *Gender and Globalisation in South Africa: Some Preliminary Reflections on Working Women and Poverty* (Cape Town, International Labour Resource and Information Group, 2000); Pearson, R, *The Global Context: Home-Based Work and Policy Options* (Mimeo NY, Home Workers Worldwide Mapping Project, 2003). See also the discussion of informalisation in Baud, ISA, 'Introduction', in ISA Baud and GA De Bruijne (eds), *Gender, Small-Scale Industry and Development Policy* (London, Intermediate Technology Publications, 1993).

[15] Hormeku, T, 'The Transformation and Development of the Informal Sector and the Role of Trade Unions', (Paper presented at OATUU/ILO/ETUF Seminar on Trade Unions and the Informal Sector, Cairo, 4–6 May, 1998).

[16] See generally International Labour Conference, 90th Session, *Decent Work and the Informal Economy: Report VI* (Geneva, International Labour Office, 2002).

[17] Other forms of segmentation in the informal economy are based on caste, ethnicity, region, training and occupation: Baud, above n 14.

earn a living via self-employment in the informal economy with the result that their participation in the informal economy is higher than their share in the total labour force.[18] Long-term gender segregation of work, discrimination in labour markets, access to credit, training, land and infrastructure, women's lower levels of education due to inequalities in social relations and the heavy burden of reproductive work account for women's greater reliance on informal economic activities. For women in formal employment, the informal economy is a source of supplementary livelihood, a phenomenon that has been growing since the economic liberalisation programmes of the 1980s.[19] In relation to domestic work, John Pape has noted that in many African countries, as a result of lower wages and social benefits and the high potential domestic labour pool, domestic labour is very cheap.[20] While this assessment is essentially correct, it is also increasingly difficult to obtain domestic workers because of growing demand, patterns of rural–urban migration and increasing commercialisation.

The policy approach to work and employment in Ghana, and much of Sub-Saharan Africa, is rooted in the economic liberalisation paradigm, a key feature of which is the downgrading of employment from a macro-economic concern to a sectoral issue. This policy approach, combined with the belief that low labour costs would attract foreign investment, has resulted in wage restraint.[21] Large-scale retrenchments of public sector workers and the demise of the tripartite system of policy negotiations involving government, employers and labour have weakened the Ghana Trades Union Congress (GTUC).[22]

The new labour code, the Labour Act, has been criticised by the GTUC for curtailing the right of workers to unionise and to take industrial action by imposing cumbersome procedures for tackling labour disputes.[23] More fundamentally, its provisions are more suited to the 20 per cent of the workforce in the formal economy despite its sweeping opening provisions that claim that the law covers all workers.[24] Recent efforts to address the

---

[18] Sethuraman, above n 14.

[19] Niger-Thomas Agbaw, M, *'Buying Futures': The Upsurge of Female Entrepreneurship Crossing the Formal/Informal Divide in South West Cameroon* (Leiden, Research School of Asian, Africa, and Amerindian Studies, University Leiden, 2000); Pearson, above n 14.

[20] Pape, above n 14.

[21] Mkandawire, T and Soludo, CC, *Our Continent, Our Future: African Perspectives on Structural Adjustment* (New Jersey, CODESRIA Press, 1999).

[22] The GTUC, which consists of 17 National Unions, is the main trade union centre for formal workers in Ghana.

[23] Under the repealed Labour Decree (NLCD 157) of 1966, it was easier to embark on industrial action as there were no detailed procedures to be followed before a strike could be declared. The Trades Union Congress has recently called for the amendment of sections on unionisation, certification of trade unions and termination of employment to remove ambiguities that are not in the interest of workers: *The Chronicle* (12 September, 2008).

[24] Section 1 of the Labour Act states that it applies to all workers and employers except those in the armed services.

problems of the informal economy have taken an enterprise rather than a labour approach, focusing on enterprise formalisation with a view to bringing more economic actors into the tax net and regulating their activities.[25] Labour relations and conditions of workers in the informal economy are not seen as a priority, partly because of the continuing belief that developing countries are competitive because of their lower labour costs.[26]

The weaknesses of the policy framework have been compounded by the lack of proper definition and documentation of informal work. This problem is particularly serious for domestic work. There is very little about domestic workers included in the last national population and housing census of 2000.[27] Out of 85 separate occupations identified in the census, only three (a) maid and related housekeeping service workers; b) building caretakers, char-workers, cleaners and related workers; c) launderers, dry cleaners and pressers) were directly connected with domestic work, and these constituted a total of 103,905 out of a 7.5 million strong working population (representing only 1.4 per cent of the labour force, 0.79 per cent male and 2.2 per cent female). It is conceivable that many more domestic workers are hidden within categories such as farmers (43.8 per cent) and hawkers, street and pavement vendors (3 per cent).[28]

The Ghana 2003 Core Welfare Indicators Questionnaire Survey,[29] which explicitly identifies domestic workers, found that in the 15 years and older age group, only 0.9 per cent were domestic workers. Unpaid family workers, however, constituted another 7.4 per cent, while students were 4.7 per cent. These categories of workers are often engaged in unpaid domestic work at different levels of intensity and, yet, would often not be classified as domestic workers.[30] A national survey on child labour found that only 1 per cent of working children were domestic workers.[31] The vast majority of them were classified as unpaid family workers (88 per cent). Given the persistent idiom of kinship surrounding domestic work, a proportion of the 88 per cent would certainly have been domestic workers who do not receive wages because of their kinship with their employers. The lack of accurate statistics for domestic workers stems from a long tradition of neglect of such workers in censuses and labour surveys. Unlike in Zambia and Zimbabwe,

---

[25] See the discussion in Baud, above n 14.

[26] Tsikata, D, 'Informalization, the Informal Economy and Urban Women's Livelihoods in Sub-Saharan Africa since the 1990s' in S Razavi (ed), *The Gendered Impacts of Liberalization: Towards 'Embedded Liberalism'?* (London, Routledge, 2009).

[27] Ghana Statistical Service, 'Ghana Population and Housing Census 2000' (Identifier GHA-GSS-PHC-2000-v1.0, 2000), available at: www.statsghana.gov.gh.

[28] *Ibid.*

[29] Ghana Statistical Service, *Ghana 2003 Core Welfare Indicators Questionnaire (CWIQ II) Survey Report: Statistical Abstract* (Accra, Ghana Statistical Service, 2005).

[30] *Ibid.*

[31] Ghana Statistical Service, *Ghana Child Labour Survey* (Accra, Ghana Statistical Service, 2003).

where statistics collected in the colonial period demonstrate the importance of domestic work,[32] most of the labour statistics in Ghana since the 1960s have been silent on domestic work.

This problem is also compounded by the challenges of defining domestic work. The Labour Act defines a domestic worker as 'a person who is not a member of the family of a person who employs him or her as house-help' (s 175). This definition excludes fostered children and persons with kinship relations with their employers, two important categories of domestic workers. The 2000 Population Census defines domestic workers as persons who are engaged to render household services with or without pay.[33] This more expansive definition captures more situations of domestic work. However, the definition of unpaid family worker by the Population Census as 'a person who helps in running an economic enterprise operated by a member of his or her family without payment of wages or salary'[34] has the effect of restricting the scope of the definition, since domestic workers are often involved in the running of informal economic enterprises. Thus, a member of the family who performs domestic work and helps in running a family business would only be included in the category of 'unpaid family worker'. Furthermore, the instruction to enumerators to exclude as family workers all persons aged 7 years and older who helped family members in their economic activities, but who were full-time students in educational institutions, and treat them instead as students[35] hides another category of domestic workers who combine work with their education. The LAWA definition of domestic workers as individuals who work in the houses of their employers and receive payment either in cash or in kind or both is useful in extending coverage to many more domestic workers.[36]

DOMESTIC WORK AND FORMAL AND INFORMAL EMPLOYMENT AGENCIES

There are several methods of recruitment of domestic workers in Ghana. These include direct hiring, recruitment through friends and family, the use

---

[32] Hansen, KT, 'Gender and Housing: The Case of Domestic Service in Lusaka, Zambia' (1992) 62 *Africa: Journal of the International African Institute* 248, 265; Pape, J, 'Still Serving the Tea: Domestic Workers in Zimbabwe 1980–90' (1993) 19 *Journal of Southern African Studies* 387.

[33] Ghana Statistical Service, *2000 Population and Housing Census Enumerator's Manual* (Accra, Ghana Statistical Service, 1999).

[34] *Ibid* at 56.

[35] *Ibid* at 49.

[36] LAWA-Ghana, above n 1. However, the distinction it makes between domestic workers and domestic assistants on grounds of age can be modified by using the term child domestic worker for all domestics under 15 (the age of majority for the purposes of work in the Labour Act).

of informal agents, formal private agencies and public sector employment offices. Apt found that 20 per cent of her respondents were recruited through relatives, 40 per cent through friends and neighbours of the employer, 16 per cent through the employers' relatives, while 18 per cent of domestics were directly recruited by their employers.[37] A 2009 study of 319 domestic workers found that 266 (83.4 per cent) found their current jobs through family and friends, while 50 (15.7 per cent) used a formal agency.[38] This finding suggests that traditional informal arrangements for procuring domestic workers have endured with the use of formal agencies only now slowly catching on. However, over the years paid middlemen or informal agents have entered into the recruitment process.[39]

Informal Agents

Informally mediated recruitment arrangements come in various forms. Mediators could be near or distant family members, neighbours, friends, and, in some cases, informal agents, who link up domestic workers and their potential employers, and in some cases assist in the negotiation of terms. For example, a family member living in an urban or another rural area could be asked to find a position for a young person living in their home town. Such individuals could also initiate the process or be approached by the parents of the potential domestic or the potential employer.

People engaged in these informal recruitment processes might perform the service of linking potential domestics with employers without remuneration, but they may also have their expenses paid by the domestic workers and the employer. Other intermediaries might establish themselves as informal agents who are paid for their services. Agents usually have communities from which they recruit domestics, who they select on the basis of affinity, proximity, ease of entry, association with a large supply of potential domestic workers and other such considerations.

Whether informal agents have introduced more formality into the recruitment of domestic workers is open to question because some elements of their transactions continue to be quite informal. For example, wages are often negotiated with the parents and other family members of the domestic, particularly when the domestic is a minor. As well, the terms and conditions often agreed do not approximate the conditions of formal workers.

---

[37] Apt, above n 4.

[38] Darkwa, A and Tsikata, D, 'Report on the Mapping of Employment Agencies in Accra, Kumasi and Tamale' (Paper presented at the Launch Workshop for the Centre for Gender Studies and Advocacy Project on the Changing Character of Women's Work in Ghana, April 2009).

[39] Apt, above n 4.

Informal agents provide a link between traditional practices of recruitment and regulation and the more formal regime of employment agencies. They are also less likely to be seen as employers of domestics. They operate at arm's length once a domestic worker is identified, and assist in negotiating salaries and terms only if requested to do so. They do not visit their placements and are often unable to insist on written agreements. While they are often called upon to settle disagreements, this is not formally required by the terms of their relationship with the parties. They provide informal services in order to maintain their links with the parties for possible future transactions.

In some cases, informal agents are connected with formal agencies. Some agencies started informally and/or use informal agents for recruiting their pool of domestics. This informality at the base of the recruitment of domestic workers has implications for efforts to institute formal processes and procedures, and renders formality and informality on a continuum and not at opposite ends of the scale.

Formal Agencies

Since 2003, registered and unregistered employment agencies have increasingly become part of the landscape for procuring domestic workers. Employment agencies were illegal in Ghana under the 1969 Labour Regulations,[40] which was consistent with Ghana's ratification of Part II of the ILO *Fee-Charging Employment Agencies Convention* (ILO C96) in 1973. This Convention required the elimination of profit-making employment agencies where public employment agencies were available. However, in 1997 the International Labour Conference adopted the *Private Employment Agencies Convention* (ILO C181), which permitted the use of regulated private employment agencies, although the Convention prohibited such agencies from charging recruitment fees to the workers they placed.[41] The current Labour Act provides for the registration of employment agencies.[42] In 2008, 35 agencies had applied to the Labour Department, out of which 19 had been granted a licence

---

[40] Labour Regulations 1969 (LI 632), para [61].

[41] *Private Employment Agencies Convention* 1997 (ILO C181) arts 7(10), 7(2). The Convention prohibits employment agencies from charging workers 'directly or indirectly, in whole or in part, for any fees or costs to workers,' although art 7(2) allows some exceptions to be justified and notified to the ILO under art 22 of the ILO Constitution.

[42] It is not clear whether Ghana has withdrawn ratification of Part II and ratified Part III of the *Fee-Charging Employment Agencies Convention* (ILO C96) which allows private agencies. A search shows that Ghana accepted the provisions of Part II in 1959. There is no entry for Part III with respect to Ghana: ILO, *International Labour Standards Department List*, available at: http://webfusion.ilo.org/public/db/standards/norms/appl/appl/byctry.cfm.

to operate.[43] The Labour Department's responsibilities are to investigate the background of the applicants, run checks, inspect their facilities and establishment, grant licences on behalf of the Minister and monitor their operations. The agencies were expected to provide quarterly reports to the Department, but were not doing this as of 2009.[44]

The growing number of sign boards in Ghana advertising the presence of recruitment agencies for domestic workers points to their increasing availability. Their entry into the sector has introduced a more formal regime between employers and domestic workers. While much of the literature suggests that formal agencies are expected to improve the conditions of domestic workers, in her study of women in an employment agency in California, Jennifer Mendez has argued that the claim that formal and more structured relations can eliminate some of the exploitative elements of domestic work is flawed.[45] Mendez found that informal and private employment arrangements secured without the assistance of an agency offer more options and allow domestics more space for negotiating their terms and conditions and exerting some control over how they work, while employment agencies seek to standardise domestic work and its terms. Indeed, Mendez's study demonstrates how not only the agencies, but also the workers, seek to establish personal relations with employers as part of a strategy to improve their terms and conditions of work.[46]

Mendez's study and her conclusions provide a useful point of departure for examining the specificities of domestic work and the operations of employment agencies in Ghana. In Ghana, formal employment agencies require potential employers of domestic workers to sign and abide by a formal contract, which includes the payment of cash wages. Formal employment agencies also assist to clarify the duties of the domestic worker and operate a wage scale in keeping with the range of skills and duties required, which is helpful in promoting recognition of the skills and experience of domestics. However, on the other hand, the wage scale ignores the range of skills that are applied by general domestic workers, who are considered unskilled.

Another way in which the arrangements of formal employment agencies in Ghana differ from more informal arrangements is with respect to the characteristics of the people they recruit. While children are commonly the targets of individual agents recruiting on behalf of employers, licensed employment agencies recruit only those who are above 15 years of age.[47]

---

[43] Only two of the 19, L'ainé Services and Tewenbo Company Limited, deal with domestic workers. Only Tewenbo Company Limited deals exclusively with domestic workers.

[44] Interview with S Dartey, Labour Department (7 July 2008).

[45] Mendez Bickham, J, 'Of Mops and Maids: Contradictions and Continuities in Bureaucratized Domestic Work' (1995) 45 *Social Problems* 114.

[46] *Ibid*. See also Bakan, A and Stasiuslis, DK, 'Making the Match: Domestic Placement Agencies and the Racialisation of Women's Household Work' (1995) 20 *Signs* 303.

[47] Interview with S Dartey, above n 44.

Agents have introduced innovations such as health checks and training for the domestics on their books. Also, there is a deliberate effort to match domestics and employers according to their needs and preferences. Employers have the liberty to express a preference for domestics of a particular gender and ethnicity and their preferences can be accommodated. They can also return a domestic to the agency and demand a replacement if they are not satisfied and do not have to justify this.

The majority of employment agencies, particularly those recruiting domestic workers, are not licensed under the Labour Code although they are registered, tax-paying limited liability companies.[48] Thus, they operate in the space between individual middlemen and the licensed agencies, avoiding regulation and scrutiny. These employment agencies have been criticised for failing to pay workers, short-changing them by making unnecessary deductions, refusing to take responsibility for domestic workers' working conditions and privileging the needs of the employers.[49]

On the other hand, employment agencies are hampered by the absence of labour regulations tailored to the particular conditions of domestic work, and the lack of enforcement mechanisms for the contracts they broker, which leads to variations and inconsistencies in their practices. While some agencies deduct monthly fees from salaries paid to them, others take a one-off payment and leave the domestic worker and the end user to deal directly with each other on questions of pay. These variations in the wages regime and related practices complicate the question about who the employer of the domestic really is, the agency or the end user?[50]

CONCLUSIONS

Mendez's argument that private and informal arrangements are superior to the use of employment agencies is not borne out in the Ghana case in spite of the many criticisms of employment agencies because of some of the key distinguishing features of domestic work in Ghana. For example, the family idiom in domestic work, which is much stronger than in situations of formalised domestic work, is so effective in Ghana because domestics are actually often extended family members of their employers. This practice

---

[48] A mapping exercise undertaken by the Centre for Gender Studies and Advocacy (CEGENSA) at the University of Ghana, in Accra, Kumasi and Tamale, three of Ghana's largest cities, identified 13 agencies recruiting only domestic workers and eight others who recruited domestic workers as part of their portfolio (Darkwa and Tsikata, above n 39).

[49] Interview with S Dartey, above n 44.

[50] And yet, the Labour Act makes a clear distinction between employment agencies and employers. Section 3, which sets out the functions of Employment Centres, states that each centre will assist persons to find suitable employment and assist employers to find suitable workers from among such persons.

has for long undermined domestic service as work that should be paid on agreed terms and conditions. Secondly, domestic work has developed in a context in which employment is largely informal and unregulated.[51] Thus, while domestic work is increasingly commodified and transformed from reproductive to productive labour,[52] many employers earn very low wages, and they barely afford to pay for domestic services. In any case, domestic employment agencies in their practice do not replace end users as employers because their relationship with domestics and users is much more limited than what pertains in other countries. The employment agency's relationship with the domestic worker appears to end once the domestic worker is placed and are paid by both parties. Further, as domestic workers predominantly live in their employers' homes, they continue to be largely supervised by their end users. Thus, employment agencies have not transformed the work process of domestic work, which continues to be similar to what pertains in direct and unmediated employment relations. The changes introduced by agencies tend to relate to wages and hours of work.

Current limitations of employment agencies notwithstanding, their operations have introduced a significant variation in the administration of domestic work in Ghana for the minority who benefit from their services. By registering and placing domestics, giving them limited training and negotiating placements backed by formal (though voluntary) agreements between employers and domestic workers, agencies are establishing new modalities and contributing to a new custom of domestic work. While this practice constitutes an improvement, it also legitimises the informality of domestic work.

---

[51] Tsikata, above n 26; Tsikata, D, *Domestic Work and Domestic Workers in Ghana: An Overview of the Legal Regime and Practice* (Working Paper No 23, Conditions of Work and Employment Programme, International Labour Office, Geneva, 2009).
[52] Mendez Bickham, above n 45.

Part IV

Regulating for Decent Work

15

Corporate Codes of Conduct in the Garment Sector in Bangalore

ROOPA MADHAV*

INTRODUCTION

SUCCESSFULLY TESTED AND implemented during the apartheid regime in South Africa,[1] Codes of Conduct for Multinational Corporations, now an important component of the corporate social responsibility framework, have steadily evolved to regulate responsible corporate behaviour by imposing labour, health, safety, social and environment standards. While the number of codes and auditors proliferate, their reach and effectiveness in regulating labour rights needs careful scrutiny from a worker's perspective. This chapter focuses on the codes regime pertaining to labour rights in the garment industry in Bangalore.

Codes of conduct gained popularity in the 1990s in the context of rapid globalisation, the resurgence of sweatshop labour as capital chased cheap labour around the world; and the expansion of brand consciousness among consumers.[2] Codes of conduct that target consumers in order to enforce

---

* I would like to thank Judy Fudge for her excellent and patient editorial support.

[1] The first governmental and inter-governmental guidelines for multinationals were created for foreign companies engaged in business in or with South Africa. In 1949, South Africa refused to endorse the ILO *Freedom of Association and Protection of the Right to Organise Convention* (ILO C87). In 1973, a delegation from the TUC General Council recommended 'Opposition to British investments in South Africa ... unless British firms operating in South Africa show in a practical way that they are encouraging and recognising genuinely independent trade unions for black workers'. Following a select committee report, the British government issued amplified guidelines in the form of a Code of Practice for British Firms with operating subsidiaries in South Africa, inviting these companies to file regular reports on progress made in raising African wages and in employment practices. This 1974 White Paper became the first issue-based code specifically focusing on South Africa (International Labour Organization, *Report on Codes of Conduct for Multinationals*, undated report), available at: http://actrav.itcilo.org/actrav-english/telearn/global/ilo/guide/main.htm.

[2] Bartley, T, 'Corporate Accountability and the Privatization of Labor Standards: Struggles Over Codes of Conduct in the Apparel Industry' (2005) 14 *Research in Political Sociology* 211.

labour standards are a form of transnational labour regulation that rest on the pillars of non-governmental organisation (NGO) activism, consumer activism, independent auditing, and the threat of market sanctions, in order to ensure compliance.

What do codes of conduct mean for workers? Have codes been effective in improving labour rights or have they operated to distract from, rather than strengthen, labour rights? This Chapter examines these questions in light of the specific experience of the garment industry in Bangalore. The Chapter is divided into two main parts. The first part identifies the main points of contention in the broader debate on the effectiveness of codes of conduct for delivering workers' rights, emphasising the shift from state regulatory mechanisms to private regulation. This part provides a broader frame for the case study in the second part, which draws upon government statistics and reports, legal documents, media reports, reports for international organisations, and interviews in order to evaluate the effectiveness of codes of conduct in protecting workers' rights in the garment sector in Bangalore. It provides the background for deeper reflection on the broader question of the efficacy of codes as a new form of regulation and highlights the need for a more comprehensive analysis of self-regulatory models and their implementation.

CORPORATE CODES OF CONDUCT: SELF-REGULATION VERSUS STATE REGULATION

Motivated largely by trade liberalisation, globalisation, and consumer activism, corporate codes are examples of 'new' models of regulatory governance that seek to improve labour conditions by supplementing or filling a gap in existing models of state regulation.[3] The claim is that these new models of self-regulation are more effective than traditional forms of top-down state regulation since they address specific issues and are flexible enough to change with rapidly evolving needs.[4] Codes, which are characterised as 'soft' law, are contrasted with 'hard' law, which is domestic labour regulation and public international law. What makes the latter law 'hard' is the existence of sanctions.[5]

It is widely believed that transnational corporations and their global supply chains operate within a regulatory gap as they conduct business across a range of geographic scales and legal jurisdictions. The goal of corporate codes is to address this regulatory gap by deploying agents or

---

[3] *Ibid.*

[4] Jenkins, R, *Corporate Codes of Conduct: Self-Regulation in a Global Economy* (Geneva, United Nations Research Institute for Social Development, 2001).

[5] Hassel, A, 'The Evolution of a Global Labor Governance Regime' (2008) 2 *Governance: An International Journal of Policy, Administration, and Institutions* 231.

involving stakeholders, such as non-governmental agencies and consumers, to enforce labour rights. Codes are a form of private, self, or soft regulation in that they do not rely on the coercive power of the state to enforce labour rights. The codes regime seeks to maintain the status quo and contains little or no scope for radical reordering of work relations and social relations for the betterment of the workers. The limited mandate of the codes regime is to ensure fair labour standards that provide minimal protection to workers. Even within the minimal protection framework, there is some hesitancy in implementing certain rights such as the right to freedom of association or the right to a living wage. This is a significant limitation of the framework within which the codes operate.

According to Bob Hepple, 'private corporate codes exist because of an absence of an enforceable internationally agreed labour regime'.[6] He identifies different phases of private regulation of TNCs, with the 1990s marking a fourth period, which he describes as an attempt 'to reassert an element of public control over private regulation by TNCs'.[7] What is new about this fourth wave of corporate codes is the attempt to tighten the link between these private forms of regulation and public international law.[8] When international institutions endorse codes of conduct they are very particular about the standards that the codes contain.

In 1998, the International Labour Organization (ILO) adopted the Declaration of Fundamental Principles and Rights at Work, which distilled four key labour rights from the broader ILO labour standards.[9] These core rights have become the standard for labour rights in inter-governmental Corporate Social Responsibility instruments; for example, the United Nations (UN) Global Compact, the ILO Tripartite Declaration of Principles concerning Multinational Enterprises and Social Policy, and the Organisation for Economic Cooperation and Development (OECD) Guidelines for Multinational Enterprises have all incorporated the ILO's core labour rights.[10]

Central to the debate on corporate codes is the changing nature of labour law, and the rapidly changing role of the state and trade unions within

---

[6] Hepple, B, *Labour Laws and Global Trade* (Hart Publishing, Oxford, 2005) 71.

[7] *Ibid*, at 72.

[8] *Ibid*.

[9] See ILO, *Declaration of Fundamental Principles and Rights at Work* (Declaration presented to the International Labour Conference, 86th Session, Geneva, 1998), available at: www.ilo.org/public/english/standards/decl/declaration/index.htm. For a rich debate on the merits and demerits of 'hard law' and 'soft law', see generally, Alston, P, '"Core Labour Standards" and the Transformation of the International Labour Rights Regime' (2004) 15 *European Journal of International Law* 457 and Langille, B, 'Core Labour Rights—The True Story (Reply to Alston)' (2005) 16 *European Journal of International Law* 409.

[10] See, generally, UN Global Compact, available at: www.unglobalcompact.org; ILO Tripartite Declaration, available at: www.ilo.org and OECD MNE guidelines, available at: www.oecd.org/daf/investment/guidelines.

the labour regulatory framework. Simultaneously, it also raises the critical question of transboundary regulation of transnational corporations and the efficacy of the newer models of regulation in filling this regulatory gap. In order to answer this question, it is important to turn to the literature, which has identified a number of limitations of, and preconditions for, using the new models such as corporate codes to protect workers' rights.

The labour standards provided in codes are both very important and highly contested. The ILO core labour standards often provide the non-negotiables to be incorporated in the codes.[11] While these standards are important because they are clear and simple, resort to the core labour standards ignores a wide range of protections that have been fought for and won by labour movements the world over. The various ILO Conventions expanding on worker rights are the direct product of these struggles. Whittling these down to a bare minimum has steadily eroded the traditional approach of progressive realisation of social and economic rights, catering more to a trade framework than a labour rights framework. As Philip Alston and James Heenan note:

> The core standards approach did not emerge in the discourse of the labor movement; this minimalist approach to international labor regulation was largely confined to the trade sphere until globalization and post Cold War neo-liberalism made trade the most pervasive and important item on the international agenda. Thereafter, the core standards approach started to spread beyond the trade sphere. Thus, international financial institutions (IFIs) are increasingly integrating core labor standards into their policy analysis, partner dialogues, and, in some cases, into lending conditionality.[12]

Two important preconditions exist for the effectiveness of corporate codes—the brand value on the one end of the continuum and the structured or 'factory' work environment on the other end. In the garment industry, it is evident that the exports to countries that have consumer awareness or brand value are the ones in which buyers seek compliance with codes. In the absence of brand value, buyers do not seek compliance and the codes regime has little or no traction. Since shaming is the only sanction when it comes to violating a code, the brand's reputation is extremely significant for the effectiveness of a code of conduct. If, however, there is no brand associated with a piece of apparel, a corporate code will have a limited impact.

---

[11] The core standards are set out in the *Declaration on Fundamental Principles and Rights at Work*, above n 9. For general discussion of the Declaration see Bellace, L, 'The ILO Declaration of Fundamental Principles and Rights at Work' (2001) 17 *International Journal of Comparative Labour Law and Industrial Relations* 269; Kellerson, H, 'The ILO Declaration of 1998 on Fundamental Principles and Rights: A Challenge for the Future?' (1998) 137 *International Labour Review* 223.

[12] Alston, P and Heenan, J, 'Shrinking the International Labor Code: An Unintended Consequence of the 1998 ILO Declaration on Fundamental Principles and Rights at Work?' (2004) 36 *New York University Journal of International Law and Politics* 221.

The codes regime has taken root in sectors and industries where unionisation and collective action by workers are at their lowest.[13] As a result, it has been necessary to create a whole new class of transnational labour code enforcers called social auditors.[14] The idea of an *Independent Social Auditor* provides an opportunity to transcend national boundaries to enforce workers' rights. However, the location of the Independent Auditor's accountability and transparency within the framework of consumer activism and corporate ethical practices discourse gives cause for concern since there is no requirement of accountability to the workers in the sector. Adelle Blackett suggests that 'by diverting attention to management monitoring systems, and away from classic voice mechanisms through labour-management dispute settlement machinery, self-regulatory initiatives run the risk of supplanting rather than buttressing democratic participation in the workplace'.[15] Moreover, trade unions and workers' collectives from the developing world rarely find a voice in formulating codes.

The *non-justiciability* of codes raises a range of potential problems. The contents of the code can be varied and changed at will. Codes can also be subject to varying interpretations, as there is no judicial process to impart finality and legitimacy. The voluntary nature of the codes and lack of deterrence in the form of effective sanctions in the event of breach, render the self-regulatory model difficult to sustain.[16]

The limitations of self-regulation are now well established. As Harry Arthurs rightly notes, state-regulation and self-regulation are neither interchangeable nor, ultimately, compatible systems. Self-regulation represents an assertion by corporations that they should be allowed to decide for themselves to what extent their interests will take priority over the claims of workers, communities and states—an assertion which has gained both popularity and credibility in a period of globalisation and neoliberal politics. State regulation, by contrast, rests on a more democratic paradigm of governance. It proceeds from the premise that communities and states must be able to respond politically, legally and practically through enforceable legislation to moral condemnation of the egregious failures of corporate self-regulation.[17]

---

[13] For a more detailed discussion on organising in the garment sector in India see, generally, Mani, M, *Garment Sector and Unionisation in India* (March 2011), available at: http://cividep.org/wp-content/uploads/garment-sector-and-unionisation-in-india-report.pdf.

[14] Don Wells discusses different types of auditors in Wells, D, 'Too Weak for the Job: Corporate Codes of Conduct, Non-Governmental organizations and the Regulation of International Labour Standards' (2007) 7 *Global Social Policy* 51.

[15] Blackett, A, 'Global Governance, Legal Pluralism and the Decentered State: A Labor Law Critique of Codes of Corporate Conduct' (2000) 8 *Indiana Journal of Global Legal Studies* 401, 420.

[16] Hepple, above n 6, at 75–6.

[17] Arthurs, H, 'Private Ordering and Workers' Rights in the Global Economy: Corporate Codes of Conduct as a Regime of Labour Market Regulation' in J Conaghan, RM Fischl and K Klare (eds), *Labour Law in an Era of Globalisation* (Oxford, Oxford University Press, 2002) 471, 484.

What *motivates* the introduction of codes is largely a desire to ensure minimal labour standards in select sectors while simultaneously seeking to satisfy the conscience of a consumer in a country abroad. However, state regulatory models seek to pursue a larger public purpose and look to protect the worker in society. The relationship of the state with the worker is that of a citizen whose welfare is of primary importance, whereas in the case of the codes, the relationship between the enforcer and the worker is that of a concerned consumer seeking to ensure some minimal protections.[18]

But, on the positive side, the new generation of codes are *multi-stakeholder initiatives*, which draw a wide range of actors into labour protection initiatives. Such initiatives enable wider social dialogue, beyond the triad of employer, employee and state, to include civil society and consumers in furthering decent work and livelihoods for workers. This development has been the most prominent and positive impact of the entire codes regime experiment, with many commentators and activists being encouraged to view any civil society engagement as precious and needing greater encouragement.

CORPORATE CODES AND THE GARMENT SECTOR IN BANGALORE: PROTECTING WORKERS' RIGHTS

In this section, I will examine specific regulatory concerns that have arisen in the decade that the codes regime has been attempted in Bangalore. After sketching the regulatory context for labour in contemporary India, I will examine the impact of codes along a number of dimensions of worker protection and rights, from health and safety through wages to collective bargaining.

Labour Regulation in India

In India, since independence, the state has played an important role in labour adjudication and labour relations providing a scheme of regulation which is tripartite in character.[19] In this regulatory model, the state seeks to balance the interests of capital in ensuring greater profits, maintaining productivity levels, and promoting growth, with that of labour in ensuring decent standards of living, creating employment, and enabling decent work. Moreover, there is a broad range of labour standards imposed by legislation

---

[18] See Seidman, G, *Beyond the Boycott: Labor Rights, Human Rights and Transnational Activism* (New York, Russell Sage Foundation Press, 2007).

[19] Ramaswamy, EA, *Power and Justice: The State in Industrial Relations* (Delhi, Oxford University Press, 1984) 3.

that applies to workers in the formal sector.[20] Trade unions favoured import substitution and protectionist policies.[21]

However, as Kamala Sankaran recounts in her chapter in this collection,[22] in the mid-1990s there was a major shift in economic and trade policies as India opened up its territory and labour force to global investment. Government policy cultivated greater foreign investment by setting up special zones and exempting corporations and transnational companies operating within them from aspects of labour regulation. For instance, the 'Special Economic Zones' (SEZ) set up in the state of Uttar Pradesh are exempt from the application of the Contract Labour (Regulation and Abolition) Act, which takes contract workers in SEZs out of the purview of labour protection.[23] This process of liberalisation resulted in a surge of economic growth and the expansion of informal employment.[24] The informal sector now constitutes nearly 93 per cent of the employment sector.[25]

Over the last two decades, demands by employers for major amendments to labour legislation to make it more flexible have met with political dissent and worker opposition. However, there are other ways of deregulating a labour market to make it more flexible than by repealing or amending legislation. A study carried out on the status of labour inspections in India paints an abysmal picture of enforcement, identifying a variety of reasons for ineffective and declining regulation: corrupt and under-resourced labour departments; subcontracting arrangements where employer–employee relationships are difficult to prove; little political commitment to improving labour standards; and poor coverage of new categories of work by existing labour laws.[26]

More troubling, in order to attract more industry and investment several states have issued directives to prevent or hinder inspection of firms. Sharma notes the example of Uttar Pradesh, where labour inspectors can carry out inspections only after the prior consent of an officer of the rank of Labour Commissioner or District Magistrate, which makes the procedure cumbersome. The states of Rajasthan and Andhra Pradesh have reduced the

---

[20] Sankaran, K, 'Labour Laws in South Asia: The Need for an Inclusive Approach' in T Teklè (ed), *Labour Law and Worker Protection in Developing Countries* (Hart Publishing, Oxford, 2010) 225, 227. For a discussion of formal and informal see Sankaran, K, 'Flexibility and Informalisation in Employment Relationships' in this collection.

[21] Sankaran, above n 20, at 228.

[22] *Ibid.*

[23] *Ibid.*

[24] *Ibid.*

[25] See Government of India, National Commission for Enterprises in the Unorganised Sector, *Conditions of Work and Promotion of Livelihood in the Unorganised Sector* (New Delhi, Government of India, 2007).

[26] Deshingkar, P, *Extending Labour Inspections to the Informal Sector and Agriculture* (Working Paper No 154, Chronic Poverty Research Centre, Overseas Development Institute, London, November 2009); Sharma, AN, 'Flexibility, Employment and Labour Market Reforms in India' (2006) 41 *Economic and Political Weekly* 2078.

scope of labour inspection, and have exempted several establishments from the purview of labour inspection.[27]

Since liberalisation, there has been a sharp decline in the incidence of strikes and lockouts, stagnant or declining real wages, increase in pro-employer court rulings and steady withdrawal of the state from its traditional role as a regulator.[28] Into the space vacated by the state, self-regulation through self-certification is now touted as a possible solution.[29] The codes regime is also presented as a workable model for future adaptation.

The Garment Industry in India and Bangalore

The Indian labour market is marked by a duality of extremes. On one end of the spectrum is a highly protected labour market with strict labour laws, while on the other, nearly 93 per cent of the workforce toils in the informal sector with little or no labour regulation. This duality is also reflected in the garment sector: Bangalore and Southern India largely comprise garment factories which generally fall within the formal sector, whereas garment production units in North India consist of small units and sub-contracted work arrangements which employ a large number of home-based informal workers.[30]

The textile and garment sector is the largest employer in India after agriculture. Production units are concentrated in cities like Delhi, Mumbai, Kolkata, Bangalore, Chennai, Jaipur, Tirupur, and Ludhiana. Bangalore is one of the centres of production of garments and has approximately 1,200 big, small and medium-sized garment factories.[31] The contribution of various clusters to the overall export market can be disaggregated thus: Delhi's contribution towards garment exports stands highest at 30 per cent, then Tirupur with 25 per cent, followed by Mumbai and Bangalore with 20 per cent and 15 per cent respectively, and Chennai contributes approximately 10 per cent.[32]

---

[27] Sharma, AN, 'Flexibility, employment and labour market reforms in India' (2006) 41 *Economic and Political Weekly* 2078, 2083.

[28] Bhattacharjea, A, 'Labour Market Regulation and Industrial Performance in India: A Critical Review of the Empirical Evidence' (2006) 49 *Indian Journal of Labour Economics* 211.

[29] See Planning Commission, *Report of Working Group on Labour Law and Other Labour Regulation* (New Delhi, Government of India, 2006), available at: http://planningcommission. nic.in/aboutus/committee/wrkgrp11/wg11_rplabr.pdf. The states of Gujarat and Punjab introduced the system of self-certification.

[30] Singh, S, 'Richer Bosses, Poorer Workers: Bangalore's Garment Industry' (Bangalore, CIVIDEP, 2009), available at: http://somo.nl/publications-en/Publication_3126/at_download/ fullfile.

[31] *Ibid.*

[32] *Ibid*, at 6.

The garment industry employs nearly 7 million workers, dominated by women, with nearly half the workers engaged in the export segment.[33] Nearly 80 per cent of Indian garment exports are sent to the United States, Canada, and the European Union. Being a major foreign exchange earner contributing nearly 17 per cent to export earnings, garment exports during 2008–09 stood at US $10.93 billion. Following the global financial meltdown, there was a dip in western markets, and export earnings overall declined marginally by 2.6 per cent to US $10.64 billion in 2009–10.[34] As a direct consequence, nearly 1 million jobs have been lost with several lay-offs and retrenchments between 2008 and 2009. However, the industry in Bangalore bucked the trend as it largely supplies the middle segment of the fashion and garment sector.[35]

Textiles and the garment industry have a fairly long history in Bangalore, dating back to the British period when the Bangalore Dressmaking Company was established in 1940 marking the beginning of ready-made garment manufacture in the city.[36] Ready-made garment manufacturing grew alongside the silk industry and flourished in the Peenya and Bommanahalli industrial areas. However, the manufacture of ready-made garments for export is relatively new and an emerging market. Significant development in the garment sector occurred in the 1970s when leading exporters like Gokaldas Export, Ashoka Export, Gokuldas Images, Continental Exports, and Leela Fashions established units in the city. Later, small industries (fabricators) grew around these large-scale operations. While there are no Special Economic Zones in the city, an Apparel Park was set up in Doddaballapur on the outskirts of Bangalore. The primary reason for the steady and rapid growth of the garment sector is the availability of export fabrics from places like Salem, Erode, and Coimbatore which are located near Bangalore.

It was only in the 1990s, post liberalisation,[37] that the country witnessed the present boom in export garment manufacturing. The exponential increase in the value of garment exports indicates the growth trajectory: the value was $2 million in 1960–1961, increasing to $696 million in

---

[33] See Press Release, *Budget 2010–11: Industry Speaks*, available at: www.cmai.in/news/apparelnews_view_index.asp?articleID=808.

[34] Press note dated 3 June 2010 issued by the Apparel Export Promotion Council, available at: www.aepcindia.com/admin/press-doc/june%203press%20releasefinal.doc.

[35] Rao, GR, *Diagnostic Study Report for Readymade Garments Cluster, Bangalore* (Bangalore, Ministry of Small Scale Industries, undated), available at: www.msmefoundation.org/DSR_temp/Diagnostic%20Study%20Report%20of%20Readymade%20Garment%20Cluster%20-%20Bangalore.pdf.

[36] *Ibid.*

[37] The post-liberalisation phase refers to the opening up of the Indian economy to international trade and investment, privatisation, deregulation and most importantly, labour reforms so as to attract greater investment in a bid to gradually move the economy from a socialist model to a capitalist economy.

1980–1981; $2,236 million in 1990–1991; and $4,765 million in 1999–2000.[38] 2005 marked another milestone for growth, when the Multi-Fibre Agreement[39] witnessed its final phase-out, marking the end of quota-based ceilings on the importation of textiles and clothing from certain developing countries.[40] According to Asiya Chaudhary:

> Readymade Garments account for approximately 41 percent of the country's total textiles exports. After the MFA phase out the textiles exports grew from US$7986.38 million in 2005–06 to US$8282.27 in 2006–07. During 2007–08 the Readymade Garments exports have amounted to US$9065.36 million, recording an increase of 9.46 percent over the exports during 2006–2007. During the period of 2008–09, the Readymade Garments exports have amounted to US$10242.08 million, recording an increase of 12.93 percent over the exports during the corresponding period of 2007.[41]

The Garment Industry Workforce in Bangalore

The garment industry workforce in Bangalore is marked by feminisation, low educational attainment, high attrition and low wages. The majority of workers in the sector are women aged between 18 and 35 years. On average, the educational qualification of these women does not exceed the 10th grade. A large number of workers are migrants from nearby villages. Many of the women workers are of marriageable age and the rate of attrition in the industry is high, as a direct consequence of marriage, pregnancy, and care responsibilities. In spite of codes and legislation[42] that mandate the establishment of crèche facilities, there is little compliance with this requirement across the sector.[43]

The average monthly income in the sector is approximately Rs 3,200/- per month (or 105.49 daily) (USD 80). The statutory minimum wage for the city of Bangalore (Zone I) is a daily rate of Rs 108.71 for highly skilled workers (designer, tailor); Rs 107.71 for skilled workers (grade 1 tailor, cutting machine operator); Rs 106.21 for semi-skilled workers (ironer,

---

[38] Chowdhary, SR, 'Labour Activism and Women in the Unorganized Sector: Garment Export Industry in Bangalore' (2005) 40 *Economic and Political Weekly* 2250.

[39] The Multi Fibre Agreement (MFA) which established such quotas was a protectionist measure and under the General Agreement on Tariffs and Trade 1994, the Agreement on Textiles and Clothing (ATC) replaced the MFA, providing for phased withdrawal of quotas under MFA by 2005.

[40] See generally, Rao, above n 35.

[41] Chaudhary, A, Changing Structure of Indian Textiles Industry after MFA (Multi Fiber Agreement) Phase-Out: A Global Perspective (2011) 2 *Far East Journal of Psychology and Business* 8; see also, Ministry of Textiles, *Annual Report 2009–10* (New Delhi, Ministry of Textiles, 2010).

[42] Section 48 of the Factories Act 1948 provides that every factory wherein more than 30 women are ordinarily employed should provide and maintain a creche for the use of children under the age of six years.

[43] Singh, above n 30.

buttonhole stitching) and Rs 101.71 for unskilled workers (packer, helper).[44] The meagre wages permit workers to rent accommodation in the poorer neighbourhoods of Bangalore, often in areas which have no civic amenities such as clean drinking water, sanitation and electricity.

A large number of these women workers support an entire family, and their meagre earnings are stretched to provide for education, medical and other household expenses. Additional benefits such as maternity benefit, retirement benefits, and gratuity[45] accrue to workers who are able to consistently work in a single factory for many years. However, the working conditions and pressure of work compel workers to quit and rejoin work at regular intervals, thus foregoing access even to these limited entitlements, as legal entitlements are linked to the number of continuous years of work with the same employer. This instability also adversely impacts on efforts to organise the workers, bettering their wages and work conditions through collective bargaining. However, despite the challenges of organising, nearly four unions are active in the garment sector in Bangalore.[46]

Corporate Codes in Bangalore

The 1990s witnessed the spread of neo-liberalism and the beginning of the era of corporate social responsibility in India.[47] Global supply chain networks saw an increase in the adoption of voluntary codes of conduct and the trickle down effects appeared in Bangalore in early 2000. In the initial phase, codes were administered primarily by an 'Independent Auditor' or management consultants, but increasingly in Bangalore (and across the world) codes are being enforced by Multi-stakeholder Initiatives (MSI) that comprise various stakeholders including workers. Some of the important MSI initiatives include the Ethical Trading Initiative (ETI), Fair Labor Association (FLA), Fair Wear Foundation (FWF), Social

---

[44] *Minimum Wage Notification No KAE 54 LMW 2001* (3 November 2001), available at: http://labour.kar.nic.in/labour/minimumwages-1948.htm.

[45] Gratuity is paid to an employee by their employer if they complete five years of continuous service with the organisation. The Payment of Gratuity Act 1972 provides the basis for calculation of the gratuity amount.

[46] Garment And Textile Workers' Union (affiliated to the New Trade Union Initiative), Indian National Trade Union Congress, Centre of Indian Trade Unions, All India Trade Union Congress and the Karnataka Garment Workers' Union.

[47] See generally Sood, A and Arora, B, *The Political Economy of Corporate Social Responsibility in India* (Programme Paper No 18, United Nations Research Institute for Social Development, Geneva, November, 2006). According to World Business Council for Sustainable Development in its publication *Making Good Business Sense* by Lord Holme and Richard Watts, 'Corporate Social Responsibility is the continuing commitment by business to behave ethically and contribute to economic development while improving the quality of life of the workforce and their families as well as of the local community and society at large'. Available at: www.wbcsd.org/DocRoot/IunSPdIKvmYH5HjbN4XC/csr2000.pdf.

Accountability International (SAI), Workers Rights Consortium (WRC), Business Social Compliance Initiative (BSCI), and Worldwide Responsible Apparel Production (WRAP). The codes regime has spawned a whole industry of 'social auditors', the prime movers of the self-regulation model of labour rights enforcement.

The codes prohibit, in no uncertain terms, any harsh or inhumane treatment including physical abuse, intimidation, and sexual abuse. Yet, a spate of women workers' deaths, following severe harassment or verbal abuse by management, has been reported in Bangalore in the recent past. Despite every code stating the need to prevent harassment (sexual and verbal), bullying continues to be a tactic used by shop floor managers to meet production targets.[48]

In 2007, the body of Ammu, a garment worker, was found on the premises of Triangle Apparels, a subsidiary of the Gokuldas Exports Group.[49] It is suspected that she committed suicide by hanging herself in the toilet of the factory on Saturday 10 February 2007. Her body was found three days later on 13 February. She had been employed in Triangle Apparels for only 21 days as a tailor. Prior to that, she was employed in the ironing section of Leela Scottish, another garment factory, where she worked for 18 months. From 2002 to 2005 she had worked in the ironing section of Arvind Mills, another garment factory located in Bangalore.[50]

Several co-workers reported that she was badly harassed by the Production Manager, Assistant Plant Manager and Plant Supervisor, and that her suicide was the result of the harassment. The management of Triangle Apparels, along with local police officers, sought to cover up the whole incident without the company accepting any accountability. Compensation of approximately Rs 200,000 (two lakhs) was paid to family members in a bid to silence them. Attempts were also made to portray Ammu as a disturbed person, and to insinuate that reasons for the suicide had nothing to do with the workplace.

Another example from 2007 involved Padmavathi, a garment worker at Shalini Creations, who died an unnatural death.[51] She started vomiting at her workplace at 9.30 am and requested the Production Manager on duty to grant her sick leave to go to a nearby hospital. She was shouted at and sent back to work. Medical help within the factory premises was not available

---

[48] The details of the case studies that follow are taken from legal documents, media reports, reports for international organisations, and interviews conducted by the author; further specific references are provided below.

[49] Gokuldas Exports is the largest garment manufacturing concern in the city. The Group employs over 30,000 workers, and has an annual turnover of over Rs 700 *crores*.

[50] *Report of the Fact Finding team of the Joint Action Committee for the Rights of Garment Workers* (6 March, 2007) (unpublished, on file with author).

[51] McVeigh, K, 'Third Death in a year at Indian factory that supplies Gap', *Guardian* (15 October 2007), available at: www.guardian.co.uk/business/2007/oct/15/india.

and a couple of hours later, when the vomiting did not stop, she was allowed to leave the factory. Barely able to walk, she collapsed outside the factory gates. People on the street moved her back into the factory and her colleagues then shifted her to hospital. She died on the same day at 1.00 pm. Shalini Creations is a subsidiary of Texport Overseas Group, which produces global brands such as GAP and Matalan. The Texport Group is regularly subject to inspections by 'Compliance Officers', but it appears that the realities of harsh treatment meted out to workers remain unchanged.

These are instances reported widely in the media. However, innumerable instances of abuse remain unrecorded. Despite codes being implemented in nearly all export-oriented factories, real change in management attitude towards workers has been slow in evolving. After a series of complaints of sexual harassment by workers, not to social auditors, but to the labour department in Bangalore, the Karnataka Government issued an order in February 2010 requiring the appointment of women labour welfare officers in factories employing women.[52] The women labour welfare officers are required to address all problems faced by women workers in factories, and in the event of specific complaints they will be required to forward the same to the labour department for further action.

Despite freedom of association and collective bargaining being core labour rights provided for by the codes, these rights are ignored. Systematic targeting of union activists has been recorded in factories even where codes have been adopted. In one instance in 2006, the General Secretary of the Garment Textile Workers' Union (GATWU), who was employed by Texport Creations Limited, was suspended for advising workers on their rights and actively pursuing legitimate claims of workers against management.[53] Following the suspension, the company approached the court for an order of injunction against the Union restraining it from communicating anything about the Company to outside agencies, including those seeking to enforce codes.[54] These actions, clearly in violation of freedom of expression and freedom of association, are examples of management attempts to prevent or subdue organising or collective action by workers. Moreover, collective bargaining is unheard of in the garment sector. Thus the spirit of freedom of association has never been actualised among garment workers.[55]

---

[52] Hunasavadi, S, 'Garment Units will get Women Labour Officers', *DNA* (3 February, 2010), available at: www.dnaindia.com/bangalore/report_garment-units-will-get-women-labour-officers_1342748.

[53] See Government of Karnataka, *Memorandum to the Ministry of Labour* (7 March 2007), available at: www.indianet.nl/070215.html.

[54] *Ibid.*

[55] For a more detailed discussion on organising in the garment sector in India see generally Mohan, M, *Garment Sector and Unionisation in India—Some Critical Issues* (Bangalore, Civil Initiatives for Development and Peace India, 2011), available at: http://cividep.org/wp-content/uploads/garment-sector-and-unionisation-in-india-report.pdf.

The limitations of the code system can be illustrated by events that took place at a company called Konega International Private Limited. The company proudly announces on its website: 'We at Konega have a capacity of producing 230,000 Pcs (cut to pack) per month. All our three production units are in compliance with the Code of Conduct for Human Rights rated by the GAP, Phillips Van Huesen, Capital Mercury, Columbia and Price Waterhouse for Disney'.[56] The company specialises in bottom wear production (such as trousers, cargos and shorts) and supplies European and US brands such as Van Heusen, Arrow, Ashworth, Guess, and Bona Parte. It declared a lockout on 7 October 2009, as recurring losses had led to massive debt, without prior notice and in clear violation of the law. The 900 workers, mostly women, who were rendered jobless, are now fighting a legal battle against the illegal lockout in the labour courts.[57] A primary cause of a large number of labour conflicts is wrongful termination, and job security is non-existent. With tough production targets that vary depending on market demands, workers are under constant pressure, and the threat of suspension or termination hangs over those unable to cope with the rigours of unscheduled long hours of work. The codes do not address the basic norms that should govern instances of termination. Even a call to ensure due process in law has been slow in coming.

Moreover, unions that seek to publicise violations of codes risk legal retaliation by employers. For example, the GATWU, CIVIDEP, Clean Clothes Campaign and the India Committee of the Netherlands were slapped with civil and criminal legal action by the company Fibres & Fabrics International (FFI/JKPL). The provocation was a public campaign which informed the Dutch and international constituencies of labour rights violations and irregularities in the application of labour laws at FFI/JKPL. The labour rights violations allegedly included sustained and high work pressure leading to extensive overtime being clocked by workers, and physical and verbal abuse of workers by the management of FFI and its subsidiary JKPL. In December 2005, the Clean Clothes Campaign (CCC) and the India Committee of Netherlands (ICN) intervened and made the labour violations public.

FFI went to court alleging that the union and the fact-finding team were spreading false information about the company and sought a 'gag' order against them.[58] The Court issued such an order in July 2006 and further extended it in February 2007.[59] The Court also issued arrest warrants

---

[56] See www.alibaba.com/member/in100306510/aboutus.html.

[57] See media reports on the illegal lockout at http://beta.thehindu.com/news/cities/Bangalore/article66396.ece; www.hinduonnet.com/2009/11/09/stories/2009110959440400.htm.

[58] Restraining order granted by the IV Additional City Civil Judge at Bangalore on 28 July 2006 in Original Suit No 16338/2006.

[59] *Ibid.*

against some of the Dutch activists. Simultaneously in November 2006, CCC and ICN filed a complaint with the Social Accountability Initiative (SAI) arguing for the withdrawal of the SA 8000 certification from FFI as the legal action against the unions violates freedom of association.[60] As the legal battle escalated, the Dutch Minister for Economic Affairs intervened and mediated an agreement the terms of which included the withdrawal of all court cases undertaken by FFI/JKPL against Indian and Dutch parties. The agreement also provided for the setting up of an Ombudsman to look into the labour-related complaints.[61] Prior to this, however, the SA 8000 certification for the FFI factories was suspended. This case study illustrates the unequal power equation in implementation of the codes regime and the potential for intimidation of trade unions and codes compliance NGOs by the garment factories.

Having listed some of the limitations of the codes regime, have the codes had any positive impact on the workers in Bangalore? In a detailed study by Ingrid Stigzelius, Linda Fredicsdotter and Cecilia Mark-Herbert of the socio-economic impact of SA 8000 in the garment sector in Bangalore and Tirupur, findings of improvement on health and safety conditions in the factories were recorded. They noted:

> The case studies indicate that in most cases an actual improvement has occurred in terms of health and safety, which leads to reduced risks. This is achieved through worker training and participation in first aid and fire fighting. The additional benefits, like canteen and medical facilities, will help the workers towards improved health, which leads to a decrease in labour turnover. However, the issues that remain hidden to the eye, such as basic needs wages and freedom of association, are still not taken seriously.[62]

Interviews with worker representatives reveal that the impact of the codes regime can be clearly seen in the physical aspects of the factory environment.[63] Factories have improved working environments with better ventilation, clean drinking water, clean toilets, and management has sought to address safety issues. But matters pertaining to wages, overtime, termination and verbal abuse continue to plague workers. Although there are claims that codes have been effective with health issues, worker representatives point to women workers having little freedom to visit the toilets leading to urinary tract infections and other reproductive health problems.

---

[60] See Complaint No 019: CCC and ICN Against Certification of FFI/JKPL factories, available at: www.saasaccreditation.org/complaint019.htm.

[61] For more particulars, see the OECD case overview available at: http://oecdwatch.org/cases/Case_109.

[62] Stigzelius, I, Fredicsdotter, L and Mark-Herbert, C, *Implementation of SA 8000 in Indian Garment Manufacturing: A Socio-economic Assessment of the Impacts on Working Conditions and Business Practices* (Paper presented to the Corporate Responsibility Research Conference, Trinity College Dublin, 4–5 September, 2006) 18.

[63] Interview with Gopinath, K, of CIVIDEP (16 June 2010).

Pre-natal and post-natal health care have not been prioritised, despite a majority of the women workers being young and in the early years of the reproductive cycle.

Factory audits rely heavily on documentary evidence (both genuine and fake) and do not amount to sustained efforts that build a relationship with workers. Workers interviewed by the auditors are often tutored by management or interviewed in the presence of managers, defeating the purpose of the engagement. Trained auditors, with a clear worker-protection focus, are equally rare. Even where code compliance requires that codes be displayed inside a factory in a prominent manner, the same is displayed in a language that is not understood by the workers concerned.[64] What is evident from a decade of implementation is that the codes regime is viewed as yet another routine set of paperwork that needs to be complied with in the course of doing business. Audit processes have also, over the years, evolved into bureaucratic exercises—a long checklist to be ticked or crossed upon finding violations, leading to the filing of detailed reports, rather than efforts to ensure compliance with the minimal norms set out in the codes. Suppliers do not have an incentive to invest in ensuring compliance with the codes regime, as buyers do not necessarily stay loyal to suppliers and could shift business according to changing needs and improved profits.

On balance, the experience over the last decade points to the limited success of the codes regime in crucial and core areas of labour rights such as wages, dispute resolution, termination and overtime, whereas it appears to have ensured improved safety standards and had some degree of success with health issues. As the National Commission for Enterprises in the Unorganised Sector (NCEUS) report notes:

> Codes may have limited success because (a) as the experience of ILO conventions (codes accepted by governments) suggests, countries bypass them; (b) as the experience of impact of trade on employment in developing countries suggests, a race to the bottom; (c) the applicability of codes is mostly limited to the formal sector; and (d) there is a sectoral limitation to the application of codes, covering mostly consumer goods sector. However, codes serve a useful purpose in so far as they keep the labour conditions on the global agenda and help labour rights campaign to be effective by raising awareness. Consumer conscientisation does have a positive linkage with political support for workers rights.[65]

Over the years, many different codes and standards have emerged in the garment sector. To deal with multifarious codes and innumerable audits, the Apparel Export Promotion Council (AEPC) has recently put in place a

---

[64] Singh, above n 30.
[65] National Commission for Enterprises in the Unorganised Sector (NCEUS), *Conditions of Work and Promotion of Livelihood in the Unorganised Sector* (Government of India, New Delhi, 2007) 171, available at: http://nceuis.nic.in/Condition_of_workers_sep_2007.pdf.

common compliance code for the industry.[66] However, a similar effort at harmonisation in Turkey called the 'Joint Initiative' met with little success.[67]

One of the most obvious benefits of codes is that they have opened up a new forum for redressing grievances for workers. In spite of criticisms that social auditors and monitors lack accountability and transparency, this new forum of appeal is seen as less corrupt and more approachable than local labour inspectorates. Another benefit of codes is that they have widened the space for social dialogue in labour relations, to include other stakeholders such as consumers and NGOs.

However, the limits of the codes regime highlight the urgent need to cultivate other forms of regulation. In fact, Nike has recognised the limits of the social audit process and has openly admitted to problems recurring once the auditing process is over. It now encourages the organisation of trade unions on the ground that it is the only stable and independent system of verification of labour standards.[68]

Perhaps the way forward is to build a hybrid form of regulation that draws upon a range of techniques and approaches taking the best of the codes regime and state regulation.[69] The codes provide simplified versions of standards that could be adopted by national regulatory regimes. Moreover, codes demonstrate how it is possible to open up national labour regulation regimes, which are closed networks, to different stakeholders. One of the strengths of the codes regime is the introduction of new actors such as consumers and NGOs into the process of social dialogue, enabling a more effective regulatory model that takes on board a wide range of groups interested in protecting the rights of workers.

However, to date, the shift away from state regulatory mechanisms to private ones has not carried a concomitant obligation to strengthen existing regulatory frameworks. Currently, in the garment industry in Bangalore there is no interface between state regulations and self-regulatory experiments. It is important to develop mechanisms to bridge the gap between the two regimes, while simultaneously leaving space for the learning and

---

[66] APEC press release (1 September 2010), available at http://www.aepcindia.com/admin/press-pdf/sep%201%20press%20release.pdf.

[67] For details see, eg, Fondation des Droits de l'Homme au Travail, *The Joint Initiative with the CCC, ETI, FLA, FWF, SAI and WRC* (11 May 2011), available at: www.fdht.org/spip.php?article26. See also Joint Initiative on Corporate Accountability and Workers Rights, *About Us*, available at: www.jo-in.org/pub/about.shtml.

[68] Makisomic, A, 'Can CSR Help Workers Organize? An Examination of Lessons Learnt and an Exploration of a New Way Forward' in K MacDonald and S Marshall, *Fair Trade, Corporate Accountability and Beyond: Experiments in Global Justice* (Farnham, Ashgate, 2010) 245, 250.

[69] See also Macklem, P and Trebilcock, M, *New Labour Standards Compliance Strategies: Corporate Codes of Conduct and Social Labeling Programs—A Research Report prepared for the Federal Labour Standards Review* (Government of Canada, 2006), available at: www.hrsdc.gc.ca/eng/labour/employment_standards/fls/research/research21/page00.shtml.

adaptation necessary for future growth and expansion. In order for the codes regime to be a success in the long run, there needs to be an effective system of state regulation and enforcement of labour standards. Codes must supplement existing labour regulatory mechanisms and not replace available protection and collective bargaining instruments.[70]

CONCLUSION

The popularity of codes regimes peaked at a time when transnational global supply chains boomed and labour law, the world over, was in transition. In India, the two pillars of labour regulation, namely, the state and trade unions, were in decline. The neo-liberal agenda propagated reforms to the labour sector, steadily reducing state capitalism and the organised (and often, unionised) formal sector labour force. Neo-liberal thinking placed greater emphasis on individual contracts to help negotiate labour relations, based on an assumption of two equal contracting parties where wages and working conditions can effectively be negotiated through contract. Yet, the lived realities of developing countries require effective state regulatory frameworks as workers continue to battle nineteenth-century industrial work relations. The battle for decent work, especially in the informal sector, is now being fought largely without the support of established trade unions and a weak labour regulatory mechanism.

Given this troubling state of affairs, the introduction of the codes regime can only be viewed as an interesting slice of labour history, experimenting with a social dialogue mechanism beyond the triad of state, employer and worker to include consumers, NGOs and auditors. In the long run, codes may reduce transparency, accountability and sustainability of inspection and enforcement models. Consequently, the future of the codes regime depends on its capacity to interface with the other two pillars of industrial relations—the state and workers. In the meantime, traditional state regulation needs to be strengthened, keeping in mind labour welfare in the garment industry and the long-term needs of citizens in society.

---

[70] Compa, L, 'Corporate Social Responsibility and Workers Rights' (2008) 30 *Comparative Labor Law and Policy Journal* 1.

16

How Britain's Low-paid Non-unionised Employees Deal with Workplace Problems

ANNA POLLERT

INTRODUCTION: BRITAIN AND NON-UNIONISM

THE CHAPTERS IN this collection illustrate how globally capital accumulation rests on diverse forms of productive and service work, many of which are so informalised as to lie beyond the reach of employment protection. This development co-exists with shifts in the advanced capitalist economies to increasing labour market flexibility under the hegemony of neo-liberalism.[1] The 'flexible' workforce in the 'core' of the capitalist system is increasingly fragmented and individualised. Even where workers under 'standard' employment contracts are formally under the aegis of employment law protection, in practice, lack of union protection leaves them vulnerable and unable to enforce their rights. Non-unionism is the experience for the majority of Britain's workers. In 2009, only 27.4 per cent of employees were unionised, the same as in 2008, but down from 28 per cent in 2007. In the private sector, membership fell by 0.6 percentage points to 15.5 per cent between 2007 and 2008; and to 15.1 per cent in 2009.[2] Sixty-four per cent of workplaces had no union members in 2004, up from 57 per cent in 1998.[3] There has been a crisis facing the identities and strategies of European unions since the 1970s,[4] but in liberal capitalist systems, such as Britain (and the US), individual membership decline has

---

[1] Pollert, A (ed), *Farewell to Flexibility?* (Oxford, Blackwell, 1991).

[2] Achur, J, *Trade Union Membership 2009* (London, Department for Business Innovation and Skills and National Statistics, 2010) 1; Barratt, C, *Trade Union Membership 2008* (London, Department of Business, Enterprise and Regulatory Reform and National Statistics, 2009) 2.

[3] Kersley, B, Alpin, C, Bryson, A, Bewley, H, Dix, G, and Oxenbridge, S, *Inside the Workplace: Findings from the 2004 Workplace Employment Relations Survey* (London, Routledge, 2006) 110.

[4] Hyman, R, 'Changing Trade Union Identities and Strategies' in R Hyman and A Ferner (eds), *New Frontiers in European Industrial Relations* (Oxford, Blackwell, 1994).

the most severe consequences for the labour movement, since there are no broad, neo-corporatist arrangements which provide protection for workers, as in many other European countries. In Britain, collective bargaining agreements, formerly 'public goods supporting much of unorganised labour' dropped from 82 per cent of employees in the mid-1990s to 33 per cent currently—covering broadly those who are union members.[5] In other parts of Europe, despite drops in membership, bargaining coverage remains at approximately 80 per cent, and some union movements with low union densities, such as France and Spain, have still exhibited political power. Whether worker vulnerability as non-unionism is defined by non-union membership, or non-coverage by collective bargaining, it has increased and includes the majority of workers.

There are differences among the non-unionised and not all are equally vulnerable. Those who lack financially and socially rewarded 'skill'[6] in 'poor-quality' jobs lack labour market power and are thus low-paid. Low pay reflects and deepens vulnerability. As Judy Fudge argues in Chapter 1 of this collection, at a global level, neo-liberalism has fuelled changes in the labour market to depress labour costs through the growth of outsourcing and the shift towards decentralised and fragmented jobs, with little or no protection either through collective labour organisation or legal regulation.[7] In Britain, changes in the structure of the labour market over the last 25 years suggest a polarisation of jobs, with an increase in both the number and proportion of low-paid, replaceable, 'lousy jobs', which indicates an increase in such vulnerable workers.[8] How 'low-pay' is defined in Britain varies. The TUC considers it to include the bottom third of the hourly income distribution, which, combined with absence of collective bargaining, meant that 5.3 million UK employees, or one in five, were vulnerable in 2006.[9] A broader approach, adopted by the research reported here, takes lower pay as that of the half of UK employees earning below median hourly earnings. If we combine low pay and a lack of union representation, this higher pay threshold means that one in three UK employees were vulnerable

---

[5] Brown, W and Nash, D, 'What Has Been Happening to Collective Bargaining Under New Labour? Interpreting WERS 2004' (2008) 39 *Industrial Relations Journal* 91, 95; Barratt, above n 2, at 37.

[6] The concept of 'skill' is commonly used in descriptive labour market literature. It is contentious, and while there may be objective measures of skill it is recognised here that it is a socially constructed concept.

[7] See Fudge, J, 'Blurring Legal Boundaries: Regulating for Decent Work' in this collection.

[8] Goos, M and Manning, A, 'Lousy and Lovely Jobs: The Rising Polarization of Work in Britain' (2007) 89 *Review of Economics and Statistics* 118; Kaplanis, I, *The Geography of Employment Polarisation in Britain* (London, Institute for Public Policy Research, 2007).

[9] Trades Union Congress, *The Hidden One-in-Five: Winning a Fair Deal for Britain's Vulnerable Workers* (London, Trades Union Congress, 2006).

in 2005 if non-coverage by collective bargaining were the criterion of non-unionism, or two fifths if non-union membership were the measure.[10] Within this definition of vulnerability, there is a spectrum. Migrant workers without legal immigration and employee status fall outside employment law protection and are among the most vulnerable.[11] Workers without employee status in general are also among the most vulnerable. These include agency workers, for whom the UK New Labour (and post-2010 Conservative–Liberal Democrat coalition) governments delayed implementation of the European Agency Worker Directive until 2011. Finally, on 1st October 2011, the Agency Workers Regulations (AWS) came into force, giving qualifying agency workers the right to be treated no less favourably in terms and conditions than if they had been directly employed by an organisation. To qualify for the regulations to apply, a 'temporary agency worker' needs to have worked in the same job with the same hirer for a period of 12 weeks. The regulations cover pay, paid annual leave, rest breaks and limits on working time, the UK National Minimum Wage, no unlawful deductions from wages, discrimination rights under the Equality Act 2010 and health and safety at work. The AWS was an advance, and culmination of trade union campaigning, on the earlier (2002) 'Fixed-Term *Employees*' Regulations, which were a restrictive British interpretation of the Fixed Term Workers' Directive, against the intentions of the European Council legislation to include all *workers*.[12] Those who move between unpaid work (primarily within home and family) and paid employment— predominantly women—are particularly vulnerable, since they are more likely to have 'non-standard' jobs (temporary, casual, fixed-term) which the courts judge as outside the contracts of employment and hence employment protection.[13] Low-paid workers earning below the lower earnings limit for national insurance contributions (primarily part-time women workers) are also excluded from a wide variety of social and employment benefits, such as incapacity benefit, statutory sick-pay and maternity pay. Thus, the most vulnerable are low-paid, 'non-standard', non-unionised workers excluded

---

[10] *Ibid* at 7; Pollert, A and Charlwood, A, 'The Vulnerable Worker in Britain and Problems at Work' (2009) 23 *Work, Employment and Society* 343, 344.

[11] Ryan, B (ed), *Labour Migration and Employment Rights* (Liverpool, Institute of Employment Rights, 2005).

[12] 2002 SI 2002/2003; (1999/70/EC); McColgan, A, 'The Fixed-Term Employees (Prevention of Less Favourable Treatment) Regulations 2002: Fiddling While Rome Burns?' (2003) 32 *Industrial Law Journal* 194.

[13] Fredman, S, 'Women at Work: The Broken Promise of Flexicurity' (2004) 33 *Industrial Law Journal* 299. On the general issue of employment protection, in Britain, it is often ambiguous as to whether workers are 'employees' and hence covered by protection for *employees* only (eg unfair dismissal protection, although some European laws, such as the Working Time Regulations, apply to all 'workers' as well as 'employees'), or whether they are only 'workers'. If they are only 'workers' they are unprotected in many areas including redundancy payments, notice pay, the right to receive written reasons for dismissal and various family leave rights.

from 'all three regulatory regimes—collective bargaining, employment protection rights, and the national insurance system'.[14]

However, while these workers are among the most vulnerable, in focusing exclusively on them there is a danger of losing sight of the mainstream, or, what happens to lower-paid, non-unionised workers who experience problems at work. This Chapter uncovers what happens to such workers in Britain. It reports on the findings of the Unrepresented Worker Survey (URWS), a telephone questionnaire in 2004 to 501 low paid, non-unionised workers about the problems that they had experienced at work in the previous three years. What problems did they have? What did they do about them? Did their actions lead to satisfactory resolutions? The findings support the contention that even workers who are employees, and primarily on 'standard' full-time, 'permanent' contracts, but without collective power are vulnerable to unilateral employer dictate in the current climate of neo-liberalism. The survey found that problems at work were widespread. A large proportion of those workers who had experienced problems felt that their rights had been violated. Despite the fact that a large majority of respondents took action to try to solve them, only a minority achieved a satisfactory resolution. The empirical section of the Chapter first outlines research methods and data, and then discusses results in terms of vulnerable workers' experience of workplace problems and dispute resolution. It provides insight into the workplace experience of dealing with individual grievances at work for the 40 per cent of the British workforce which is lower paid and non-unionised.

CONCEPTUALISING 'PROBLEMS' AND RESEARCH METHODS

The URWS aimed to capture both the nature of, and responses to, workplace 'problems'. It cognitively tested the word 'problem' and found it excluded eligible respondents who, when asked about work in terms such as 'worries' or 'concerns', recalled a range of workplace grievances. This demonstrated that the threshold for registering workplace experiences as 'problems' can be high, especially at the lower end of the labour market, where habituation to experiences such as work intensification, insecurity, low pay and coercion lower expectations of working life.[15] The URWS began with terms such as 'difficulty, concern or worry' and then focused on 10 prompted potential grievance areas experienced in the previous three years.

---

[14] *Ibid*, at 308.
[15] Wright, T and Pollert, A, *The Experience of Ethnic Minority Workers in the Hotel and Catering Industry: Routes to Support and Advice on Workplace Problems* (London, ACAS, 2006).

Who, then, has problems at work? An indication was given in the first phase of the URWS, which began with regionally representative sampling of households containing workers.[16] After exclusion of refusals and households without workers, 1,971 workers were screened for having had any one of 10 prompted employment workplace grievances in the previous three years. Of these, 48.6 per cent had experienced some. While caution is required in interpretation, this suggests that almost half of Britain's workers have experienced a problem at work, which is similar to the 42 per cent demonstrated in earlier research.[17] The URWS survey then excluded unionised workers earning above the median and focused on a sample of 501 lower paid, unrepresented workers with problems at work over the past three years.

WHO ARE THE LOWER-PAID, NON-UNIONISED WITH PROBLEMS AT WORK?

The URWS sample provides an indication of who experiences and/or reports problems (although the two cannot be distinguished) by comparison with the 2004 Labour Force Survey (LFS)[18] and a sub-sample of non-unionised workers earning below the median in the workforce (the 'vulnerable' in the LFS) (Table 16.1). Women workers were significantly more likely to be present in the URWS than in the LFS, but, partly reflecting women's low pay, their over-representation in the URWS was similar to their dominance among the vulnerable in the LFS.[19] However, young workers (24 years or less) were under-represented in the URWS compared to the vulnerable in the LFS—possibly through sampling error due to telephone interviewing depending on fixed lines, which may be less common for young workers. Ethnic minority workers were significantly more likely to be present in the URWS than in the LFS and the vulnerable in it, which suggests a higher occurrence of problems. Workers in small workplaces (10–24 workers) were more

---

[16] This Chapter is based on an ESRC project: *The Unorganised Worker, Routes to Support, Views on Representation*. Working Papers, including details on methodology, can be found at: www.uwe.ac.uk/bbs/research/cesr/workingpapers.shtml.

[17] Casebourne, J, Regan, J, Neathey, F, and Tuohy, S, Institute of Employment Studies, *Employment Rights at Work—Survey of Employees 2005* (London, Department of Trade and Industry, 2006, Employment Relations Research Series No 51) 98.

[18] The Labour Force Survey (LFS) is a quarterly sample survey of households living at private addresses in Great Britain. Its purpose is to provide information on the UK labour market that can then be used to develop, manage, evaluate and report on labour market policies. The questionnaire design, sample selection, and interviewing are carried out by the Social and Vital Statistics Division of the Office for National Statistics (ONS) on behalf of the Statistical Outputs Group of the ONS. ONS publishes full UK LFS results. However, the fieldwork is carried out separately; by ONS for GB, and by the Central Survey Unit of the Department of Finance and Personnel in Northern Ireland on behalf of the Department of Trade and Investment (DETINI), available at: www.statistics.gov.uk/statbase/Source.asp?vlnk=358.

[19] Results based on Chi squared tests. Further details in Working Papers, n 16.

Table 16.1: Comparison of selected characteristics of the URWS (low-paid unrepresented workers with problems) with low-paid, all unrepresented workers in the LFS (2004) and the workforce as a whole (LFS).

	Vulnerable workers: unrepresented workers survey	Low-paid, unrepresented workers (Labour Force Survey)	All workers (Labour Force Survey)
Individual characteristics			
Male	39.12	42.14	53.77***
Female	60.88	57.86	46.23***
Age			
<25	16.53	29.71***	14.27**
25–34	20.36	19.63	21.83
35–44	23.79	20.1	26.32
45–54	24.4	15.89***	21.91
55+	14.92	14.86	15.67
Ethnicity			
Non-white ethnic minorities	8.78	6.42***	7.07**
White	91.22	93.58***	92.93**
Job characteristics			
Sector[2]			
Public sector	17.67	15.87	24.19***
Private sector	82.33	84.13	75.81***
Industry			
Agriculture, forestry and fishing	1.44	1.61	1.34
Manufacturing	14.43	13.42	13.57
Construction	3.3	6.9***	8.07***
Retail, wholesale and distribution	18.76	25.69***	13.45**
Hotels and restaurants	7.01	8.75	4.35***
Transport and communications	4.95	5.27	6.75
Financial intermediation	3.51	2.7	4.18
Other business services	9.07	8.97	11.46

(*continued*)

Table 16.1:   *Continued*

	Vulnerable workers: unrepresented workers survey	Low-paid, unrepresented workers (Labour Force Survey)	All workers (Labour Force Survey)
Public administration	5.98	3.34***	7.04
Education	8.04	6.42	9.09
Health and social services	17.11	11.38***	12.09***
Other community services	6.39	6.52	5.6
Workplace size			
<10 employees	21.76	29.87***	19.01**
10–24 employees	20.39	18.23	12.63***
25–49 employees	14.87	15.25	12.66*
50–249 employees	28.72	21.22***	21.48***
250–499 employees	6.11	6.3	7.11
>499 employees	8.15	8.31	15.75***
Full-time job	78.34	61.97***	76.11
Part-time job	21.66	38.03***	23.89
Non-standard employment contract	11.45	7.77***	5.27***

Source: 3rd quarter (autumn) of 2004 Labour Force Survey and Unrepresented Workers Survey

Notes:
1. Responses here are not strictly comparable as the LFS asks a much more detailed set of questions about qualifications. Because of these differences, no significance tests were performed on these variables.
2. Differences between the URWS and LFS here may arise from differences in the questions. The URWS asks if workers work for private contractors in the public sector, respondents who are categorised in the URWS column as being in the private sector. In the LFS workers in these jobs may classify themselves as working in the public sector.

* Difference compared to the unrepresented workers sample is statistically significant at the 10 per cent level or better.
** Difference compared to the unrepresented workers sample is statistically significant at the 5 per cent level or better.
*** Difference compared to the unrepresented workers sample is statistically significant at the 1 per cent level or better.
Results are based on Chi^2 tests.

likely to be in the URWS than in the LFS, but not its non-union, low-paid sub-sample, which partly reflects low unionisation in small workplaces.[20] Interestingly, full-time workers had a similar presence in the URWS to the LFS, but a higher one than among the vulnerable in the LFS—suggesting more problems or a higher perception of them. Retail, hotels and catering had a stronger presence in the URWS than in the LFS and interestingly, those in Health and social services had a significantly higher presence in the URWS than in either LFS comparators, which suggests a concentration of problems here. Most strikingly, workers with less than six months' tenure were much more likely to be in the URWS than in the LFS or its low-paid, non-unionised sub-sample, as were temporary and agency workers, which supports the discussion (above) of their heightened vulnerability.

Finally the majority of the URWS sample, 58 per cent, had never been union members, 34 per cent had been members at some time and 6 per cent were members when they had their problems, but without union recognition or representation.

WHAT PROBLEMS ARE EXPERIENCED AND DID WORKERS DO ANYTHING TO RESOLVE THEM?

The URWS asked respondents about all problems experienced at work in any job in the previous three years, then about details of problems in *one* job and finally about *one* problem (the 'main problem'), prioritised as one which the worker 'pushed hardest' to resolve. Table 16.2 summarises the results and shows that problems with pay, work relations, such as stress and bullying, workload, working hours and job security were the chief problems, although all workers suffered from multiple problems.

Respondents were asked 'Do you feel your problems were an infringement of your rights?' This question was deliberately framed to probe beyond a sense or knowledge of legal rights alone. While responses could include reference to infringement of employment rights, they also encompassed 'rights' in terms of a sense of 'fairness'—as expressed in 'fair treatment of employees' in the New Labour Government's White Paper 'Fairness at Work', and in its 2006 statement on 'Success at Work'.[21] In total, 55 per cent thought that one or more of their problems were an infringement of their rights.

Only 14 per cent of respondents said they did nothing about their problems. These respondents were more likely to have been in their job for less

---

[20] Kersley *et al*, above n 3, at 110.
[21] Department of Trade and Industry, *Fairness at Work*, Cm 3968 (London, The Stationery Office, 1998) para [1.9]; Department of Trade and Industry, *Success at Work: Protecting Vulnerable Workers, Supporting Good Employers. A Policy Statement for this Parliament* (London, The Stationery Office, 2006) 5.

Table 16.2: The nature of the problems, percentage of respondents.

	All problems experienced in all jobs in past 3 years		All problems experienced in screened job		Main problem pushed hardest to solve	
	Number	Per cent	Number	Per cent	Number	Per cent
1. *Pay* (1)	191	38.1	181	36.1	80	16
2. *Work relations, such as stress or bullying*	184	36.7	172	34.3	76	15.2
3. *Workload*	160	31.9	143	28.5	46	9.2
4. *Job security*	152	30.3	124	24.8	32	6.4
5. *Working hours*	143	28.5	127	25.3	32	6.4
6. *Contract or job description*	133	26.5	115	22.8	24	4.8
7. *Health and safety*	122	24.4	109	21.8	42	8.4
8. *Opportunities*	121	24.2	102	20.4	27	5.4
9. *Taking time off*	120	24.0	109	21.8	30	6
10. *Discrimination* (2)	89	17.8	76	15.2	19	3.8
Multiple problems					7	1.4
Unspecified problems which at first said did not act upon (3)					86	17.2

Notes: Results rounded to one decimal place.
(1) Such as not being paid the correct amount, not being paid regularly, or not receiving pay for holidays or overtime etc.
(2) Towards yourself.
(3) 86 people at first said they did not try to do anything about their main problem, so were not asked about it. Sixteen of these did in fact take action, reducing the 'non-actors' from 86 to 70 (14 per cent of the sample).

than a year and to be in semi-skilled manual occupations. Pessimism and fear were their main rationales, particularly, 'I did not think I would be successful' (12 per cent), 'others at work had the same problem, and that made me put up with it' (12 per cent) and 'I was worried I might lose my job' (11 per cent). This refutes any preconceptions that vulnerable, powerless workers are passive.

Before acting to resolve their main problem, 61 per cent took advice. Those with pay, opportunities, discrimination, workload, health and safety, contract and work relations problems, and women, disabled workers and those who perceived that their rights had been violated were significantly more likely to seek advice than others. Several sources of advice were sought, with a third approaching managers and friends and work colleagues. A significant minority approached Citizens' Advice (13 per cent), but few sought trade unions, ACAS (the Advisory, Conciliation and Arbitration Service) or Law Centres (5, 3 and 1 per cent respectively). Interestingly, workers were most strongly influenced by the advice of friends or colleagues (20 per cent), followed by family and friends (16 per cent). Managers had greatest influence for only a tenth of respondents. The majority (91 per cent) of those who took advice then went on to take action, but three quarters of those who did not take advice also went on to act.

A major finding of the URWS was that the vast majority of all respondents acted to resolve their main problem—86 per cent—with discrimination and pay problems leading to an even greater predilection to act (95 and 91 per cent took action respectively). While a sense of rights infringed did not make action more probable, regression analysis showed that respondents with multiple problems—and three fifths had more than one problem—were more likely to act than those with just one.

What did they do? Respondents were first asked about all actions to resolve their main problem and then about the most important one taken (Table 16.3).

Most tried several options (the mean number of actions was 2.2) and Table 16.3 shows that the majority tried to solve matters informally with line managers, followed by senior managers, and very few used formal grievance procedures. It could be that this was because these were not available. Only 62 per cent of respondents reported having formal grievance procedures compared with the British average of 96 per cent of employees.[22] However, unavailability of formal procedures did not explain their low use: 12 per cent of workers reported that they used formal procedures whether or not they stated that they had them. External recourse for help was also

---

[22] The question asked on grievance procedures was 'In the workplace where you were/are having problems, if a problem came up between you and your employer, are there set rules for how they should be dealt with?' (Prompt if necessary: for example, the making of a written statement or warning, or a formal meeting); compare Kersley *et al*, above n 3, at 213.

Table 16.3: What actions did respondents take?

Type of Action	All actions taken % respondents		Most important action % respondents	
	% (base: whole sample)	% (base: all who took any action)	% (base: whole sample)	% (base: all who took action)
Informal approach to line manager	69.3	80.8	37.7	44.1
Informal approach to senior manager	42.7	49.9	21.8	25.4
Joined together with other workers	24.2	28.2	6.8	7.9
Used formal complaints procedure	11.6	13.5	2.4	2.8
Went to Citizens Advice Bureau	9.2	10.7	3	3.5
Sought help from friends or family	8	9.3	2.6	3.0
Sought help from a trade union	6	7	2.4	2.8
Approach to co-workers responsible for the problem	5.2	6.1	3	3.5
Began Employment Tribunal proceedings	2.4	2.8	1.6	1.9

very low, the highest being to a Citizens Advice Bureau (11 per cent of the sample). Finally application to an Employment Tribunal was extremely rare (2 per cent of the sample).

The second surprising finding of the URWS was the frequency of informal *collective voice*. A quarter of the URWS and 28 per cent of those who took action responded positively when asked: 'Did you join with others in your workplace who share your concerns, to get together as a group to pursue your claims?' This was significantly more likely among workers in the transport, storage and communication industries and in health and social work. Interestingly, the more problems a respondent had experienced, the more likely they were to take informal collective action, possibly because this increased the likelihood that some of these problems were shared. Team-working also made informal collective action more likely, with 30 per cent of those working in a team attempting it.

The URWS also explored collective identity more broadly by asking respondents whether they felt their problem was shared by others. Three-quarters thought that it was, and among these, three-quarters also said that they attempted group solutions. Collective action was, however, limited: for 78 per cent, it meant discussing with others what to do about the problem, although 19 per cent went as a group to management, and 13 per cent organised a group meeting—arguably more advanced forms of mobilisation. Nevertheless, the evidence points to the persistence of collectivity in the workplace, which had no place in the New Labour Government's approach to vulnerability, which emphasised worker individualism and passive need for help.

OUTCOMES: THE PAUCITY OF CONCLUSIONS

The third major finding of the URWS was the paucity of outcome to action. The 86 per cent of sample respondents who took action were asked, 'Did this action lead to any conclusion with your employer?'—a question framed to identify any conclusion at all, which is broader than resolution to the problem. Of the 429 respondents who took action, 47 per cent had no outcome. Just 38 per cent reported that their problem was brought to a conclusion and only 49 per cent of these were satisfied. In total, almost half of those who acted had no result and 18.6 per cent reached a satisfactory resolution—16 per cent the whole sample. These low levels of satisfactory resolution resonate with other research findings, such as Genn's in 1999, which showed that 52 per cent of those who took action on an employment problem with potential legal redress reached no agreement and no resolution,[23] and a West Midlands employment advice line survey of its users, which found that just under half of respondents resolved their problem.[24] The URWS provides a snapshot of what happens to non-unionised workers who primarily attempt to resolve their grievances without recourse to the law. This broadens the picture of worker powerlessness which Barmes fleshes out in her analysis of the processes of legal obfuscation which diminish the chances of workers who do enter the Employment Tribunal system of achieving justice.[25] Both analyses show that, without strong collective organisation, both the informal workplace route to employment rights and the legal route fail the isolated and vulnerable worker.

---

[23] Genn, H, *Paths to Justice: What People Do and Think About Going To The Law* (Oxford, Hart Publishing, 1999) 157.

[24] Russell, C and Eyers, D, *Clutching at Straws: Rights at Work* (Briefing Paper No 53, West Midlands Employment and Low Pay Unit, Birmingham, January 2002) 2.

[25] Barmes, L, 'Learning from Case Law Accounts of Marginalised Working' in this collection.

Table 16.4: Outcomes by the presence of workplace grievance procedures and consultation.

	Consultation procedure		Grievance procedure	
	% Yes	% No	% Yes	% No
Respondents who took action (base 429)				
No outcome	59	67.3*	63.2	60.6
Any outcome	41	32.7*	36.8	39.4
Respondents who took action (base 429)				
No outcome/unsatisfactory outcome	77.3	88***	80.7	82.5
Satisfactory outcome	22.7	12***	19.3	17.5
Respondents with an outcome (base 162)				
Unsatisfactory outcome	43.1	62.8**	46.4	54.1
Satisfactory outcome	56.9	37.3**	53.6	45.9

* Statistically significant at the 10 per cent level.
** Statistically significant at the 5 per cent level.
*** Statistically significant at the 1 per cent level.

In workplaces with mechanisms for regular consultation and communication between employees and management, problems were more likely to reach a conclusion, and to be resolved satisfactorily.[26] However, respondents who had a formal grievance procedure were not significantly more likely to get a conclusion or a satisfactory resolution than those who worked in a workplace without such a procedure (Table 16.4).

Taking informal collective action was more likely than other actions to result in a conclusion to the problem, but not to result in a satisfactory resolution. This cannot be easily interpreted, although it appears that it produces 'voice' in forcing some kind of an outcome, but the limited forms

[26] The survey question for Joint Consultation was 'Could/can staff or their representatives meet regularly with managers to discuss workplace issues?' It thus covered both representative organisations and forms of direct communication, such as briefing meetings. Again, response depended on respondents' perceptions. Only 3 per cent said they did not know, and 60 per cent said they had such a mechanism. This is not directly comparable to WERS 2004, which found that only 42 per cent of employees worked in workplaces with a joint consultative committee— down from 46 per cent in 1998 (Kersley *et al*, above n 3, at 127). In the URWS, 73 per cent of respondents had consultation procedures in workplaces of over 500 workers, but only 54 per cent of those in workplaces with below 25 workers. These accounted for 41 per cent of the sample.

of collective action suggest it is not effective in terms of a satisfactory resolution to those with problems.

What happened to workers unable to bring satisfactory resolution to their problems? Most vulnerable workers tried to overcome difficulties, failed in their efforts but remained in their job—58 per cent were in the 'problem' job when interviewed. Two-fifths took action and left their jobs. Regression analysis showed that respondents who took their problem to a senior manager and respondents who took a case to an Employment Tribunal were more likely to have left their jobs, possibly because these actions suggest heightened confrontation or more serious problems. Workers who had experienced the problem within the first six months of employment and ethnic minority respondents were also more likely to resign, but interestingly, those workers who took informal collective action were less likely to resign. This suggests a paradoxical outcome for collective action: on the one hand, it was associated with reduced turnover, but the fact that it produced conclusions, but not satisfactory resolutions, may contribute to frustration.

It was also observed that there was a positive relationship between having a mechanism for regular consultation with management and resolution to problems, but none between having grievance procedures and reaching an outcome. Workers were less likely to quit if their workplace had a joint consultation mechanism and also if they had a grievance procedure. This suggests that regular consultation may benefit dispute resolution and increase retention, but grievance procedures do not do much for workers in terms of bringing about satisfactory resolutions to problems, although they serve management by reducing labour turnover with its associated costs.

CONCLUSION

Britain's New Labour Government during its period of office (1997–2010) turned its attention to vulnerable work following evidence of employment abuse, but insisted on a narrow view, providing a list of the loci and symptoms of where 'vulnerability' is more likely, and further, arguing that potential vulnerability is only a problem if it is 'exploited'.[27] This narrow interpretation is no accident. A treatment of vulnerability that avoids conflict of interest in the employment relationship is consistent with the 'partnership' conceptualisation of the employment relationship, and with a neo-liberal discourse of the 'third way'—a modernised unitary perspective.[28] This restricted view allows vulnerable employment to be regarded as a marginal issue not

---

[27] DTI 2006, above n 21, at 25.
[28] Fox, A, *Industrial Sociology and Industrial Relations: Royal Commission on Trade Unions and Employers' Associations* (Research Paper No 3, London, HMSO, 1966) 3; Smith, P and Morton, G, 'Nine Years of New Labour: Neoliberalism and Workers' Rights' (2006) 44 *British Journal of Industrial Relations* 401, 402.

associated with the decline in collectivism in industrial relations and the fact that 72 per cent of the UK workforce is non-unionised. The assumption is that, for the majority of workers, industrial relations are fair and harmonious. The establishment in May 2010 of the Conservative–Liberal Democrat Coalition Government continues the neo-liberal discourse and policy of de-collectivised industrial relations and the primacy of free markets, started with the Thatcher and Major Conservative Governments between 1979 and 1997, and continued by New Labour.[29]

This Chapter shares the fundamental analysis of pluralist, radical and Marxist approaches to industrial relations, that the individual employee or worker is weak in relation to the greater power of the employer, and argues that this is the root of vulnerability. To narrow the definition for empirical research, vulnerability can be exacerbated by weak labour market power, which is demonstrated in low pay. The TUC has calculated that one in five or 5.3 million UK employees are vulnerable in terms of absence of collective bargaining coverage and being in the bottom third of the hourly income distribution. The URWS reported here takes for its definition a broader pay threshold as the bottom half of the earnings distribution and non-union membership, which means that 40 per cent of the workforce is in vulnerable employment. Within both definitions, there is a spectrum, with migrant workers and those with non-employee status among the most vulnerable.

In 2001, the former New Labour Government asserted that the rise in applications to Employment Tribunals indicated that workers were becoming increasingly litigious in a new 'compensation' culture.[30] It has subsequently been demonstrated that these assertions were premised on selective use of evidence.[31] Although the statutory dismissal, disciplinary and grievance procedures of the Employment Act 2002, which had been introduced to minimise recourse to the Employment Tribunal system, were repealed in 2009,[32] the New Labour Government remained committed to 'seeking to resolve more

---

[29] Wedderburn, KW, 'Freedom of Association and Philosophies of Labour Law' (1989) 18 *Industrial Law Journal* 1; Smith, P and Morton, G, 'Union Exclusion and the Decollectivisation of Industrial Relations in Contemporary Britain' (1991) 31 *British Journal of Industrial Relations* 99; Smith, P and Morton, G, 'New Labour's Reform of Britain's Employment Law: The Devil is Not Only in the Detail but in the Values and Policy Too' (2001) 38 *British Journal of Industrial Relations* 119.

[30] Department of Trade and Industry, *Routes to Resolution: Improving Dispute Resolution in Britain* (London, The Stationery Office, 2001).

[31] Hepple, B and Morris, G, 'The Employment Act 2002 and the Crisis of Individual Employment Rights' (2002) 31 *Industrial Law Journal* 245; Pollert, A, 'The Unorganised Worker, the Decline in Collectivism and New Hurdles to Individual Employment Rights' (2005) 34 *Industrial Law Journal* 217; Pollert, A, 'Individual Employment Rights:"Paper Tigers, Fierce in Appearance but Missing in Tooth and Claw"' (2007) 28 *Economic and Industrial Democracy* 110.

[32] Department of Trade and Industry, *Better Dispute Resolution: A Review of Employment Dispute Resolution in Great Britain* (London, The Stationery Office, 2007); Employment Act 2008 (UK) s 24.

disputes in the workplace'.[33] Our research sheds light on how this system operated for the non-unionised, who comprise the majority of employees. The findings suggest that almost half of workers in Britain have had problems at work in the previous three years, a finding consistent with research commissioned by the former Labour Government.[34] Around half of the 501 workers interviewed with problems at work felt that these had been an infringement of their rights. When details of problems were examined, aspects of work intensification emerged as the main ones: stress; being given too much work without enough time; and management taking advantage or bullying.

The URWS was equally concerned with responses to problems as with their nature. Most workers (61 per cent) sought advice about what to do. Most sought advice from managers, colleagues and friends and family, and the latter two categories had the most influence. A significant minority also approached Citizens Advice (13 per cent), especially if they felt that their rights were violated, and if their problems concerned discrimination, pay, job security, taking time off and working hours.

Most (58 per cent) were still in the job in which they had their main problem, which indicates that the assumption that the first response to problems among the vulnerable unorganised is to resign is wrong. One of the most striking findings of the URWS is that passive acceptance is not the dominant response either: 86 per cent of the sample tried to do something within their workplace to resolve their problem, primarily by approaching line and senior managers. Additionally, the more problems a person had, and certain problems experienced (for example, discrimination and pay problems), further increased the likelihood of taking action. Importantly, those who had left and those who remained in their job were equally likely to have acted. For policy makers, a further significant result was the low proportion who used the official grievance procedure, in spite of the fact that the survey took place after the statutory grievance procedures were put into place in October 2004. The even lower percentage which began employment tribunal proceedings is less surprising in view of similar survey evidence.[35] One of the most surprising findings, considering that this study focused on the non-unionised and the majority of the sample had no union experience, was the high proportion (28 per cent of those who took action) who attempted collective solutions to their problems, primarily through group discussion, but also with a minority organising group delegations to management or organising group meetings. This underlines the fact that managerial initiatives to individualise employment relations have not destroyed the collective nature of labour.

The final finding is that very few vulnerable workers found a satisfactory resolution to their problems. Indeed, for 47 per cent, nothing happened

---

[33] DTI 2006, above n 21, at 39.
[34] Casebourne *et al*, above n 17.
[35] Kersley *et al*, above n 3, at 227.

after all their efforts. Only 18 per cent of those who took action and 16 per cent of all those with problems had a satisfactory outcome. Problems that respondents perceived to be violations of their rights were even less likely to be satisfactorily resolved. Collective action increased the likelihood of there being an outcome, but not a satisfactory one, and decreased the likelihood of exit. Thus, spontaneous collectivity is not dead, but without being harnessed into organised power, it may only improve employment stability and force outcomes to problems better than other strategies, but not in workers' interests. The existence of grievance and disciplinary procedures did not increase the likelihood of conclusions to problems, or satisfactory resolutions, but decreased the likelihood of exit. They thus appeared to serve managerial interests in reducing turnover, but not in achieving their purpose of assisting dispute resolution. By contrast, when workplaces had mechanisms for regular consultation and communication between employees and management, problems were more likely to be resolved, and to be resolved satisfactorily.

While we found that temporary and agency workers were over-represented in the URWS compared with the 2004 LFS, the majority in the sample were full-time workers on standard contracts. The breadth of problems and low success rate of workplace resolution among non-unionised, 'lower'-paid employees (note—they were not even the least well-off, since we used a broader definition of low-paid than the more frequently used definition of the bottom third of the income distribution) indicate that vulnerability extends beyond those who are most disadvantaged—for example those working in non-standard contracts, in the informal economy, the self-employed eking a living at the bottom of and dependent on global supply chains, those shifting between paid and unpaid work and those outside any labour law regulatory regimes.[36] Furthermore, young workers, probably the least informed and most insecure, were under-represented in the URWS, which suggests our findings possibly underestimate the extent of problems and of poor resolution.

Overall, these expose the double disadvantage of the low-paid, non-unionised: not only do they suffer from multiple problems at work, but when they try to resolve them, the overwhelming majority fail. The majority do not exit. When workers resigned, they had first taken action to try to get a resolution. This survey identified processes of unresolved problems at work which are likely to build a store of resentment and frustration among Britain's vulnerable workers which are illustrated in qualitative research on those seeking justice at work.[37]

---

[36] See further Chapters by Chikarmane, P and Narayan, L, 'Transform or Perish: Changing Conceptions of Work in Recycling'; Tsikata, D, 'Employment Agencies and Domestic Work in Ghana'; Mundlak, G, 'The Wages of Care-Workers: From Structure to Agency'; and Bernstein, S, 'Sector-based Collective Bargaining Regimes and Gender Segregation: A Case Study of Self-employed Home Childcare Workers in Quebec' in this collection.

[37] Pollert, A, 'The Lived Experience of Isolation for Vulnerable Workers Facing Workplace Grievances in 21st Century Britain' (2010) 31 *Economic and Industrial Democracy* 62.

17

Learning from Case Law Accounts of Marginalised Working

LIZZIE BARMES

INTRODUCTION

IN THIS CHAPTER I analyse case law accounts as qualitative evidence better to understand the treatment in the UK of workers whose labour market position is weak. Primary legal sources are mined, not for the legal answers they give, but for the stories they tell about the lives of workers at the margins of economic, legal, political and social structures. I concentrate on the qualitative reading of one case through its various appeal stages, *Kalwak & Ors v Consistent Group Ltd and Welsh Country Foods*,[1] because research by other social scientists establishes that the story it tells is emblematic of workplace vulnerability in the UK. I contend that analysis even of this one case is revelatory, while also pointing to the usefulness of more wide-ranging and comparative work of this type.

First, qualitative examination of this case tells us something about the experiences in the UK of workers who, for whatever reason, are vulnerable to mistreatment. Second, it demonstrates how judicial decision-making interacts with other sources of state power in constructing what happens to people whose labour market position is weak. Most importantly, adjudication is revealed to be functional to the UK government and legislature, as well as UK society more widely, evading the acute economic, moral and political dilemmas raised by marginalised working. The analysis not only demonstrates similarities in the exploitation that occurs in richer and poorer countries, but illustrates mechanisms by which judicial decision-making distracts from societal failures purposefully to address this. The need that emerges most urgently for the goal of this collection[2] is to expose what is

---

[1] *Kalwak & Ors v Consistent Group Ltd; Kalwak & Ors v Welsh Country Foods Limited* (*Kalwak & Ors*) Case Numbers 2101855/05 etc at first instance, Reserved Judgment, 2 August 2006 (unreported), (on file with the author); UKEAT/0535/06/DM on appeal, 18 May 2007 (unreported); and [2008] EWCA Civ 430, [2008] IRLR 505 on further appeal.

[2] Fudge, J, 'Blurring Legal Boundaries: Regulating for Decent Work' in this collection.

really happening to people at the 'bottom end' of the UK labour market and the widespread shared responsibility for this state of affairs. The hope, although perhaps forlorn, is that shining a light in this way would catalyse more effective argumentation, pressure and mobilisation to raise the floor of labour standards.

THE CASE FOR QUALITATIVE ENQUIRY INTO CASE LAW ACCOUNTS OF MARGINALISED WORKING

This is a vibrant time in the UK for research, within and across disciplines, about the experience of working people whose labour market position is weak. There have also been significant campaigns and initiatives to alter the conditions in which such people work and live, sometimes with official impetus or involvement.[3]

The vocabulary of vulnerability has been used, particularly in the official elements of this discourse, to denote the category of workers concerned. This begs questions about what qualifies or disqualifies a worker from vulnerability. I sidestep these because my interest is in anyone with minimal labour market power. This might, as Judy Fudge made clear in Chapter 1, be related, for example, to characteristics personal to the worker, result from a person's structural location in the marketplace or be the effect of regulation. Arguably all workers are implicated because the structural subordination of labour to capital in the globalised economy weakens everyone who sells their own labour. Yet there are some groups, and often endurably, whose labour market power is especially marginal, and these are the focus of my interest.

---

[3] See, eg, Pollert, A, 'The Unorganised Worker: The Decline in Collectivism and New Hurdles to Individual Employment Rights' (2007) 34 *Industrial Law Journal* 217; Pollert, A, *The Unorganised Vulnerable Worker: The Case for Union Organising* (London, Institute of Employment Rights, 2007); Department for Business, Enterprise and Regulatory Reform (BERR), *Vulnerable Worker Enforcement Forum—Final Report and Government Conclusions* (London, BERR, 2008); McCann, D, *Regulating Flexible Work* (Oxford, Oxford University Press, 2008); Trades Union Congress (TUC) on Vulnerable Employment, *Hard Work, Hidden Lives* (TUC, 2008); and see further, including for underlying research studies: www.vulnerableworkers.org.uk; Countouris, N and Horton, R, 'The Temporary Agency Work Directive: Another Broken Promise?' (2009) 38 *Industrial Law Journal* 329; McKay, S, *Agency and Migrant Workers* (London, Institute of Employment Rights, 2009); Pollert, A and Charlwood, A, 'The Vulnerable Worker in Britain and Problems at Work' (2009) 23 *Work, Employment and Society* 343; Wynn, M, 'Regulating Rogues? Employment Agency Enforcement and Sections 15–18 of the Employment Act 2008' (2009) 38 *Industrial Law Journal* 64; Pollert, A, 'The Lived Experience of Isolation for Vulnerable Workers Facing Workplace Grievances in 21st Century Britain' (2010) 31 *Economic and Industrial Democracy* 62; Wills, J, Datta, K, Evans, Y, Herbert, J, May, J & McIlwaine, C, *Global Cities at Work: New Migrant Divisions of Labour* (London, Pluto Press, 2010); see also www.londoncitizens.org.uk/; www.london.gov.uk/mayor/economic_unit/workstreams/living-wage.jsp.

The inspiration for my particular enquiry came from noticing disconnects between non-legal accounts of working lives at the 'bottom end' of the labour market and the approach of judges in claims brought by UK workers in this position. I have been especially struck by the richness of qualitative evidence about the lived reality of people working in London's worst jobs, as well as by insights from relating such accounts to broader national and international trends.[4] Apart from anything else, this work has spoken very directly to my students, echoing their experiences at the sharp end of the UK labour market. While my students have tended to be philosophical about their deplorable treatment, perceiving that they have a way out, they have made clear that oppressive exercises of managerial power are a commonplace to them and their families. As other Chapters in this collection show, there are also striking parallels between the working experiences described and those in other cities across the globe.

The richness of non-legal accounts and analyses starkly contrast with the abstracted, convoluted and, with respect, frequently baffling, reflections of judges in categorising different kinds of workers in order to determine the statutory rights they have (or more typically, especially the more needful of external protection the working person, that they don't have). Labour law students must quickly adapt to a system of thought, an epistemic world, in which it is often hard to categorise people even though they work in paradigmatically subordinated and subjugated ways, at times for years and indistinguishably from more legally favoured others doing identical work. It doesn't take long for this counter-intuitive way of seeing working life to become at least one of the lenses through which labour lawyers see a varied cast of working people. In the UK this includes, to name just a few, banquet waiters at a premier London hotel,[5] bank nurses,[6] tour guides to a nuclear power station,[7] dockworkers,[8] labourers,[9] local authority cleaners[10] and delivery workers for a courier firm.[11]

Naturally there are different ways of deploying the dark legal arts that come from familiarity with the statutes and case law. One route is to

---

[4] On London see Toynbee, P, *Hard Work: Life in Low-Pay Britain* (London, Bloomsbury, 2003) and Wills *et al*, above n 3. In the US and comparatively, see, eg, Ehrenreich, B, *Nickel and Dimed: Undercover in Low-Wage USA* (London, Granta, 2002); Ehrenreich, B and Hochschild, AR (eds), *Global Woman: Nannies, Maids and Sex Workers in the New Economy* (London, Granta, 2003); Hochschild, AR, *The Commercialization of Intimate Life: Notes from Home and Work* (Berkeley, University of California Press, 2003); Smith, A, Stenning, A and Willis, K, *Social Justice and Neoliberalism: Global Perspectives* (London, 2008, Zed Books).

[5] *O'Kelly v Trusthouse Forte* [1984] QB 90.

[6] *Clark v Oxfordshire Health Authority* [1998] IRLR 125.

[7] *Carmichael v National Power plc* [1999] ICR 1226.

[8] *Stevedoring & Haulage Services Ltd v Fuller* [2001] IRLR 627.

[9] *Byrne Brothers (Formwork) Ltd v Baird & Ors* [2002] IRLR 96.

[10] *Dacas v Brook Street Bureau (UK) Ltd* [2004] EWCA Civ 217; [2004] ICR 1437; *James v London Borough of Greenwich* [2008] EWCA Civ 35; [2008] ICR 545.

[11] *James v Redcats (Brands) Ltd* [2007] ICR 1006.

assist organisations in manipulating parts of their workforce, typically the weakest, into the categories that are most advantageous to those for whom they work. But much legal endeavour has also been devoted to internal and external analysis of legal doctrine, past and present, to show up its manifold weaknesses from a range of points of view.[12]

Reading qualitative social science accounts of the experiences of marginalised workers, however, led me to ask if there is additional understanding to be gained from glimpses that case law provides into working lives, as well as from the manner in which disputes before the courts are framed and recounted. Viewed in this light, the decades of case law we have is a source of data about the treatment of workers over time, and importantly one that illuminates what happens when law is invoked to resist poor treatment. Case law constitutes a set of uniquely documented, 'real time' accounts of state power being wielded, for good or ill, over working people. It is important that each case brought by a worker (or set of workers) in a weak labour market position is, by definition, a remarkable encounter. Somehow the claimant has transcended their subordinated position, not only to assert a claim against those for whom they work, but to invoke the apparatus of the state in pursuing this. From the point of view of the working person the stakes are necessarily extremely high: failure not only means Goliath triumphing over David, but the state in the guise of judges legitimating and reinforcing the claimant's subjugated position.

I was also influenced by Hazel Genn's recent observations about the dearth in the UK of systematic social scientific research into myriad important questions about civil justice.[13] In relation to adjudication in particular she argued that: 'the failure of the academy to scrutinise, describe and explain the work of judges is an astonishing void in our understanding of the essential functioning of the civil justice system'.[14] She explained this absence in part with reference to the legal academy's 'preoccupation with the law, with its substance and its philosophical and moral foundations, rather than any particular interest in the *doing* of justice'.[15] The focus on appeal court decisions at the cost of studying judicial behaviour was also argued to be in part because doctrinal lawyers lack empirical research skills and, drawing on Marc Galanter, that legal scholars' intellectual styles mirror those of judges and lawyers.[16] A further suggested explanation was that political and social scientists in the UK 'who do have the necessary repertoire of research

---

[12] See, eg, in the UK, the work of Hugh Collins, Nicola Countouris, Bob Hepple, Sandra Fredman and Mark Freedland.

[13] Genn, H, *Judging Civil Justice* (Cambridge, Cambridge University Press, 2010) 52, 62–8, 129–43, 183–86.

[14] *Ibid*, at 135–6.

[15] *Ibid*, at 136, emphasis in original.

[16] *Ibid*, at 137–8, citing Galanter, M, 'In the Winter of our Discontent: Law, Anti-Law and Social Science' (2006) 2 *Annual Review of Law and Social Science* 1.

skills have shown no interest in the judiciary, or indeed the legal system as a whole'.[17] It seems to me that the specific subject matter of this Chapter is one in relation to which Genn's observations have resonance. While we have many instances of innovative enquiry on the general topic of workers' legal status, there is more to be done by legal scholars in terms of social science enquiry into litigation by working people. My suggestion therefore in some sense takes up the challenge that Genn has laid down, seeking to explore whether lawyers could develop qualitative methods that build on their existing research capacity to fill some knowledge gaps. I recognise, however, that this is only a partial response. Undoubtedly our capacity to understand the impact of law and legal processes on working life is significantly dependent on knowing more about which working people litigate and how this tends to turn out.[18] Work in recent years by Anna Pollert has emphasised this by illuminating the many difficulties that workers who are vulnerable to ill-treatment have in obtaining knowledge or advice about their legal rights, let alone in accessing enforcement mechanisms.[19]

THE EMPIRICAL AND POLICY BACKGROUND TO *KALWAK & ORS V CONSISTENT GROUP LTD AND WELSH COUNTRY FOODS*

Evidently I have not chosen to concentrate on *Kalwak & Ors v Consistent Group Limited (Consistent) and Welsh Country Foods* (WCF) for the legal outcomes in the Employment Tribunal (ET), Employment Appeal Tribunal (EAT) or Court of Appeal (CA), nor for the legal discussion that gave rise to them. Apart from anything, there has since been a change of direction on the critical legal point.[20] To explain this a little further, the central legal question in the case was whether Ms Kalwak and the other claimants, all migrant workers from Poland, had the legal status of 'employees'. If Ms Kalwak and the others were 'employees', whether of Consistent, WCF or both, the

---

[17] *Ibid*, at 138.

[18] An important starting point, including regarding employment disputes, is provided by Genn, H, *Paths to Justice: What People Do and Think About Going to Law* (Oxford, Hart Publishing, 1999). There is also useful quantitative data in the results of two successive research studies. First are the WERS surveys, including most recently, Forth, J, Bewley, H and Bryson, A, *Small and Medium-Sized Enterprises: Findings from the 2004 Workplace Employment Relations Survey* (London, Department of Trade and Industry, 2006) and Kersley, B, Alpin, C, Forth, J, Bryson, A, Bewley, H, Dix, G & Oxenbridge, S, *Inside the Workplace: Findings from the 2004 Workplace Employment Relations Survey* (London, Routledge, 2006). Secondly there are the SETA surveys, most recently, Peters, M, Seeds, K, Harding, C & Garnett, E, *Findings from the Survey of Employment Tribunal Applications 2008* (London, Department for Business, Innovation and Skills, Employment Relations, 2010).

[19] See Pollert, n 3 above and Pollert, A, 'How Britain's Low Paid Non-Unionised Employees Deal with Workplace Problems' in this collection.

[20] See *Protectacoat Firthglow Ltd v Szilagyi* [2009] EWCA Civ 98; [2009] ICR 835 (and the discussion of it in Davies, ACL, 'Sensible Thinking About Sham Transactions' (2009) 38 *Industrial Law Journal* 318 and now *Autoclenz Ltd v Belcher* [2011] UKSC 41).

relevant statute accorded the legal entitlements they sought to assert. If they were not, they did not qualify for these protections and their claims had to be dismissed without further consideration.

The fact that the claimants were 'supplied' by Consistent to work for WCF was, in legal terms, important factual background. UK law on agency contractual arrangements that split, on the one hand, day-to-day control of work processes and, on the other hand, day-to-day securing and paying of people to work, prima facie prevent those working from being legally classified as anyone's 'employees'. Note also that it is commonplace in the UK, pursuant to the dark legal arts mentioned above, for agencies to take additional measures to ensure that agency workers do not acquire 'employee' status. This is particularly done by requiring people who register to work through an agency to sign standard form contracts specifying that the agency is not required to offer work and the working person is not obliged to accept work.[21] The overall effect is that people who work via this sort of 'triangular' contractual structure frequently have no, or very few, statutory employment rights.

There are, of course, exceptional cases. A working person might have sufficient labour market power genuinely to negotiate the various contracts underpinning an agency arrangement. Evidently, however, this possibility is not relevant to the workers under consideration here. The more salient possible exception is where the law disrupts the ostensible contractual position. But whether this happens is within the control of the state. And UK employment legislation continues to be structured such that statutory protection of agency workers by this route is significantly dependent on judicial interpretation and development of the law. For example, in *Kalwak* the agency worker claimants argued they were 'employees' on the basis that contractual terms, which would otherwise have determined that they were not, were shams. The *Kalwak* claimants managed on this basis to persuade the ET and the EAT that they were 'employees' of Consistent. But the CA overturned those decisions, at the same time shutting down this avenue for legal redress by taking a highly restrictive approach to the law governing when a sham could be found. It is on this point that later authorities have now taken a quite different tack, reverting to the EAT in *Kalwak's* more open approach.[22] The litigation thereby demonstrated the significance of judicial power to the protection in the UK of working people with a weak labour market position. Critically to the analysis here, moreover, this is the result of the legislature choosing to leave the precise definition of the boundary of protection to judges.

---

[21] Burchell, B, Deakin, S and Honey, S, *The Employment Status of Individuals in Non-Standard Employment* (London, Department of Trade and Industry, 1999) para [8.4].
[22] See *Protectacoat* and *Autoclenz*, above n 20.

The particular facts of the case also provided a useful occasion for observing this power in action, since the situation of the claimants epitomised several of the factors that make people working in the UK vulnerable to exploitation. Ms Kalwak and the six other claimants were in low-paid, low-skilled (although this does not necessarily connote the workers themselves being low-skilled) agency work. They were recently arrived migrant workers with, at this point, no access to UK welfare entitlements and with limited English. It is important, however, that factors associated with the worst instances of UK worker vulnerability were absent. In particular, being Polish, these were legal migrants working legally, and they would in time acquire welfare entitlements. They were also not from a visible ethnic minority, they were not working in a traditionally female occupation and they belonged to a trade union that supported their legal action. So the position of these workers in the UK labour market was bad, but it was nowhere near as bad as it gets.

Geographers at Queen Mary have recently completed extensive research into the lives of migrant workers at the 'bottom end' of the London labour market.[23] This paints a detailed picture of this world, making it possible to situate the individual experiences of Ms Kalwak and the other claimants, albeit that they didn't work in London, in relation to broader national and international developments. First, Wills *et al*, in keeping with the work discussed by Fudge in this collection, showed how neo-liberal principles and practices, and particularly sub-contracting, have tended to increase the sum of international migration and also to create new flows from South to North and from East to West. In their argument, while sub-contracting has made it easier for multinational corporations to exploit the opportunities associated with new sources of cheap labour in the global South and has contributed to economic growth in that region, it has 'generated the widening inequalities and impoverishment that have further encouraged international migration'.[24]

Important examples of new migration flows to the UK (amongst other countries) in response to economic restructuring in sending and receiving countries have been, first, increased movement from Ghana since the 1980s and, second, wholly new migration from countries of central and eastern Europe, particularly Poland, since the 1990s. While it is possible to understand such migration 'as an attempt by both individual households and the state to manage the fallout of neoliberal restructuring',[25] May *et al* argue

---

[23] Wills *et al*, above n 3.
[24] *Ibid*, at 5–6, and on this issue generally, see 2–6.
[25] May, J, Datta, K, Evans, Y, Herbert, J, McIlwaine, C, and Wills, J, 'Travelling Neoliberalism: Polish and Ghanaian Migrant Workers in London' in Smith *et al*, above n 3, at 67. See further at 65–7 on the migration effects of structural adjustment and poverty reduction strategies in the global South and of 'transition' in eastern and central Europe.

that a more nuanced account requires consideration of the specific historical, social and cultural background to national trends.[26] Restructuring in the UK has also been important, on the one hand, increasing the demand for workers to do unskilled work and, on the other hand, contributing generally to poor and insecure employment conditions in 'low-end' jobs owing especially to extensive sub-contracting.[27] But there are specificities of experience in this respect too. Notable here is that agencies have played a particular role for some Polish workers, both facilitating their migration to the UK and substantially influencing their employment experience on arrival.[28]

Second, uneven welfare entitlements as between local and migrant workers in the UK, between different categories of EU migrants and between EU and non-EU migrants have given rise to new labour hierarchies, the operation in London of which Wills *et al* uncovered in rich detail.[29] The overall picture is of restructuring creating pressures and incentives for workers to move from poor countries in Europe and the global South to earn higher wages in the UK. In consequence there have been pools of migrant workers in the UK willing to meet the growing demand for unskilled labour, whereas many in the local workforce, including settled migrants from earlier periods, have opted instead to draw on their welfare entitlements. These new or enlarged migration flows have made it possible for organisations to meet their needs for low-skill work without change to the poor and downgraded (and often sub-contracted) terms upon which it is offered. Moreover, migrants with the least access to state support, and especially those working illegally (estimated at 500,000, mostly based in London), have been most vulnerable to exploitative working practices.[30]

Third, it is important that the precise nature of these hierarchies has been influenced by the change in UK policy orientation towards managing migration for instrumental economic purposes.[31] This shift is in a context in which the EU in recent years required Member States, subject to certain regulatory options, to allow free movement to workers from the central and eastern European countries, notably Poland, which acceded to the Union in

---

[26] *Ibid*, at 70.

[27] See further McDowell, L, Batnitzky, A and Dyer, S, 'Internationalization and the Spaces of Temporary Labour: The Global Assembly of a Local Workforce' (2008) 46 *British Journal of Industrial Relations* 750; McKay, S, above n 3, generally and at 28–36, 41–47; and Wills *et al*, above n 3, generally and at 1–4, 26, 37–8, 51–2, ch 3 on particular industries, especially at 81–93; May *et al*, above n 25, at 73–82.

[28] See Sumption, M and Somerville, W, *The UK's New Europeans: Progress and Challenges Five Years After Accession* (Equality and Human Rights Commission, 2010) 18–19, 27–8.

[29] See Wills *et al*, above n 3, 52, 66–7 and, now in respect of migrants from Bulgaria and Romania, Sumption and Somerville, above n 28, at 9–11, 20, 42–3.

[30] Wills *et al*, above n 3, generally and at 7–8, 15 (on the numbers living and working illegally in the UK) 19, 26, 38–58, 190–5.

[31] *Ibid*, at 11–17.

2004 (the so-called 'A8') and then from those which joined in 2007, namely Bulgaria and Romania (the 'A2'). The UK was in fact one of only three European countries to allow unrestricted migration from the A8 countries from the date of accession. More restricted access to those from Bulgaria and Romania then followed. Linked to these developments, the UK moved to a points-based immigration system which severely limits the legal possibilities for unskilled workers from outside the EU to come to the UK. Wills *et al* made the following point on current increases to border controls:

> It is thus tempting to suggest that, now that employers have a strong supply of low-waged labour from central and eastern Europe, they no longer need workers from further afield. Now that employers can recruit 'white' Europeans, the state has been able to crack down on those from beyond the EU who were doing the work—albeit without the correct papers—before this new labour supply materialised.[32]

Certainly the scale of the migration flow of A8 workers to the UK, of whom Poles make up two-thirds, was significant (and unpredicted), with total migration from the A8 countries estimated at 1.5 million people, of whom 700,000 remained in 2010.[33]

Unsurprisingly tensions have emerged between different groups of migrants as the effects of this complex of changes have been felt.[34] Equally there are resentments between local workers and migrants, which have grown in vehemence with the economic crisis.[35] A depressing expression of this trend was the deeply negative reaction to Nick Clegg's advocacy during the 2010 election of the Liberal Democrat proposal to regularise the position of migrants who had been working illegally in the UK for 10 years.[36] The Coalition Government now plans further to restrict non-EU migration to the UK,[37] adding to heightened controls for those working illegally that were already being undertaken.[38]

Fourth, other variables intersect with economic, welfare and immigration policy in influencing the labour market experiences of migrant workers. As Wills *et al* said about the trends they found in London:

> We argue that the emergence of a new migrant division of labour in London is the result of a convergence—and the (sometimes unforeseen) consequences—of the

---

[32] *Ibid*, at 16.

[33] See Sumption and Somerville, above n 28, at 13–15.

[34] See May *et al*, above n 25, generally, and especially 75–6, 80–1, 83; Wills *et al*, above n 3, at 56–7, 104–12, 119–20.

[35] See Wills *et al*, above n 3, at 8, 17–21, 190–5.

[36] *Ibid*, at 181–6 on the background in community organisation to adoption by the Liberal Democrats of this policy.

[37] UK Border Agency, *Employment-Related Settlement, Tier 5 and Overseas Domestic Workers: A Consultation* (London, Home Office, June 2011).

[38] See Wills *et al*, above n 3, at 12, 14–15, 190–1.

semi-autonomous actions of policy-makers, politicians, employers and migrant workers themselves.[39]

Examples of particular factors affecting some A8 workers (including the majority of Poles) are, first, their frequent need to learn English, which at least temporarily worsens their labour market position,[40] and second, whether individuals or groups have short- or long-term plans to stay in the UK, which also seems important to migrants' labour market experience.[41] It is also striking that, while employers have generally supported liberalised immigration regimes,[42] their attitudes to A8 workers are especially positive.[43] Interestingly, including in relation to tensions between local and migrant workers, these positive attitudes have at times been associated with highly punitive and critical opinions about local workers and settled migrants, the latter often from non EU countries and from visible minorities.[44]

Trade unions have also tended to be upbeat about migration to the UK. At the same time, despite some efforts to recruit and organise margina-lised workers,[45] including by the TGWU which supported the claimants in the *Kalwak* litigation, they have made little headway in this respect.[46] But there are new coalitions, particularly drawing on faith-based groups, which have made some progress in representing and campaigning on behalf of low-wage migrant workers.[47] The fact remains, however, as Wills *et al* eloquently argue, that only undifferentiated improvements in working con-ditions in 'bottom end' work in the UK is capable of reversing the damaging consequences of the multiple divisions amongst people doing this work and others who might, if conditions were better, opt to do it.[48]

LEARNING FROM *KALWAK & ORS V CONSISTENT GROUP LTD AND WELSH COUNTRY FOODS*

Against this background, can anything be learned from analysis of the judg-ments in *Kalwak & Ors v Consistent Group Ltd and Welsh Country Foods*

---

[39] *Ibid*, at 30–1, 47–8.

[40] See Sumption and Somerville, above n 28, at 28–9, 32–3, although see generally on the higher education levels, on average, of migrants to date from the A8 countries (of whom Poles are the majority) than the UK born at 16–7.

[41] *Ibid*, at 17–18, 21, 30–3.

[42] *Ibid*, at 8. While Wills *et al*, above n 3, at 47, 49, 52–5 make the point that there is typically a strong preference for temporary schemes.

[43] Sumption and Somerville, above n 28, at 24, 33.

[44] See *ibid*, at 19–21.

[45] See Fitzgerald, I and Hardy, J, 'Thinking Outside the Box'? Trade Union Organizing Strategies and Polish Migrant Workers in the United Kingdom' (2010) 48 *British Journal of Industrial Relations* 131.

[46] Consider *ibid* and Wills *et al*, above n 3, at 171, 190–5.

[47] See Wills *et al*, above n 3, at 169–85.

[48] *Ibid*, at 195.

as qualitative evidence of the treatment in the UK of marginalised workers? An important preliminary point is that only the EAT and CA judgments are readily available. This reflects that the ET was meant to be an easily accessible, informal, specialist tribunal. Legally qualified and lay judges, the latter drawn from the two sides of industry, sit on panels together, although it is permitted for some decisions to be taken by a legally qualified judge sitting alone. In line with this set-up, ET judgments have no precedential value and are not straightforward to obtain. The EAT is the specialist labour appeal court sitting above the ET, also with legally qualified and lay judges sitting together. Its judgments, however, are binding on courts below, particularly ETs, and hence easy to access. Further appeal is to the CA, the second highest court in the UK, whose judgments are also public. This system means that the one judgment that is difficult for third parties to scrutinise is that by the court which actually saw and heard the parties and their witnesses. Still, I was able to obtain the *Kalwak* judgment in the ET by approaching the legal representatives in the case.

The Distancing Effect

The first striking feature of the three judgments is that it is remarkably difficult to discern from the accounts given more than the barest facts about the part played by the claimants in the litigation. Reading the judgments leaves you none the wiser about how these claims got to the ET, let alone the EAT and the CA, nor about the effect on the claimants of the decisions at each instance.

The ET judgment simply relates that Katarzyna Kalwak, Jaroslaw Babicki, Kararzyna Bachorska, Michal Albinski, Tomasz Skubis, Marta Majder and Piotr Szymanski brought ET proceedings against both Consistent and WCF. They claimed that they had been unfairly dismissed, arguing that their dismissal was automatically unfair being for a reason related to their trade union membership or activities and/or that they had asserted a statutory right. They further claimed that their employer had breached their contracts of employment by failing to pay them for their period of notice and that the two companies had made unlawful deductions from their wages. As we have seen, the presentation of these claims raised the question, considered as a preliminary point, whether the claimants were 'employees' of either of the companies, since only then would they have the statutory rights asserted. When Ms Kalwak etc finally lost in the CA, it was ordered that this preliminary issue be re-heard in the ET.

The ET hearing took place in Liverpool on 27 March, 9 May and 5 July 2006 before an Employment Judge sitting alone. The claimants were represented by a solicitor, Consistent by a barrister and WCF by someone whose profession is not given (suggesting she was not a lawyer). Only Ms Bachorska gave evidence such that it cannot be known if the other claimants were in court. It seems likely, however, that they were, because the Judge noted that their command of English was 'at best only limited'.[49] He related that everyone agreed that an interpreter was needed. A Polish-speaking TGWU official volunteered for this task on the first day, after which a qualified and experienced interpreter was appointed by the Tribunal. Unfortunately she was prevented at the last minute from attending on the third day, but the advocates agreed to the case proceeding seeing as most of the evidence had by then been heard. Judgment was reserved and sent to the parties on 2 August 2006.

There was a hearing of Consistent's appeal in the EAT on 2 May 2007 with reserved judgment on 18 May 2007. All three parties were this time represented by Counsel. Finally, there was a hearing of Consistent's further appeal to the CA on 5 February 2008 with reserved judgment on 29 April 2008. Consistent was now represented by a QC, Ms Kalwak etc by the same barrister as in the EAT and WCF did not appear. There was no mention of the workers being present in either the EAT or CA nor, in turn, of any need for an interpreter.

At this point the trail of the worker litigants goes entirely cold. On the basis of my enquiries it seems there was not in fact a re-hearing in the ET, since by the end of the case the claimants were apparently no longer in the country. Equally, while the only mention of trade union involvement was regarding an interpreter on the first day, I'm told that the TGWU funded the litigation as part of a recruitment campaign. About the experience of the claimants of the litigation, therefore, the case law accounts raise a raft of questions which only direct enquiry of them, their lawyers and their union could answer. What was it in the claimants, the union and the surrounding circumstances that enabled these claims to get to court? What did the claimants understand of what went on, either in the ET or thereafter, and how did it subjectively affect them? Could the claims have been presented differently such as to secure a better ultimate outcome, even if only one that was more intelligible to those directly affected? How much did all this cost and who ultimately paid what?

This absence of information, however, is important in itself. It is true that the time, money and concern focused on the claimants' predicament through the litigation process was in stark contrast to the treatment they otherwise received during their time in the UK. Even so, the unevenness of the information about them in the judgments reveals the law's attention to be oddly distanced. The claimants themselves seem quite quickly to have become superfluous to the machinery trundling on. The impression is certainly given, especially higher up the court hierarchy, that the effect in practice on the

---

[49] *Kalwak & Ors* (ET decision), above n 1, at para [1.1].

claimants was a peripheral or incidental concern. While it was a premise of the final order for a re-hearing that the claimants should again become actively involved, it was apparently by then obvious that the CA decision marked the end of the line. In keeping with the general approach to the claimants, however, this merited no official recognition or comment.

From the point of view of those schooled in the law this is all perfectly appropriate. They read the case as a primary legal source, from which point of view what really mattered was the exposition of some tricky points of law. But considering the judgments as an account of how workers like Ms Kalwak are treated in the UK, what hits home is the dislocation between the sophisticated, elaborate analysis of the legal problem that their situation raised and the distinct lack of interest in anything about these workers beyond that narrow frame.

The Truth Effect

The next notable aspect of reading these cases as qualitative evidence is that the approach taken to establishing basic facts was, to say the least, patchy. The ET judgment described Consistent as being agents who provide staff for food processing factories and hotels, deploying mostly Polish nationals and working predominantly with hotels. It further described WCF as producers of food products with a factory in Winsford. But it went on to say that WCF also ran hotels and largely used staff provided by Consistent. The proposition that WCF ran hotels is highly dubious. I can find no support for it in reports about this well-established food company. Doubt may also be cast on the second finding about its relationship with Consistent, seeing as there are indications that the workforce at WCF is unionised.[50] Yet observations about WCF's hotel business were repeated in the courts above.[51] This was despite the EAT having appreciated that WCF was part of the Grampian group,[52] a large and well-known Scottish food company, later taken over by an even larger and better known Netherlands food company, Vion.[53]

---

[50] Hughes, OR, 'WCF abattoir staff go on strike' *North Wales News* (16 August 2008); 'Anglesey abattoir tells 480 staff jobs are threatened' *Daily News* (12 February 2009); 'Meat plant set to shed 200 jobs', *BBC News* (12 January 2010).

[51] *Kalwak & Ors* (EAT decision), above n 1, at para [10] and CA, above n 1, at para [3].

[52] *Ibid*, at paras [1], [10], [49].

[53] See Kleinman, M and Harrington, B, 'Grampian to be swallowed up by Dutch food giant Vion', *Daily Telegraph* (6 April 2008); Vass, S, 'Who led Grampian to the slaughter', *Herald Scotland* (12 April 2008); 'Vion lands Grampian Country Foods for £380m', *The Daily Record* (17 June 2008); Davies, J, 'Vion pledges investment after Grampian takeover', *Farmers' Guardian* (20 June 2008), noting that: 'As well as taking control of Grampian's pig and poultry operations, the deal includes red meat processors St Merryn Meat, McIntosh Donald and Welsh Country Foods—major suppliers to UK supermarkets including Tesco, Sainsbury's, Asda, Morrisons, the Co-op, Somerfield and Marks & Spencer.'

Laxness about facts is, however, most evident in the approach to the documentation put before the court as recording the agreement between Consistent and WCF for the provision of agency workers. Ms Kalwak and the others had come to the UK in April 2005 and worked at WCF from 6 May until June 2005. But the document produced to the Tribunal as relating Consistent and WCF's agreement was dated 12 September 2005 and dealt only with the provision by Consistent of agency staff to do hotel work for WCF. While noting these points, the Employment Judge merely observed: 'But I did not hear that when [the September 2005 contract] was made, there was any wish or need materially to alter any term of the existing relationship between [Consistent and WCF]'. He accepted the document as representing 'no great new departure' in their arrangements and that it applied to all the people sent by Consistent to work at WCF, noting that he had certainly seen no agreement covering WCF's food-processing activity.[54]

This set of findings is really very striking when it is remembered that the entire claim turned on the correct legal classification of the arrangements under which the claimants did work for WCF. Moreover, as noted above, the claimants' essential contention was that the paperwork that governed the provision of their labour was a sham. The Tribunal's lackadaisical approach to this aspect of the facts was nonetheless repeated without question by the EAT and the CA. This was so despite Lord Justice Rimer further noticing that 'the agreement in fact purported to describe its commencement date as 6 January 2005'.[55]

What this all put to one side was the possibility that the claimants' version of the true relationships between these parties was supported by the absence either of a contemporaneous agreement between Consistent and WCF or of one relating to the subject matter of their collaboration regarding these claimants. A more careful rendering of the facts would surely at least have perceived that possibility. Even allowing that this was a preliminary hearing and that supervision on appeal of factual findings is limited, the higher courts' complacency on this issue notably contrasts with their exhaustive analyses of the rest of the documentation.

This exposition of the claimants' stories in the judgments was nevertheless authoritative in law. In legal terms the courts' findings officially recorded what had happened, even where they were obviously and significantly questionable. Unpicking the judgment in this way thereby discloses how court decisions not only selectively narrate workers' experiences, but do so with authority irrespective of whether they depict 'truth'.

---

[54] *Kalwak & Ors* (ET decision), above n 1, at paras [3.5]–[3.6].
[55] *Kalwak & Ors* (EAT decision), above n 1, at para [10]; *Kalwak & Ors* (CA decision), above n 1, at para [3].

The Muting Effect

Finally there is the detail given in the judgment pertaining to Ms Kalwak and the others' working experiences in the UK. The Employment Judge treated Ms Bachorska's case as though it applied to all the claimants, saying that there were only immaterial differences between them. He recorded that the claimants arranged with Consistent to be placed in work before leaving Poland. There is then the brief, somewhat disturbing statement that:

> On arrival [in April 2005], they stayed in a house in Liverpool provided by [Consistent], but in the night they came under attack from local people. To prevent further trouble, the first respondents had them driven to Wrexham where they were, in a hurry, accommodated at a Travel Lodge.[56]

On the next day they were said to have signed contracts with Consistent in English and Polish versions. The contract included the clause often included with the aim of preventing agency workers being 'employees', that Consistent were not required to provide work and the 'sub-contractor' (as each claimant was described) was not required to accept work if offered. There were, however, other provisions that made the correct legal categorisation of these particular contracts debatable. The Judge also recorded that the claimants were later given a further, non-contractual document called 'Being Self-Employed—What It Means'.

The Judge in the ET went on to note that £56.40 was deducted each week from the claimant's pay for accommodation and cleaning, with the latter being found rarely, if at all, to have been done. The workers were accommodated in a house in Crewe where six other Poles were already living. After a health check they started work as meatpackers at WCF's factory in Winsford. The Judge found that in practice the claimants were required to work when required, were discouraged from joining the TGWU and told it consisted of 'bad people' and, finally, on the claimants' giving two weeks' notice as provided by their contract, were required to finish the next day and to vacate their accommodation. The Judge also recorded that Consistent ensured the claimants were registered with the Home Office as self-employed.

In the EAT a summary of this account was repeated, with more detail given of the written contracts between the claimants and Consistent. In particular it noted the provision for further payments from the claimants to Consistent, on which the CA, in addition to essentially repeating the ET's account of the facts, elaborated. From the CA judgment we know that the pay rate for the first 40 hours of work in a week was £3.44 if only accommodation was provided and £2.92 if there was a hot meal per shift. After 40 hours the pay rose in each case to £4.85, the then national minimum wage.

---

[56] *Kalwak & Ors* (EAT decision), above n 1, at para [3.8].

There was also a £25 charge per year for use of Consistent's translation services and £100 per year for their accountancy service. Finally there was a deposit to occupy the accommodation provided, payable by four £75 weekly instalments. By my reckoning this would leave the claimants earning either £137.60 or £116.80 per week before overtime or tax, reduced to £62.60 or £41.80 in the first four weeks when the accommodation deposit was subtracted.

This official recounting of the minutiae of how these individuals were treated is of interest in itself. But the facts recorded would need to be aggregated with other case law accounts to build a fuller picture. Equally, evaluation is needed of how far it matters that judicial accounts are at several removes from the actors themselves.

But more than this, there is a chilling, eerie quality to the bland recounting of these happenings. The stories the judgments tell are reminiscent of Gaskell's accounts of Northern English work practices during the Industrial Revolution, and of the attitudes of some within social and economic elites to these.[57] This seems far removed from what might now be expected in a country of the UK's riches and professed adherence to humane, democratic values. No overt comment or reaction from the judges was elicited, however, whatever their private thoughts might have been.

This becomes even more telling when it is remembered, as set out above, that these claimants were far from being amongst the workers who are most disadvantaged in the UK labour market. In particular, their experiences were short-lived and they had important support available to them, reflecting various factors, including their legal status in Europe, that combined to give them realistic exit (and, to some extent, voice) options. What then, it might be asked, would it take for judicial disapprobation of work practices to be expressed?

But this agnosticism was again entirely comprehensible from a legal point of view. While judges quite often comment in asides on cases before them, their legal conclusions are meant not, implicitly or explicitly, to draw on their personal thoughts and feelings. So it is quite proper for judges to refrain from making any comment in a case such as this. But the upshot was that an official light was shone on a situation meriting wider deliberation without anything beyond the legal technicalities attracting even comment. The judgments can thereby be seen as illustrating the potentially muting, distracting effect of litigation. While enabling important stories to be aired and analysed, litigation risks their full import or significance being dissipated or lost.

---

[57] See, eg, Gaskell, E, *North and South*, first published 1854–1855.

CONCLUSION

Reading these judgments as qualitative evidence of the treatment of workers like Ms Kalwak is instructive in a number of ways. It tells us something about what happens when they challenge their treatment at work, including, first, about the law's selective interest in them and their stories, and second, how the official re-telling gives authority to even garbled versions of their experiences. There is also potentially useful information in the accounts by the various judges of the detail of these workers' lives. The recounting is also striking for its potential to dilute the wider impact that the underlying facts should have.

Even still, we know that the ET and the EAT judges accepted that the contractual terms that effectively denied the claimants 'employee' status were shams. This followed from the judges in those courts to some extent contextualising their consideration of the legal issue. While not drawing on broader knowledge, they did consider the relationship in practice between these particular claimants and these particular companies. The analysis of Elias J (as he then was) in turn demonstrated that the common law could defensibly be interpreted so as to find for the claimants, as is now borne out by the shift in the subsequent cases.

The CA judgment, on the other hand, was, with respect, based on a reading of the situation before the court that was far removed from any plausible version of reality. After crushing criticism of the ET judgment and less trenchant disagreement with that of the EAT, Rimer LJ, with the concurrence of Wilson and May LJJ, made the following remarkable statement:

> If a term solemnly agreed in writing is to be rejected in favour of a different one, that can only be done by a clear finding that the real agreement was to that different effect and that the term in the contract was included by the [parties to it] so as to present a misleadingly different impression.[58]

By these words Rimer, Wilson and May LJJ exercised the power the legislature accorded them, notwithstanding ambiguity in the legal position, to hold that a sham could only be found in a case like this if there had been deliberate collusion between the parties to the contractual documentation to deceive third parties. This is despite it seeming almost satirical to imply that the agreement at stake was 'solemnly' made, let alone that workers like Ms Kalwak would ever be in a position deliberately to collude with an agency in like circumstances. The implicit hypothetical is in fact yet more fanciful in that to qualify as a sham the collusion would have to be with the aim of misleading third parties, including public authorities (and courts), on whom marginalised workers may well come to rely. In effect, therefore, the CA held that the law could never recognise that agreements

---

[58] *Kalwak & Ors* (CA decision), above n 1, at para [40].

in situations like the one before the court were a sham. This is despite the CA so carefully relating that this contract was made by workers who barely spoke English, had no access to legal advice, had arrived in the UK the day before as economic migrants from a poorer country, had been moved in the night to escape attack and were to take up low-skill, low-paid work that they relied on Consistent to provide and on which their accommodation, and perhaps safety, depended.

In reaching this conclusion the CA judgment exhibited the distancing, truth and muting effects identified above to a startling degree and it is perhaps unsurprising that later decisions resiled from its approach. But it is perhaps more important that these elements were present in all the judgments, impeding them to differing degrees from being fully intelligible, informed or able usefully to signpost the need for broader reflection on the issues raised.

The qualitative evidence in these judgments thereby demonstrated different ways in which courts are disabled from making good determinations of questions like those raised in *Kalwak*. The most important lesson, especially given the wealth of non-legal knowledge about life in the 'bottom end' of the UK labour market, is that whatever courts decide, the nature of adjudication forces them into ruling on the UK's migrant divisions of labour in ways that are more or less sub-optimal. Whatever the ramifications of their rulings, judges cannot duck making a decision. Yet the process of adjudication does not permit or enable all relevant learning and analyses systematically to be taken into account. At the same time the fact of litigation likely neutralises the impact of the stories told to courts, dissipating the wider beneficial influence that the public recounting of them might have. What emerges as most significant, therefore, is that the legislature has set up judicial decision-making in this area to be functional to society avoiding the economically technical, political contested and morally troubling choices posed by marginalised work in its modern incarnation.

Index